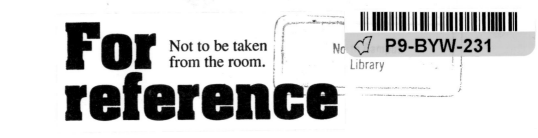

AMERICAN
GENERATIONS

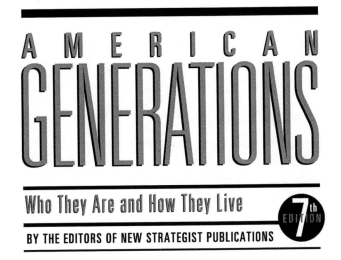

AMERICAN GENERATIONS

Who They Are and How They Live

7th EDITION

BY THE EDITORS OF NEW STRATEGIST PUBLICATIONS

New Strategist Publications, Inc.

Ithaca, New York

New Strategist Publications, Inc.
P.O. Box 242, Ithaca, New York 14851
800/848-0842; 607/273-0913
www.newstrategist.com

ISBN 978-1-935114-78-9 (hardcover)
ISBN 978-1-935114-79-6 (paper)

Printed in the United States of America

Table of Contents

Chapter 8. Living Arrangements

Chapter 9. Population

Chapter 10. Spending

Chapter 11. Time Use

Chapter 12. Wealth

List of Tables

Chapter 3. Education

Chapter 4. Health

Chapter 5. Housing

Chapter 6. Income

Chapter 9. Population

Chapter 10. Spending

Chapter 11. Time Use

Chapter 12. Wealth

List of Charts

Chapter 5. Housing

Chapter 6. Income

Chapter 7. Labor Force

Chapter 8. Living Arrangements

Chapter 9. Population

Chapter 10. Spending

Chapter 11. Time Use

Chapter 12. Wealth

Introduction

In the past, when the pace of change was slow, the concept of generations had little importance for society, public policy, or commerce. But today, the world changes rapidly and people who are as little as 10 years apart in age may have very different experiences growing up—making them unlike one another in significant ways. *American Generations: Who They Are and How They Live* reveals the differences and similarities among the six living generations of Americans.

For decades, the U.S. population has been fragmented by generation. The seventh edition of *American Generations* is an important tool for piecing together those fragments and seeing the whole. The generational profiles contained in this book are of value not only to marketers, but also to social scientists and policymakers. Each generation, after all, makes its demands on public policy just as it does on business. And those seeking to understand societal or consumer change must address how attitudes and values, wants and needs, evolve with generational replacement.

American Generations examines both generations and age groups. Age groups are static, never changing; generations pass through age groups. People aged 40 today are members of Generation X, but in another decade the Millennial generation will occupy the age group. Since each generation has a distinct character, the policy issues, products, services, advertising, and media that resonate with people aged 40 today may not work for 40-year-olds a decade from now.

Explaining generational differences

Several factors account for generational differences. One is education, which greatly influences people's attitudes and values, wants and needs. The generations born after World War II are much better educated than older Americans. This fact alone means that middle-aged and younger generations will think and behave differently from the way their parents did at the same age. Another important difference is the greater degree of diversity among younger generations. Accustomed to a wide variety of cultures, younger generations are more likely to view the nation as a "salad bowl" rather than a melting pot. Technology also divides the generations. The Internet and cell phones are integral parts of the lives of younger generations, setting them apart from their elders.

Differences in attitudes and behavior are not the only factors that make each generation unique. The relative size of the generations affects the age distribution of the population. When generations are of uneven size, as they are today, the social and economic effects can be far-reaching. In the 1950s, for example, schools that were adequate for educating the relatively small Swing generation suddenly were flooded with students as Boomers arrived. As the last classes of Boomers graduated from high school, the public schools were forced to adapt to the smaller Generation X. Many of them sold their school buildings in the belief that the crush was over. Wrong. Behind Generation X came the much larger Millennial generation, rivaling the Baby Boom in size and straining school budgets and facilities all over again.

This expansion and contraction can catch business and public policy off guard. But it is possible to look down the road and know what's coming. That is what *American Generations* is all about—preparing businesses and policymakers for what lies ahead, helping them plan as the generations move through the age structure and change our society.

Much of the social change of the past half-century has been caused by "generational replacement." As older generations die and are replaced by new generations, society adopts the attitudes and values of the living generations. From the expanding roles of women to the increased acceptance of homosexuality, attitudes are changing because new generations are taking over.

Using age group data

Differences among generations are too often buried in statistics that look only at the population as a whole, or divide it by a characteristic such as sex, but not age. Overall, 30 percent of Americans aged 25 or older have a bachelor's degree, but this single statistic fails to tell an important part of the story—there is a distinct generational difference in education. Only 18 percent of women in the older generations (Swing and World War II) have a bachelor's degree, for example, compared with 36 percent of Millennial women. Incomes, labor force participation, living arrangements, spending patterns, and even time use all vary by generation.

Because generations do not always fit easily into the age group data collected by the Census Bureau and other organizations, much of the statistical information presented in this book approximates the generations. Millennials were aged 16 to 33 in 2010, for example. They do not fit precisely into the standard five- or ten-year age groups, such as 25-to-34-year-olds, for which researchers typically collect data. When generations are split by age groupings, the text of this book discusses the generation that accounts for the majority of the age group's members. In many of the book's tables, New Strategist's editors have estimated the size of each generation, allowing readers to see at a glance the differing educational attainment, household income, living arrangements, and labor force status of the generations.

This edition of *American Marketplace* includes a chapter revealing the major attitudinal differences among the generations, based on 2008 General Social Survey data. The book also contains the latest income, spending, housing, and labor force statistics as well as an updated look at time use based on unpublished 2008 data from the American Time Use Survey.

How to use this book

American Generations is divided into 12 chapters: The Generations, Attitudes, Education, Health, Housing, Income, Labor Force, Living Arrangements, Population, Spending, Time Use, and Wealth. Each chapter includes tables and text describing the most important trends, including what to expect in the future.

Most of the tables in *American Generations* are based on data collected by the federal government, in particular the Census Bureau, the Bureau of Labor Statistics, the National Center for Education Statistics, the National Center for Health Statistics, and the Federal Reserve Board. The federal government continues to be the best source of up-to-date, reliable information on the changing characteristics of Americans.

Several government surveys are of particular importance to *American Generations*. One is the Census Bureau's Current Population Survey. The CPS is a nationally representative survey of the civilian noninstitutional population aged 15 or older. The Census Bureau takes it monthly, collecting information on employment and unemployment from more than 50,000 households. Each year, the March survey includes a demographic supplement that is the source of most national data on the characteristics of Americans, such as their educational attainment, living arrangements, and incomes. CPS data appear in many tables of this book.

The American Community Survey is another important source of data for *American Generations*. The ACS is an ongoing nationwide survey of 250,000 households per month that provides detailed demographic data at the community level. Designed to replace the census long-form questionnaire, the ACS includes more than 60 questions that formerly appeared on the long form, such as ones asking about language spoken at home, income, and education. ACS data are available for the nation, regions, states, counties, metropolitan areas, and smaller geographic units.

The Consumer Expenditure Survey is the data source for the Spending chapter. Sponsored by the Bureau of Labor Statistics, the CEX is an ongoing study of the day-to-day spending of American households. The data collected by the survey are used to update prices for the consumer price index. The CEX includes an interview survey and a diary survey administered to two separate, nationally representative samples. The average spending figures shown in the Spending chapters of this book are the integrated data from both the diary and interview components of the survey. For the interview survey, about 7,000 consumer units are interviewed on a rotating panel basis each quarter for five consecutive quarters. For the diary survey, another 7,000 consumer units keep weekly diaries of spending for two consecutive weeks.

The Bureau of Labor Statistics' American Time Use Survey is the source of data for the Time Use chapter. Through telephone interviews with a nationally representative sample of noninstitutionalized Americans aged 15 or older, ATUS collects information in minute detail about what survey respondents did during the previous 24 hours. Time use data allow social scientists to better understand our economy and lifestyle and how policy decisions affect our lives.

The data in the Wealth chapter comes from the Survey of Consumer Finances, a triennial survey taken by the Federal Reserve Board. The SCF collects data on the assets, debt, and net worth of American households. The latest data available are from the 2007 survey, for which the Federal Reserve Board interviewed a representative sample of more than 4,000 households. These data were collected just before the Great Recession took hold. Consequently, the Wealth chapter shows the economic status of households before the plunge in the stock and housing markets.

To explore changes in attitudes, New Strategist extracted data from the nationally representative General Social Survey of the University of Chicago's National Opinion Research Center. NORC conducts the biennial survey through face-to-face interviews with an independently drawn, representative sample of 3,000 to 4,000 noninstitutionalized people aged 18 or older who live in the United States. The GSS is one of the best sources of attitudinal data on Americans available today.

Value added

While the government collected most of the data presented in *American Generations*, the tables published here are not reprints from government reports—as is the case in many reference books. Instead, New Strategist's editors spent hundreds of hours scouring web sites, compiling numbers into meaningful statistics, and creating tables with calculations that reveal the trends. Those who want spreadsheet versions of the tables in this book should visit www.newstrategist.com to buy and download the pdf file with links to each table in Excel format.

Government web sites are useful for obtaining summary data and for tapping into complex databases. But too often summary data are not enough, and those complex databases usually require analysis by statistical program. With this volume, New Strategist has done the work for you, delving into the data and providing analysis and comparisons, placing the important information about the generations at your fingertips. The text and chart accompanying most of the tables tell a story about the generations, explaining past and future trends. Researchers who want even more can use the source listed at the bottom of each table to explore the original data. The book contains a comprehensive table list to help readers locate the information they need. For a more detailed search, use the index at the back of the book. Also in the back of the book is the glossary, which defines most of the terms commonly used in the tables and text.

With *American Generations* in hand, you will discover the many ways in which the six generations of living Americans differ. Those who know the differences will better understand the change in store for the decades ahead.

The Generations

The six generations of Americans are, from youngest to oldest, the iGeneration, the Millennial generation, Generation X, the Baby Boom, the Swing generation, and the World War II generation. Below is a brief overview of the generations, followed by a more detailed look at their demographics.

• **iGeneration** After a decades-long rollercoaster ride, the annual number of births stabilized in the mid-1990s at about 4 million a year. The oldest members of the generation born out of this stability, dubbed the iGeneration to mark the technological engine to which they are harnessed, turns 15 in 2010. The attitudes and values of the iGeneration are still forming, so stay tuned for what they will become.

• **Millennial Generation** Like the Baby Boom, this generation, which was born between 1977 and 1994, is marked by its large size and the intense peer competition for a foothold in the middle class. But the world that Millennials are navigating in their twenties and thirties is very different from the one Boomers faced at the same age. Boomers entered adulthood in an expanding economy. Millennials face the highest unemployment rate on record for their age group. They are coping with a battered economy, falling housing prices, and burdensome student loan debt. But they are more optimistic than Boomers about their chances of achieving the American Dream.

Millennials are the most liberal of the generations, they rank among the best-educated Americans, and they are the first generation born into the high-tech world. These characteristics should help them succeed despite the difficulties that lie ahead.

• **Generation X** Born between 1965 and 1976, this well-educated, media-savvy generation now makes up the largest share of the nation's parents with children under age 18. The small size of Generation X has made it relatively easy to overlook—and it is painfully aware of this fact. When Gen Xers were teenagers, attention was focused on the Baby Boom. Businesses retailored youth-oriented offerings to suit the tastes of Boomer families. Now that Generation X has entered middle age, businesses are focusing on young adults to capture the spending of the large Millennial generation.

As parents, Gen Xers face the same problems that confronted Boomers—a conflict between work and family roles. They have an additional burden, however, because many bought houses during the peak of the housing bubble. Many are deeply in debt, with mortgage payments much higher than any other generation. With Boomers postponing retirement and clogging the promotional pipeline at work, many Gen Xers wonder when their day will come.

• **Baby-Boom Generation** Born between 1946 and 1964, this is no longer the largest generation of Americans because Millennials surpassed them in size in 2010. Because of their numbers, Boomers have been the focus of attention since their birth. Businesses that sold diapers, baby food, and grade-school books rejoiced at their arrival. But as Boomers matured into new stages of life, the businesses they left behind had to choose between tracking them or shifting their loyalties to a new generation.

Boomers were raised by young, stay-at-home mothers who followed Dr. Spock's every word. They were taught to be independent and to believe they could control their own destinies. During the 1960s, this upbringing manifested itself in the anti-authoritarian counterculture movement. In the 1980s, it translated into see-how-fast-I-can-get-rich materialism. In 2010, Boomers are realizing that they may not have as much control over their lives as they once believed. Their retirement savings have been decimated by the Great Recession, many own houses that are worth less than they paid for them, their children have outsized college expenses and remain financially dependent well into adulthood, and their own health care costs have ballooned. Consequently, most are postponing retirement as their once empty nest refills.

Baby Boomers have been affected by their generation's immense size throughout their lives. In turn, the massive generation has had an enormous influence on the American economy and culture. This influence will continue for at least two more decades.

• **Swing Generation** This generation was born between 1933 and 1945. It is a small cohort of Americans caught between two powerful forces—the Boomers and the World War II generation. Consequently, the generation has swung between the attitudes and lifestyles of the generations on either side, which accounts for its name. Some members adopted the more casual lifestyle commonly associated with Boomers. Many leaders of the civil rights, women's, and antiwar movements in the 1960s were members of the Swing generation. Other Swing generation members are as conservative as their World War II elders. Many of the nation's politicians and CEOs are members of the Swing generation.

The Swing generation came of age during a period of quiet prosperity. Its relatively small size benefited its members—companies needed entry-level workers when they were young adults and managers as they reached middle age. Achieving a middle-class lifestyle seemed easy when the economy was expanding and corporations were feeling generous. This is the most affluent group of older Americans in history—and likely will remain so, a footnote in the history books.

• **World War II Generation** Born before 1933, these are the oldest living Americans. Many members of the generation fought in the war that gave the generation its name. The Great Depression and World War II shaped their attitudes and values more than anything else. Sometimes called the Greatest Generation, they were once a major force in the United States. The World War II generation is less educated than younger Americans because a high school diploma was once sufficient to get a good-paying, secure job. This generation's lower level of education is one reason why its members see things differently from younger Americans.

The iGeneration: Growing Up

The oldest members of the youngest generation are now in their teens.

After decades of ups and downs in births, the rollercoaster finally came to a halt. The annual number of births leveled out in the mid-1990s at around 4 million a year. These young people have been dubbed the iGeneration—destined to be the most diverse and yet connected birth cohort in history. Today the iGeneration includes everyone in the United States under age 16.

The unique attitudes and values of the iGeneration are still forming. Because they are so young, they are not yet counted in labor force and other economic statistics. Even their time use is unknown since they are just entering the 15-to-19 age group. Yet some of their characteristics can be seen in household and family statistics and by looking at economic trends among families with children.

■ The iGeneration is close to being a minority majority generation, even more diverse than Millennials.

■ The iGeneration could be the first to be raised in a United States with a shrinking middle class as their parents struggle with outsized mortgages, high levels of unemployment, and burdensome student loan debt.

Table 1.1 Birth of the iGeneration, 1995 to Present

(annual number of births, 1995 to present; numbers in thousands)

	number
Total births	**65,148**
1995	3,890
1996	3,981
1997	3,881
1998	3,942
1999	3,959
2000	4,059
2001	4,026
2002	4,022
2003	4,070
2004	4,112
2005	4,138
2006	4,266
2007	4,315
2008	4,247
2009	4,120
2010	4,120

Note: Figures for 2009 and 2010 are projected based on trends through July 2009.
Source: National Center for Health Statistics, various reports, Internet site http://www.cdc.gov/nchs/products/nvsr.htm

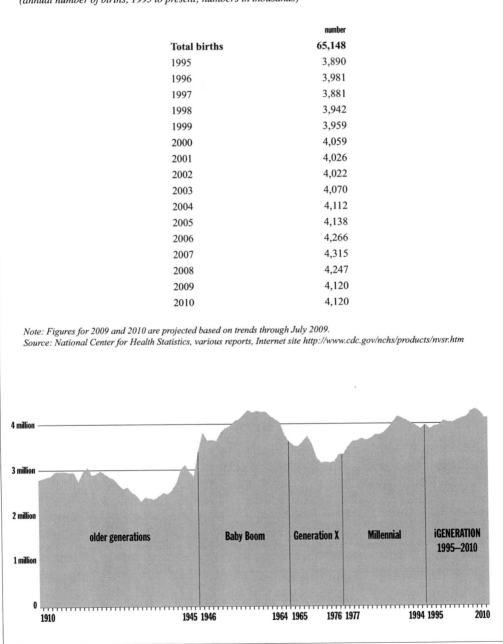

Table 1.2 Size of the iGeneration, 2010

(number of people in the iGeneration by single year of age, 2010)

	number
iGeneration (aged 0 to 15)	**66,593,915**
Under age 1	4,261,083
Aged 1	4,236,682
Aged 2	4,214,386
Aged 3	4,198,061
Aged 4	4,189,309
Aged 5	4,186,867
Aged 6	4,183,737
Aged 7	4,162,453
Aged 8	4,162,444
Aged 9	4,190,254
Aged 10	4,067,842
Aged 11	4,055,383
Aged 12	4,042,092
Aged 13	4,072,414
Aged 14	4,157,603
Aged 15	4,213,305

Source: Bureau of the Census, Internet site http://www.census.gov/population/www/projections/2009projections.html; calculations by New Strategist

Table 1.3 iGeneration by Age, 2000 to 2020

(age of oldest member of the iGeneration, 2000 to 2020)

	age of oldest member
2000	5
2001	6
2002	7
2003	8
2004	9
2005	10
2006	11
2007	12
2008	13
2009	14
2010	15
2011	16
2012	17
2013	18
2014	19
2015	20
2016	21
2017	22
2018	23
2019	24
2020	25

Source: Calculations by New Strategist

Table 1.4 iGeneration Share of Population, 2010

(number and percent distribution of the total population and the population aged 18 or older by generation, 2010)

	number	share of total population	share of adult* population
Total people	**310,232,863**	**100.0%**	–
IGENERATION (aged 0 to 15)	**66,593,915**	**21.5**	**0.0%**
Millennial (aged 16 to 33)	77,247,589	24.9	29.2
Generation X (aged 34 to 45)	49,651,298	16.0	21.1
Baby Boom (aged 46 to 64)	76,511,349	24.7	32.6
Older generations (aged 65 or older)	40,228,712	13.0	17.1

* Population aged 18 or older, projected to be 235,015,757 in 2010.
Source: Bureau of the Census, Internet site http://www.census.gov/population/www/projections/2009projections.html; calculations by New Strategist

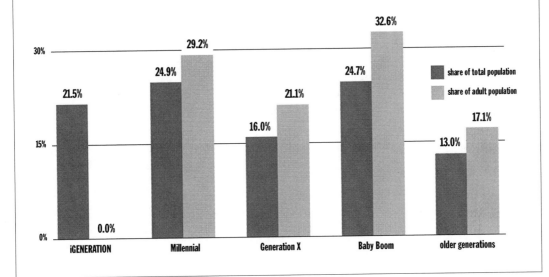

The Millennial Generation: Another Baby Boom

The young adult generation now outnumbers Boomers.

In 1977, a new birth boom began when 3.3 million babies were born—159,000 more than in the previous year. This large rise in the number of births followed the 12-year lull that is commonly called Generation X. By 1980, annual births had risen to 3.6 million. By 1989, they topped 4 million. Altogether, nearly 68 million babies were born between 1977 and 1994—when births once again dropped below the 4 million mark.

The large Millennial generation—the name for those born between 1977 and 1994—spanned the ages from 16 to 33 in 2010. Because of their numbers, Millennials command the nation's attention. As of 2010, the 77 million Millennials accounted for 24.9 percent of the total population, a slightly greater share than the Boomers' 24.7 percent. Millennials aged 18 or older are a substantial 29.2 percent of the nation's adults—greater than Generation X's 21.1 percent share.

Like the Boomers before them, Millennials are transforming markets as they age. They crowded the nation's public schools in their youth and boosted college enrollments as they entered the young-adult age group. Now, with the oldest entering their thirties, the generation is trying to gain a foothold in the American middle class. The task is daunting because they face a record level of unemployment for their age group and many are burdened by student debt. Millennials hold promise for the struggling housing market, but many do not have the jobs necessary to support a mortgage payment.

■ The Millennial generation has diversified the youth market. Asians, blacks, and Hispanics account for a large share of Millennials—affecting everything from fashion to politics.

■ The first generation to be raised on cell phones and the Internet, Millennials are always connected.

■ Millennials must compete against their many peers for colleges and jobs. This competitive crush shapes the attitudes and lifestyles of Millennials and is one of the factors that distinguishes them from Generation X.

Table 1.5 Birth of the Millennial Generation, 1977 to 1994

(annual number of births, 1977 to 1994; numbers in thousands)

	number
Total births	**67,949**
1977	3,327
1978	3,333
1979	3,494
1980	3,612
1981	3,629
1982	3,681
1983	3,639
1984	3,669
1985	3,761
1986	3,757
1987	3,809
1988	3,910
1989	4,041
1990	4,158
1991	4,111
1992	4,065
1993	4,000
1994	3,953

Source: National Center for Health Statistics, Report of Final Natality Statistics, Monthly Vital Statistics Report, Vol. 45, No. 11 Supplement, 1997

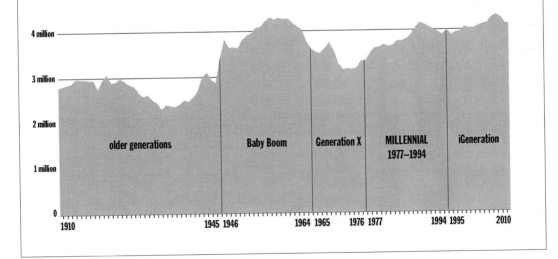

Table 1.6 Size of the Millennial Generation, 2010

(number of people in the Millennial generation by single year of age, 2010)

	number
Millennial, aged 16 to 33	**77,247,589**
Aged 16	4,266,403
Aged 17	4,356,788
Aged 18	4,428,312
Aged 19	4,505,016
Aged 20	4,524,865
Aged 21	4,399,321
Aged 22	4,321,924
Aged 23	4,259,822
Aged 24	4,273,548
Aged 25	4,260,440
Aged 26	4,222,570
Aged 27	4,269,237
Aged 28	4,298,928
Aged 29	4,366,874
Aged 30	4,331,902
Aged 31	4,156,461
Aged 32	4,045,728
Aged 33	3,959,450

Source: Bureau of the Census, Internet site http://www.census.gov/population/www/projections/2009projections.html; calculations by New Strategist

Table 1.7 Millennial Generation by Age, 2000 to 2020

(age range of the Millennial generation, 2000 to 2020)

	age range
2000	6–23
2001	7–24
2002	8–25
2003	9–26
2004	10–27
2005	11–28
2006	12–29
2007	13–30
2008	14–31
2009	15–32
2010	16–33
2011	17–34
2012	18–35
2013	19–36
2014	20–37
2015	21–38
2016	22–39
2017	23–40
2018	24–41
2019	25–42
2020	26–43

Source: Calculations by New Strategist

Table 1.8 Millennial Share of Population, 2010

(number and percent distribution of the total population and the population aged 18 or older by generation, 2010)

	number	share of total population	share of adult* population
Total people	**310,232,863**	**100.0%**	–
iGeneration (aged 0 to 15)	66,593,915	21.5	0.0%
MILLENNIAL (aged 16 to 33)	**77,247,589**	**24.9**	**29.2**
Generation X (aged 34 to 45)	49,651,298	16.0	21.1
Baby Boom (aged 46 to 64)	76,511,349	24.7	32.6
Older generations (aged 65 or older)	40,228,712	13.0	17.1

* Population aged 18 or older, projected to be 235,015,757 in 2010.
Source: Bureau of the Census, Internet site http://www.census.gov/population/www/projections/2009projections.html; calculations by New Strategist

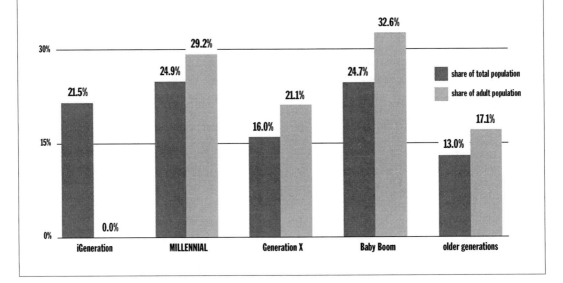

Generation X: Now in Middle Age

Though small, Generation X is a powerhouse in the marketplace.

It is the fate of Generation X, born between 1965 and 1976, to be overshadowed by the large generations on either side of it—the Millennial and Baby Boom generations. The reason is simple arithmetic.

After the 19-year birth fest that created the Baby Boom, the annual number of births declined. In 1964, the last year of the Baby Boom, more than 4 million babies were born. In 1965, there were only 3.8 million births. The annual number of births continued to slide in a generally downward direction through 1976 before beginning to rise again. This period of fewer births resulted in a numerically small generation sandwiched between two much larger ones.

In 2010, there were nearly 50 million Generation Xers, aged 34 to 45. The generation accounts for 16 percent of the population, well below the 25 percent share accounted for by Millennials. Generation X makes up 21 percent of the adult population compared with Boomers' 33 percent and Millennials' 29 percent.

Although the media often overlook Generation Xers, they are vital to the American economy in a variety of ways. Generation X dominates family life, heading the largest share (45 percent) of households with children. Consequently, they are the biggest spenders on a range of products and services needed by crowded-nest families, including mortgage interest.

■ Generation Xers are now the nation's parents, and they are entering their peak earning and spending years.

■ Generation X is well-educated. The women of Generation X have a higher level of educational attainment than any other group of Americans.

■ Generation X is struggling because many bought homes during the housing bubble. Their outsized debt and falling incomes could spell trouble for the many businesses that market products and services for families with children.

Table 1.9 Birth of Generation X, 1965 to 1976

(annual number of births, 1965 to 1976; numbers in thousands)

	number
Total births	**41,143**
1965	3,760
1966	3,606
1967	3,521
1968	3,502
1969	3,600
1970	3,731
1971	3,556
1972	3,258
1973	3,137
1974	3,160
1975	3,144
1976	3,168

Source: National Center for Health Statistics, Report of Final Natality Statistics, Monthly Vital Statistics Report, Vol. 45, No. 11 Supplement, 1997

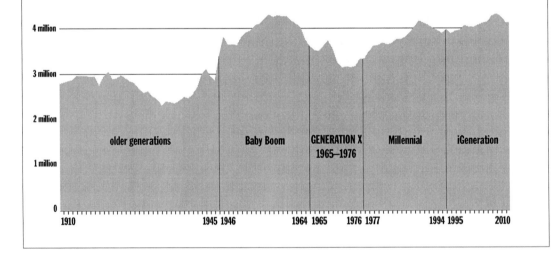

Table 1.10 Size of Generation X, 2010

(number of people in Generation X by single year of age, 2010)

	number
Total, aged 34 to 45	**49,651,298**
Aged 34	3,906,015
Aged 35	3,963,126
Aged 36	3,881,076
Aged 37	3,957,695
Aged 38	4,123,923
Aged 39	4,341,575
Aged 40	4,416,869
Aged 41	4,199,196
Aged 42	4,095,240
Aged 43	4,094,590
Aged 44	4,203,765
Aged 45	4,468,228

Source: Bureau of the Census, Internet site http://www.census.gov/population/www/projections/2009projections.html; calculations by New Strategist

Table 1.11 Generation X by Age, 2000 to 2020

(age range of Generation X, 2000 to 2020)

	age range
2000	24–35
2001	25–36
2002	26–37
2003	27–38
2004	28–39
2005	29–40
2006	30–41
2007	31–42
2008	32–43
2009	33–44
2010	34–45
2011	35–46
2012	36–47
2013	37–48
2014	38–49
2015	39–50
2016	40–51
2017	41–52
2018	42–53
2019	43–54
2020	44–55

Source: Calculations by New Strategist

Table 1.12 Generation X Share of Population, 2010

(number and percent distribution of the total population and the population aged 18 or older by generation, 2010)

	number	share of total population	share of adult* population
Total people	**310,232,863**	**100.0%**	–
iGeneration (aged 0 to 15)	66,593,915	21.5	0.0%
Millennial (aged 16 to 33)	77,247,589	24.9	29.2
GENERATION X (aged 34 to 45)	**49,651,298**	**16.0**	**21.1**
Baby Boom (aged 46 to 64)	76,511,349	24.7	32.6
Older generations (aged 65 or older)	40,228,712	13.0	17.1

* Population aged 18 or older, projected to be 235,015,757 in 2010.
Source: Bureau of the Census, Internet site http://www.census.gov/population/www/projections/2009projections.html; calculations by New Strategist

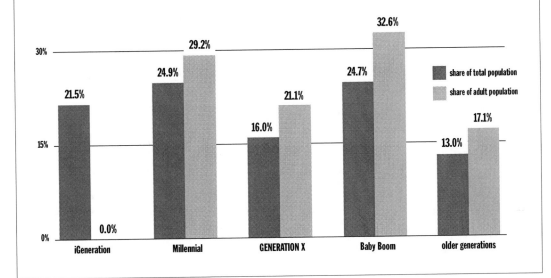

The Baby-Boom Generation: Still Center Stage

In middle age, Boomers dominate the nation's politics and economy.

Nine months after the end of World War II, the nation's maternity wards filled with babies—and no one so much as blinked, for this is the sort of thing demographers expect following the end of a war. But no one anticipated that the boom in births would last an astonishing 19 years. In 1957, the peak birth year, 4.3 million babies were born.

Today, the Baby Boom generation numbers just over 76 million. The youngest Boomers turn 46 in 2010. The oldest celebrate their 64th birthday in 2010, many probably wondering whether the country will still love them when they begin to enroll en masse in Medicare in 2011. The Great Recession has devastated the retirement plans of millions of Boomers, a misfortune that is not only rocking the economy overall but in particular is rewriting the business plans of the many companies that had been eagerly anticipating waves of Boomer retirees with time and money on their hands.

Because of its size, the Baby-Boom generation has been the focus of business and media attention since its birth. It is hard to ignore a generation that accounts for 25 percent of the total population and 33 percent of adults—a larger share of adults than any other generation. In turn, Boomers have transformed American culture and the economy.

Time moves on, however. As of 2010, Boomers are no longer the largest generation. They are outnumbered by the 77 million–strong Millennial generation. Millennials account for another 25 percent of the population and 29 percent of adults. Although they are drawing the spotlight away from Boomers, this has not stirred resentment among Boomers because most Millennials are their beloved children. And besides, the economic clout of the Baby-Boom generation—even after being knocked to their knees by the Great Recession—guarantees that it will be a force to be reckoned with for decades to come.

■ Boomers will be the prime customers of the health care industry just as it is being transformed by health insurance reform.

■ Most Boomers are empty-nesters, for whom free time and discretionary income are supposed to increase. But the Great Recession has diminished their retirement savings, reduced their standard of living, and forced Boomers to postpone retirement.

■ Even as empty-nesters, the primary focus of many Boomers is the well-being of their adult children. Helping their children cope with the Great Recession is straining the resources of middle-aged Boomers.

Table 1.13 Birth of the Baby-Boom Generation, 1946 to 1964

(annual number of births, 1946 to 1964; numbers in thousands)

	number
Total births	**75,862**
1946	3,411
1947	3,817
1948	3,637
1949	3,649
1950	3,632
1951	3,820
1952	3,909
1953	3,959
1954	4,071
1955	4,097
1956	4,210
1957	4,300
1958	4,246
1959	4,286
1960	4,258
1961	4,268
1962	4,167
1963	4,098
1964	4,027

Source: Bureau of the Census, Historical Statistics of the United States—Colonial Times to 1970, Part 1, 1975

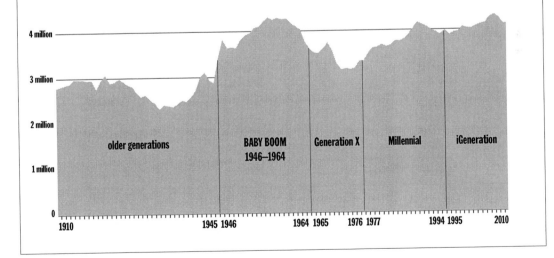

Table 1.14 Size of the Baby-Boom Generation, 2010

(number of people in the Baby-Boom generation by single year of age, 2010)

	number
Total, aged 46 to 64	**76,511,349**
Aged 46	4,528,943
Aged 47	4,514,791
Aged 48	4,525,611
Aged 49	4,558,142
Aged 50	4,629,668
Aged 51	4,460,629
Aged 52	4,444,284
Aged 53	4,347,297
Aged 54	4,227,142
Aged 55	4,211,049
Aged 56	4,020,634
Aged 57	3,894,794
Aged 58	3,765,043
Aged 59	3,625,633
Aged 60	3,611,517
Aged 61	3,467,474
Aged 62	3,463,670
Aged 63	3,409,970
Aged 64	2,805,058

Source: Bureau of the Census, Internet site http://www.census.gov/population/www/projections/2009projections.html; calculations by New Strategist

Table 1.15 Baby-Boom Generation by Age, 2000 to 2020

(age range of the Baby-Boom generation, 2000 to 2020)

	age range
2000	36–54
2001	37–55
2002	38–56
2003	39–57
2004	40–58
2005	41–59
2006	42–60
2007	43–61
2008	44–62
2009	45–63
2010	46–64
2011	47–65
2012	48–66
2013	49–67
2014	50–68
2015	51–69
2016	52–70
2017	53–71
2018	54–72
2019	55–73
2020	56–74

Source: Calculations by New Strategist

Table 1.16 Baby-Boom Share of Population, 2010

(number and percent distribution of the total population and the population aged 18 or older by generation, 2010)

	number	share of total population	share of adult* population
Total people	**310,232,863**	**100.0%**	–
iGeneration (aged 0 to 15)	66,593,915	21.5	0.0%
Millennial (aged 16 to 33)	77,247,589	24.9	29.2
Generation X (aged 34 to 45)	49,651,298	16.0	21.1
BABY BOOM (aged 46 to 64)	**76,511,349**	**24.7**	**32.6**
Older generations (aged 65 or older)	40,228,712	13.0	17.1

* Population aged 18 or older, projected to be 235,015,757 in 2010.
Source: Bureau of the Census, Internet site http://www.census.gov/population/www/projections/2009projections.html; calculations by New Strategist

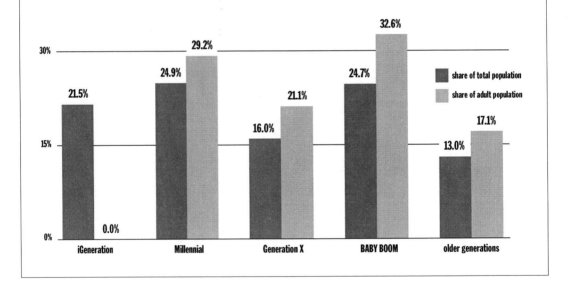

Older Generations: The Wealthiest Retirees

Younger generations are not likely to experience the comfortable, leisurely retirement enjoyed by the Swing and World War II generations.

Two living generations precede the Baby Boom: the Swing and World War II generations. Today, the youngest members of the older generations are turning 65. The oldest members are more than 100 years old.

A century ago, the annual number of births in the United States varied only slightly, ranging between 2.7 million and 3.0 million per year. In the late 1920s, the number of births began to fall, coinciding with the Great Depression. Today, the World War II generation, whose members were born in the years prior to 1933, is aged 78 or older and numbers more than 14 million. Although the World War II generation struggled through the Great Depression and World War II, it prospered in the aftermath. The lifestyles of the nation's oldest Americans were improved by generous government benefits and private-sector retirement plans. The financial security and relative good health of the World War II generation enabled it to enjoy a long, comfortable, and leisurely lifestyle in retirement.

As the stock market fell in the 1930s, so too did the annual number of births, dropping to 2.3 million in 1933. The number of births remained below 2.5 million from 1933 until 1940, when it began to climb again, although only slightly. It was not until the early 1940s that the annual number of births again matched the level of the early years of the 20th century. Altogether, 34 million babies were born between 1933 and 1945.

The Swing generation now numbers 26 million and is aged 65 to 77. Although the Swing generation was relatively small compared to the generations on either side of it, its small size belied its influence on American society. The women of the Swing generation were the first to move into the workforce in substantial proportions. Many leaders of the social movements of the 1960s and 1970s were members of the generation, including Gloria Steinem, Jesse Jackson, and Abbie Hoffman. Much of the popular culture credited to the Baby Boom was actually created by the Swing generation. Bob Dylan, for example, is a member of the Swing generation.

■ The two older generations account for only 13 percent of the overall population and 17 percent of adults.

■ Although most members of the Swing generation are retired, many still hold powerful positions in government and business.

■ The older generations will go down in history as the wealthiest retirees America has ever seen thanks to generous government and corporate retirement benefits that have now been sharply reduced or eliminated entirely.

Table 1.17 Birth of the Older Generations, 1910 to 1945

(annual number of births, 1910 to 1945; numbers in thousands)

	number
World War II generation	**64,968**
1910	2,777
1911	2,809
1912	2,840
1913	2,869
1914	2,966
1915	2,965
1916	2,964
1917	2,944
1918	2,948
1919	2,740
1920	2,950
1921	3,055
1922	2,882
1923	2,910
1924	2,979
1925	2,909
1926	2,839
1927	2,802
1928	2,674
1929	2,582
1930	2,618
1931	2,506
1932	2,440
Swing generation	**33,962**
1933	2,307
1934	2,396
1935	2,377
1936	2,355
1937	2,413
1938	2,496
1939	2,466
1940	2,559
1941	2,703
1942	2,989
1943	3,104
1944	2,939
1945	2,858

Source: Bureau of the Census, Historical Statistics of the United States—Colonial Times to 1970, Part 1, 1975

Table 1.18 Size of the Older Generations, 2010

(number of people in the older generations by single year of age, 2010)

	number
TOTAL, AGED 65 OR OLDER	**40,228,712**
Swing generation (aged 65 to 77)	**26,005,645**
Aged 65	2,616,759
Aged 66	2,590,421
Aged 67	2,578,205
Aged 68	2,340,647
Aged 69	2,134,646
Aged 70	2,033,433
Aged 71	1,928,300
Aged 72	1,844,892
Aged 73	1,729,795
Aged 74	1,665,501
Aged 75	1,622,276
Aged 76	1,484,580
Aged 77	1,436,190
World War II generation (aged 78 or older)	**14,223,067**
Aged 78	1,387,386
Aged 79	1,351,396
Aged 80	1,307,116
Aged 81	1,214,245
Aged 82	1,152,533
Aged 83	1,071,256
Aged 84	987,836
Aged 85	916,831
Aged 86	820,333
Aged 87	717,701
Aged 88	643,266
Aged 89	551,900
Aged 90	461,530
Aged 91	372,766
Aged 92	302,236
Aged 93	241,679
Aged 94	191,573
Aged 95	151,161
Aged 96	114,193
Aged 97	84,654
Aged 98	59,953
Aged 99	42,422
Aged 100 or older	79,101

Source: Bureau of the Census, Internet site http://www.census.gov/population/www/projections/2009projections.html; calculations by New Strategist

Table 1.19 Older Generations by Age, 2000 to 2020

(age range of the older generations, 2000 to 2020)

	Swing	World War II
2000	55–67	68+
2001	56–68	69+
2002	57–69	70+
2003	58–70	71+
2004	59–71	72+
2005	60–72	73+
2006	61–73	74+
2007	62–74	75+
2008	63–75	76+
2009	64–76	77+
2010	65–77	78+
2011	66–78	79+
2012	67–79	80+
2013	68–80	81+
2014	69–81	82+
2015	70–82	83+
2016	71–83	84+
2017	72–84	85+
2018	73–85	86+
2019	74–86	87+
2020	75–87	88+

Source: Calculations by New Strategist

Table 1.20 Older Generations Share of Population, 2010

(number and percent distribution of the total population and the population aged 18 or older by generation, 2010)

	number	share of total population	share of adult* population
Total people	**310,232,863**	**100.0%**	–
iGeneration (aged 0 to 15)	66,593,915	21.5	0.0%
Millennial (aged 16 to 33)	77,247,589	24.9	29.2
Generation X (aged 34 to 45)	49,651,298	16.0	21.1
Baby Boom (aged 46 to 64)	76,511,349	24.7	32.6
OLDER GENERATIONS (aged 65 or older)	**40,228,712**	**13.0**	**17.1**
Swing generation (aged 65 to 77)	26,005,645	8.4	11.1
World War II generation (aged 78 or older)	14,223,067	4.6	6.1

* Population aged 18 or older, projected to be 235,015,757 in 2010.
Source: Bureau of the Census, Internet site http://www.census.gov/population/www/projections/2009projections.html; calculations by New Strategist

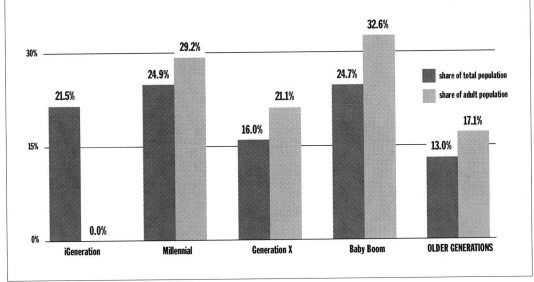

Attitudes

The Baby-Boom generation has long been credited with rebelling against its elders. But over the years the National Opinion Research Center's General Social Survey has consistently shown that the rebels were a small portion of Boomers, and that the majority of the Baby-Boom generation held middle-of-the-road or even conservative positions on many issues. Interestingly, the latest results from the General Social Survey suggest that the Baby-Boom's children—the Millennial generation—may turn out to be the real rebels.

Whether the topic is the Bible in the public schools, gay marriage, or political leanings, Millennial attitudes are distinctly more liberal than those of older generations. Will they retain these attitudes as they age? Chances are the answer is yes. Boomer attitudes on most issues have barely shifted over the years, nor have the attitudes of each succeeding older generation changed much with age. If the attitudes of Millennials continue into middle and old age, then American society will become more scientifically oriented, politically liberal, and socially tolerant in the years ahead.

What to expect in the future

■ Sweeping change in media consumption is underway as Millennials adopt the Internet as their primary source of scientific and other news.

■ Americans will become increasingly tolerant of homosexuality as a growing share of the population sees nothing wrong with it.

■ Politics will be redefined as the most liberal generation in modern history becomes a political powerhouse.

Daily Newspapers Have Lost the Youngest Generation

For the Millennial generation, the Internet is a more important source for news.

When asked where they get most of their information about current news events, 38 percent of Millennials say the Internet and only 10 percent say newspapers, according to the 2008 General Social Survey. Among Millennials, the Internet is a more important source of news than television.

Generation Xers, Boomers, and older Americans name television as the number-one medium from which they get news about current events. More than half of Boomers and older Americans say television is number one. The Internet is the number-two choice for Gen Xers. Among Boomers and older generations, newspapers rank second as the source of news.

Among Millennials, only 16 percent say they read a newspaper every day. Among older Americans, the figure is 62 percent.

■ The media preferences of the Millennial generation are revolutionizing the news industry.

Media use varies sharply by generation

(percent of people aged 18 or older who name medium as their most important source of information about current events, by generation, 2008)

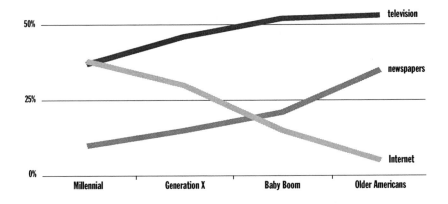

Table 2.1 Main Source of News, 2008

"Where do you get most of your information about current news events?"

(percent of people aged 18 or older responding by generation, 2008)

	television	Internet	newspapers	radio	other
Total people	**47.5%**	**22.0%**	**19.6%**	**6.1%**	**4.8%**
Millennial (18 to 31)	36.8	38.3	9.8	8.4	6.7
Generation X (32 to 43)	46.3	30.0	15.2	3.1	5.4
Baby Boom (44 to 62)	52.4	14.8	21.5	7.6	3.7
Older Americans (63 or older)	53.1	5.0	34.5	3.5	3.9

Source: Survey Documentation and Analysis, Computer-assisted Survey Methods Program, University of California, Berkeley, General Social Survey, 1972–2008 Cumulative Data Files, Internet site http://sda.berkeley.edu/cgi-bin/hsda?harcsda+gss08; calculations by New Strategist

Table 2.2 Daily Newspaper Readership, 2008

"How often do you read the newspaper?"

(percent of people aged 18 or older responding by generation, 2008)

	everyday	few times a week	once a week	less than once a week	never
Total people	**32.2%**	**22.9%**	**17.3%**	**14.3%**	**13.2%**
Millennial (18 to 31)	16.4	27.7	20.3	20.5	15.1
Generation X (32 to 43)	20.9	24.2	23.5	16.3	15.2
Baby Boom (44 to 62)	35.6	22.7	15.4	13.3	13.0
Older Americans (63 or older)	61.7	14.5	10.1	5.8	7.9

Source: Survey Documentation and Analysis, Computer-assisted Survey Methods Program, University of California, Berkeley, General Social Survey, 1972–2008 Cumulative Data Files, Internet site http://sda.berkeley.edu/cgi-bin/hsda?harcsda+gss08; calculations by New Strategist

The Internet Is an Important Source of Science News

Television is number one, but not among Millennials.

When asked where they get most of their information about science and technology, the largest share of Millennials (45 percent) say the Internet. A smaller 32 percent of Millennials name television as their primary source of information about science and technology, according to the 2008 General Social Survey. Among Gen Xers and Boomers, television is the number-one source of science news, and the Internet is number two. Among older Americans, television is in first place, newspapers and magazines are in second and third place, and the Internet ranks a lowly fourth.

Most Millennials, Gen Xers, and Boomers do not agree with the notion that science makes our way of life change too fast, 52 to 55 percent being in disagreement with the statement. In contrast, the 51 percent majority of older Americans think that science makes things change too fast.

Sixty-two percent of Millennials believe in evolution. Among Gen Xers, the slim majority (52 percent) believes in evolution. Among Boomers and older Americans, most do not believe that humans developed from earlier species of animals.

■ Not only do Millennials depend on the Internet for most of their science and technology news, but they are most welcoming of the changes brought about by scientific progress.

Millennials are most likely to believe in evolution

(percent of people aged 18 or older who say human beings developed from earlier species of animals, by generation, 2008)

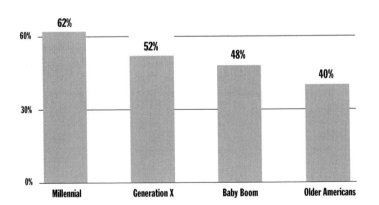

Table 2.3 Main Source of Information about Science and Technology, 2008

"Where do you get most of your information about science and technology?"

(percent of people aged 18 or older responding by generation, 2008)

	television	Internet	newspapers	magazines	books	other
Total people	**41.6%**	**28.0%**	**10.9%**	**10.9%**	**3.2%**	**5.4%**
Millennial (18 to 31)	32.2	44.9	4.9	7.3	2.1	8.6
Generation X (32 to 43)	42.2	35.5	9.6	7.6	2.0	3.1
Baby Boom (44 to 62)	42.8	21.6	12.7	12.5	4.4	6.0
Older Americans (63 or older)	51.3	9.4	16.8	16.2	3.9	2.4

Source: Survey Documentation and Analysis, Computer-assisted Survey Methods Program, University of California, Berkeley, General Social Survey, 1972–2008 Cumulative Data Files, Internet site http://sda.berkeley.edu/cgi-bin/hsda?harcsda+gss08; calculations by New Strategist

Table 2.4 Science Makes Our Way of Life Change Too Fast, 2008

"Science makes our way of life change too fast."

(percent of people aged 18 or older responding by generation, 2008)

	agree	disagree
Total people	**47.8%**	**52.2%**
Millennial (18 to 31)	44.6	55.4
Generation X (32 to 43)	47.8	52.2
Baby Boom (44 to 62)	48.4	51.6
Older Americans (63 or older)	51.0	49.0

Source: Survey Documentation and Analysis, Computer-assisted Survey Methods Program, University of California, Berkeley, General Social Survey, 1972–2008 Cumulative Data Files, Internet site http://sda.berkeley.edu/cgi-bin/hsda?harcsda+gss08; calculations by New Strategist

Table 2.5 Human Evolution, 2008

"Human beings, as we know them today, developed from earlier species of animals. Is this true or false?"

(percent of people aged 18 or older responding by generation, 2008)

	true	false
Total people	**50.9%**	**49.1%**
Millennial (18 to 31)	62.1	37.9
Generation X (32 to 43)	51.8	48.2
Baby Boom (44 to 62)	47.8	52.2
Older Americans (63 or older)	39.8	60.2

Source: Survey Documentation and Analysis, Computer-assisted Survey Methods Program, University of California, Berkeley, General Social Survey, 1972–2008 Cumulative Data Files, Internet site http://sda.berkeley.edu/cgi-bin/hsda?harcsda+gss08; calculations by New Strategist

Religious Beliefs Shape the Perspectives of Older Americans

Younger generations are more secular in their outlook.

Technology is not the only thing that separates young from old. On religious issues, Millennials and older Americans are often far apart. Only 39 percent of Millennials identify themselves as Protestant, for example, compared with 60 percent of older Americans. Twenty-seven percent of Millennials say they have no religion compared with just 7 percent of the oldest generation.

Most Millennials believe in God without a doubt (53 percent), but the figure is well below the percentage that has no doubt among older Americans (71 percent). The 55 percent majority of Millenials say they are only slightly or not at all religious. Among older Americans, 76 percent say they are moderately or very religious.

Most Americans heartily disagree with the decades-old Supreme Court decision banning the Bible from the public schools. Overall, only 42 percent approve. But among Millennials, the 53 percent majority agrees with the decision.

■ Millennials may become more religious as they get older, or they could usher in a more secular society.

Older Americans are the most religious

(percent of people aged 18 or older who say they are moderately or very religious, by generation, 2008)

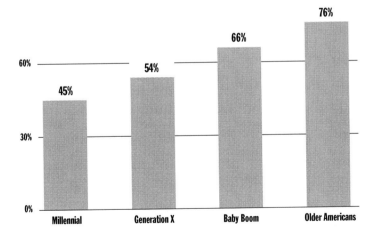

Table 2.6 Religious Preference, 2008

"What is your religious preference?"

(percent of people aged 18 or older responding by generation, 2008)

	Protestant	Catholic	Jewish	Buddhism	Moslem/ Islam	Hinduism	other	none
Total people	**49.8%**	**25.1%**	**1.7%**	**0.6%**	**0.7%**	**0.4%**	**4.9%**	**16.8%**
Millennial (18 to 31)	39.0	26.3	1.2	0.5	1.0	–	4.9	27.1
Generation X (32 to 43)	39.1	28.1	2.9	0.7	1.4	1.8	7.1	18.9
Baby Boom (44 to 62)	58.4	21.1	0.9	0.8	0.5	0.1	4.7	13.6
Older Americans (63 or older)	60.1	27.3	2.6	0.4	–	–	2.5	7.2

Note: "–" means sample is too small to make a reliable estimate.
Source: Survey Documentation and Analysis, Computer-assisted Survey Methods Program, University of California, Berkeley, General Social Survey, 1972–2008 Cumulative Data Files, Internet site http://sda.berkeley.edu/cgi-bin/hsda?harcsda+gss08; calculations by New Strategist

Table 2.7 Attendance at Religious Services, 2008

"How often do you attend religious services?"

(percent of people aged 18 or older responding by generation, 2008)

	more than once a week	every week	nearly every week	two or three times a month	once a month	several times a year	once a year	less than once a year	never
Total people	**7.8%**	**17.6%**	**4.6%**	**9.1%**	**7.5%**	**11.1%**	**13.5%**	**6.9%**	**21.8%**
Millennial (18 to 31)	4.7	11.0	3.6	7.3	9.2	11.4	17.7	5.6	29.5
Generation X (32 to 43)	6.5	14.9	4.1	14.7	6.3	11.1	12.8	6.3	23.3
Baby Boom (44 to 62)	7.7	18.5	5.5	7.6	7.8	12.3	13.5	8.8	18.3
Older Americans (63 or older)	13.7	28.5	4.5	7.4	6.2	8.5	8.4	5.8	17.2

Source: Survey Documentation and Analysis, Computer-assisted Survey Methods Program, University of California, Berkeley, General Social Survey, 1972–2008 Cumulative Data Files, Internet site http://sda.berkeley.edu/cgi-bin/hsda?harcsda+gss08; calculations by New Strategist

Table 2.8 Confidence in the Existence of God, 2008

"Which statement comes closest to expressing what you believe about God: 1) I don't believe in God. 2) I don't know whether there is a God and I don't believe there is any way to find out. 3) I don't believe in a personal God, but I do believe in a Higher Power of some kind. 4) I find myself believing in God some of the time, but not at others. 5) While I have doubts, I feel that I do believe in God. 6) I know God really exists and I have no doubts about it."

(percent of people aged 18 or older responding by generation, 2008)

	1 don't believe	2 no way to find out	3 higher power	4 believe sometimes	5 believe but doubts	6 know God exists
Total people	**3.1%**	**4.9%**	**10.1%**	**3.4%**	**16.9%**	**61.6%**
Millennial (18 to 31)	3.6	7.1	13.0	5.2	18.2	53.0
Generation X (32 to 43)	3.1	5.6	12.2	2.6	15.3	61.3
Baby Boom (44 to 62)	3.2	3.6	9.6	2.2	18.8	62.6
Older Americans (63 or older)	1.9	4.2	4.7	4.6	13.5	71.1

Source: Survey Documentation and Analysis, Computer-assisted Survey Methods Program, University of California, Berkeley, General Social Survey, 1972–2008 Cumulative Data Files, Internet site http://sda.berkeley.edu/cgi-bin/hsda?harcsda+gss08; calculations by New Strategist

Table 2.9 Degree of Religiosity, 2008

"To what extent do you consider yourself a religious person?"

(percent of people aged 18 or older responding by generation, 2008)

	very	moderately	slightly	not
Total people	**18.2%**	**42.2%**	**23.4%**	**16.2%**
Millennial (18 to 31)	12.1	33.1	28.1	26.7
Generation X (32 to 43)	13.8	40.6	25.7	19.9
Baby Boom (44 to 62)	20.1	45.9	22.1	11.9
Older Americans (63 or older)	27.7	48.6	17.4	6.3

Source: Survey Documentation and Analysis, Computer-assisted Survey Methods Program, University of California, Berkeley, General Social Survey, 1972–2008 Cumulative Data Files, Internet site http://sda.berkeley.edu/cgi-bin/hsda?harcsda+gss08; calculations by New Strategist

Table 2.10 Bible in Public Schools, 2008

"The United States Supreme Court has ruled that no state or local government may require the reading of the Lord's Prayer or Bible verses in public schools. Do you approve or disapprove of the court ruling?"

(percent of people aged 18 or older responding by generation, 2008)

	approve	disapprove
Total people	**41.8%**	**58.2%**
Millennial (18 to 31)	52.8	47.2
Generation X (32 to 43)	48.0	52.0
Baby Boom (44 to 62)	36.2	63.8
Older Americans (63 or older)	30.7	69.3

Source: Survey Documentation and Analysis, Computer-assisted Survey Methods Program, University of California, Berkeley, General Social Survey, 1972–2008 Cumulative Data Files, Internet site http://sda.berkeley.edu/cgi-bin/hsda?harcsda+gss08; calculations by New Strategist

Younger Generations Spurn Traditional Sex Roles

The percentage that sees nothing wrong with homosexuality grows with each succeeding younger generation.

There is no longer any controversy about working women in our society. That is because most Americans disagree that traditional sex roles—whereby men go to work and women stay home—are best. More than two-thirds of Millennials, Gen Xers, and Boomers disagree that traditional sex roles are best. This compares with a smaller 48 percent of older Americans. The oldest generation is the only one in which the majority thinks there is something wrong with premarital sex.

Americans are still ambivalent about homosexuality. But the Millennial generation is far more tolerant than older Americans. In fact, the 52 percent majority of Millennials thinks there is nothing wrong with sexual relations between adults of the same sex. Fifty-two percent believe homosexual couples should have the right to marry.

■ Among Millennials, 5 percent identify themselves as gay, lesbian, or bisexual—a larger percentage than in any older generation probably because of their greater willingness to acknowledge their sexual orientation.

Millennials support gay marriage

(percent of people aged 18 or older who agree that homosexuals should have the right to marry one another, by generation, 2008)

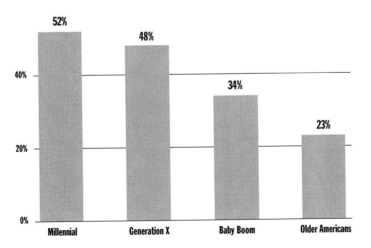

Table 2.11 Sex Roles, 2008

"It is much better for everyone involved if the man is the achiever outside the home and the woman takes care of the home and family."

(percent of people aged 18 or older responding by generation, 2008)

	strongly agree	agree	disagree	strongly disagree
Total people	**8.2%**	**27.0%**	**47.2%**	**17.5%**
Millennial (18 to 31)	7.3	24.0	44.5	24.2
Generation X (32 to 43)	8.4	25.2	47.8	18.6
Baby Boom (44 to 62)	7.5	24.0	50.7	17.8
Older Americans (63 or older)	11.3	40.5	42.6	5.5

Source: Survey Documentation and Analysis, Computer-assisted Survey Methods Program, University of California, Berkeley, General Social Survey, 1972–2008 Cumulative Data Files, Internet site http://sda.berkeley.edu/cgi-bin/hsda?harcsda+gss08; calculations by New Strategist

Table 2.12 Mother Worked While You Were Growing Up, 2008

"Did your mother ever work for pay for as long as a year while you were growing up?"

(percent of people aged 18 or older responding by generation, 2008)

	yes	no
Total people	**68.8%**	**31.2%**
Millennial (18 to 31)	80.6	19.4
Generation X (32 to 43)	74.9	25.1
Baby Boom (44 to 62)	67.6	32.4
Older Americans (63 or older)	48.9	51.1

Source: Survey Documentation and Analysis, Computer-assisted Survey Methods Program, University of California, Berkeley, General Social Survey, 1972–2008 Cumulative Data Files, Internet site http://sda.berkeley.edu/cgi-bin/hsda?harcsda+gss08; calculations by New Strategist

Table 2.13 Premarital Sex, 2008

"If a man and a woman have sex relations before marriage, do you think it is always wrong, almost always wrong, sometimes wrong, or not wrong at all?"

(percent of people aged 18 or older responding by generation, 2008)

	always wrong	almost always wrong	sometimes wrong	not wrong at all
Total people	**22.6%**	**7.2%**	**15.4%**	**54.8%**
Millennial (18 to 31)	17.5	6.9	15.8	59.8
Generation X (32 to 43)	21.0	4.9	17.7	56.5
Baby Boom (44 to 62)	23.0	6.5	12.4	58.1
Older Americans (63 or older)	31.0	11.7	18.9	38.4

Source: Survey Documentation and Analysis, Computer-assisted Survey Methods Program, University of California, Berkeley, General Social Survey, 1972–2008 Cumulative Data Files, Internet site http://sda.berkeley.edu/cgi-bin/hsda?harcsda+gss08; calculations by New Strategist

Table 2.14 Homosexuality, 2008

"What about sexual relations between two adults of the same sex? Is it always wrong, almost always wrong, sometimes wrong, or not wrong at all?"

(percent of people aged 18 or older responding by generation, 2008)

	always wrong	almost always wrong	sometimes wrong	not wrong at all
Total people	**52.4%**	**3.1%**	**6.7%**	**37.8%**
Millennial (18 to 31)	41.4	1.9	5.3	51.5
Generation X (32 to 43)	47.0	4.3	3.9	44.8
Baby Boom (44 to 62)	53.0	3.3	10.0	33.8
Older Americans (63 or older)	72.6	2.8	5.4	19.2

Source: Survey Documentation and Analysis, Computer-assisted Survey Methods Program, University of California, Berkeley, General Social Survey, 1972–2008 Cumulative Data Files, Internet site http://sda.berkeley.edu/cgi-bin/hsda?harcsda+gss08; calculations by New Strategist

Table 2.15 Gay Marriage, 2008

"Do you agree or disagree? Homosexual couples should
have the right to marry one another."

(percent of people aged 18 or older responding by generation, 2008)

	agree	neither agree nor disagree	disagree
Total people	**39.3%**	**13.0%**	**47.7%**
Millennial (18 to 31)	51.7	12.5	35.8
Generation X (32 to 43)	48.2	14.1	37.8
Baby Boom (44 to 62)	33.8	14.9	51.3
Older Americans (63 or older)	22.8	8.8	68.4

Source: Survey Documentation and Analysis, Computer-assisted Survey Methods Program, University of California, Berkeley, General Social Survey, 1972–2008 Cumulative Data Files, Internet site http://sda.berkeley.edu/cgi-bin/hsda?harcsda+gss08; calculations by New Strategist

Table 2.16 Sexual Orientation, 2008

"Which of the following best describes you?"

(percent of people aged 18 or older responding by demographic characteristic, 2008)

	gay, lesbian, or homosexual	bisexual	heterosexual or straight
Total people	**1.6%**	**1.1%**	**97.3%**
Millennial (18 to 31)	3.0	2.5	94.6
Generation X (32 to 43)	0.9	1.7	97.4
Baby Boom (44 to 62)	1.5	0.3	98.2
Older Americans (63 or older)	0.6	0.3	99.1

Source: Survey Documentation and Analysis, Computer-assisted Survey Methods Program, University of California, Berkeley, General Social Survey, 2008 Cumulative Data Files, Internet site http://sda.berkeley.edu/cgi-bin/hsda?harcsda+gss08; calculations by New Strategist

Most Americans Do Not Trust Others

Younger generations are less trusting than older ones.

When Americans are asked whether most people can be trusted, the 64 percent majority says no. The percentage of people who say others cannot be trusted ranges from a high of 71 percent among Millennials to a low of 55 percent among older Americans.

Only 47 percent of the public says that life is exciting, while a slightly larger 48 percent say it is pretty routine despite the technological, political, and economic change that has occurred in the United States. There are almost no differences in response to this question by generation. Differences emerge when people are asked how happy they are, however. Older Americans are much happier than middle-aged and younger people. Forty percent of people aged 63 or older say they are very happy compared with just 27 to 31 percent of younger people.

■ Trust in others has eroded significantly in every age group over the past few decades.

Older Americans are the happiest

(percent of people aged 18 or older who say they are very happy, by generation, 2008)

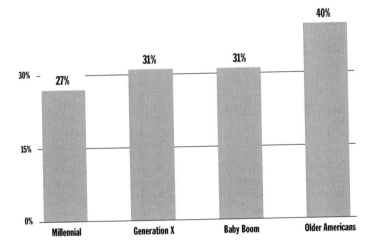

Table 2.17 **Trust in Others, 2008**

"Generally speaking, would you say that most people can be trusted
or that you can't be too careful in life?"

(percent of people aged 18 or older responding by generation, 2008)

	can trust	cannot trust	depends
Total people	**31.9%**	**63.9%**	**4.3%**
Millennial (18 to 31)	24.5	71.1	4.4
Generation X (32 to 43)	29.3	66.7	4.1
Baby Boom (44 to 62)	34.3	61.5	4.2
Older Americans (63 or older)	40.5	55.4	4.1

Source: Survey Documentation and Analysis, Computer-assisted Survey Methods Program, University of California, Berkeley, General Social Survey, 1972–2008 Cumulative Data Files, Internet site http://sda.berkeley.edu/cgi-bin/hsda?harcsda+gss08; calculations by New Strategist

Table 2.18 **Life Exciting or Dull, 2008**

"In general, do you find life exciting, pretty routine, or dull?"

(percent of people aged 18 or older responding by generation, 2008)

	exciting	pretty routine	dull
Total people	**47.2%**	**48.1%**	**3.8%**
Millennial (18 to 31)	47.4	48.5	3.8
Generation X (32 to 43)	48.6	46.5	3.1
Baby Boom (44 to 62)	46.7	49.0	3.9
Older Americans (63 or older)	46.4	47.7	4.4

Note: Numbers do not sum to 100 because "other response" is not shown.
Source: Survey Documentation and Analysis, Computer-assisted Survey Methods Program, University of California, Berkeley, General Social Survey, 1972–2008 Cumulative Data Files, Internet site http://sda.berkeley.edu/cgi-bin/hsda?harcsda+gss08; calculations by New Strategist

Table 2.19 General Happiness, 2008

"Taken all together, how would you say things are these days—would you
say that you are very happy, pretty happy, or not too happy?"

(percent of people aged 18 or older responding by generation, 2008)

	very happy	pretty happy	not too happy
Total people	**31.6%**	**54.4%**	**13.9%**
Millennial (18 to 31)	27.4	55.8	16.8
Generation X (32 to 43)	31.0	57.0	12.0
Baby Boom (44 to 62)	30.8	55.6	13.6
Older Americans (63 or older)	39.7	47.2	13.1

Source: Survey Documentation and Analysis, Computer-assisted Survey Methods Program, University of California, Berkeley, General Social Survey, 1972–2008 Cumulative Data Files, Internet site http://sda.berkeley.edu/cgi-bin/hsda?harcsda+gss08; calculations by New Strategist

Among the Generations, Millennials Are the Most Liberal

Older Americans are the most conservative.

There is a common misconception that people become increasingly conservative with age. In fact, political outlook develops in early adulthood and tends to remain stable throughout life. This stability in political leanings over the life course makes the current findings from the General Social Survey especially interesting. The 2008 results show Millennials to be the most liberal generation and the only one in which liberals outnumber conservatives. In 2008, 34 percent of Millennials identified themselves as liberal compared with a smaller 28 percent who identified themselves as conservative. Conservatism grows in each successive older generation. Among the oldest Americans, 45 percent are conservative and only 17 percent are liberal.

Millennials also are more likely than older generations to identify themselves as Democrats, with the 52 percent majority placing themselves on the Democratic end of the spectrum. Only 24 percent of Millennials identify themselves as Republican compared with 37 to 40 percent of older Americans.

■ Millennials are more likely than older generations to think the government should help people pay for medical care. Older Americans, who are almost universally covered by the government's Medicare health insurance program, are least supportive of government help.

Older Americans are least likely to think the government should help with medical care

(percent of people aged 18 or older who believe the federal government should help people pay for their medical care, by generation, 2008)

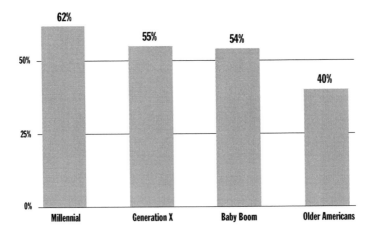

Table 2.20 Political Leanings, 2008

"We hear a lot of talk these days about liberals and conservatives. Where would you place yourself on a seven-point scale from extremely liberal (1) to extremely conservative (7)?"

(percent of people aged 18 or older responding by generation, 2008)

	liberal (1 to 3)	moderate (4)	conservative (5 to 7)
Total people	**25.7%**	**38.6%**	**35.7%**
Millennial (18 to 31)	34.4	37.6	28.0
Generation X (32 to 43)	27.7	39.4	32.9
Baby Boom (44 to 62)	23.5	38.4	38.1
Older Americans (63 or older)	16.8	38.4	44.8

Source: Survey Documentation and Analysis, Computer-assisted Survey Methods Program, University of California, Berkeley, General Social Survey, 1972–2008 Cumulative Data Files, Internet site http://sda.berkeley.edu/cgi-bin/hsda?harcsda+gss08; calculations by New Strategist

Table 2.21 Political Party Affiliation, 2008

"Generally speaking, do you usually think of yourself as a Republican, Democrat, Independent, or what?"

(percent of people aged 18 or older responding by generation, 2008)

	strong Democrat	not strong Democrat	independent, near Democrat	independent	independent, near Republican	not strong Republican	strong Republican	other party
Total people	**18.9%**	**17.1%**	**12.1%**	**15.7%**	**8.1%**	**15.7%**	**10.5%**	**1.8%**
Millennial (18 to 31)	14.2	21.2	16.6	21.0	5.5	12.9	5.6	2.9
Generation X (32 to 43)	20.4	16.7	9.1	15.5	9.2	17.9	9.4	1.8
Baby Boom (44 to 62)	18.7	17.1	10.9	15.0	9.6	16.8	10.9	1.1
Older Americans (63 or older)	23.5	12.2	12.6	10.4	7.4	14.8	17.9	1.2

Source: Survey Documentation and Analysis, Computer-assisted Survey Methods Program, University of California, Berkeley, General Social Survey, 1972–2008 Cumulative Data Files, Internet site http://sda.berkeley.edu/cgi-bin/hsda?harcsda+gss08; calculations by New Strategist

Table 2.22 Government Should Help Pay for Medical Care, 2008

"In general, some people think that it is the responsibility of the government in Washington to see to it that people have help in paying for doctors and hospital bills; they are at point 1. Others think that these matters are not the responsibility of the federal government and that people should take care of these things themselves; they are at point 5. Where would you place yourself on the scale?"

(percent of people aged 18 or older responding by generation, 2008)

	1 government should help	2	3 agree with both	4	5 people should help themselves
Total people	**34.9%**	**18.7%**	**30.0%**	**9.3%**	**7.1%**
Millennial (18 to 31)	39.0	23.1	25.9	5.2	6.8
Generation X (32 to 43)	35.0	19.8	30.7	9.4	5.1
Baby Boom (44 to 62)	35.2	18.5	28.0	11.4	7.0
Older Americans (63 or older)	28.7	11.2	39.1	10.0	11.0

Source: Survey Documentation and Analysis, Computer-assisted Survey Methods Program, University of California, Berkeley, General Social Survey, 1972–2008 Cumulative Data Files, Internet site http://sda.berkeley.edu/cgi-bin/hsda?harcsda+gss08; calculations by New Strategist

Boomers Have Hit Hard Times

They are most likely to have lost their faith in the American Dream.

Boomers are in their peak earning years and most likely to think their family income is above average, 25 percent feeling that way. But the peak earning years have not insulated Boomers from hard times. Thirty-two percent of Boomers say their financial situation has gotten worse over the past few years, a greater share than the 31 percent who say their finances have improved.

When it comes to the American Dream, Boomers are the most jaded. Thirty-one percent disagree with the statement, "The way things are in America, people like me and my family have a good chance of improving our standard of living," a higher share than in any other generation. Only 12 percent strongly agree that they have a good chance of improving their standard of living.

■ Despite their economic struggles, Boomers are more likely than Gen Xers to be satisfied with their financial situation.

Older Americans are most satisfied with their financial situation

(percent of people aged 18 or older who say they are satisfied with their financial situation, by generation, 2008)

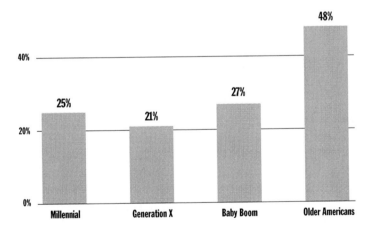

Table 2.23 Family Income Relative to Others, 2008

"Compared with American families in general, would you say your family income is far below average, below average, average, above average, or far above average?"

(percent of people aged 18 or older responding by generation, 2008)

	far below average	below average	average	above average	far above average
Total people	**6.3%**	**25.2%**	**46.7%**	**19.8%**	**2.0%**
Millennial (18 to 31)	6.6	26.8	49.4	16.5	0.7
Generation X (32 to 43)	7.8	25.5	43.9	20.7	2.2
Baby Boom (44 to 62)	5.6	22.8	46.2	22.4	3.1
Older Americans (63 or older)	5.0	27.8	47.9	17.9	1.4

Source: Survey Documentation and Analysis, Computer-assisted Survey Methods Program, University of California, Berkeley, General Social Survey, 1972–2008 Cumulative Data Files, Internet site http://sda.berkeley.edu/cgi-bin/hsda?harcsda+gss08; calculations by New Strategist

Table 2.24 Change in Financial Situation, 2008

"During the last few years, has your financial situation been getting better, worse, or has it stayed the same?"

(percent of people aged 18 or older responding by generation, 2008)

	better	worse	stayed same
Total people	**31.7%**	**28.3%**	**40.0%**
Millennial (18 to 31)	40.3	22.4	37.3
Generation X (32 to 43)	36.8	27.2	36.0
Baby Boom (44 to 62)	30.9	31.8	37.3
Older Americans (63 or older)	15.9	30.2	54.0

Source: Survey Documentation and Analysis, Computer-assisted Survey Methods Program, University of California, Berkeley, General Social Survey, 1972–2008 Cumulative Data Files, Internet site http://sda.berkeley.edu/cgi-bin/hsda?harcsda+gss08; calculations by New Strategist

Table 2.25 Satisfaction with Financial Situation, 2008

"We are interested in how people are getting along financially these days. So far as you and your family are concerned, would you say that you are pretty well satisfied with your present financial situation, more or less satisfied, or not satisfied at all?"

(percent of people aged 18 or older responding by generation, 2008)

	satisfied	more or less satisfied	not at all satisfied
Total people	**28.9%**	**41.7%**	**29.4%**
Millennial (18 to 31)	24.8	43.7	31.5
Generation X (32 to 43)	20.5	43.7	35.7
Baby Boom (44 to 62)	27.3	44.2	28.4
Older Americans (63 or older)	48.0	31.6	20.4

Source: Survey Documentation and Analysis, Computer-assisted Survey Methods Program, University of California, Berkeley, General Social Survey, 1972–2008 Cumulative Data Files, Internet site http://sda.berkeley.edu/cgi-bin/hsda?harcsda+gss08; calculations by New Strategist

Table 2.26 Standard of Living Will Improve, 2008

"The way things are in America, people like me and my family have a good chance of improving our standard of living. Do you agree or disagree?"

(percent of people aged 18 or older responding by generation, 2008)

	strongly agree	agree	neither	disagree	strongly disagree
Total people	**14.7%**	**44.7%**	**13.9%**	**22.9%**	**3.8%**
Millennial (18 to 31)	19.6	52.2	11.3	14.0	2.9
Generation X (32 to 43)	15.2	44.7	13.7	21.7	4.6
Baby Boom (44 to 62)	12.0	44.9	11.8	27.9	3.4
Older Americans (63 or older)	13.2	33.6	22.3	26.0	4.9

Source: Survey Documentation and Analysis, Computer-assisted Survey Methods Program, University of California, Berkeley, General Social Survey, 1972–2008 Cumulative Data Files, Internet site http://sda.berkeley.edu/cgi-bin/hsda?harcsda+gss08; calculations by New Strategist

Millennials Socialize the Most

Socializing with relatives is more common than socializing with friends.

Thirty-eight percent of Americans socialize with relatives at least weekly. Millennials are most likely to do so, 52 percent spending a social evening with relatives at least several times a week. Millennials are also most likely to socialize at least weekly with friends (44 percent). About one-third of Gen Xers, Boomers, and older Americans socialize with relatives on a weekly basis, but only 14 to 16 percent get together with friends that frequently.

A 36 percent minority of the public owns a gun, the proportion rising with age. Among older Americans, the 54 percent majority has a gun in their home. Among Millennials, only 19 percent are gun owners.

■ In every generation, the majority opposes the legalization of marijuana, but younger Americans are less opposed than older.

Millennials are most supportive of legalizing marijuana

(percent of people aged 18 or older who think marijuana should be made legal, by generation, 2008)

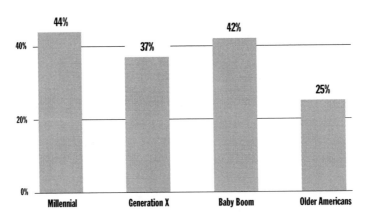

Table 2.27 Spend Evening with Relatives, 2008

"How often do you spend a social evening with relatives?"

(percent of people aged 18 or older responding by generation, 2008)

	almost daily	several times a week	several times a month	once a month	several times a year	once a year	never
Total people	**13.8%**	**24.3%**	**19.7%**	**15.1%**	**16.6%**	**6.5%**	**4.0%**
Millennial (18 to 31)	24.5	27.5	15.3	14.1	9.4	5.1	4.2
Generation X (32 to 43)	12.5	23.1	23.7	16.0	15.9	6.0	2.7
Baby Boom (44 to 62)	9.4	24.2	21.7	16.2	17.5	7.8	3.1
Older Americans (63 or older)	10.3	21.3	16.7	13.4	25.7	5.4	7.2

Source: Survey Documentation and Analysis, Computer-assisted Survey Methods Program, University of California, Berkeley, General Social Survey, 1972–2008 Cumulative Data Files, Internet site http://sda.berkeley.edu/cgi-bin/hsda?harcsda+gss08; calculations by New Strategist

Table 2.28 Spend Evening with Friends, 2008

"How often do you spend a social evening with friends
who live outside the neighborhood?"

(percent of people aged 18 or older responding by generation, 2008)

	almost daily	several times a week	several times a month	once a month	several times a year	once a year	never
Total people	**4.5%**	**17.6%**	**20.4%**	**21.2%**	**18.7%**	**7.8%**	**9.8%**
Millennial (18 to 31)	13.9	30.4	21.4	18.0	7.3	4.6	4.4
Generation X (32 to 43)	1.4	13.5	24.7	27.0	19.2	8.5	5.6
Baby Boom (44 to 62)	1.5	12.8	19.8	22.8	23.1	8.1	11.8
Older Americans (63 or older)	1.7	14.6	15.4	14.8	24.2	11.0	18.2

Source: Survey Documentation and Analysis, Computer-assisted Survey Methods Program, University of California, Berkeley, General Social Survey, 1972–2008 Cumulative Data Files, Internet site http://sda.berkeley.edu/cgi-bin/hsda?harcsda+gss08; calculations by New Strategist

Table 2.29 Have Gun in Home, 2008

"Do you happen to have in your home (or garage) any guns or revolvers?"

(percent of people aged 18 or older responding by generation, 2008)

	yes	no	refused
Total people	**36.0%**	**63.0%**	**1.1%**
Millennial (18 to 31)	18.7	81.2	0.1
Generation X (32 to 43)	33.0	65.7	1.3
Baby Boom (44 to 62)	39.9	58.4	1.7
Older Americans (63 or older)	54.5	44.8	0.7

Source: Survey Documentation and Analysis, Computer-assisted Survey Methods Program, University of California, Berkeley, General Social Survey, 1972–2008 Cumulative Data Files, Internet site http://sda.berkeley.edu/cgi-bin/hsda?harcsda+gss08; calculations by New Strategist

Table 2.30 Should Marijuana Be Made Legal, 2008

"Do you think the use of marijuana should be made legal or not?"

(percent of people aged 18 or older responding by generation, 2008)

	legal	not legal
Total people	**38.3%**	**61.7%**
Millennial (18 to 31)	43.8	56.2
Generation X (32 to 43)	36.6	63.4
Baby Boom (44 to 62)	41.5	58.5
Older Americans (63 or older)	24.8	75.2

Source: Survey Documentation and Analysis, Computer-assisted Survey Methods Program, University of California, Berkeley, General Social Survey, 1972–2008 Cumulative Data Files, Internet site http://sda.berkeley.edu/cgi-bin/hsda?harcsda+gss08; calculations by New Strategist

Education

Increasingly, job success depends upon being able to research, understand, and manage information. In today's complex, information-rich world, having at least an associate's degree has become a minimum requirement for obtaining jobs that provide a middle-class lifestyle. As a result, education no longer ends with a high school diploma for most young people. The majority starts college, and one-third eventually obtains a bachelor's or higher degree.

The higher educational attainment of younger generations is a factor in many of the changes in our economy and society during the past half-century. This is because education influences a person's attitudes, lifestyle, expectations, and consumer behavior. As growing numbers of Baby Boomers celebrate their 60th birthdays over the next few years, the educational differences between older and younger generations will disappear. This will greatly diminish the generation gap in attitudes and lifestyles that has characterized relations among the generations for the past few decades.

What to expect in the future

■ Success in the information age depends on the continuous updating of skills. Consequently, middle-aged and older adults are becoming increasingly important consumers of education.

■ As Americans become better educated, they are less willing to leave decision-making to experts. This hands-on attitude is reshaping institutions in fields ranging from education to finance and medicine.

Generation X Is the Most Highly Educated

By age group, 30-to-39-year-olds are most likely to have a bachelor's degree.

The educational attainment of the Swing and World War II generations is considerably lower than that of younger generations. Because education influences attitudes, this difference is the key element in the enduring gap between older and younger Americans.

A substantial 21 percent of the Swing and World War II generations never graduated from high school. This compares with only 11 to 12 percent of Boomers, Generation Xers, and Millennials who do not have a high school diploma.

Generation X is the best-educated generation, with 33 percent of its members having completed a bachelor's degree. This compares with a slightly smaller 32 percent of Millennials and 30 percent of Baby Boomers. In contrast, only 23 percent of the members of the Swing and World War II generations are college graduates. The 58 to 60 percent majority of Millennials, Gen Xers, and Boomers have at least some college experience compared with only 43 percent of the Swing and World War II generations.

■ College credentials—at least an associate's degree—are a requirement for a growing number of jobs.

The Swing and World War II generations are the least educated

(percent of people with a bachelor's degree or more, by generation, 2009)

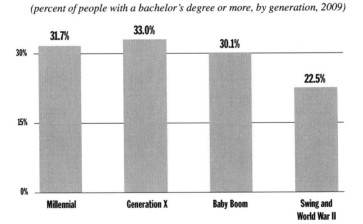

Table 3.1 Educational Attainment by Age, 2009

(number and percent distribution of people aged 25 or older by educational attainment and age, 2009; numbers in thousands)

	total	25 to 29	30 to 34	35 to 39	40 to 44	45 to 49	50 to 54	55 to 59	60 to 64	65+
Total people	198,285	21,256	19,264	20,445	20,877	22,712	21,654	18,755	15,534	37,788
Not a high school graduate	26,414	2,420	2,330	2,447	2,370	2,478	2,378	2,046	1,760	8,190
High school graduate only	61,626	6,113	5,239	5,506	6,336	7,348	6,930	5,691	4,681	13,783
Some college, no degree	33,832	4,361	3,422	3,472	3,387	3,824	3,705	3,413	2,695	5,553
Associate's degree	17,838	1,856	1,769	2,086	2,136	2,420	2,353	1,823	1,323	2,071
Bachelor's degree	37,635	4,927	4,314	4,487	4,367	4,350	3,981	3,466	2,908	4,835
Master's degree	15,118	1,258	1,622	1,754	1,646	1,615	1,655	1,722	1,579	2,268
Professional degree	3,206	204	341	403	338	346	390	301	311	572
Doctoral degree	2,614	117	228	290	300	330	262	292	278	515
High school graduate or more	171,869	18,836	16,935	17,998	18,510	20,233	19,276	16,708	13,775	29,597
Some college or more	110,243	12,723	11,696	12,492	12,174	12,885	12,346	11,017	9,094	15,814
Associate's degree or more	76,411	8,362	8,274	9,020	8,787	9,061	8,641	7,604	6,399	10,261
Bachelor's degree or more	58,573	6,506	6,505	6,934	6,651	6,641	6,288	5,781	5,076	8,190
Total people	100.0%	100.0%	100.0%	100.0%	100.0%	100.0%	100.0%	100.0%	100.0%	100.0%
Not a high school graduate	13.3	11.4	12.1	12.0	11.4	10.9	11.0	10.9	11.3	21.7
High school graduate only	31.1	28.8	27.2	26.9	30.3	32.4	32.0	30.3	30.1	36.5
Some college, no degree	17.1	20.5	17.8	17.0	16.2	16.8	17.1	18.2	17.3	14.7
Associate's degree	9.0	8.7	9.2	10.2	10.2	10.7	10.9	9.7	8.5	5.5
Bachelor's degree	19.0	23.2	22.4	21.9	20.9	19.2	18.4	18.5	18.7	12.8
Master's degree	7.6	5.9	8.4	8.6	7.9	7.1	7.6	9.2	10.2	6.0
Professional degree	1.6	1.0	1.8	2.0	1.6	1.5	1.8	1.6	2.0	1.5
Doctoral degree	1.3	0.6	1.2	1.4	1.4	1.5	1.2	1.6	1.8	1.4
High school graduate or more	86.7	88.6	87.9	88.0	88.7	89.1	89.0	89.1	88.7	78.3
Some college or more	55.6	59.9	60.7	61.1	58.3	56.7	57.0	58.7	58.5	41.8
Associate's degree or more	38.5	39.3	43.0	44.1	42.1	39.9	39.9	40.5	41.2	27.2
Bachelor's degree or more	29.5	30.6	33.8	33.9	31.9	29.2	29.0	30.8	32.7	21.7

Source: Bureau of the Census, Educational Attainment in the United States: 2009, Internet site http://www.census.gov/population/www/socdemo/education/cps2009.html; calculations by New Strategist

Table 3.2 Educational Attainment by Generation, 2009

(number and percent distribution of people aged 15 or older by educational attainment and generation, 2009; numbers in thousands)

	total	Millennial (25 to 32)	Generation X (33 to 44)	Baby Boom (45 to 63)	Swing and World War II (64 or older)
Total people	**198,285**	**32,814**	**49,028**	**75,548**	**40,895**
Not a high school graduate	26,414	3,818	5,749	8,310	8,542
High school graduate only	61,626	9,256	13,938	23,714	14,719
Some college, no degree	33,832	6,414	8,228	13,098	6,092
Associate's degree	17,838	2,917	4,930	7,654	2,336
Bachelor's degree	37,635	7,515	10,580	14,123	5,417
Master's degree	15,118	2,231	4,049	6,255	2,584
Professional degree	3,206	409	877	1,286	634
Doctoral degree	2,614	254	681	1,106	571
High school graduate or more	171,869	28,997	43,282	67,237	32,352
Some college or more	110,243	19,741	29,344	43,523	17,633
Associate's degree or more	76,411	13,326	21,117	30,425	11,541
Bachelor's degree or more	58,573	10,409	16,187	22,771	9,205
Total people	**100.0%**	**100.0%**	**100.0%**	**100.0%**	**100.0%**
Not a high school graduate	13.3	11.6	11.7	11.0	20.9
High school graduate only	31.1	28.2	28.4	31.4	36.0
Some college, no degree	17.1	19.5	16.8	17.3	14.9
Associate's degree	9.0	8.9	10.1	10.1	5.7
Bachelor's degree	19.0	22.9	21.6	18.7	13.2
Master's degree	7.6	6.8	8.3	8.3	6.3
Professional degree	1.6	1.2	1.8	1.7	1.6
Doctoral degree	1.3	0.8	1.4	1.5	1.4
High school graduate or more	86.7	88.4	88.3	89.0	79.1
Some college or more	55.6	60.2	59.9	57.6	43.1
Associate's degree or more	38.5	40.6	43.1	40.3	28.2
Bachelor's degree or more	29.5	31.7	33.0	30.1	22.5

Note: Educational attainment by generation is calculated by New Strategist.
Source: Bureau of the Census, Educational Attainment in the United States: 2009, Internet site http://www.census.gov/population/www/socdemo/education/cps2009.html; calculations by New Strategist

Under Age 50, Women Are Better Educated than Men

Among Millennials and Gen Xers, women are more likely than men to be college graduates.

Among both men and women, middle-aged and younger adults are better educated than their elders. But college graduation rates differ for men and women in interesting ways.

Millennial women are better educated than women in any other generation. Thirty-six percent have a bachelor's degree, more than double the percentage with a bachelor's degree among women in the Swing and World War II generations. Among men, Gen Xers are about equally likely as Boomers to have a bachelor's degree.

By age group, men aged 55 or older are better educated than their female counterparts. Among people aged 65 or older, 28 percent of men and a much smaller 17 percent of women have a bachelor's degree. Under age 50, however, women are more likely than men to be college graduates. The gap is greatest in the 30-to-34 age group where 37.6 percent of women and only 29.9 percent of men have a bachelor's degree.

■ Because young and middle-aged women are more highly educated than their male counterparts, the earnings gap between men and women should continue to shrink.

Among Millennials and Generation X, women are better educated than men

(percent of people aged 25 or older with a bachelor's degree or more, by generation and sex, 2009)

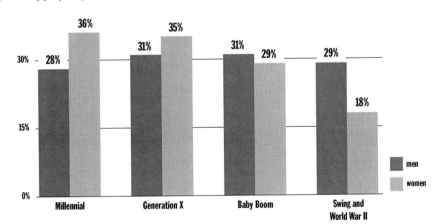

Table 3.3 Educational Attainment of Men by Age, 2009

(number and percent distribution of men aged 25 or older by educational attainment and age, 2009; numbers in thousands)

	total	25 to 29	30 to 34	35 to 39	40 to 44	45 to 49	50 to 54	55 to 59	60 to 64	65+
Total men	**95,518**	**10,867**	**9,574**	**10,169**	**10,322**	**11,162**	**10,611**	**9,083**	**7,423**	**16,308**
Not a high school graduate	13,153	1,363	1,323	1,357	1,293	1,380	1,206	1,046	845	3,339
High school graduate only	30,025	3,565	2,931	2,957	3,355	3,794	3,539	2,656	2,013	5,216
Some college, no degree	16,093	2,196	1,683	1,753	1,535	1,811	1,821	1,657	1,261	2,377
Associate's degree	7,541	856	773	883	916	988	962	798	582	782
Bachelor's degree	18,101	2,228	1,931	2,100	2,082	2,020	1,918	1,756	1,526	2,539
Master's degree	7,009	516	637	754	778	767	771	779	791	1,215
Professional degree	1,953	93	160	206	173	204	234	214	231	438
Doctoral degree	1,643	52	136	157	190	199	158	177	174	401
High school graduate or more	82,365	9,506	8,251	8,810	9,029	9,783	9,403	8,037	6,578	12,968
Some college or more	52,340	5,941	5,320	5,853	5,674	5,989	5,864	5,381	4,565	7,752
Associate's degree or more	36,247	3,745	3,637	4,100	4,139	4,178	4,043	3,724	3,304	5,375
Bachelor's degree or more	28,706	2,889	2,864	3,217	3,223	3,190	3,081	2,926	2,722	4,593
Total men	**100.0%**	**100.0%**	**100.0%**	**100.0%**	**100.0%**	**100.0%**	**100.0%**	**100.0%**	**100.0%**	**100.0%**
Not a high school graduate	13.8	12.5	13.8	13.3	12.5	12.4	11.4	11.5	11.4	20.5
High school graduate only	31.4	32.8	30.6	29.1	32.5	34.0	33.4	29.2	27.1	32.0
Some college, no degree	16.8	20.2	17.6	17.2	14.9	16.2	17.2	18.2	17.0	14.6
Associate's degree	7.9	7.9	8.1	8.7	8.9	8.9	9.1	8.8	7.8	4.8
Bachelor's degree	19.0	20.5	20.2	20.7	20.2	18.1	18.1	19.3	20.6	15.6
Master's degree	7.3	4.7	6.7	7.4	7.5	6.9	7.3	8.6	10.7	7.5
Professional degree	2.0	0.9	1.7	2.0	1.7	1.8	2.2	2.4	3.1	2.7
Doctoral degree	1.7	0.5	1.4	1.5	1.8	1.8	1.5	1.9	2.3	2.5
High school graduate or more	86.2	87.5	86.2	86.6	87.5	87.6	88.6	88.5	88.6	79.5
Some college or more	54.8	54.7	55.6	57.6	55.0	53.7	55.3	59.2	61.5	47.5
Associate's degree or more	37.9	34.5	38.0	40.3	40.1	37.4	38.1	41.0	44.5	33.0
Bachelor's degree or more	30.1	26.6	29.9	31.6	31.2	28.6	29.0	32.2	36.7	28.2

Source: Bureau of the Census, Educational Attainment in the United States: 2009, Internet site http://www.census.gov/ population/www/socdemo/education/cps2009.html; calculations by New Strategist

Table 3.4 Educational Attainment of Men by Generation, 2009

(number and percent distribution of men aged 25 or older by educational attainment and generation, 2009; numbers in thousands)

	total	Millennials (25 to 32)	Generation X (33 to 44)	Baby Boom (45 to 63)	Swing and World War II (64 or older)
Total men	**95,518**	**16,611**	**24,321**	**36,794**	**17,793**
Not a high school graduate	13,153	2,157	3,179	4,308	3,508
High school graduate only	30,025	5,324	7,484	11,599	5,619
Some college, no degree	16,093	3,206	3,961	6,298	2,629
Associate's degree	7,541	1,320	2,108	3,214	898
Bachelor's degree	18,101	3,387	4,954	6,915	2,844
Master's degree	7,009	898	1,787	2,950	1,373
Professional degree	1,953	189	443	837	484
Doctoral degree	1,643	134	401	673	436
High school graduate or more	82,365	14,457	21,139	32,485	14,284
Some college or more	52,340	9,133	13,655	20,886	8,665
Associate's degree or more	36,247	5,927	9,694	14,588	6,036
Bachelor's degree or more	28,706	4,607	7,586	11,375	5,137
Total men	**100.0%**	**100.0%**	**100.0%**	**100.0%**	**100.0%**
Not a high school graduate	13.8	13.0	13.1	11.7	19.7
High school graduate only	31.4	32.0	30.8	31.5	31.6
Some college, no degree	16.8	19.3	16.3	17.1	14.8
Associate's degree	7.9	7.9	8.7	8.7	5.0
Bachelor's degree	19.0	20.4	20.4	18.8	16.0
Master's degree	7.3	5.4	7.3	8.0	7.7
Professional degree	2.0	1.1	1.8	2.3	2.7
Doctoral degree	1.7	0.8	1.7	1.8	2.4
High school graduate or more	86.2	87.0	86.9	88.3	80.3
Some college or more	54.8	55.0	56.1	56.8	48.7
Associate's degree or more	37.9	35.7	39.9	39.6	33.9
Bachelor's degree or more	30.1	27.7	31.2	30.9	28.9

Note: Educational attainment by generation is calculated by New Strategist.
Source: Bureau of the Census, Educational Attainment in the United States: 2009, Internet site http://www.census.gov/population/www/socdemo/education/cps2009.html; calculations by New Strategist

Table 3.5 Educational Attainment of Women by Age, 2009

(number and percent distribution of women aged 25 or older by educational attainment and age, 2009; numbers in thousands)

	total	25 to 29	30 to 34	35 to 39	40 to 44	45 to 49	50 to 54	55 to 59	60 to 64	65+
Total women	**102,767**	**10,389**	**9,691**	**10,275**	**10,556**	**11,550**	**11,043**	**9,671**	**8,112**	**21,480**
Not a high school graduate	13,262	1,057	1,006	1,089	1,075	1,099	1,171	1,000	913	4,851
High school graduate only	31,601	2,548	2,308	2,549	2,981	3,555	3,391	3,035	2,668	8,565
Some college, no degree	17,739	2,165	1,739	1,719	1,852	2,013	1,884	1,756	1,435	3,176
Associate's degree	10,296	1,000	996	1,202	1,221	1,431	1,390	1,026	742	1,288
Bachelor's degree	19,534	2,699	2,383	2,387	2,284	2,330	2,063	1,710	1,382	2,296
Master's degree	8,110	743	985	1,000	867	848	884	943	787	1,054
Professional degree	1,253	111	180	197	165	142	155	87	80	135
Doctoral degree	971	65	92	133	110	132	105	115	104	115
High school graduate or more	89,504	9,331	8,683	9,187	9,480	10,451	9,872	8,672	7,198	16,629
Some college or more	57,903	6,783	6,375	6,638	6,499	6,896	6,481	5,637	4,530	8,064
Associate's degree or more	40,164	4,618	4,636	4,919	4,647	4,883	4,597	3,881	3,095	4,888
Bachelor's degree or more	29,868	3,618	3,640	3,717	3,426	3,452	3,207	2,855	2,353	3,600
Total women	**100.0%**	**100.0%**	**100.0%**	**100.0%**	**100.0%**	**100.0%**	**100.0%**	**100.0%**	**100.0%**	**100.0%**
Not a high school graduate	12.9	10.2	10.4	10.6	10.2	9.5	10.6	10.3	11.3	22.6
High school graduate only	30.8	24.5	23.8	24.8	28.2	30.8	30.7	31.4	32.9	39.9
Some college, no degree	17.3	20.8	17.9	16.7	17.5	17.4	17.1	18.2	17.7	14.8
Associate's degree	10.0	9.6	10.3	11.7	11.6	12.4	12.6	10.6	9.1	6.0
Bachelor's degree	19.0	26.0	24.6	23.2	21.6	20.2	18.7	17.7	17.0	10.7
Master's degree	7.9	7.2	10.2	9.7	8.2	7.3	8.0	9.8	9.7	4.9
Professional degree	1.2	1.1	1.9	1.9	1.6	1.2	1.4	0.9	1.0	0.6
Doctoral degree	0.9	0.6	0.9	1.3	1.0	1.1	1.0	1.2	1.3	0.5
High school graduate or more	87.1	89.8	89.6	89.4	89.8	90.5	89.4	89.7	88.7	77.4
Some college or more	56.3	65.3	65.8	64.6	61.6	59.7	58.7	58.3	55.8	37.5
Associate's degree or more	39.1	44.5	47.8	47.9	44.0	42.3	41.6	40.1	38.2	22.8
Bachelor's degree or more	29.1	34.8	37.6	36.2	32.5	29.9	29.0	29.5	29.0	16.8

Source: Bureau of the Census, Educational Attainment in the United States: 2009, Internet site http://www.census.gov/population/www/socdemo/education/cps2009.html; calculations by New Strategist

Table 3.6 Educational Attainment of Women by Generation, 2009

(number and percent distribution of women aged 25 or older by educational attainment and generation, 2009; numbers in thousands)

	total	Millennials (25 to 32)	Generation X (33 to 44)	Baby Boom (45 to 63)	Swing and World War II (64 or older)
Total women	**102,767**	**16,204**	**24,707**	**38,754**	**23,102**
Not a high school graduate	13,262	1,661	2,566	4,000	5,034
High school graduate only	31,601	3,933	6,453	12,115	9,099
Some college, no degree	17,739	3,208	4,267	6,801	3,463
Associate's degree	10,296	1,598	2,821	4,441	1,436
Bachelor's degree	19,534	4,129	5,624	7,209	2,572
Master's degree	8,110	1,334	2,261	3,305	1,211
Professional degree	1,253	219	434	448	151
Doctoral degree	971	120	280	435	136
High school graduate or more	89,504	14,541	22,140	34,753	18,069
Some college or more	57,903	10,608	15,687	22,638	8,970
Associate's degree or more	40,164	7,400	11,420	15,837	5,507
Bachelor's degree or more	29,868	5,802	8,599	11,396	4,071
Total women	**100.0%**	**100.0%**	**100.0%**	**100.0%**	**100.0%**
Not a high school graduate	12.9	10.2	10.4	10.3	21.8
High school graduate only	30.8	24.3	26.1	31.3	39.4
Some college, no degree	17.3	19.8	17.3	17.5	15.0
Associate's degree	10.0	9.9	11.4	11.5	6.2
Bachelor's degree	19.0	25.5	22.8	18.6	11.1
Master's degree	7.9	8.2	9.2	8.5	5.2
Professional degree	1.2	1.4	1.8	1.2	0.7
Doctoral degree	0.9	0.7	1.1	1.1	0.6
High school graduate or more	87.1	89.7	89.6	89.7	78.2
Some college or more	56.3	65.5	63.5	58.4	38.8
Associate's degree or more	39.1	45.7	46.2	40.9	23.8
Bachelor's degree or more	29.1	35.8	34.8	29.4	17.6

Note: Educational attainment by generation is calculated by New Strategist.
Source: Bureau of the Census, Educational Attainment in the United States: 2009, Internet site http://www.census.gov/ population/www/socdemo/education/cps2009.html; calculations by New Strategist

Asians Are Well Educated

Many Hispanics have not even graduated from high school.

The educational attainment of Hispanics lags far behind that of Asians, blacks, and non-Hispanic whites. Overall, only 62 percent of Hispanics aged 25 or older have a high school diploma, and just 13 percent are college graduates. Younger Hispanics are better educated than older ones, but even among the youngest adults fewer than 70 percent have a high school diploma. One reason for the low level of educational attainment among Hispanics is that many are recent immigrants with little formal schooling.

More than 84 percent of blacks have a high school diploma, a figure that ranges from a low of 64 percent among the oldest blacks to a high of 89 to 90 percent among blacks under age 45. More than one in four blacks has at least an associate's degree and 19 percent have a bachelor's degree. The proportion of blacks with a bachelor's degree peaks at 26 percent among black women aged 30 to 34.

Asians are by far the best-educated Americans. More than half of Asian men—55 percent—have a bachelor's degree. Among women, the proportion is 49 percent. Asians are far better educated than non-Hispanic whites, only 33 percent of whom have a bachelor's degree.

■ With tuition expenses rising rapidly, young blacks and Hispanics—many from low-income families—face a particularly difficult time paying for college.

Among 30-to-34-year-olds, educational attainment varies sharply by race and Hispanic origin

(percent of 30-to-34-year-olds who have a bachelor's degree, by race and Hispanic origin, 2009)

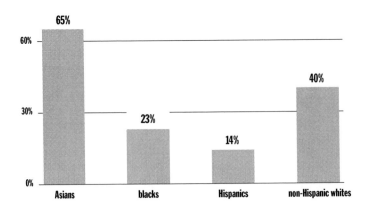

Table 3.7 High School and College Graduates by Age, Race, and Hispanic Origin, 2009: Total People

(percent of total people aged 25 or older with at least a high school diploma, at least an associate's degree, and at least a bachelor's degree, by age, race, and Hispanic origin, 2009; numbers in thousands)

	total	Asian	black	Hispanic	non-Hispanic white
HIGH SCHOOL DIPLOMA OR MORE					
Total people	**86.7%**	**88.3%**	**84.1%**	**61.9%**	**91.6%**
Aged 25 to 29	88.6	95.2	88.8	68.9	94.6
Aged 30 to 34	87.9	94.8	88.9	63.4	95.0
Aged 35 to 39	88.0	92.6	90.3	62.9	94.6
Aged 40 to 44	88.7	90.6	89.4	64.6	94.0
Aged 45 to 49	89.1	91.8	86.8	63.5	93.9
Aged 50 to 54	89.0	89.7	86.2	59.9	93.6
Aged 55 to 59	89.1	84.3	84.1	61.9	93.5
Aged 60 to 64	88.7	82.2	81.1	58.1	93.2
Aged 65 or older	78.3	72.1	63.9	45.9	83.1
ASSOCIATE'S DEGREE OR MORE					
Total people	**38.5**	**58.6**	**28.5**	**19.3**	**42.5**
Aged 25 to 29	39.3	64.7	27.8	18.4	47.1
Aged 30 to 34	43.0	71.0	31.7	20.1	50.4
Aged 35 to 39	44.1	67.1	33.4	21.5	50.8
Aged 40 to 44	42.1	63.7	31.1	21.3	47.6
Aged 45 to 49	39.9	60.5	29.5	20.6	43.8
Aged 50 to 54	39.9	57.0	28.9	17.3	44.1
Aged 55 to 59	40.5	51.7	29.8	21.9	43.9
Aged 60 to 64	41.2	53.0	27.2	18.8	44.7
Aged 65 or older	27.2	35.7	19.1	13.2	28.9
BACHELOR'S DEGREE OR MORE					
Total people	**29.5**	**51.8**	**19.4**	**13.2**	**32.9**
Aged 25 to 29	30.6	58.1	19.1	12.2	37.2
Aged 30 to 34	33.8	65.2	22.7	13.6	39.8
Aged 35 to 39	33.9	60.4	22.7	14.6	39.3
Aged 40 to 44	31.9	56.6	19.6	14.6	36.5
Aged 45 to 49	29.2	51.3	20.2	13.8	32.1
Aged 50 to 54	29.0	50.3	19.5	11.8	31.9
Aged 55 to 59	30.8	45.5	20.5	15.6	33.6
Aged 60 to 64	32.7	44.8	18.2	13.6	36.1
Aged 65 or older	21.7	30.3	13.6	9.5	23.3

Note: Asians and blacks are those who identify themselves as being of the race alone and those who identify themselves as being of the race in combination with other races. Hispanics may be of any race. Non-Hispanic whites are those who identify themselves as being white alone and not Hispanic.
Source: Bureau of the Census, Educational Attainment in the United States: 2009, Internet site http://www.census.gov/ population/www/socdemo/education/cps2009.html; calculations by New Strategist

Table 3.8 High School and College Graduates by Age, Race, and Hispanic Origin, 2009: Men

(percent of men aged 25 or older with at least a high school diploma, at least an associate's degree, and at least a bachelor's degree, by age, race, and Hispanic origin, 2009; numbers in thousands)

	total	Asian	black	Hispanic	non-Hispanic white
HIGH SCHOOL DIPLOMA OR MORE					
Total men	**86.2%**	**90.5%**	**83.9%**	**60.5%**	**91.4%**
Aged 25 to 29	87.5	95.8	88.5	66.2	94.4
Aged 30 to 34	86.2	93.9	88.4	59.5	94.3
Aged 35 to 39	86.6	92.1	91.0	60.6	93.6
Aged 40 to 44	87.5	91.1	90.5	62.7	92.7
Aged 45 to 49	87.6	93.9	84.2	62.1	92.5
Aged 50 to 54	88.6	89.8	84.9	59.7	93.4
Aged 55 to 59	88.5	85.9	83.5	59.8	92.8
Aged 60 to 64	88.6	88.6	78.3	55.8	93.1
Aged 65 or older	79.5	81.4	63.7	49.3	83.7
ASSOCIATE'S DEGREE OR MORE					
Total men	**37.9**	**61.8**	**25.3**	**17.7**	**42.4**
Aged 25 to 29	34.5	64.2	21.9	15.9	41.8
Aged 30 to 34	38.0	68.4	25.9	15.2	45.8
Aged 35 to 39	40.3	66.3	28.3	19.4	46.8
Aged 40 to 44	40.1	65.9	29.4	19.8	45.3
Aged 45 to 49	37.4	64.6	25.6	19.8	40.8
Aged 50 to 54	38.1	57.9	26.3	16.7	41.9
Aged 55 to 59	41.0	58.9	27.7	21.3	44.3
Aged 60 to 64	44.5	55.7	26.5	18.0	48.6
Aged 65 or older	33.0	49.2	17.6	15.8	35.3
BACHELOR'S DEGREE OR MORE					
Total men	**30.1**	**54.8**	**17.8**	**12.4**	**33.9**
Aged 25 to 29	26.6	56.8	15.0	11.0	32.6
Aged 30 to 34	29.9	62.7	18.5	10.2	36.1
Aged 35 to 39	31.6	59.5	20.2	13.4	36.8
Aged 40 to 44	31.2	60.9	19.5	13.5	35.8
Aged 45 to 49	28.6	53.9	19.1	13.7	31.2
Aged 50 to 54	29.0	51.9	17.4	11.9	32.1
Aged 55 to 59	32.2	52.0	20.4	16.0	34.9
Aged 60 to 64	36.7	48.3	17.6	13.9	40.8
Aged 65 or older	28.2	42.6	13.3	11.7	30.5

Note: Asians and blacks are those who identify themselves as being of the race alone and those who identify themselves as being of the race in combination with other races. Hispanics may be of any race. Non-Hispanic whites are those who identify themselves as being white alone and not Hispanic.
Source: Bureau of the Census, Educational Attainment in the United States: 2009, Internet site http://www.census.gov/population/www/socdemo/education/cps2009.html; calculations by New Strategist

Table 3.9 High School and College Graduates by Age, Race, and Hispanic Origin, 2009: Women

(percent of women aged 25 or older with at least a high school diploma, at least an associate's degree, and at least a bachelor's degree, by age, race, and Hispanic origin, 2009; numbers in thousands)

	total	Asian	black	Hispanic	non-Hispanic white
HIGH SCHOOL DIPLOMA OR MORE					
Total women	**87.1%**	**86.4%**	**84.2%**	**63.3%**	**91.9%**
Aged 25 to 29	89.8	94.5	89.0	72.5	94.8
Aged 30 to 34	89.6	95.0	89.4	67.7	95.8
Aged 35 to 39	89.4	93.4	89.6	65.3	95.6
Aged 40 to 44	89.8	89.9	88.5	66.7	95.3
Aged 45 to 49	90.5	89.5	88.8	64.9	95.3
Aged 50 to 54	89.4	89.8	87.3	60.2	93.8
Aged 55 to 59	89.7	83.3	84.4	63.9	94.1
Aged 60 to 64	88.7	76.9	83.4	60.1	93.1
Aged 65 or older	77.4	65.8	64.2	43.3	82.7
ASSOCIATE'S DEGREE OR MORE					
Total women	**39.1**	**55.8**	**31.0**	**20.9**	**42.6**
Aged 25 to 29	44.5	64.8	32.9	21.6	52.5
Aged 30 to 34	47.8	73.0	36.5	25.5	55.1
Aged 35 to 39	47.9	68.3	37.2	23.8	54.8
Aged 40 to 44	44.0	61.8	32.4	22.7	49.8
Aged 45 to 49	42.3	56.6	32.7	21.4	46.8
Aged 50 to 54	41.6	56.4	31.0	17.7	46.1
Aged 55 to 59	40.1	45.5	31.4	22.5	43.6
Aged 60 to 64	38.2	50.8	27.7	19.3	41.1
Aged 65 or older	22.8	26.5	20.0	11.1	24.0
BACHELOR'S DEGREE OR MORE					
Total women	**29.1**	**49.2**	**20.7**	**14.0**	**31.9**
Aged 25 to 29	34.8	59.3	22.6	13.8	42.0
Aged 30 to 34	37.6	66.9	26.2	17.4	43.6
Aged 35 to 39	36.2	61.5	24.7	15.8	41.9
Aged 40 to 44	32.5	52.9	19.7	15.8	37.3
Aged 45 to 49	29.9	49.0	21.1	13.8	33.1
Aged 50 to 54	29.0	49.2	21.3	11.7	31.7
Aged 55 to 59	29.5	40.1	20.6	15.2	32.3
Aged 60 to 64	29.0	41.8	18.7	13.2	31.6
Aged 65 or older	16.8	21.6	13.7	7.7	17.8

Note: Asians and blacks are those who identify themselves as being of the race alone and those who identify themselves as being of the race in combination with other races. Hispanics may be of any race. Non-Hispanic whites are those who identify themselves as being white alone and not Hispanic.
Source: Bureau of the Census, Educational Attainment in the United States: 2009, Internet site http://www.census.gov/ population/www/socdemo/education/cps2009.html; calculations by New Strategist

Young Adults Are Much More Likely to Be in School

The biggest gain has been among 20-to-21-year-olds.

More than half of preschoolers are enrolled in school, a proportion that continues to inch upwards. Working mothers are behind the increase, the majority of mothers with preschoolers now being in the labor force.

The percentage of young adults enrolled in school grew sharply between 2000 and 2008. Among those aged 18 to 19, the share rose by 5 percentage points. The gain was an even larger 6 percentage points among those aged 20 to 21. Many young adults are delaying entry into the labor force because of the recession.

■ Rising college costs are becoming a hardship for many young adults, and they may limit school enrollment in the coming years.

The majority of 20-to-21-year-olds are now in school

(percent of people aged 18 to 21 enrolled in school, 2000 and 2008)

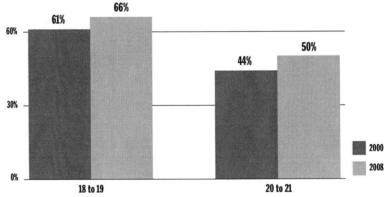

Table 3.10 School Enrollment by Age, 2000 and 2008

(percent of people aged 3 or older enrolled in school, by age, 2000 and 2008; percentage point change, 2000–08)

	2008	2000	percentage point change 2000–08
Total, aged 3 or older	**26.6%**	**27.5%**	**–0.9**
Aged 3 to 4	52.8	52.1	0.7
Aged 5 to 6	93.8	95.6	–1.8
Aged 7 to 9	98.3	98.1	0.2
Aged 10 to 13	98.9	98.3	0.6
Aged 14 to 15	98.6	98.7	–0.1
Aged 16 to 17	95.2	92.8	2.4
Aged 18 to 19	66.0	61.2	4.8
Aged 20 to 21	50.1	44.1	6.0
Aged 22 to 24	28.2	24.6	3.6
Aged 25 to 29	13.2	11.4	1.8
Aged 30 to 34	7.3	6.7	0.6
Aged 35 or older	2.0	1.9	0.1

Source: Bureau of the Census, School Enrollment, Historical Tables, Internet site http://www.census.gov/population/www/socdemo/school.html; calculations by New Strategist

More than One in Four Americans Are in School

The majority of people ranging in age from 3 to 21 is in school.

Twenty-seven percent of Americans aged 3 or older are enrolled in school. Not surprisingly, enrollment peaks among school-aged children. More than 95 percent of 7-to-17-year-olds are in school.

Enrollment drops to 66 percent among 18-to-19-year-olds, most of whom are in college. Although about two out of three young adults enroll in college, many do not graduate as evidenced by lower school enrollment among people aged 20 to 21. Nevertheless, half of 20-to-21-year-olds are still in school.

Women are more likely than men to go to school as adults. Overall, 51 percent of people enrolled in school are female. The figure rises to a peak of 65 percent among 35-to-44-year-olds.

■ Because education is strongly linked to higher incomes, many of those who do not complete high school or college eventually return to school to get their degree.

Many young adults are in school

(percent of people aged 18 or older enrolled in school, by age, 2008)

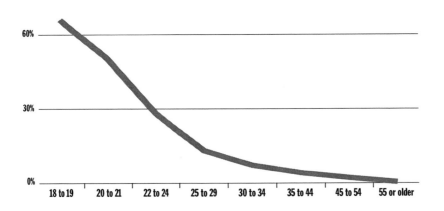

Table 3.11 School Enrollment by Age and Sex, 2008

(number and percent of people aged 3 or older enrolled in school, by age and sex, and females as a percent of total, 2008; numbers in thousands)

	total		female		male		female share of total
	number	percent	number	percent	number	percent	
Total people	**76,353**	**26.6%**	**38,598**	**26.3%**	**37,755**	**26.9%**	**50.6%**
Aged 3 to 4	4,458	52.8	2,212	53.3	2,246	52.3	49.6
Aged 5 to 6	7,651	93.8	3,752	93.7	3,900	93.8	49.0
Aged 7 to 9	11,827	98.3	5,812	98.7	6,014	98.0	49.1
Aged 10 to 13	15,854	98.9	7,753	99.2	8,101	98.7	48.9
Aged 14 to 15	7,965	98.6	3,869	98.2	4,096	99.0	48.6
Aged 16 to 17	8,202	95.2	4,035	95.4	4,167	94.9	49.2
Aged 18 to 19	5,607	66.0	2,864	68.1	2,743	64.0	51.1
Aged 20 to 21	4,052	50.1	2,087	53.0	1,964	47.4	51.5
Aged 22 to 24	3,488	28.2	1,879	30.1	1,609	26.3	53.9
Aged 25 to 29	2,764	13.2	1,491	14.3	1,273	12.1	53.9
Aged 30 to 34	1,407	7.3	802	8.3	605	6.3	57.0
Aged 35 to 44	1,760	4.2	1,143	5.4	616	3.0	64.9
Aged 45 to 54	970	2.2	702	3.1	267	1.2	72.4
Aged 55 or older	349	0.5	196	0.5	153	0.5	56.2

Source: Bureau of the Census, School Enrollment—Social and Economic Characteristics of Students: October 2008, Detailed Tables, Internet site http://www.census.gov/population/www/socdemo/school/cps2008.html; calculations by New Strategist

Millennials Are Boosting College Enrollment

The number of students on the nation's college campuses grew by 22 percent between 2000 and 2008.

College enrollment has been expanding steadily since 1950, when only 2 million people were enrolled in an institution of higher education. By 2008, college enrollment exceeded 18 million. Three factors are behind the increase: the large size of the Millennial generation, which is now in the age group most likely to be in college; rising college enrollment rates for both men and women as young adults delay entering the labor force because of the recession; and a growing number of older students. On college campuses today, students aged 22 or older outnumber those aged 18 to 21, which is the traditional age of college enrollment.

Women account for the 55 percent majority of college students. The female share is even greater among students aged 35 or older, at 66 percent.

■ As the Millennial generation ages into its thirties and forties, campuses across the nation are likely to see a continuing increase in older students.

Most students on college campuses are aged 22 or older

(percent distribution of college students by age, 2008)

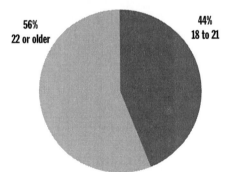

56%
22 or older

44%
18 to 21

Table 3.12 College Students by Age, 2000 and 2008

(number and percent distribution of people aged 14 or older enrolled in institutions of higher education, by age, 2000 and 2008; percent and percentage point change, 2000–08; numbers in thousands)

	2008	2000	percent change 2000–08
Total students	**18,632**	**15,314**	**21.7%**
Under age 20	4,367	3,748	16.5
Aged 20 to 21	3,920	3,169	23.7
Aged 22 to 24	3,420	2,683	27.5
Aged 25 to 29	2,657	1,962	35.4
Aged 30 to 34	1,356	1,244	9.0
Aged 35 or older	2,911	2,507	16.1

	2008	2000	percentage point change 2000–08
Total students	**100.0%**	**100.0%**	–
Under age 20	23.4	24.5	–1.0
Aged 20 to 21	21.0	20.7	0.3
Aged 22 to 24	18.4	17.5	0.8
Aged 25 to 29	14.3	12.8	1.4
Aged 30 to 34	7.3	8.1	–0.8
Aged 35 or older	15.6	16.4	–0.7

Note: "–" means not applicable.
Source: Bureau of the Census, School Enrollment, Historical Tables, Internet site http://www.census.gov/population/www/socdemo/school.html; calculations by New Strategist

Table 3.13 College Students by Age and Sex, 2008

(number of people aged 14 or older enrolled in institutions of higher education, by age and sex, and female share of total, 2008; numbers in thousands)

	total	female	male	female share of total
Total students	**18,632**	**10,321**	**8,311**	**55.4%**
Under age 20	4,367	2,325	2,042	53.2
Aged 20 to 21	3,920	2,013	1,908	51.4
Aged 22 to 24	3,420	1,854	1,566	54.2
Aged 25 to 29	2,657	1,428	1,229	53.7
Aged 30 to 34	1,356	779	577	57.4
Aged 35 or older	2,911	1,922	989	66.0

Source: Bureau of the Census, School Enrollment, Historical Tables, Internet site http://www.census.gov/population/www/socdemo/school.html; calculations by New Strategist

Part-Time Study Is the Norm for Older Students

With families to support, older students cannot afford full-time study.

Among students at four-year institutions of higher education, 83 percent attend full-time. The proportion of full-timers is a smaller 64 percent among students attending two-year schools. About half of graduate students attend school part-time.

The atmosphere of a college campus is largely determined by the age and attendance status of its student body. Four-year schools are much more likely to provide the stereotypical college experience, as full-time students under age 25 constitute the 71 percent majority of the student body. At two-year schools, in contrast, just under half of students are full-timers under age 25.

■ Rising college costs require many students to attend college part-time as they juggle work and school.

Full-time attendance falls with age

(percent of college students at four-year institutions who attend school full-time, by age, 2008)

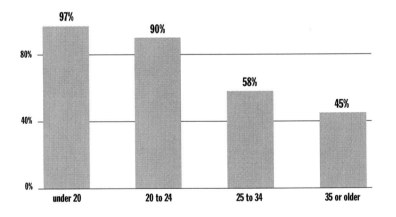

Table 3.14 College Students by Type of School, Age, and Attendance Status, 2008

(number, percent, and percent distribution of people aged 15 or older enrolled in institutions of higher education, by type of school, age, and attendance status, 2008; numbers in thousands)

	total	full-time number	full-time share of total
Total students	**18,632**	**13,245**	**71.1%**
Aged 15 to 19	4,367	4,020	92.1
Aged 20 to 24	7,340	6,161	83.9
Aged 25 to 34	4,013	2,091	52.1
Aged 35 or older	2,911	972	33.4
Total, two-year	**5,344**	**3,397**	**63.6**
Aged 15 to 19	1,731	1,450	83.8
Aged 20 to 24	1,727	1,217	70.5
Aged 25 to 34	1,095	466	42.6
Aged 35 or older	792	263	33.2
Total, four-year	**9,611**	**7,981**	**83.0**
Aged 15 to 19	2,616	2,549	97.4
Aged 20 to 24	4,735	4,245	89.7
Aged 25 to 34	1,336	774	57.9
Aged 35 or older	924	412	44.6
Total, graduate school	**3,676**	**1,867**	**50.8**
Aged 15 to 19	21	21	100.0
Aged 20 to 24	878	699	79.6
Aged 25 to 34	1,583	851	53.8
Aged 35 or older	1,195	296	24.8

Source: Bureau of the Census, School Enrollment—Social and Economic Characteristics of Students: October 2008, Detailed Tables, Internet site http://www.census.gov/population/www/socdemo/school/cps2008.html; calculations by New Strategist

Millennials Will Boost the Number of Older College Students

A smaller proportion of college students will be under age 25.

According to projections by the National Center for Education Statistics (NCES), the number of college students will grow by 11 percent between 2008 and 2018. The number of women on campus should expand much more rapidly than the number of men—up 17 and 2 percent, respectively, during those years.

The fastest increase in college students is projected to occur among 30-to-34-year-olds as the large Millennial generation passes through the age group. The NCES projects that the number of college students aged 30 to 34 will expand by 37 percent between 2008 and 2018. The number of students aged 20 to 21 is projected to rise by just 5 percent during those years, and the number of male college students in the age group is projected to decline.

■ The Great Recession may reduce college enrollment if young adults cannot afford the cost, or it may boost college enrollment because the unemployed go to school.

College students are projected to increase in almost every age group

(percent change in number of college students by age, 2008 to 2018)

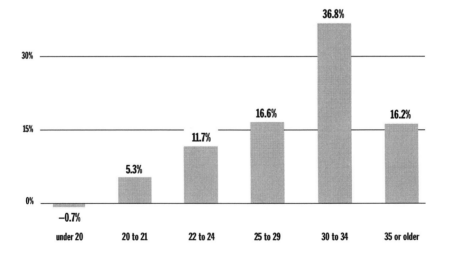

Table 3.15 Projections of College Students by Sex and Age, 2008 and 2018

(number and percent distribution of people aged 14 or older enrolled in institutions of higher education, by sex and age, 2008 and middle series projection for 2018; percent change in number, 2008–18; numbers in thousands)

	2008		2018		percent change in number 2008–2018
	number	percent distribution	number	percent distribution	
Total students	**18,632**	**100.0%**	**20,620**	**100.0%**	**10.7%**
Under age 20	4,367	23.4	4,336	21.0	−0.7
Aged 20 to 21	3,920	21.0	4,128	20.0	5.3
Aged 22 to 24	3,420	18.4	3,820	18.5	11.7
Aged 25 to 29	2,657	14.3	3,097	15.0	16.6
Aged 30 to 34	1,356	7.3	1,856	9.0	36.8
Aged 35 or older	2,911	15.6	3,383	16.4	16.2
Female students	**10,321**	**100.0**	**12,115**	**100.0**	**17.4**
Under age 20	2,325	22.5	2,471	20.4	6.3
Aged 20 to 21	2,013	19.5	2,356	19.4	17.0
Aged 22 to 24	1,854	18.0	2,151	17.8	16.0
Aged 25 to 29	1,428	13.8	1,854	15.3	29.8
Aged 30 to 34	779	7.5	1,044	8.6	34.1
Aged 35 or older	1,922	18.6	2,239	18.5	16.5
Male students	**8,311**	**100.0**	**8,505**	**100.0**	**2.3**
Under age 20	2,042	24.6	1,865	21.9	−8.7
Aged 20 to 21	1,908	23.0	1,773	20.8	−7.1
Aged 22 to 24	1,566	18.8	1,669	19.6	6.6
Aged 25 to 29	1,229	14.8	1,243	14.6	1.1
Aged 30 to 34	577	6.9	811	9.5	40.6
Aged 35 or older	989	11.9	1,144	13.5	15.7

Source: National Center for Education Statistics, Projections of Education Statistics to 2018, Internet site http://nces.ed.gov/ programs/projections/tables.asp; calculations by New Strategist

4

Health

In many ways, Americans are healthier than ever, thanks to lifestyle changes spearheaded by well-educated and health-conscious younger generations. Far fewer Americans smoke today, for example, than in the 1960s. Fewer people have high cholesterol, although the percentage of Americans with high blood pressure has risen.

Some things have not changed, however. The young are still most likely to die from accidents, the old from cancer and heart disease. And in spite of millions of dollars spent on diet products, health clubs, and exercise equipment, Americans of all ages are losing the battle of the bulge. Sedentary jobs, fast food, and labor-saving appliances all conspire to keep everyone running a calorie surplus.

One trend that is particularly troubling is the growing number of people without health insurance, but health care reform legislation passed in 2010 may alleviate this problem.

What to expect in the future

■ Obesity has become a major health issue as Americans put on the pounds. Problems with weight affect everyone, making it certain that eating less and exercising more will be top priorities for all age groups in the coming years.

■ The debate over the nation's health care system is just beginning. As aging Boomers face more health problems, costs will soar. So will continuing demands for improvement in the health care system.

Most Americans Feel "Very Good" or "Excellent"

Adults under age 55, however, have become less likely to rate their health highly.

Overall, 55 percent of adults say their health is "very good" or "excellent," ranging from a high of 63 percent among people aged 25 to 34 to a low of 38 percent among people aged 65 or older. The percentage of adults under age 55 who rate their health highly has fallen over the past few years for unknown reasons. The decline was particularly steep among adults ranging in age from 25 to 54, with the percentage who rate their health very good or excellent falling by 4 to 7 percentage points between 1995 and 2008. The number of days that adults report experiencing poor mental health also increased during those years among people under age 65, rising by an additional full day of poor mental health for those aged 55 to 64.

The 56 percent majority of parents say their children's health is excellent—a figure that does not vary much by age of child. Interestingly, however, while 53 percent of parents with children aged 12 to 17 say their children's health status is excellent, a much smaller 25 percent of 18-to-24-year-olds say they are in excellent health.

■ The health of middle-aged and younger adults may be declining because of the stress of maintaining a middle-class lifestyle in a rapidly changing economy.

Adults of prime working age do not feel as good as they once did

(percent of people aged 25 to 54 who say their health is "very good" or "excellent," by age, 1995 and 2008)

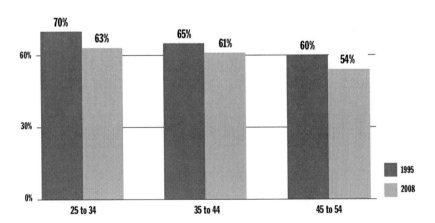

Table 4.1 Health Status of Adults by Age, 2008

"How is your general health?"

(percent of people aged 18 or older responding by age, 2008)

	excellent	very good	good	fair	poor
Total people	**20.2%**	**34.9%**	**30.1%**	**10.6%**	**3.8%**
Aged 18 to 24	25.1	35.8	29.7	6.7	1.1
Aged 25 to 34	24.9	38.1	29.0	7.3	1.4
Aged 35 to 44	23.8	37.3	28.4	8.0	2.2
Aged 45 to 54	19.6	34.5	29.1	10.3	4.3
Aged 55 to 64	17.3	31.5	30.3	13.8	5.7
Aged 65 or older	11.5	26.8	34.1	18.0	7.4

Source: Centers for Disease Control and Prevention, Behavioral Risk Factor Surveillance System, Prevalence Data, Internet site http://apps.nccd.cdc.gov/brfss/index.asp; calculations by New Strategist

Table 4.2 Health Status, 1995 to 2008

"How is your general health?"

(percent of noninstitutionalized people aged 18 or older responding "excellent" or "very good," by age, 1995 to 2008; percentage point change, 1995–2008)

	percent responding "excellent" or "very good"			percentage point change
	2008	2000	1995	1995 to 2008
Total people	**55.1%**	**56.2%**	**58.7%**	**–3.6**
Aged 18 to 24	60.9	62.8	63.1	–2.2
Aged 25 to 34	63.0	67.1	69.8	–6.8
Aged 35 to 44	61.1	63.2	65.1	–4.0
Aged 45 to 54	54.1	56.4	59.5	–5.4
Aged 55 to 64	48.8	49.1	49.9	–1.1
Aged 65 or older	38.3	36.2	37.2	1.1

Source: Centers for Disease Control and Prevention, Behavioral Risk Factor Surveillance System, Prevalence Data, Internet site http://apps.nccd.cdc.gov/brfss/index.asp; calculations by New Strategist

Table 4.3 Mental Health Status in Past Month, 1995 to 2008

"Thinking about your mental health, which includes stress, depression,
and problems with emotions, for how many days during the past
30 days was your mental health not good?"

*(average number of days during the past 30 days when mental health was not good among noninstitutionalized
people aged 18 or older, by selected characteristics, 1995 to 2008; change in days, 1995–2008)*

	average number of days			change in days,
	2008	2000	1995	1995 to 2008
Total people	**3.4**	**3.2**	**2.9**	**0.5**
Aged 18 to 24	4.0	4.1	3.6	0.4
Aged 25 to 34	3.7	3.4	3.1	0.6
Aged 35 to 44	3.6	3.5	3.3	0.3
Aged 45 to 54	3.9	3.5	3.0	0.9
Aged 55 to 64	3.4	2.7	2.4	1.0
Aged 65 to 74	2.2	2.0	2.1	0.1
Aged 75 or older	2.0	2.0	2.0	0.0

*Source: Centers for Disease Control and Prevention, Health-Related Quality of Life, Behavioral Risk Factor Surveillance
System, Prevalence Data, Internet site http://apps.nccd.cdc.gov/HRQOL/; calculations by New Strategist*

Table 4.4 Health Status of Children by Age, 2008

(percent distribution of children under age 18 by parent-reported health status, by age, 2008)

	excellent	very good	good	fair/poor
Total children	**55.5%**	**26.9%**	**15.6%**	**1.8%**
Aged 0 to 4	59.4	25.2	13.9	1.2
Aged 5 to 11	54.5	27.6	16.0	1.8
Aged 12 to 17	53.4	27.5	16.6	2.3

*Source: National Center for Health Statistics, Summary Health Statistics for U.S. Children: National Health Interview Survey,
2008, Vital and Health Statistics, Series 10, No. 244, 2009, Internet site http://www.cdc.gov/nchs/nhis/nhis_series.htm*

Birth Rate Fell between 2007 and 2008

Despite the decline, the rate was higher in 2008 than in 2000.

Between 2000 and 2008, the birth rate (the number of live births per 1,000 women aged 15 to 44) increased from 65.9 to 68.7. The birth rate fell among women under age 25, but climbed among women aged 25 or older. The increase was especially large among older women, with the birth rate climbing 40 percent among women aged 45 or older.

Between 2007 and 2008, the birth rate fell among women under age 40. Behind the decline was the recession, as many couples postponed having children because money was tight. Despite the decline between 2007 and 2008, the birth rate among women ranging in age from 25 to 39 was higher in 2008 than in 2000.

■ The birth rate among women aged 40 or older is rising because of postponed childbearing.

Birth rate has fluctuated among women aged 25 to 29

(number of births per 1,000 women aged 25 to 29, for selected years, 2000 to 2008)

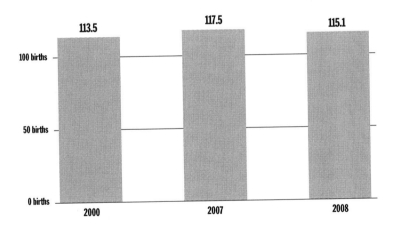

Table 4.5 Birth Rate by Age, 2000 to 2008

(number of live births per 1,000 women aged 15 to 44 by age, 2000 to 2008; percent change in rate for selected years)

	total*	15 to 19	20 to 24	25 to 29	30 to 34	35 to 39	40 to 44	45 or older
2008	68.7	41.5	103.1	115.1	99.3	46.9	9.9	0.7
2007	69.5	42.5	106.4	117.5	99.9	47.5	9.5	0.6
2006	68.5	41.9	105.9	116.7	97.7	47.3	9.4	0.6
2005	66.7	40.4	102.2	115.6	95.9	46.3	9.1	0.6
2004	66.3	41.1	101.7	115.5	95.3	45.4	8.9	0.5
2003	66.1	41.7	102.6	115.7	95.2	43.8	8.7	0.5
2002	64.8	43.0	103.6	113.6	91.5	41.4	8.3	0.5
2001	65.3	45.3	106.2	113.4	91.9	40.6	8.1	0.5
2000	65.9	47.7	109.7	113.5	91.2	39.7	8.0	0.5
Percent change								
2000 to 2008	4.2%	–13.0 %	–6.0%	1.4%	8.9%	18.1%	23.8%	40.0%

* Total is the number of births per 1,000 women aged 15 to 44.
Source: National Center for Health Statistics, Births: Final Data for 2006, National Vital Statistics Reports, Vol. 57, No. 7, 2009, and Births: Preliminary Data for 2008, National Vital Statistics Report, Vol. 58, No. 16, 2010, Internet site http://www.cdc.gov/nchs/products/nvsr.htm; calculations by New Strategist

Blacks and Hispanics Have Children at a Younger Age

Asian and non-Hispanic white women are more likely to delay childbearing.

Among all women giving birth in 2008, the 53 percent majority were in their twenties. But there is great variation in the age of childbearing by race and Hispanic origin. Asian and non-Hispanic white women have children at an older age than American Indian, black, or Hispanic women.

Among Asian women who gave birth in 2008, most (57 percent) were aged 30 or older. Among non-Hispanic whites, the figure was a smaller but still substantial 40 percent. In contrast, only 26 percent of black women and 31 percent of Hispanic women who gave birth in 2008 were aged 30 or older.

Nearly half—49 percent—of black women who gave birth in 2008 were younger than age 25, as were 42 percent of Hispanics. In contrast, just 15 percent of Asian women giving birth in that year were under age 25.

■ Variation in the timing of childbearing creates lifestyle differences by race and Hispanic origin.

Most Asian women delay childbearing until their thirties

(percent of births to women aged 30 or older, by race and Hispanic origin, 2008)

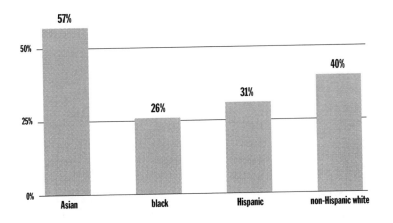

Table 4.6 Births by Age, Race, and Hispanic Origin, 2008

(number and percent distribution of births by age, race, and Hispanic origin, 2008)

	total	American Indian	Asian	non-Hispanic black	Hispanic	non-Hispanic white
Total births	4,251,095	49,540	253,396	625,314	1,038,933	2,273,220
Under age 15	5,775	126	81	2,140	2,328	1,108
Aged 15 to 19	435,000	8,817	7,545	104,794	144,702	168,865
Aged 20 to 24	1,052,928	16,798	31,074	198,699	292,595	512,538
Aged 25 to 29	1,196,713	12,653	71,294	157,051	280,716	671,977
Aged 30 to 34	957,567	7,169	85,572	98,524	199,401	563,755
Aged 35 to 39	489,357	3,205	47,660	50,823	96,889	288,629
Aged 40 to 44	106,090	730	9,458	12,464	21,141	61,603
Aged 45 to 54	7,666	42	713	818	1,161	4,746

PERCENT DISTRIBUTION BY RACE AND HISPANIC ORIGIN

	total	American Indian	Asian	non-Hispanic black	Hispanic	non-Hispanic white
Total births	100.0%	1.2%	6.0%	14.7%	24.4%	53.5%
Under age 15	100.0	2.2	1.4	37.1	40.3	19.2
Aged 15 to 19	100.0	2.0	1.7	24.1	33.3	38.8
Aged 20 to 24	100.0	1.6	3.0	18.9	27.8	48.7
Aged 25 to 29	100.0	1.1	6.0	13.1	23.5	56.2
Aged 30 to 34	100.0	0.7	8.9	10.3	20.8	58.9
Aged 35 to 39	100.0	0.7	9.7	10.4	19.8	59.0
Aged 40 to 44	100.0	0.7	8.9	11.7	19.9	58.1
Aged 45 to 54	100.0	0.5	9.3	10.7	15.1	61.9

PERCENT DISTRIBUTION BY AGE

	total	American Indian	Asian	non-Hispanic black	Hispanic	non-Hispanic white
Total births	100.0%	100.0%	100.0%	100.0%	100.0%	100.0%
Under age 15	0.1	0.3	0.0	0.3	0.2	0.0
Aged 15 to 19	10.2	17.8	3.0	16.8	13.9	7.4
Aged 20 to 24	24.8	33.9	12.3	31.8	28.2	22.5
Aged 25 to 29	28.2	25.5	28.1	25.1	27.0	29.6
Aged 30 to 34	22.5	14.5	33.8	15.8	19.2	24.8
Aged 35 to 39	11.5	6.5	18.8	8.1	9.3	12.7
Aged 40 to 44	2.5	1.5	3.7	2.0	2.0	2.7
Aged 45 to 54	0.2	0.1	0.3	0.1	0.1	0.2

Note: Births by race and Hispanic origin do not add to total because Hispanics may be of any race and "not stated" is not shown.
Source: National Center for Health Statistics, Births: Preliminary Data for 2008, National Vital Statistics Report, Vol. 58, No. 16, 2010, Internet site http://www.cdc.gov/nchs/products/nvsr.htm; calculations by New Strategist

More than 40 Percent of New Mothers Are Not Married

The proportion of babies born out-of-wedlock bottoms out among women in their thirties.

In 2008, a substantial 41 percent of the nation's births were to unmarried women, up from just 11 percent in 1970. More than 1.7 million single women gave birth in 2008.

Among new mothers under age 15, virtually all are unmarried. Among those aged 20 to 24, the figure is 87 percent. The proportion is above 60 percent in the 20-to-24 age group. The share falls to 33 percent in the 25-to-29 age group and bottoms out at 18 percent among women aged 35 to 39.

■ Unmarried women are approaching half of all new mothers. Their wants and needs differ significantly from those of married mothers.

Women in their late thirties are most likely to be married when they give birth

(percent of births to unmarried women, by age, 2008)

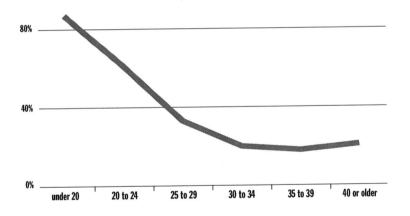

Table 4.7 Births to Unmarried Women by Age, 2008

(total number of births and number and percent to unmarried women, by age, 2008)

		unmarried women		
	total	number	percent distribution	percent of total
Total births	**4,251,095**	**1,727,950**	**100.0%**	**40.6%**
Under age 15	5,775	5,721	0.3	99.1
Aged 15 to 19	435,000	377,058	21.8	86.7
Aged 20 to 24	1,052,928	641,245	37.1	60.9
Aged 25 to 29	1,196,713	397,679	23.0	33.2
Aged 30 to 34	957,567	193,618	11.2	20.2
Aged 35 to 39	489,357	88,953	5.1	18.2
Aged 40 to 54	113,756	23676	1.4	20.8

Source: National Center for Health Statistics, Births: Preliminary Data for 2008, National Vital Statistics Report, Vol. 58, No. 16, 2010, Internet site http://www.cdc.gov/nchs/products/nvsr.htm; calculations by New Strategist

Most First-Time Mothers Are Young

Few first children are born to mothers aged 30 or older.

Among the 4.3 million babies born in 2008, 40 percent were first births, 31 percent were second births, 17 percent were third births, and 11 percent were fourth or higher-order births.

Older mothers make interesting media stories, but in reality the great majority of women who are having their first child are under age 30—76 percent in 2008. Among women having their second child, 61 percent are under age 30. Even among women having their third child, most are younger than age 30. Among women having their fourth or later child, however, the 60 percent majority is aged 30 or older.

■ Although women are delaying childbearing, few wait until their thirties to start families.

Three out of four first-borns have a mother under age 30

(percent of babies born to mothers under age 30, by birth order, 2008)

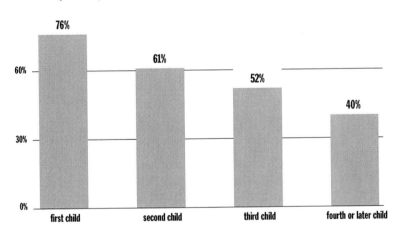

Table 4.8 Births by Age of Mother and Birth Order, 2008

(number and percent distribution of births by age of mother and birth order, 2008)

	total	first child	second child	third child	fourth or later child
Total births	**4,251,095**	**1,705,270**	**1,331,563**	**705,683**	**481,916**
Under age 15	5,775	5,642	81	6	0
Aged 15 to 19	435,000	349,473	71,053	10,590	1,387
Aged 20 to 24	1,052,928	512,489	347,646	135,741	50,506
Aged 25 to 29	1,196,713	431,690	394,016	224,046	139,666
Aged 30 to 34	957,567	270,581	328,455	199,260	153,311
Aged 35 to 39	489,357	110,234	158,675	112,631	104,402
Aged 40 to 44	106,090	23,127	29,791	22,037	30,315
Aged 45 to 54	7,666	2,036	1,846	1,372	2,328

PERCENT DISTRIBUTION BY BIRTH ORDER

Total births	**100.0%**	**40.1%**	**31.3%**	**16.6%**	**11.3%**
Under age 15	100.0	97.7	1.4	0.1	0.0
Aged 15 to 19	100.0	80.3	16.3	2.4	0.3
Aged 20 to 24	100.0	48.7	33.0	12.9	4.8
Aged 25 to 29	100.0	36.1	32.9	18.7	11.7
Aged 30 to 34	100.0	28.3	34.3	20.8	16.0
Aged 35 to 39	100.0	22.5	32.4	23.0	21.3
Aged 40 to 44	100.0	21.8	28.1	20.8	28.6
Aged 45 to 54	100.0	26.6	24.1	17.9	30.4

PERCENT DISTRIBUTION BY AGE

Total births	**100.0%**	**100.0%**	**100.0%**	**100.0%**	**100.0%**
Under age 15	0.1	0.3	0.0	0.0	0.0
Aged 15 to 19	10.2	20.5	5.3	1.5	0.3
Aged 20 to 24	24.8	30.1	26.1	19.2	10.5
Aged 25 to 29	28.2	25.3	29.6	31.7	29.0
Aged 30 to 34	22.5	15.9	24.7	28.2	31.8
Aged 35 to 39	11.5	6.5	11.9	16.0	21.7
Aged 40 to 44	2.5	1.4	2.2	3.1	6.3
Aged 45 to 54	0.2	0.1	0.1	0.2	0.5

Note: Numbers do not add to total because "not stated" is not shown.
Source: National Center for Health Statistics, Births: Preliminary Data for 2008, National Vital Statistics Report, Vol. 58, No. 16, 2010, Internet site http://www.cdc.gov/nchs/products/nvsr.htm; calculations by New Strategist

Many Women Have Not Had Children

Postponing pregnancy sometimes results in no pregnancy.

A growing proportion of women are childless. Among women aged 15 to 44, a larger share (45 percent) is childless today than in 1990 (42 percent). Among women aged 20 to 24, the childless proportion climbed from 65 to 69 percent between 1990 and 2006. Among women aged 25 to 29, the figure increased from 42 to 46 percent during those years. Most of the childless in these age groups will eventually have children.

In the 40-to-44 age group, 20 percent of women were childless in 2006, up from 16 percent in 1990. Most of these women will never have children.

Some of the increase in childlessness among older women is the result of fertility problems associated with delayed childbearing, but changing attitudes toward parenthood also play a role.

■ The higher fertility of Hispanic women may lower rates of childlessness in the younger age groups in the years ahead.

More women aged 40 to 44 are childless

(percent of women aged 40 to 44 who have had no children, 1990 and 2006)

Table 4.9 Childless Women by Age, 1990 to 2006

(percent of women aged 15 to 44 who have not had a live birth, by age, selected years 1990 to 2006)

	total aged 15 to 44	15 to 19	20 to 24	25 to 29	30 to 34	35 to 39	40 to 44
2006	45.1%	93.3%	68.6%	45.6%	26.2%	18.9%	20.4%
2004	44.6	93.3	68.9	44.2	27.6	19.6	19.3
2002	43.5	91.2	67.0	45.2	27.6	20.2	17.9
2000	42.8	90.5	63.6	44.2	28.1	20.1	19.0
1998	42.2	90.1	64.0	43.5	27.4	19.8	19.0
1995	41.8	90.7	64.3	43.8	26.7	19.7	17.5
1994	42.0	91.6	65.3	43.6	26.3	19.6	17.5
1992	41.2	92.7	65.9	41.3	26.1	18.8	15.7
1990	41.6	91.9	64.6	42.1	25.7	17.7	16.0

Source: Bureau of the Census, Fertility of American Women, Historical Time Series Tables, Internet site http://www.census .gov/population/www/socdemo/fertility.html#hist

Most Adults Are Overweight

No one is immune from weight problems, regardless of age.

Americans are losing the battle of the bulge. Desk jobs and fast food are taking their toll. Regardless of age, Americans weigh much more than they did a generation ago. The average man, in fact, weighs 21 pounds more than in 1976–80. The average woman weighs 19 pounds more.

In 2003–06, nearly 73 percent of men and 61 percent of women were overweight, up from 53 and 42 percent, respectively, in 1976–80. Thirty-three percent of men and 35 percent of women are now obese, more than double the 13 and 17 percent, respectively, of 1976–80.

■ As restaurants compete to offer ever-larger portions to a population that appears to have little will power, it is an uphill battle to reduce the nation's collective girth.

The average woman weighs 165 pounds

(average weight in pounds of people aged 20 or older, by sex, 2003–06)

Table 4.10 **Average Measured Weight by Sex and Age, 1976–80 and 2003–06**

(average weight in pounds of people aged 20 or older, by sex and age, 1976–80 and 2003–06; change in pounds 1976–80 to 2003–06)

	2003–06	1976–80*	change in pounds
Men aged 20 or older	**194.7**	**173.8**	**20.9**
Aged 20 to 29	188.3	167.9	20.4
Aged 30 to 39	194.1	175.5	18.6
Aged 40 to 49	202.3	179.7	22.6
Aged 50 to 59	198.8	176.0	22.8
Aged 60 to 69	198.3	167.5**	–
Aged 70 to 79	187.4	–	–
Aged 80 or older	168.1	–	–
Women aged 20 or older	**164.7**	**145.4**	**19.3**
Aged 20 to 29	155.9	135.7	20.2
Aged 30 to 39	164.7	145.5	19.2
Aged 40 to 49	171.3	148.8	22.5
Aged 50 to 59	172.1	150.4	21.7
Aged 60 to 69	170.5	146.9**	–
Aged 70 to 79	155.6	–	–
Aged 80 or older	142.2	–	–

* People aged 20 to 74.
** People aged 60 to 74.
Note: Data are based on the measured weight of a sample of the civilian noninstitutionalized population. "–" means data are not available.
Source: National Center for Health Statistics, Mean Body Weight, Height, and Body Mass Index, United States 1960–2002, Advance Data, No. 347, 2004, Internet site http://www.cdc.gov/nchs/pressroom/04news/americans.htm; and Anthropometric Reference Data for Children and Adults: United States, 2003–2006, National Health Statistics Reports, No. 10, 2008, Internet site http://www.cdc.gov/nchs/products/nhsr.htm; calculations by New Strategist

Table 4.11 Adults Measured as Overweight or Obese by Sex and Age, 1976–80 and 2003–06

(percent of people aged 20 to 74 who are overweight or obese, by sex and age, 1976–80 and 2003–06; percentage point change, 1976–80 to 2003–06)

	overweight			obese		
	2003–06	1976–80	percentage point change	2003–06	1976–80	percentage point change
Men aged 20 to 74	**72.6%**	**52.9%**	**19.7**	**33.1%**	**12.8%**	**20.3**
Aged 20 to 34	61.6	41.2	20.4	26.2	8.9	17.3
Aged 35 to 44	75.2	57.2	18.0	37.0	13.5	23.5
Aged 45 to 54	78.5	60.2	18.3	34.6	16.7	17.9
Aged 55 to 64	79.7	60.2	19.5	39.3	14.1	25.2
Aged 65 to 74	78.0	54.2	23.8	33.0	13.2	19.8
Women aged 20 to 74	**61.2**	**42.0**	**19.2**	**35.2**	**17.1**	**18.1**
Aged 20 to 34	50.9	27.9	23.0	28.4	11.0	17.4
Aged 35 to 44	60.7	40.7	20.0	36.1	17.8	18.3
Aged 45 to 54	67.3	48.7	18.6	40.0	19.6	20.4
Aged 55 to 64	69.6	53.7	15.9	41.0	22.9	18.1
Aged 65 to 74	70.5	59.5	11.0	36.4	21.5	14.9

Note: Overweight is defined as a body mass index of 25 or higher. Obesity is defined as a body mass index of 30 or higher. Body mass index is calculated by dividing weight in kilograms by height in meters squared. Data are based on measured height and weight of a representative sample of the civilian noninstitutionalized population.
Source: National Center for Health Statistics, Health, United States, 2009, Internet site http://www.cdc.gov/nchs/hus.htm; calculations by New Strategist

Weight Problems Start Young

Many teenagers are trying to lose weight.

The weight problems of adults could become even worse as today's children grow up. A significant proportion of the nation's school children are overweight. According to measurements taken by the National Center for Health Statistics, 18 percent of teenagers aged 12 to 19 are overweight.

Among high school students, 15 percent of boys and 16 percent of girls are overweight, according to the Centers for Disease Control and Prevention. More than one-third of girls think they are overweight and 60 percent are trying to lose weight. A smaller 24 percent of boys think they are overweight and 30 percent are trying to lose weight.

■ Ready access to soft drinks and fast food, as well as a couch-potato lifestyle, are putting the pounds on the nation's children.

Most high school girls are trying to lose weight

(percent of high school students who say they are trying to lose weight, by sex, 2007)

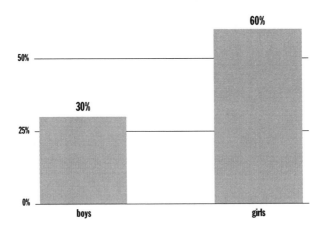

Table 4.12 Children Measured as Overweight by Sex, Race, Hispanic Origin, and Age, 2003–06

(percent of people aged 6 to 19 who are overweight, by sex, race, Hispanic origin, and age, 2003–06)

	6 to 11	12 to 19
TOTAL OVERWEIGHT	**17.0%**	**17.6%**
Boys	**18.0**	**18.2**
Black, non-Hispanic	18.6	18.5
Hispanic (Mexican)	27.5	22.1
White, non-Hispanic	15.5	17.3
Girls	**15.8**	**16.8**
Black, non-Hispanic	24.0	27.7
Hispanic (Mexican)	19.7	19.9
White, non-Hispanic	14.4	14.5

Note: Overweight is defined as a body mass index of 25 or higher. Body mass index is calculated by dividing weight in kilograms by height in meters squared. Data are based on measured height and weight of a representative sample of the civilian noninstitutionalized population.
Source: National Center for Health Statistics, Health, United States, 2009, Internet site http://www.cdc.gov/nchs/hus.htm; calculations by New Strategist

Table 4.13 Weight Problems and Dieting Behavior of 9th to 12th Graders by Sex, 2007

(percent of 9th to 12th graders by weight status and dieting behavior, by sex and grade, 2007)

	total	9th grade	10th grade	11th grade	12th grade
BOYS					
Overweight*	16.4%	17.0%	17.7%	15.9%	14.9%
Described themselves as overweight	24.2	24.3	24.8	25.8	21.6
Were trying to lose weight	30.4	31.0	31.6	30.1	28.7
Ate less food, fewer calories, or foods low in fat to lose weight or to avoid gaining weight in past 30 days	28.3	27.3	29.1	29.8	27.4
Exercised to lose weight or to avoid gaining weight in past 30 days	55.0	58.7	54.2	54.9	51.1
Went without eating for at least 24 hours to lose weight or to avoid gaining weight in past 30 days	7.3	6.5	6.5	8.1	8.0
Took diet pills, powders, or liquids without a doctor's advice to lose weight or avoid gaining weight in past 30 days	4.2	2.9	3.8	5.0	5.7
Vomited or took a laxative to lose weight or to avoid gaining weight in past 30 days	2.2	2.1	1.8	2.1	2.6
GIRLS					
Overweight*	15.1	18.3	14.2	14.2	13.1
Described themselves as overweight	34.5	33.6	33.8	36.2	34.9
Were trying to lose weight	60.3	58.6	50.2	61.3	61.6
Ate less food, fewer calories, or foods low in fat to lose weight or to avoid gaining weight in past 30 days	53.2	50.5	53.0	54.0	56.4
Exercised to lose weight or to avoid gaining weight in past 30 days	67.0	70.6	67.7	65.0	63.7
Went without eating for at least 24 hours to lose weight or to avoid gaining weight in past 30 days	16.3	16.8	19.1	14.8	13.6
Took diet pills, powders, or liquids without a doctor's advice to lose weight or avoid gaining weight in past 30 days	7.5	6.1	6.9	7.4	10.2
Vomited or took a laxative to lose weight or to avoid gaining weight in past 30 days	6.4	5.5	7.6	5.7	6.6

* Students were classified as overweight if they were at or above the 95th percentile for body mass index, by age and sex, based on reference data.
Source: Centers for Disease Control and Prevention, Youth Risk Behavior Surveillance—United States, 2007, Mortality and Morbidity Weekly Report, Vol. 57/SS-4, June 6, 2008; Internet site http://www.cdc.gov/HealthyYouth/yrbs/index.htm

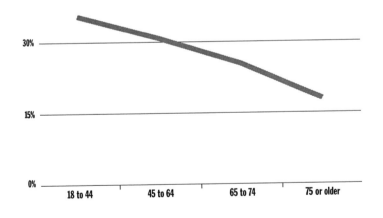

Most Americans Do Not Get Enough Exercise

Many are physically inactive.

No wonder Americans are gaining weight. Most do not exercise enough—meaning less than 30 minutes of light to moderate physical activity at least five times a week or 20 minutes of vigorous physical activity at least three times a week. Only 32 percent of adults are classified as getting regular leisure-time physical activity, 30 percent get only some, and the 36 percent plurality are physically inactive.

Participation in regular leisure-time physical activity declines with age. It is highest among 18-to-44-year-olds, at 35.5 percent. It falls to just 18 percent among people aged 75 or older. The percentage of people who are physically inactive rises from 30 percent among 18-to-44-year-olds to the 54.5 percent majority among people aged 75 or older.

■ Government efforts to get people to eat less and exercise more have so far failed to change people's sedentary lifestyles.

Young adults are most likely to get regular exercise

(percent of people aged 18 or older who get regular leisure-time physical activity, by age, 2008)

Table 4.14 Physical Activity Status of People Aged 18 or Older, 2008

(number of people aged 18 or older and percent distribution by leisure-time physical activity status, by age, 2008; numbers in thousands)

| | total | | physically inactive | some leisure-time physical activity | regular leisure-time physical activity |
	number	percent			
Total people	225,227	100.0%	35.6%	30.3%	31.6%
Aged 18 to 44	110,615	100.0	30.4	31.9	35.5
Aged 45 to 64	77,335	100.0	36.4	30.0	30.8
Aged 65 to 74	19,869	100.0	44.8	27.1	25.4
Aged 75 or older	17,409	100.0	54.5	24.8	18.0

Note: Adults classified as inactive reported no sessions of light to moderate or vigorous leisure-time activity of at least 10 minutes' duration. Adults classified as having some leisure-time activity reported at least one session of light to moderate or vigorous physical activity of at least 10 minutes but did not meet the definition of regular leisure-time activity. Adults classified as having regular leisure-time activity reported three or more sessions per week of vigorous activity lasting at least 20 minutes or five or more sessions per week of light to moderate activity lasting at least 30 minutes. Numbers may not add to total because "unknown" is not shown.
Source: National Center for Health Statistics, Summary Health Statistics for U.S. Adults: National Health Interview Survey, 2008, Series 10, No. 242, 2009, Internet site http://www.cdc.gov/nchs/nhis/nhis_series.htm; calculations by New Strategist

New Drugs Help Lower Cholesterol Levels

Cholesterol levels have declined in most age groups.

Thanks to screening programs, dietary changes, and the development of new medications, high cholesterol is becoming less of a health problem. The proportion of adults who have high cholesterol fell 3 percentage points between 1988–94 and 2003–06. Declines occurred in most age groups.

Older women have had the most success in bringing down their cholesterol, although they are still more likely than men to have high cholesterol. The percentage of women aged 65 to 74 with high cholesterol fell 17 points between 1988–94 and 2003–06. The decline was 20 percentage points among women aged 75 or older.

For some younger adults, cholesterol levels have risen. Twenty-one percent of men aged 35 to 44 have high cholesterol, a slightly higher share than in the late 1980s. Women aged 20 to 34 also saw an increase in the percentage with high cholesterol since 1988–94, the figure rising from 7 to 10 percent.

■ The significant decline in the proportion of the population with high cholesterol may help lower mortality from heart disease in the future.

Older women are most likely to have high cholesterol

(percent of people aged 20 or older with high serum cholesterol, by age and sex, 2003–06)

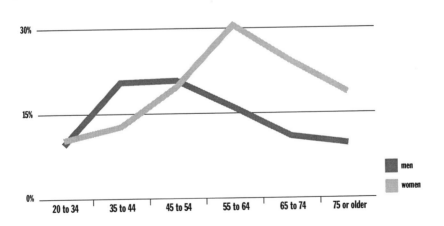

Table 4.15 High Cholesterol by Sex and Age, 1988–94 and 2003–06

(percent of people aged 20 or older who have high serum cholesterol, by sex and age, 1988–94 and 2003–06; percentage point change, 1988–94 to 2003–06)

	2003–06	1988–94	percentage point change
TOTAL PEOPLE	**16.4%**	**19.6%**	**–3.2**
Total men	**15.2**	**17.7**	**–2.5**
Aged 20 to 34	9.5	8.2	1.3
Aged 35 to 44	20.5	19.4	1.1
Aged 45 to 54	20.8	26.6	–5.8
Aged 55 to 64	16.0	28.0	–12.0
Aged 65 to 74	10.9	21.9	–11.0
Aged 75 or older	9.6	20.4	–10.8
Total women	**17.5**	**21.3**	**–3.8**
Aged 20 to 34	10.3	7.3	3.0
Aged 35 to 44	12.7	12.3	0.4
Aged 45 to 54	19.7	26.7	–7.0
Aged 55 to 64	30.5	40.9	–10.4
Aged 65 to 74	24.2	41.3	–17.1
Aged 75 or older	18.6	38.2	–19.6

Note: High cholesterol is defined as 240 mg/dL or more.
Source: National Center for Health Statistics, Health, United States, 2009, Internet site http://www.cdc.gov/nchs/hus.htm; calculations by New Strategist

Blood Pressure Is Up

The biggest increase has been among older women.

Americans are more likely to have high blood pressure today than they were a decade ago. The proportion of adults with high blood pressure rose from 24 to 32 percent between 1988–94 and 2003–06. Behind the rise is a substantial increase in the proportion of older men and women with high blood pressure.

Among women aged 45 to 74, the percentage with high blood pressure rose 11 to 15 percentage points between 1988–94 and 2003–06. Most men and women aged 55 or older have high blood pressure.

■ As the population ages, the proportion of Americans with high blood pressure is likely to rise, boosting demand for antihypertensive medications.

High blood pressure is more likely with increasing age

(percent of people aged 20 or older who have hypertension, by age and sex, 2003–06)

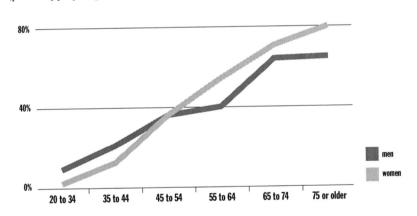

Table 4.16 Hypertension by Sex and Age, 1988–94 and 2003–06

(percent of people aged 20 or older who have hypertension or take antihypertensive medication, by sex and age, 1988–94 and 2003–06; percentage point change, 1988–94 to 2003–06)

	2003–06	1988–94	percentage point change
TOTAL PEOPLE	**32.1%**	**24.1%**	**8.0**
Total men	**31.3**	**23.8**	**7.5**
Aged 20 to 34	9.2	7.1	2.1
Aged 35 to 44	21.1	17.1	4.0
Aged 45 to 54	36.2	29.2	7.0
Aged 55 to 64	50.2	40.6	9.6
Aged 65 to 74	64.1	54.4	9.7
Aged 75 or older	65.0	60.4	4.6
Total women	**32.9**	**24.4**	**8.5**
Aged 20 to 34	2.2	2.9	−0.7
Aged 35 to 44	12.6	11.2	1.4
Aged 45 to 54	36.2	23.9	12.3
Aged 55 to 64	54.4	42.6	11.8
Aged 65 to 74	70.8	56.2	14.6
Aged 75 or older	80.2	73.6	6.6

Note: People by definition have hypertension if they have a systolic pressure of at least 140 mmHg or a diastolic pressure of at least 90 mmHg or take antihypertensive medication.
Source: National Center for Health Statistics, Health, United States, 2009, Internet site http://www.cdc.gov/nchs/hus.htm; calculations by New Strategist

Diabetes Is a Growing Problem

Nearly one in four older adults have diabetes.

Diabetes is a growing problem as Americans put on weight. In 2003–06, one in 10 adults aged 20 or older had been diagnosed with diabetes or had a fasting blood glucose level that indicated diabetes. The percentage of Americans with diabetes has grown by 2.5 percentage points since 1988–94.

The percentage of adults with diabetes increased in every age group between 1988–94 and 2003–06. The biggest increase has been among people aged 60 or older, with the proportion rising from 19 to 23 percent during those years.

■ As Americans continue to put on the pounds, the percentage with diabetes will grow.

The percentage of people with diabetes rises with age

(percent of people aged 20 or older with diabetes, by age, 2003–06)

Table 4.17 Diabetes by Age, 1988–94 and 2003–06

(percent of people aged 20 or older with diabetes, by age, 1988–94 and 2003–06, and percentage point change 1988–94 to 2003–06)

	2003–06	1988–94	percentage point change
Total people	**10.3%**	**7.8%**	**2.5**
Aged 20 to 39	2.5	1.6	0.9
Aged 40 to 59	10.6	8.9	1.7
Aged 60 or older	22.9	18.9	4.0

Note: People with diabetes include those diagnosed by a physician and those who have not been diagnosed but who have a fasting blood glucose of at least 126 mg/dL.
Source: National Center for Health Statistics, Health, United States, 2009, Internet site http://www.cdc.gov/nchs/hus.htm; calculations by New Strategist

More than One in Five Americans Smoke

Most high school students have tried cigarettes.

Most Americans try cigarettes at some point in their lives—often as teenagers. Among the population aged 12 or older, 24 percent have smoked a cigarette in the past month. Smoking peaks among people in their twenties. More than one-third of people aged 19 to 29 have smoked a cigarette in the past month. Smoking declines with age, in part because some people quit and also because smokers have a higher mortality rate than nonsmokers.

The majority of high school students have tried cigarettes, but only 20 percent have smoked a cigarette in the past month. Evidently, teens have no problem procuring cigarettes, with 16 percent able to purchase cigarettes from a store during the past month.

■ Despite extensive antismoking campaigns, most young adults try cigarettes and many adopt the habit.

Many high school students smoke regularly

(percent of high school students who have smoked cigarettes during the past 30 days, by grade, 2007)

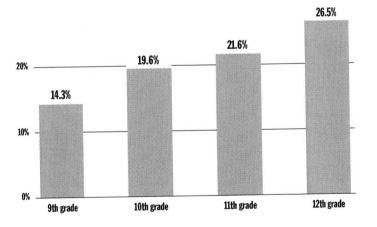

Table 4.18 Cigarette Smoking by People Aged 12 or Older, 2008

(percent of people aged 12 or older who reported any, past year, or past month use of cigarettes, 2008)

	ever smoked	smoked in past year	smoked in past month
Total people	**65.1%**	**28.0%**	**23.9%**
Aged 12	5.0	2.4	1.2
Aged 13	10.1	5.9	2.9
Aged 14	16.9	9.9	5.0
Aged 15	25.5	17.2	10.1
Aged 16	34.4	22.9	14.1
Aged 17	42.0	29.0	19.4
Aged 18	53.2	41.6	30.2
Aged 19	60.9	46.0	34.3
Aged 20	62.0	45.0	36.9
Aged 21	65.2	46.6	38.5
Aged 22	66.5	47.0	37.7
Aged 23	68.4	45.0	36.0
Aged 24	69.3	43.9	36.0
Aged 25	71.5	45.4	37.6
Aged 26 to 29	72.1	44.1	37.1
Aged 30 to 34	68.5	35.4	30.4
Aged 35 to 39	68.3	29.7	26.1
Aged 40 to 44	71.7	30.2	27.4
Aged 45 to 49	73.8	31.1	28.8
Aged 50 to 54	72.6	30.1	27.1
Aged 55 to 59	75.5	22.3	20.6
Aged 60 to 64	73.8	20.4	18.0
Aged 65 or older	65.3	11.2	10.3

Source: SAMHSA, Office of Applied Studies, National Survey on Drug Use and Health, 2008, Internet site http://www.oas .samhsa.gov/NSDUH/2K8NSDUH/tabs/toc.htm

Table 4.19 Tobacco Use among 9th to 12th Graders, 2007

(percent of 9th to 12th graders by tobacco use status, by grade, 2007)

	total	9th grade	10th grade	11th grade	12th grade
Lifetime cigarette use (ever tried a cigarette)	50.3%	42.7%	48.8%	53.4%	59.3%
Lifetime daily cigarette use (ever smoked a cigarette every day for 30 days)	12.4	8.3	12.0	13.8	16.8
Current cigarette use (smoked a cigarette in the past 30 days)	20.0	14.3	19.6	21.6	26.5
Current frequent cigarette use (smoked a cigarette on 20 of the past 30 days)	8.1	4.3	7.0	10.1	12.2
Smoked more than 10 cigarettes a day on the days they smoked in past 30 days (among current smokers)	10.7	10.1	9.0	9.0	13.6
Tried to quit smoking during past year (among current smokers)	49.7	48.6	51.9	49.9	48.5
Purchased cigarettes at a store or gas station during the past 30 days	16.0	9.7	15.0	17.8	25.6
Used chewing tobacco, snuff, or dip during the past 30 days	7.9	6.3	8.7	7.6	8.9
Smoked cigars, cigarillos, or little cigars in the past 30 days	13.6	9.9	12.5	15.5	17.6
Used tobacco of any kind in the past 30 days	25.7	18.6	24.8	28.2	33.4

Source: Centers for Disease Control and Prevention, Youth Risk Behavior Surveillance—United States, 2007, Mortality and Morbidity Weekly Report, Vol. 57/SS-4, June 6, 2008, Internet site http://www.cdc.gov/HealthyYouth/yrbs/index.htm

Many Young Adults Are Binge Drinkers

Alcohol use is widespread among teenagers.

Although parents worry that their children will use illegal drugs, alcohol use is a bigger threat. The percentage of teenagers who have had an alcoholic beverage in the past month rises into the double digits by age 14, according to the federal government's National Survey on Drug Use and Health. By age 19, the majority has had a drink in the past month.

Among 9th graders, 36 percent have had a drink in the past month, according to a survey by the Centers for Disease Control and Prevention. The figure rises to 55 percent among high school seniors. More than one-third of high school seniors have had a binge-drinking episode in the past month.

■ Alcohol is currently the drug of choice on college campuses, sometimes leading to injury or death.

Most young adults do not wait for legal drinking age

(percent of 18-to-20-year-olds who have consumed alcoholic beverages during the past month, 2008)

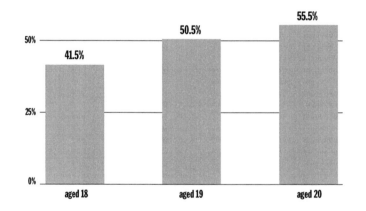

Table 4.20 Alcohol Use by People Aged 12 or Older, 2008

(percent of people aged 12 or older who drank alcoholic beverages during their lifetime, during the past year, and during the past month, by age, 2008)

	lifetime	past year	past month
Total people	**82.2%**	**66.1%**	**51.6%**
Aged 12	9.9	6.2	2.1
Aged 13	17.8	12.7	4.6
Aged 14	32.3	23.9	10.6
Aged 15	44.5	36.9	15.5
Aged 16	56.8	47.0	22.2
Aged 17	63.3	53.5	30.3
Aged 18	73.6	63.6	41.5
Aged 19	79.8	72.0	50.5
Aged 20	82.4	74.8	55.5
Aged 21	89.1	84.5	70.6
Aged 22	90.4	83.7	70.4
Aged 23	90.4	82.8	69.0
Aged 24	91.1	84.6	69.8
Aged 25	91.5	82.5	67.8
Aged 26 to 29	90.8	81.5	67.4
Aged 30 to 34	89.3	77.2	59.9
Aged 35 to 39	90.2	74.5	59.4
Aged 40 to 44	89.9	74.8	60.3
Aged 45 to 49	90.6	73.2	59.6
Aged 50 to 54	87.7	68.5	54.9
Aged 55 to 59	92.0	68.7	54.6
Aged 60 to 64	86.9	64.1	50.3
Aged 65 or older	77.5	50.7	39.7

Source: SAMHSA, Office of Applied Studies, National Survey on Drug Use and Health, 2008, Internet site http://www.oas .samhsa.gov/NSDUH/2K8NSDUH/tabs/toc.htm

Table 4.21 Alcohol Use by 9th to 12th Graders, 2007

(percent of 9th to 12th graders who have ever used or currently use acohol, and percent who have drunk heavily in past 30 days, by grade, 2007)

	lifetime use (ever had one or more drinks)	current use (one or more drinks in past 30 days)	episodic heavy drinking (drank 5 or more drinks in a row in past 30 days)
Total in 9th to 12th grade	**75.0%**	**44.7%**	**26.0%**
9th graders	65.5	35.7	17.0
10th graders	74.7	41.8	23.7
11th graders	79.4	49.0	29.9
12th graders	82.8	54.9	36.5

Source: Centers for Disease Control and Prevention, Youth Risk Behavior Surveillance—United States, 2007, Mortality and Morbidity Weekly Report, Vol. 57/SS-4, June 6, 2008, Internet site http://www.cdc.gov/HealthyYouth/yrbs/index.htm

Many Adults Have Used Illicit Drugs

Lifetime illicit drug use surpasses 50 percent among people ranging in age from 19 to 59.

Teens and young adults are most likely to experiment with drugs. More than 20 percent of people aged 18 to 22 used some type of an illicit drug during the past month. (An illicit drug is defined as an illegal drug or the nonmedical use of a prescription drug.) The figure falls below 10 percent among people aged 30 or older.

Marijuana has long been the most popular illicit drug. The percentage of 18-to-25-year-olds who had ever used marijuana exceeded 50 percent for the first time in 1978. Although most young adults still try marijuana, few continue to use it as they age into their thirties. Fewer than 10 percent of adults aged 30 or older have used marijuana in the past month. Forty-nine percent of high school seniors have tried marijuana, and a smaller 25 percent have used marijuana in the past month.

■ Although most people do not regularly use illicit drugs, the large percentage who have ever tried them attests to the difficulty of winning the war on drugs.

Marijuana use became common among young adults in the 1970s

(percent of people aged 18 to 25 who have ever used marijuana, by age, 1965 to 2008)

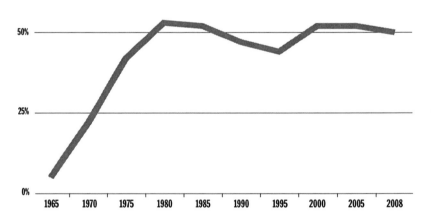

Table 4.22 Illicit Drug Use by People Aged 12 or Older, 2008

(percent of people aged 12 or older who ever used any illicit drug, who used an illicit drug in the past year, and who used an illicit drug in the past month, by age, 2008)

	ever used	used in past year	used in past month
Total people	**47.0%**	**14.2%**	**8.0%**
Aged 12	11.2	7.2	3.1
Aged 13	15.2	9.9	3.4
Aged 14	21.5	14.9	6.7
Aged 15	28.4	20.4	10.5
Aged 16	35.8	27.5	13.5
Aged 17	42.0	31.8	17.0
Aged 18	47.5	34.7	20.3
Aged 19	52.5	37.6	22.2
Aged 20	55.7	36.9	22.3
Aged 21	59.0	35.6	20.9
Aged 22	60.1	34.8	20.7
Aged 23	59.1	28.8	17.3
Aged 24	59.9	29.6	17.4
Aged 25	61.7	28.7	15.4
Aged 26 to 29	61.1	23.4	13.0
Aged 30 to 34	55.4	16.4	9.6
Aged 35 to 39	55.2	14.6	8.6
Aged 40 to 44	60.2	12.9	6.3
Aged 45 to 49	62.7	11.5	7.0
Aged 50 to 54	58.0	8.1	4.3
Aged 55 to 59	51.9	7.7	5.0
Aged 60 to 64	41.3	5.2	3.0
Aged 65 or older	13.5	1.4	1.0

Note: Illicit drugs include marijuana, hashish, cocaine (including crack), heroin, hallucinogens, inhalants, and any prescription-type psychotherapeutic used nonmedically.
Source: SAMHSA, Office of Applied Studies, National Survey on Drug Use and Health, 2008, Internet site http://www.oas
.samhsa.gov/NSDUH/2K8NSDUH/tabs/toc.htm

Table 4.23 Lifetime Marijuana Use by People Aged 12 to 25, 1965 to 2008

(percent of people aged 12 to 25 who have ever used marijuana, selected years 1965 to 2008)

	12 to 17	18 to 25
2008	16.5%	50.4%
2005	17.4	52.4
2000	20.4	51.8
1995	16.4	44.1
1990	11.9	46.6
1985	15.4	51.5
1980	19.4	53.0
1975	15.8	41.6
1970	7.4	22.0
1965	1.8	5.1

Source: SAMHSA, Office of Applied Studies, National Survey on Drug Use and Health, 2008, Internet site http://www.oas .samhsa.gov/NSDUH/2K8NSDUH/tabs/toc.htm

Table 4.24 Marijuana Use by People Aged 12 or Older, 2008

(percent of people aged 12 or older who ever used marijuana, who used marijuana in the past year, and who used marijuana in the past month, by age, 2008)

	ever used	used in past year	used in past month
Total people	**41.0%**	**10.3%**	**6.1%**
Aged 12	1.5	1.1	0.5
Aged 13	4.6	3.8	1.4
Aged 14	9.8	8.1	3.6
Aged 15	19.2	14.8	7.7
Aged 16	26.5	21.2	10.9
Aged 17	34.4	26.6	14.5
Aged 18	40.6	29.3	17.8
Aged 19	46.0	32.2	19.4
Aged 20	49.8	31.5	18.9
Aged 21	52.7	30.4	17.8
Aged 22	53.6	28.5	17.3
Aged 23	53.4	22.4	14.0
Aged 24	54.2	23.3	13.3
Aged 25	55.8	21.9	12.5
Aged 26 to 29	54.6	18.2	10.5
Aged 30 to 34	48.3	11.8	7.2
Aged 35 to 39	48.5	10.0	6.1
Aged 40 to 44	55.1	7.9	4.1
Aged 45 to 49	57.6	7.6	4.7
Aged 50 to 54	53.2	5.3	3.0
Aged 55 to 59	47.5	5.1	3.9
Aged 60 to 64	34.6	3.2	2.3
Aged 65 or older	9.3	0.4	0.3

Source: SAMHSA, Office of Applied Studies, National Survey on Drug Use and Health, 2008, Internet site http://www.oas .samhsa.gov/NSDUH/2K8NSDUH/tabs/toc.htm

Table 4.25 Marijuana Use by 9th to 12th Graders, 2007

(percent of 9th to 12th graders who have ever used marijuana or have used marijuana in the past 30 days, by grade, 2007)

	lifetime	past month
Total in 9th to 12th grade	**38.1%**	**19.7%**
9th graders	27.5	14.7
10th graders	36.9	19.3
11th graders	42.4	21.4
12th graders	49.1	25.1

Source: Centers for Disease Control and Prevention, Youth Risk Behavior Surveillance—United States, 2007, Mortality and Morbidity Weekly Report, Vol. 57/SS-4, June 6, 2008, Internet site http://www.cdc.gov/HealthyYouth/yrbs/index.htm

Most Women of Childbearing Age Use Contraceptives

The pill and female sterilization are the most popular contraceptives.

Among the nation's women of childbearing age—15 to 44—the 62 percent majority uses contraceptives. The pill is most popular, with 19 percent of women taking it, according to the federal government's National Survey of Family Growth. Female sterilization is the contraceptive choice of 17 percent of women, while condoms rank third at 11 percent. Use of the pill peaks at 32 percent among women aged 20 to 24, while women aged 35 or older are more likely to use female sterilization than the pill.

For most Americans, sexual activity begins in high school. Fifty-seven percent of 11th grade boys and 54 percent of 11th grade girls have had sexual intercourse. Most sexually active teens used birth control the last time they had sex.

■ Sexual activity being the norm among high school students, sex education is a necessity.

The pill is popular among young women

(percent of women aged 15 to 44 who are using the contraceptive pill, 2002)

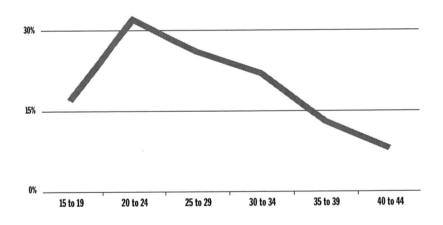

Table 4.26 Contraceptive Use by Age, 2002

(total number of women aged 15 to 44 and percent distribution by contraceptive status and age, 2002; numbers in thousands)

	total	15 to 19	20 to 24	25 to 29	30 to 34	35 to 39	40 to 44
Total women aged 15 to 44 (number)	61,561	9,834	9,840	9,249	10,272	10,853	11,512
Total women aged 15 to 44 (percent)	100.0%	100.0%	100.0%	100.0%	100.0%	100.0%	100.0%
Using contraception	**61.9%**	**31.5%**	**60.7%**	**68.0%**	**69.2%**	**70.8%**	**69.1%**
Female sterilization	16.7	0.0	2.2	10.3	19.0	29.2	34.7
Male sterilization	5.7	0.0	0.5	2.8	6.4	10.0	12.7
Pill	18.9	16.7	31.9	25.6	21.8	13.2	7.6
Implant, Lunelle, or Patch	0.8	0.4	0.9	1.7	0.9	0.5	0.2
Three-month injectable (Depo-Provera)	3.3	4.4	6.1	4.4	2.9	1.5	1.1
Intrauterine device (IUD)	1.3	0.1	1.1	2.5	2.2	1.0	0.8
Diaphragm	0.2	0.0	0.1	0.3	0.1	0.0	0.4
Condom	11.1	8.5	14.0	14.0	11.8	11.1	8.0
Periodic abstinence—calendar rhythm method	0.7	0.0	0.8	0.3	0.9	1.1	1.2
Periodic abstinence—natural family planning	0.2	0.0	0.0	0.4	0.2	0.3	0.4
Withdrawal	2.5	0.8	3.1	5.3	2.6	2.4	1.0
Other methods	0.6	0.6	0.2	0.4	0.4	0.5	1.1
Not using contraception	**38.1**	**68.5**	**39.3**	**32.0**	**30.8**	**29.2**	**30.9**
Surgically sterile female (noncontraceptive)	1.5	0.0	0.0	0.4	0.9	2.1	4.9
Nonsurgically sterile, male or female	1.6	0.7	0.7	0.9	1.4	1.2	4.4
Pregnant or postpartum	5.3	3.5	9.5	8.4	6.9	3.8	0.8
Seeking pregnancy	4.2	1.2	2.8	5.5	7.0	5.1	3.3
Other nonuse							
Never had intercourse or no intercourse in past three months	18.1	56.2	17.9	8.9	7.6	9.1	10.8
Had intercourse during past three months	7.4	6.9	8.4	8.0	7.0	7.7	6.7

Note: "Other methods" includes Today sponge, cervical cap, female condom, and other methods.
Source: National Center for Health Statistics, Use of Contraception and Use of Family Planning Services in the United States: 1982–2002, Advance Data, No. 350, 2004, Internet site http://www.cdc.gov/nchs/nsfg.htm

Table 4.27 Sexual Behavior of 9th to 12th Graders by Sex, 2007

(percent of 9th to 12th graders engaging in selected sexual activities, by sex and grade, 2007)

	total	9th grade	10th grade	11th grade	12th grade
BOYS					
Ever had sexual intercourse	**49.8%**	**38.1%**	**45.6%**	**57.3%**	**62.8%**
Currently sexually active*	34.3	22.2	29.4	42.0	48.3
First sexual intercourse before age 13	10.1	13.5	9.1	9.9	6.7
Four or more sex partners during lifetime	17.9	11.9	16.7	20.6	24.7
Condom use during last sexual intercourse	68.5	75.8	73.2	69.3	59.6
Birth control pill use before last sexual intercourse	13.1	8.3	9.5	11.0	20.8
GIRLS					
Ever had sexual intercourse	**45.9**	**27.4**	**41.9**	**53.6**	**66.2**
Currently sexually active*	35.6	18.0	31.8	41.5	56.7
First sexual intercourse before age 13	4.0	4.9	4.7	3.4	2.4
Four or more sex partners during lifetime	11.8	5.5	10.2	13.1	20.1
Condom use during last sexual intercourse	54.9	61.0	59.5	55.1	49.9
Birth control pill use before last sexual intercourse	18.7	9.2	13.7	18.9	25.6

* Had sexual intercourse during the three months preceding the survey.
Source: Centers for Disease Control and Prevention, Youth Risk Behavior Surveillance—United States, 2007, Mortality and Morbidity Weekly Report, Vol. 57/SS-4, June 6, 2008, Internet site http://www.cdc.gov/HealthyYouth/yrbs/index.htm

Most Teens Avoid Risky Behavior

The Millennial generation lives neither recklessly nor risk free.

A survey of teen behavior by the Centers for Disease Control and Prevention shows that most 9th through 12th graders do not participate in risky activities—although many do. Most teens wear seat belts, but 14 percent of boys say they rarely or never use them. Most do not drink and drive, but 13 percent of boys say they have done so in the past month. Nearly 30 percent of boys say they have carried a weapon in the past 30 days, and 44 percent have been in a physical fight in the past year.

Teenage boys are more likely than girls to engage in most risk behaviors. Boys are considerably more likely than girls to carry a weapon (28.5 versus 7.5 percent) or get in a physical fight (44.4 versus 26.5 percent). Girls, on the other hand, are more likely to have contemplated suicide (19 versus 10 percent).

■ Teenagers are notoriously unaware of the risks of reckless behavior. This is why accidents (particularly motor vehicle accidents) are one of the leading causes of death among young people.

Many teens say they rode with a driver who had been drinking

(percent of 9th through 12th graders who, in the past 30 days, rode with a driver who had been drinking, by sex, 2007)

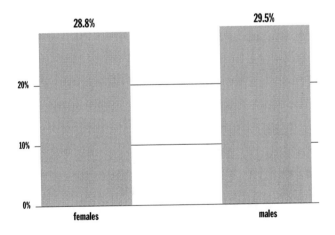

Table 4.28   Risk Behavior among 9th to 12th Graders by Sex, 2007

(percent of 9th to 12th graders engaging in selected risk behaviors, by sex, 2007)

	total	9th grade	10th grade	11th grade	12th grade
Rarely or never use seat belts when riding in car driven by someone else					
Total	11.1%	12.3%	10.8%	10.6%	10.5%
Female	8.5	9.2	8.3	8.9	7.3
Male	13.6	15.1	13.2	12.2	13.8
Rode in past 30 days with driver who had been drinking					
Total	29.1	27.6	28.7	29.2	31.5
Female	28.8	27.6	30.4	26.8	30.5
Male	29.5	27.6	27.1	31.4	32.5
Drove in past 30 days after drinking					
Total	10.5	5.5	8.7	11.5	18.3
Female	8.1	4.1	7.3	9.1	13.1
Male	12.8	6.8	10.0	13.7	23.6
Carried a weapon (gun, knife, club, etc.) in past 30 days					
Total	18.0	20.1	18.8	16.7	15.5
Female	7.5	8.9	8.1	6.0	6.2
Male	28.5	31.0	29.3	27.7	25.0
Carried a gun in past 30 days					
Total	5.2	5.2	5.5	4.6	5.0
Female	1.2	1.4	1.1	1.2	0.9
Male	9.0	8.9	9.8	8.1	9.2
Seriously considered attempting suicide during past 12 months					
Total	14.5	14.8	15.6	13.5	13.5
Female	18.7	19.0	22.0	16.3	16.7
Male	10.3	10.8	9.3	10.7	10.2
Attempted suicide during past 12 months					
Total	6.9	7.9	8.0	5.8	5.4
Female	9.3	10.5	11.2	7.8	6.5
Male	4.6	5.3	4.9	3.7	4.2
Was in a physical fight during past 12 months					
Total	35.5	40.9	36.2	34.8	28.0
Female	26.5	31.8	27.2	23.5	21.8
Male	44.4	49.6	45.1	46.3	34.3
Was hit, slapped, or physically hurt on purpose by a boyfriend or girlfriend during the past 12 months					
Total	9.9	8.5	8.9	10.6	12.1
Female	8.8	6.3	8.8	10.2	10.1
Male	11.0	10.5	9.1	10.8	14.1
Was forced to have sexual intercourse					
Total	7.8	6.6	8.2	8.5	8.3
Female	11.3	9.2	13.1	12	10.9
Male	4.5	4.1	3.4	5	5.7

Source: Centers for Disease Control and Prevention, Youth Risk Behavior Surveillance—United States, 2007, Mortality and Morbidity Weekly Report, Vol. 57/SS-4, June 6, 2008, Internet site http://www.cdc.gov/HealthyYouth/yrbs/index.htm

Many Older Americans Have Physical Difficulties

The biggest problem is standing for two hours.

A 2008 survey by the National Center for Health Statistics estimated that 33 million Americans—15 percent of people aged 18 or older—have physical difficulties. The difficulties range from walking a quarter mile, to climbing stairs and grasping small objects. Not surprisingly, older Americans are much more likely than younger adults they have physical difficulties.

Just 5 percent of people aged 18 to 44 reported having any physical difficulty. The proportion rises to 18 percent among 45-to-64-year-olds, and peaks at 45 percent among people aged 75 or older. The most common problem is standing for two hours, with 9 percent of people aged 18 or older saying this would be "very difficult" for them or they "can't do it at all." Almost the same proportion of adults say they would have difficulty stooping, bending, or kneeling.

Among people aged 75 or older, 30 percent say they would have difficulty standing for two hours. Twenty-seven percent say it would be very difficult or impossible for them to walk a quarter of a mile. People aged 75 or older account for one in four Americans with physical difficulties.

■ Although Americans aged 65 or older are most likely to report physical difficulties, younger adults account for the majority of those with physical difficulties.

Physical difficulties rise with age

(percent of people with physical difficulties, by age, 2008)

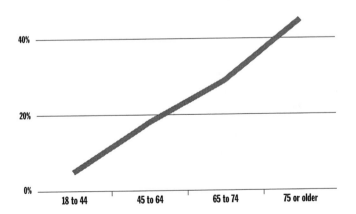

Table 4.29 Difficulties in Physical Functioning among Adults by Age, 2008

(number of people aged 18 or older with difficulties in physical functioning, by type of difficulty and age, 2008; numbers in thousands)

	total	18 to 44	45 to 64	aged 65 or older total	65 to 74	75 or older
TOTAL PEOPLE	225,227	110,615	77,335	37,278	19,869	17,409
Total with any physical difficulty	33,131	5,587	13,986	13,557	5,676	7,881
Walk quarter of a mile	16,010	1,908	6,552	7,550	2,791	4,759
Climb 10 steps without resting	11,334	1,197	4,718	5,418	1,960	3,458
Stand for two hours	19,938	3,126	8,105	8,706	3,543	5,163
Sit for two hours	6,921	1,754	3,421	1,745	833	912
Stoop, bend, or kneel	19,512	2,876	8,275	8,361	3,734	4,627
Reach over head	5,044	534	2,129	2,381	833	1,548
Grasp or handle small objects	3,722	524	1,595	1,603	605	998
Lift or carry 10 pounds	9,295	1,304	3,745	4,247	1,405	2,842
Push or pull large objects	13,222	2,205	5,599	5,418	2,137	3,281
PERCENT WITH PHYSICAL DIFFICULTY						
Total people	100.0%	100.0%	100.0%	100.0%	100.0%	100.0%
Total with any physical difficulty	14.7	5.1	18.1	36.4	28.6	45.3
Walk quarter of a mile	7.1	1.7	8.5	20.3	14.0	27.3
Climb 10 steps without resting	5.0	1.1	6.1	14.5	9.9	19.9
Stand for two hours	8.9	2.8	10.5	23.4	17.8	29.7
Sit for two hours	3.1	1.6	4.4	4.7	4.2	5.2
Stoop, bend, or kneel	8.7	2.6	10.7	22.4	18.8	26.6
Reach over head	2.2	0.5	2.8	6.4	4.2	8.9
Grasp or handle small objects	1.7	0.5	2.1	4.3	3.0	5.7
Lift or carry 10 pounds	4.1	1.2	4.8	11.4	7.1	16.3
Push or pull large objects	5.9	2.0	7.2	14.5	10.8	18.8
PERCENT DISTRIBUTION BY AGE						
Total people	100.0%	49.1%	34.3%	16.6%	8.8%	7.7%
Total with any physical difficulty	100.0	16.9	42.2	40.9	17.1	23.8
Walk quarter of a mile	100.0	11.9	40.9	47.2	17.4	29.7
Climb 10 steps without resting	100.0	10.6	41.6	47.8	17.3	30.5
Stand for two hours	100.0	15.7	40.7	43.7	17.8	25.9
Sit for two hours	100.0	25.3	49.4	25.2	12.0	13.2
Stoop, bend, or kneel	100.0	14.7	42.4	42.9	19.1	23.7
Reach over head	100.0	10.6	42.2	47.2	16.5	30.7
Grasp or handle small objects	100.0	14.1	42.9	43.1	16.3	26.8
Lift or carry 10 pounds	100.0	14.0	40.3	45.7	15.1	30.6
Push or pull large objects	100.0	16.7	42.3	41.0	16.2	24.8

Note: Respondents were classified as having difficulties if they responded "very difficult" or "can't do at all."
Source: National Center for Health Statistics, Summary Health Statistics for U.S. Adults: National Health Interview Survey, 2008, Series 10, No. 242, 2009, Internet site http://www.cdc.gov/nchs/nhis/nhis_series.htm; calculations by New Strategist

Health Problems Are Common among Older Americans

Lower back pain is one of the most frequently reported health conditions.

Twenty-seven percent of Americans aged 18 or older have experienced lower back pain for at least one full day in the past three months, making it one of the most frequently reported health problems. Chronic joint symptoms also affect 27 percent of adults, while arthritis has been officially diagnosed in 23 percent. Twenty-five percent have hypertension.

Many ailments are more common among older than younger Americans. Fifty-four percent of people aged 75 or older have been diagnosed with arthritis, for example, compared with fewer than 10 percent of 18-to-44-year-olds. Forty-three percent of the oldest Americans have hearing problems. But only 3 percent of people aged 75 or older suffer from migraines or severe headaches compared with a larger 17 percent of people aged 18 to 44.

■ As the Baby-Boom generation ages into its sixties, the number of people with arthritis or hearing problems will soar.

Most people aged 75 or older have arthritis

(percent of people diagnosed with arthritis, by age, 2008)

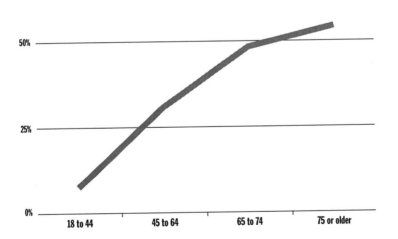

Table 4.30 Number of Health Conditions among Adults by Age, 2008

(number of people aged 18 or older with selected health conditions, by type of condition and age, 2008; numbers in thousands)

	total	18 to 44	45 to 64	aged 65 or older total	65 to 74	75 or older
TOTAL PEOPLE	**225,227**	**110,615**	**77,335**	**37,278**	**19,869**	**17,409**
Selected circulatory diseases						
Heart disease, all types	26,628	5,067	9,469	12,092	5,287	6,805
Coronary	14,428	1,258	5,205	7,965	3,337	4,628
Hypertension	56,159	9,643	25,126	21,390	10,774	10,616
Stroke	6,460	714	2,260	3,486	1,248	2,238
Selected respiratory conditions						
Emphysema	3,789	222	1,573	1,994	1,124	870
Asthma, ever	28,260	14,888	9,265	4,107	2,376	1,731
Asthma, still	16,380	7,949	5,768	2,664	1,548	1,116
Hay fever	18,022	7,379	7,823	2,820	1,537	1,283
Sinusitis	30,621	12,850	12,072	5,699	3,362	2,337
Chronic bronchitis	9,832	3,486	4,251	2,094	1,172	922
Cancer						
Any cancer	17,866	2,521	6,838	8,507	3,814	4,693
Breast cancer	3,134	120	1,233	1,782	877	905
Cervical cancer	1,637	699	725	213	141	72
Prostate cancer	2,160	–	620	1,516	707	809
Other selected diseases and conditions						
Diabetes	18,651	2,553	9,223	6,875	3,940	2,935
Ulcers	19,321	6,065	8,045	5,212	2,719	2,493
Kidney disease	3,731	795	1,372	1,564	601	963
Liver disease	3,262	1,060	1,680	522	330	192
Arthritis	51,233	8,306	23,900	19,028	9,574	9,454
Chronic joint symptoms	61,656	18,481	27,067	16,106	8,533	7,573
Migraines or severe headaches	30,262	18,352	10,260	1,650	1,121	529
Pain in neck	31,447	14,017	12,744	4,686	2,618	2,068
Pain in lower back	61,719	27,136	22,778	11,806	6,359	5,447
Pain in face or jaw	9,753	5,092	3,523	1,138	649	489
Selected sensory problems						
Hearing	34,750	7,637	14,190	12,923	5,499	7,424
Vision	25,150	7,980	10,673	6,498	2,831	3,667
Absence of all natural teeth	19,134	3,097	6,558	9,479	4,028	5,451

Note: The conditions shown are those that have ever been diagnosed by a doctor, except as noted. Hay fever, sinusitis, and chronic bronchitis have been diagnosed in the past 12 months. Kidney and liver disease have been diagnosed in the past 12 months and exclude kidney stones, bladder infections, and incontinence. Chronic joint symptoms are shown if respondent had pain, aching, or stiffness in or around a joint (excluding back and neck) and the condition began more than three months ago. Migraines, pain in neck, lower back, face, or jaw are shown only if pain lasted a whole day or more. "–" means sample is too small to make a reliable estimate.
Source: National Center for Health Statistics, Summary Health Statistics for U.S. Adults: National Health Interview Survey, 2008, Series 10, No. 242, 2009, Internet site http://www.cdc.gov/nchs/nhis/nhis_series.htm; calculations by New Strategist

Table 4.31 Percent Distribution of Health Conditions among Adults by Age, 2008

(percent distribution of people aged 18 or older with selected health conditions, by type of condition and age, 2008)

	total	18 to 44	45 to 64	aged 65 or older total	65 to 74	75 or older
TOTAL PEOPLE	**100.0%**	**49.1%**	**34.3%**	**16.6%**	**8.8%**	**7.7%**
Selected circulatory diseases						
Heart disease, all types	100.0	19.0	35.6	45.4	19.9	25.6
Coronary	100.0	8.7	36.1	55.2	23.1	32.1
Hypertension	100.0	17.2	44.7	38.1	19.2	18.9
Stroke	100.0	11.1	35.0	54.0	19.3	34.6
Selected respiratory conditions						
Emphysema	100.0	5.9	41.5	52.6	29.7	23.0
Asthma, ever	100.0	48.5	35.2	16.3	9.5	6.8
Asthma, still	100.0	40.9	43.4	15.6	8.5	7.1
Hay fever	100.0	42.0	39.4	18.6	11.0	7.6
Sinusitis	100.0	35.5	43.2	21.3	11.9	9.4
Chronic bronchitis						
Cancer						
Any cancer	100.0	14.1	38.3	47.6	21.3	26.3
Breast cancer	100.0	3.8	39.3	56.9	28.0	28.9
Cervical cancer	100.0	42.7	44.3	13.0	8.6	4.4
Prostate cancer	100.0	–	28.7	70.2	32.7	37.5
Other selected diseases and conditions						
Diabetes	100.0	13.7	49.5	36.9	21.1	15.7
Ulcers	100.0	31.4	41.6	27.0	14.1	12.9
Kidney disease	100.0	21.3	36.8	41.9	16.1	25.8
Liver disease	100.0	32.5	51.5	16.0	10.1	5.9
Arthritis	100.0	16.2	46.6	37.1	18.7	18.5
Chronic joint symptoms	100.0	30.0	43.9	26.1	13.8	12.3
Migraines or severe headaches	100.0	60.6	33.9	5.5	3.7	1.7
Pain in neck	100.0	44.6	40.5	14.9	8.3	6.6
Pain in lower back	100.0	44.0	36.9	19.1	10.3	8.8
Pain in face or jaw	100.0	52.2	36.1	11.7	6.7	5.0
Selected sensory problems	**100.0**	**22.0**	**40.8**	**37.2**	**15.8**	**21.4**
Hearing	100.0	31.7	42.4	25.8	11.3	14.6
Vision	100.0	16.2	34.3	49.5	21.1	28.5
Absence of all natural teeth	100.0	12.2	30.9	56.9	24.0	32.9

Note: The conditions shown are those that have ever been diagnosed by a doctor, except as noted. Hay fever, sinusitis, and chronic bronchitis have been diagnosed in the past 12 months. Kidney and liver disease have been diagnosed in the past 12 months and exclude kidney stones, bladder infections, and incontinence. Chronic joint symptoms are shown if respondent had pain, aching, or stiffness in or around a joint (excluding back and neck) and the condition began more than three months ago. Migraines, pain in neck, lower back, face, or jaw are shown only if pain lasted a whole day or more. "–" means sample is too small to make a reliable estimate.
Source: National Center for Health Statistics, Summary Health Statistics for U.S. Adults: National Health Interview Survey, 2008, Series 10, No. 242, 2009, Internet site http://www.cdc.gov/nchs/nhis/nhis_series.htm; calculations by New Strategist

Table 4.32 Percent of Adults with Health Conditions by Age, 2008

(percent of people aged 18 or older with selected health conditions, by type of condition and age, 2008)

	total	18 to 44	45 to 64	65 to 74	75 or older
TOTAL PEOPLE	100.0%	100.0%	100.0%	100.0%	100.0%
Selected circulatory diseases					
Heart disease, all types	11.8	4.6	12.3	26.7	39.2
Coronary	6.4	1.1	6.7	16.9	26.7
Hypertension	25.0	8.7	32.5	54.4	61.1
Stroke	2.9	0.6	2.9	6.3	12.9
Selected respiratory conditions					
Emphysema	1.7	0.2	2.0	5.7	5.0
Asthma, ever	12.6	13.5	12.0	12.0	10.0
Asthma, still	7.3	7.2	7.5	7.8	6.4
Hay fever	8.0	6.7	10.1	7.7	7.4
Sinusitis	13.6	11.6	15.6	16.9	13.4
Chronic bronchitis	4.4	3.2	5.5	5.9	5.3
Cancer					
Any cancer	7.9	2.3	8.9	19.2	27.0
Breast cancer	1.4	0.1	1.6	4.4	5.2
Cervical cancer	1.4	1.3	1.8	1.3	0.7
Prostate cancer	2.0	–	1.7	7.7	11.8
Other selected diseases and conditions					
Diabetes	8.4	2.3	12.1	20.4	17.3
Ulcers	8.6	5.5	10.4	13.7	14.4
Kidney disease	1.7	0.7	1.8	3.0	5.5
Liver disease	1.4	1.0	2.2	1.7	1.1
Arthritis	22.8	7.5	30.9	48.3	54.4
Chronic joint symptoms	27.4	16.7	35.0	43.0	43.6
Migraines or severe headaches	13.4	16.6	13.3	5.7	3.0
Pain in neck	14.0	12.7	16.5	13.2	11.9
Pain in lower back	27.4	24.5	29.5	32.1	31.3
Pain in face or jaw	4.3	4.6	4.6	3.3	2.8
Selected sensory problems					
Hearing	15.4	6.9	18.4	27.8	42.7
Vision	11.2	7.2	13.8	14.3	21.1
Absence of all natural teeth	8.5	2.8	8.5	20.4	31.5

Note: The conditions shown are those that have ever been diagnosed by a doctor, except as noted. Hay fever, sinusitis, and chronic bronchitis have been diagnosed in the past 12 months. Kidney and liver disease have been diagnosed in the past 12 months and exclude kidney stones, bladder infections, and incontinence. Chronic joint symptoms are shown if respondent had pain, aching, or stiffness in or around a joint (excluding back and neck) and the condition began more than three months ago. Migraines, pain in neck, lower back, face, or jaw are shown only if pain lasted a whole day or more. "–" means sample is too small to make a reliable estimate.
Source: National Center for Health Statistics, Summary Health Statistics for U.S. Adults: National Health Interview Survey, 2008, Series 10, No. 242, 2009, Internet site http://www.cdc.gov/nchs/nhis/nhis_series.htm; calculations by New Strategist

Men Aged 25 to 44 Account for Most AIDS Cases

Only 19 percent of those who have been diagnosed with AIDS are women.

Through 2007, more than 1 million people had been diagnosed with AIDS. While new drug therapies have been successful in reducing the AIDS mortality rate, the number of AIDS cases continues to climb.

Men accounted for 80 percent of people diagnosed with AIDS through 2007, and the 57 percent majority were aged 25 to 44 at the time of diagnosis. Men aged 35 to 44 account for the largest share of people diagnosed with AIDS—32 percent of the total through 2007. Men aged 25 to 34 account for another 25 percent.

■ Although AIDS mortality has been reduced, the disease is still a devastating diagnosis that requires expensive drug regimens to manage.

Men aged 25 to 44 dominate AIDS cases

(percent distribution of people diagnosed with AIDS by sex and age at diagnosis, through 2007)

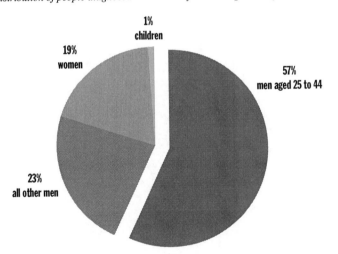

Table 4.33 AIDS Cases by Sex and Age, through 2007

(cumulative number and percent distribution of AIDS cases by age at diagnosis and sex for those aged 13 or older, 2007)

	number	percent distribution
Total cases	**1,018,428**	**100.0%**
Under age 13	9,209	0.9
Aged 13 to 14	1,168	0.1
Aged 15 to 24	44,264	4.3
Aged 25 to 34	322,369	31.7
Aged 35 to 44	396,851	39.0
Aged 45 to 54	176,304	17.3
Aged 55 to 64	52,409	5.1
Aged 65 or older	15,853	1.6
MEN		
Total, aged 13 or older	**810,676**	**79.6**
Aged 13 to 14	643	0.1
Aged 15 to 24	30,454	3.0
Aged 25 to 34	256,477	25.2
Aged 35 to 44	323,350	31.7
Aged 45 to 54	144,758	14.2
Aged 55 to 64	42,768	4.2
Aged 65 or older	12,225	1.2
WOMEN		
Total, aged 13 or older	**198,544**	**19.5**
Aged 13 to 14	525	0.1
Aged 15 to 24	13,810	1.4
Aged 25 to 34	65,892	6.5
Aged 35 to 44	73,501	7.2
Aged 45 to 54	31,546	3.1
Aged 55 to 64	9,641	0.9
Aged 65 or older	3,628	0.4

Note: Numbers do not add to total because of methodology and unknown sex.
Source: National Center for Health Statistics, Health, United States, 2009, Internet site http://www.cdc.gov/nchs/hus.htm

Asthma and Allergies Affect Many Children

Boys are more likely than girls to have learning disabilities.

Asthma is a growing problem among children. Nearly 14 percent of the nation's 74 million children under age 18 have been diagnosed with asthma. Nine percent have had asthma in the past year. Boys are more likely than girls to have asthma (16.5 versus 11.2 percent), and blacks more than whites (21.2 versus 13.0 percent).

Five million children aged 3 to 17 (8 percent) have been diagnosed with a learning disability, and about the same number have attention deficit hyperactivity disorder. Boys, who are far more likely than girls to have these conditions, account for nearly two-thirds of those with learning disabilities and nearly three-fourths of those with attention deficit hyperactivity disorder.

Many children use prescription medications. Nine million children have taken prescription medications regularly for at least three months during the past year—that is a substantial 13 percent of the nation's children. Among 12-to-17-year-olds, the figure is an even higher 16 percent.

■ Prescription drug use is growing, even among children.

Asthma is a big problem for black children

(percent of people under age 18 diagnosed with asthma, by race and Hispanic origin, 2008)

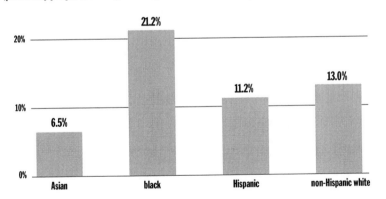

Table 4.34 Health Conditions among Children by Selected Characteristics, 2008

(number of people under age 18 with selected health conditions, by selected characteristics and type of condition, 2008; numbers in thousands)

	total children	asthma		in last 12 months			prescription medication taken
		ever had	still have	hay fever	respiratory allergies	other allergies	regularly at least 3 months
TOTAL CHILDREN	73,859	10,190	6,953	7,069	8,254	10,514	9,449
Sex							
Female	36,109	4,006	2,660	3,027	3,667	5,149	3,747
Male	37,750	6,184	4,293	4,042	4,587	5,365	5,702
Age							
Aged 0 to 4	20,800	1,499	1,276	957	1,713	3,173	1,490
Aged 5 to 11	28,250	4,573	3,159	3,198	3,400	4,220	4,005
Aged 12 to 17	24,809	4,118	2,518	2,915	3,141	3,121	3,954
Race and Hispanic origin							
Asian	2,911	191	107	143	232	401	224
Black	11,337	2,384	1,753	881	1,215	1,900	1,360
Hispanic	15,803	1,725	1,055	1,039	1,161	1,954	1,191
Non-Hispanic white	41,294	5,356	3,638	4,685	5,314	5,756	6,282
Family structure							
Mother and father	52,026	6,193	4,204	5,282	5,967	7,085	6,440
Mother, no father	17,287	3,255	2,262	1,506	1,961	2,984	2,355
Father, no mother	2,377	256	138	125	115	167	237
Neither mother nor father	2,169	486	349	157	211	278	417
Parent's education							
Less than high school diploma	9,255	929	688	423	555	918	797
High school diploma	15,437	2,088	1,372	1,173	1,293	1,737	1,734
More than high school	46,749	6,667	4,535	5,288	6,196	7,573	6,497
Household income							
Less than $35,000	21,285	3,913	2,696	1,642	2,095	3,161	2,845
$35,000 to $54,999	10,230	1,148	809	711	943	1,382	1,239
$55,000 to $74,999	12,980	1,401	939	1,361	1,453	1,598	1,538
$75,000 to $99,999	8,719	1,324	849	996	1,200	1,242	1,048
$100,000 or more	15,555	1,955	1,357	2,020	2,239	2,444	2,342

Note: Mother and father include biological, adoptive, step, in-law, and foster relationships. Legal guardians are classified as neither mother nor father. Parent's education is the education level of the parent with the higher level of education. Other allergies include food or digestive allergies, eczema, and other skin allergies. Numbers of education and income may not add to total because "unknown" is not shown. Numbers by race do not add to total because not all races are shown and Hispanics may be of any race.
Source: National Center for Health Statistics, Summary Health Statistics for U.S. Children: National Health Interview Survey, 2008, Vital and Health Statistics, Series 10, No. 244, 2009, Internet site http://www.cdc.gov/nchs/nhis/nhis_series.htm

Table 4.35 Distribution of Health Conditions by Selected Characteristics of Children, 2008

(percent distribution of people under age 18 with health condition by selected characteristics, 2008)

| | total children | asthma | | in last 12 months | | | prescription medication taken |
		ever had	still have	hay fever	respiratory allergies	other allergies	regularly at least 3 months
TOTAL CHILDREN	100.0%	100.0%	100.0%	100.0%	100.0%	100.0%	100.0%
Sex							
Female	48.9	39.3	38.3	42.8	44.4	49.0	39.7
Male	51.1	60.7	61.7	57.2	55.6	51.0	60.3
Age							
Aged 0 to 4	28.2	14.7	18.4	13.5	20.8	30.2	15.8
Aged 5 to 11	38.2	44.9	45.4	45.2	41.2	40.1	42.4
Aged 12 to 17	33.6	40.4	36.2	41.2	38.1	29.7	41.8
Race and Hispanic origin							
Asian	3.9	1.9	1.5	2.0	2.8	3.8	2.4
Black	15.3	23.4	25.2	12.5	14.7	18.1	14.4
Hispanic	21.4	16.9	15.2	14.7	14.1	18.6	12.6
Non-Hispanic white	55.9	52.6	52.3	66.3	64.4	54.7	66.5
Family structure							
Mother and father	70.4	60.8	60.5	74.7	72.3	67.4	68.2
Mother, no father	23.4	31.9	32.5	21.3	23.8	28.4	24.9
Father, no mother	3.2	2.5	2.0	1.8	1.4	1.6	2.5
Neither mother nor father	2.9	4.8	5.0	2.2	2.6	2.6	4.4
Parent's education							
Less than high school diploma	12.5	9.1	9.9	6.0	6.7	8.7	8.4
High school diploma	20.9	20.5	19.7	16.6	15.7	16.5	18.4
More than high school	63.3	65.4	65.2	74.8	75.1	72.0	68.8
Household income							
Less than $20,000	28.8	38.4	38.8	23.2	25.4	30.1	30.1
$20,000 to $34,999	13.9	11.3	11.6	10.1	11.4	13.1	13.1
$35,000 to $54,999	17.6	13.7	13.5	19.3	17.6	15.2	16.3
$55,000 to $74,999	11.8	13.0	12.2	14.1	14.5	11.8	11.1
$75,000 or more	21.1	19.2	19.5	28.6	27.1	23.2	24.8

Note: Mother and father include biological, adoptive, step, in-law, and foster relationships. Legal guardians are classified as neither mother nor father. Parent's education is the education level of the parent with the higher level of education. Other allergies include food or digestive allergies, eczema, and other skin allergies. Numbers of education and income may not add to total because "unknown" is not shown. Numbers by race do not add to total because not all races are shown and Hispanics may be of any race.
Source: National Center for Health Statistics, Summary Health Statistics for U.S. Children: National Health Interview Survey, 2008, Vital and Health Statistics, Series 10, No. 244, 2009, Internet site http://www.cdc.gov/nchs/nhis/nhis_series.htm

Table 4.36 Percent of Children with Health Conditions by Selected Characteristics, 2008

(percent of people under age 18 with selected health conditions, by type of condition and selected characteristics, 2008)

| | total children | asthma | | in last 12 months | | | prescription medication taken |
		ever had	still have	hay fever	respiratory allergies	other allergies	regularly at least 3 months
TOTAL CHILDREN	**100.0%**	**13.8%**	**9.4%**	**9.6%**	**11.2%**	**14.2%**	**12.8%**
Sex							
Female	100.0	11.2	7.4	8.5	10.2	14.3	10.4
Male	100.0	16.5	11.5	10.9	12.2	14.2	15.2
Age							
Aged 0 to 4	100.0	7.2	6.2	4.6	8.2	15.3	7.2
Aged 5 to 11	100.0	16.2	11.2	11.4	12.1	14.9	14.2
Aged 12 to 17	100.0	16.6	10.2	11.8	12.7	12.6	15.9
Race and Hispanic origin							
Asian	100.0	6.5	3.6	4.8	7.9	13.7	7.6
Black	100.0	21.2	15.6	7.9	10.8	16.8	12.1
Hispanic	100.0	11.2	6.8	6.7	7.4	12.3	7.6
Non-Hispanic white	100.0	13.0	8.8	11.4	12.9	14.0	15.2
Family structure							
Mother and father	100.0	12.2	8.2	10.4	11.7	13.6	12.6
Mother, no father	100.0	19.1	13.3	8.8	11.3	17.4	13.6
Father, no mother	100.0	8.7	5.0	4.1	5.4	8.0	9.6
Neither mother nor father	100.0	21.3	15.7	7.8	10.8	13.9	18.1
Parent's education							
Less than high school diploma	100.0	10.4	7.7	4.6	6.0	9.9	8.9
High school diploma	100.0	13.7	8.9	7.7	8.4	11.3	11.3
More than high school	100.0	14.4	9.8	11.4	13.3	16.2	14.0
Household income							
Less than $20,000	100.0	19.3	13.2	8.2	10.1	14.9	13.9
$20,000 to $34,999	100.0	11.2	7.9	6.9	9.3	13.5	12.1
$35,000 to $54,999	100.0	10.7	7.2	10.5	11.2	12.3	11.8
$55,000 to $74,999	100.0	14.9	9.6	11.3	13.8	14.3	11.9
$75,000 or more	100.0	12.5	8.7	12.8	14.2	15.7	14.6

Note: Mother and father include biological, adoptive, step, in-law, and foster relationships. Legal guardians are classified as neither mother nor father. Parent's education is the education level of the parent with the higher level of education. Other allergies include food or digestive allergies, eczema, and other skin allergies.
Source: National Center for Health Statistics, Summary Health Statistics for U.S. Children: National Health Interview Survey, 2008, Vital and Health Statistics, Series 10, No. 244, 2009, Internet site http://www.cdc.gov/nchs/nhis/nhis_series.htm

Table 4.37 Children with a Learning Disability or Attention Deficit Hyperactivity Disorder, 2008

(total number of children aged 3 to 17 and number and percent who have been told they have a learning disability or attention deficit hyperactivity disorder, by selected characteristics, 2008; numbers in thousands)

	total	learning disability		attention deficit hyperactivity disorder	
		number	percent	number	percent
TOTAL CHILDREN	**61,907**	**5,012**	**8.1%**	**4,968**	**8.0%**
Sex					
Female	30,183	1,839	6.2	1,459	4.9
Male	31,724	3,174	10.1	3,508	11.2
Age					
Aged 3 to 4	8,848	206	2.3	171	1.9
Aged 5 to 11	28,250	2,485	8.8	2,059	7.3
Aged 12 to 17	24,809	2,321	9.4	2,738	11.1
Race and Hispanic origin					
Asian	2,491	30	1.2	–	–
Black	9,596	860	9.2	792	8.3
Hispanic	12,922	750	5.9	535	4.2
Non-Hispanic white	34,836	3,158	9.1	3,425	9.8
Family structure					
Mother and father	42,931	2,930	6.9	2,907	6.9
Mother, no father	14,715	1,585	11.0	1,422	9.7
Father, no mother	2,256	189	8.3	298	12.6
Neither mother nor father	2,006	308	15.9	341	18.0
Parent's education					
Less than high school diploma	7,666	703	9.6	458	6.3
High school diploma	12,767	1,265	10.0	1,126	8.9
More than high school	39,240	2,736	7.0	3,038	7.8
Household income					
Less than $35,000	16,954	1,907	11.7	1,759	10.7
$35,000 to $54,999	8,821	782	9.0	746	8.7
$55,000 to $74,999	10,920	833	7.6	741	6.8
$75,000 to $99,999	7,555	546	7.3	569	7.6
$100,000 or more	13,461	743	5.5	960	6.9
Health insurance coverage					
Private	36,461	2,081	5.6	2,448	6.6
Medicaid/other public	17,815	2,442	14.3	2,120	12.4
Other	1,479	144	9.7	111	7.7
Uninsured	5,896	339	6.1	283	4.8

Note: Mother and father include biological, adoptive, step, in-law, and foster relationships. Legal guardians are classified as neither mother nor father. Parent's education is the education level of the parent with the higher level of education. Other allergies include food or digestive allergies, eczema, and other skin allergies. "–" means sample is too small to make a reliable estimate.
Source: National Center for Health Statistics, Summary Health Statistics for U.S. Children: National Health Interview Survey, 2008, Vital and Health Statistics, Series 10, No. 244, 2009, Internet site http://www.cdc.gov/nchs/nhis/nhis_series.htm

More People Do Not Have Health Insurance

Thanks to Medicare, older Americans are most likely to be insured.

Eighty-five percent of Americans were covered by public or private health insurance in 2008, leaving 46 million people without insurance. The percentage of people without health insurance rose from 14 to 15 percent between 2000 and 2008. In some age groups the increase was much steeper. The proportion of people aged 25 to 34 without health insurance climbed from 21 to 27 percent between 2000 and 2008. Cost is the number-one reason for not having health insurance, cited by 48 percent of those under age 65 without insurance.

Only 31 percent of Americans are covered by employment-based health insurance through their own employer. Overall, 58 percent are covered by their own or the employment-based health insurance of a spouse or parent. Only 9 percent buy their own private health insurance. The government's Medicare program covers 93 percent of Americans aged 65 or older. Medicaid, the health insurance program for the poor, covers 14 percent of all Americans—including 30 percent of children.

■ With so many Americans covered by the employment-based insurance of a spouse or parent, many people are only a lay-off, a divorce, or a birthday away from no coverage at all.

Twenty-nine percent of 18-to-24-year-olds do not have health insurance

(percent of people without health insurance, by age, 2008)

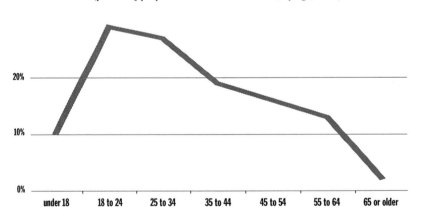

Table 4.38 Health Insurance Coverage by Age, 2008: Private Health Insurance Type

(number and percent distribution of people by age and health insurance coverage status, 2008; numbers in thousands)

		with any health insurance	with private health insurance	employment-based		direct	government	no
	total	total	total	total	own	purchase	insurance	insurance
Total people	**301,483**	**255,143**	**200,992**	**176,332**	**92,901**	**26,777**	**87,411**	**46,340**
Under age 65	263,695	218,002	178,705	163,119	82,885	16,673	51,977	45,693
Under age 18	74,510	67,161	47,282	43,874	228	3,812	24,767	7,348
Aged 18 to 24	28,688	20,488	16,947	13,450	5,052	1,700	4,741	8,200
Aged 25 to 34	40,520	29,766	25,879	24,130	18,632	2,189	5,086	10,754
Aged 35 to 44	41,322	33,287	29,780	27,899	19,702	2,444	4,685	8,035
Aged 45 to 54	44,366	37,312	33,234	30,861	22,393	3,182	5,797	7,054
Aged 55 to 64	34,289	29,989	25,584	22,906	16,877	3,346	6,901	4,301
Aged 65 or older	37,788	37,142	22,287	13,212	10,016	10,103	35,434	646

PERCENT DISTRIBUTION BY COVERAGE STATUS

Total people	**100.0%**	**84.6%**	**66.7%**	**58.5%**	**30.8%**	**8.9%**	**29.0%**	**15.4%**
Under age 65	100.0	82.7	67.8	61.9	31.4	6.3	19.7	17.3
Under age 18	100.0	90.1	63.5	58.9	0.3	5.1	33.2	9.9
Aged 18 to 24	100.0	71.4	59.1	46.9	17.6	5.9	16.5	28.6
Aged 25 to 34	100.0	73.5	63.9	59.6	46.0	5.4	12.6	26.5
Aged 35 to 44	100.0	80.6	72.1	67.5	47.7	5.9	11.3	19.4
Aged 45 to 54	100.0	84.1	74.9	69.6	50.5	7.2	13.1	15.9
Aged 55 to 64	100.0	87.5	74.6	66.8	49.2	9.8	20.1	12.5
Aged 65 or older	100.0	98.3	59.0	35.0	26.5	26.7	93.8	1.7

PERCENT DISTRIBUTION BY AGE

Total people	**100.0%**	**100.0%**	**100.0%**	**100.0%**	**100.0%**	**100.0%**	**100.0%**	**100.0%**
Under age 65	87.5	85.4	88.9	92.5	89.2	62.3	59.5	98.6
Under age 18	24.7	26.3	23.5	24.9	0.2	14.2	28.3	15.9
Aged 18 to 24	9.5	8.0	8.4	7.6	5.4	6.3	5.4	17.7
Aged 25 to 34	13.4	11.7	12.9	13.7	20.1	8.2	5.8	23.2
Aged 35 to 44	13.7	13.0	14.8	15.8	21.2	9.1	5.4	17.3
Aged 45 to 54	14.7	14.6	16.5	17.5	24.1	11.9	6.6	15.2
Aged 55 to 64	11.4	11.8	12.7	13.0	18.2	12.5	7.9	9.3
Aged 65 or older	12.5	14.6	11.1	7.5	10.8	37.7	40.5	1.4

Note: Numbers may not add to total because some people have more than one type of health insurance coverage.
Source: Bureau of the Census, Historical Health Insurance Tables, Internet site http://www.census.gov/hhes/www/cpstables/032009/health/toc.htm; calculations by New Strategist

Table 4.39 Health Insurance Coverage by Age, 2008: Government Health Insurance Type

(number and percent distribution of people by age and health insurance status, 2008; numbers in thousands)

		with any health insurance					private insurance	no insurance
			with government health insurance					
	total	total	total	Medicaid	Medicare	military		
Total people	**301,483**	**255,143**	**87,411**	**42,641**	**43,029**	**11,560**	**200,992**	**46,340**
Under age 65	263,695	218,002	51,977	39,213	7,725	8,740	178,705	45,693
Under age 18	74,510	67,161	24,767	22,555	623	2,241	47,282	7,348
Aged 18 to 24	28,688	20,488	4,741	3,798	254	868	16,947	8,200
Aged 25 to 34	40,520	29,766	5,086	3,748	546	1,104	25,879	10,754
Aged 35 to 44	41,322	33,287	4,685	3,155	970	1,097	29,780	8,035
Aged 45 to 54	44,366	37,312	5,797	3,313	1,967	1,371	33,234	7,054
Aged 55 to 64	34,289	29,989	6,901	2,644	3,365	2,059	25,584	4,301
Aged 65 or older	37,788	37,142	35,434	3,428	35,304	2,821	22,287	646

PERCENT DISTRIBUTION BY COVERAGE STATUS

Total people	**100.0%**	**84.6%**	**29.0%**	**14.1%**	**14.3%**	**3.8%**	**66.7%**	**15.4%**
Under age 65	100.0	82.7	19.7	14.9	2.9	3.3	67.8	17.3
Under age 18	100.0	90.1	33.2	30.3	0.8	3.0	63.5	9.9
Aged 18 to 24	100.0	71.4	16.5	13.2	0.9	3.0	59.1	28.6
Aged 25 to 34	100.0	73.5	12.6	9.2	1.3	2.7	63.9	26.5
Aged 35 to 44	100.0	80.6	11.3	7.6	2.3	2.7	72.1	19.4
Aged 45 to 54	100.0	84.1	13.1	7.5	4.4	3.1	74.9	15.9
Aged 55 to 64	100.0	87.5	20.1	7.7	9.8	6.0	74.6	12.5
Aged 65 or older	100.0	98.3	93.8	9.1	93.4	7.5	59.0	1.7

Percent distribution by age

Total people	**100.0%**	**100.0%**	**100.0%**	**100.0%**	**100.0%**	**100.0%**	**100.0%**	**100.0%**
Under age 65	87.5	85.4	59.5	92.0	18.0	75.6	88.9	98.6
Under age 18	24.7	26.3	28.3	52.9	1.4	19.4	23.5	15.9
Aged 18 to 24	9.5	8.0	5.4	8.9	0.6	7.5	8.4	17.7
Aged 25 to 34	13.4	11.7	5.8	8.8	1.3	9.6	12.9	23.2
Aged 35 to 44	13.7	13.0	5.4	7.4	2.3	9.5	14.8	17.3
Aged 45 to 54	14.7	14.6	6.6	7.8	4.6	11.9	16.5	15.2
Aged 55 to 64	11.4	11.8	7.9	6.2	7.8	17.8	12.7	9.3
Aged 65 or older	12.5	14.6	40.5	8.0	82.0	24.4	11.1	1.4

Note: Numbers may not add to total because some people have more than one type of health insurance coverage.
Source: Bureau of the Census, Historical Health Insurance Tables, Internet site http://www.census.gov/hhes/www/cpstables/032009/health/toc.htm; calculations by New Strategist

Table 4.40 People without Health Insurance by Age, 2000 and 2008

(number and percent of people without health insurance coverge by age, 2000 and 2008; percent change in number and percentage point change in share, 2000–08; numbers in thousands)

	2008	2000	percent change 2000–08
Number without insurance	**46,340**	**38,426**	**20.6%**
Under age 18	7,348	8,385	–12.4
Aged 18 to 24	8,200	7,203	13.8
Aged 25 to 34	10,754	8,318	29.3
Aged 35 to 44	8,035	6,746	19.1
Aged 45 to 54	7,054	4,492	57.0
Aged 55 to 64	4,301	3,031	41.9
Aged 65 or older	646	251	157.4

	2008	2000	percentage point change 2000–08
Percent without insurance	**15.4%**	**13.7%**	**1.7**
Under age 18	9.9	11.6	–1.7
Aged 18 to 24	28.6	26.9	1.7
Aged 25 to 34	26.5	21.4	5.1
Aged 35 to 44	19.4	15.1	4.3
Aged 45 to 54	15.9	11.6	4.3
Aged 55 to 64	12.5	12.3	0.2
Aged 65 or older	1.7	0.7	1.0

Source: Bureau of the Census, Historical Health Insurance Tables, Current Population Survey, Internet site http://www.census .gov/hhes/www/hlthins/historic/index.html

Table 4.41 Reason for Lack of Health Insurance Coverage by Age, 2008

(number of people under age 65 without health insurance and percent distribution by reason for lack of coverage, by age, 2008; numbers in thousands)

	total people under age 65 without health insurance		cost	lost job or change in employment	employer didn't offer or insurance company refused	Medicaid stopped	ineligible due to age or left school	change in marital status or death of parent	other reason
	number	percent							
Total under age 65	**43,675**	**100.0%**	**48.0%**	**22.1%**	**13.1%**	**9.7%**	**8.0%**	**2.3%**	**6.9%**
Under age 12	4,037	100.0	37.7	17.5	8.1	21.6	0.5	1.5	15.4
Aged 12 to 17	2,597	100.0	48.5	15.2	7.5	15.1	2.2	3.3	11.3
Aged 18 to 44	26,622	100.0	47.1	19.9	15.0	9.4	12.6	1.9	6.2
Aged 45 to 64	10,420	100.0	54.0	31.0	11.8	4.5	0.7	3.6	4.0

Note: Numbers may not sum to total because people can report more than one reason. "Other reason" includes moved, self-employed, never had coverage, did not want or need coverage, and other unspecified reasons.
Source: National Center for Health Statistics, Summary Health Statistics for U.S. Adults: National Health Interview Survey, 2008, Series 10, No. 242, 2009, Internet site http://www.cdc.gov/nchs/nhis/nhis_series.htm; calculations by New Strategist

More than One Billion Health Care Visits Occurred in 2006

Most health care visits are made by people aged 45 or older.

Americans visited a doctor 902 million times in 2006. They visited emergency rooms 119 million times and made 102 million trips to hospital outpatient departments. Older Americans dominate doctor visits. People aged 45 or older accounted for the 51 percent majority of doctor visits in 2006. They accounted for a smaller 44 percent share of visits to hospital outpatient departments and for an even smaller 36 percent of visits to emergency rooms.

The 80 percent majority of health care visits in 2006 were to physicians' offices. Only 9 percent were to hospital outpatient departments and 11 percent to emergency rooms. The likelihood of visiting an emergency room rather than a doctor varies by age. Among health care visits by people aged 15 to 24, a substantial 19 percent are to emergency rooms. Among visits by people aged 65 or older, only 7 percent are to emergency rooms.

■ As the population ages, health care visits of all types will continue to rise.

Emergency rooms account for a large share of health care visits by young adults

(emergency room visits as a percentage of total health care visits, by age, 2006)

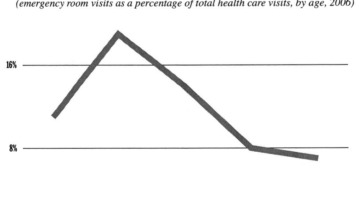

Table 4.42 Health Care Visits by Age, 2006

(number and percent distribution of visits to physicians' offices, hospital outpatient departments, and emergency rooms, by age, 2006; numbers in thousands)

	total	physicians' offices	hospital outpatient departments	hospital emergency departments
NUMBER				
Total visits	**1,123,354**	**901,954**	**102,208**	**119,191**
Under age 15	199,646	157,906	19,864	21,876
Aged 15 to 24	103,948	72,411	12,012	19,525
Aged 25 to 44	245,443	185,305	25,104	35,034
Aged 45 to 64	310,667	256,494	28,707	25,466
Aged 65 or older	263,649	229,837	16,522	17,290
PERCENT DISTRIBUTION BY PLACE OF CARE				
Total visits	**100.0%**	**80.3%**	**9.1%**	**10.6%**
Under age 15	100.0	79.1	9.9	11.0
Aged 15 to 24	100.0	69.7	11.6	18.8
Aged 25 to 44	100.0	75.5	10.2	14.3
Aged 45 to 64	100.0	82.6	9.2	8.2
Aged 65 or older	100.0	87.2	6.3	6.6
PERCENT DISTRIBUTION BY AGE				
Total visits	**100.0%**	**100.0%**	**100.0%**	**100.0%**
Under age 15	17.8	17.5	19.4	18.4
Aged 15 to 24	9.3	8.0	11.8	16.4
Aged 25 to 44	21.8	20.5	24.6	29.4
Aged 45 to 64	27.7	28.4	28.1	21.4
Aged 65 or older	23.5	25.5	16.2	14.5

Source: National Center for Health Statistics, Ambulatory Medical Care Utilization Estimates for 2006, National Health Statistics Reports, No. 8, 2008, Internet site http://www.cdc.gov/nchs/ahcd/ahcd_reports.htm; calculations by New Strategist

Table 4.43 Physician Office Visits by Sex and Age, 2006

(total number, percent distribution, and number of physician office visits per person per year, by sex and age, 2006; numbers in thousands)

	total	percent distribution	average visits per person per year
Total visits	**901,954**	**100.0%**	**3.1**
Under age 15	157,906	17.5	2.6
Aged 15 to 24	72,411	8.0	1.7
Aged 25 to 44	185,305	20.5	2.3
Aged 45 to 64	256,494	28.4	3.5
Aged 65 or older	229,837	25.5	6.5
Aged 65 to 74	108,063	12.0	5.8
Aged 75 or older	121,774	13.5	7.2
Visits by females	**533,292**	**59.1**	**3.6**
Under age 15	76,300	8.5	2.6
Aged 15 to 24	49,641	5.5	2.4
Aged 25 to 44	122,261	13.6	3.0
Aged 45 to 64	149,778	16.6	3.9
Aged 65 to 74	60,699	6.7	6.0
Aged 75 or older	74,613	8.3	7.3
Visits by males	**368,662**	**40.9**	**2.6**
Under age 15	81,607	9.0	2.6
Aged 15 to 24	22,770	2.5	1.1
Aged 25 to 44	63,044	7.0	1.6
Aged 45 to 64	106,716	11.8	3.0
Aged 65 to 74	47,364	5.3	5.5
Aged 75 or older	47,161	5.2	7.1

Source: National Center for Health Statistics, National Ambulatory Medical Care Survey: 2006 Summary, National Health Statistics Reports, No. 3, 2008, Internet site http://www.cdc.gov/nchs/ahcd/ahcd_reports.htm

One in 12 Americans Had a Hospital Stay in 2008

Older Americans are most likely to be hospitalized.

As health insurance companies try to cut costs, hospitals have changed their strategy. They are less likely to keep patients overnight and more likely to care for them through outpatient services.

In 2008, only 8 percent of people aged 18 or older were hospitalized overnight. People aged 65 or older are most likely to experience a hospital stay, 17 percent doing so in 2008. This compares with only 2 percent of teenagers—the 12-to-17 age group is least likely to be hospitalized.

■ Children under age 12 are more likely than teens to be hospitalized because of the greater likelihood of health problems in infancy.

Hospitalization is least likely among teenagers

(percent of people who experienced an overnight hospital stay in the past 12 months, by age, 2008)

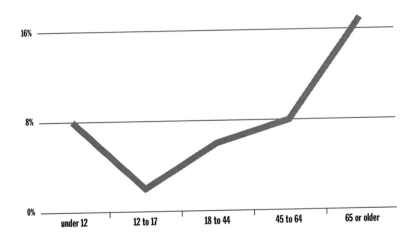

Table 4.44 Overnight Hospital Stays by Age, 2008

(total number of people and percent distribution by experience of an overnight hospital stay in past 12 months, by age, 2008; numbers in thousands)

	total		number of stays	
	number	percent	none	one or more
Total people	**299,082**	**100.0%**	**92.0%**	**8.0%**
Under age 12	49,087	100.0	92.3	7.7
Aged 12 to 17	24,771	100.0	97.6	2.4
Aged 18 to 44	110,613	100.0	93.6	6.4
Aged 45 to 64	77,489	100.0	92.2	7.8
Aged 65 or older	19,858	100.0	82.6	17.4

Source: National Center for Health Statistics, Summary Health Statistics for the U.S. Population: National Health Interview Survey, 2008, Vital and Health Statistics, Series 10, No. 243, 2009, Internet site http://www.cdc.gov/nchs/nhis/nhis_series.htm

Heart Disease Is the Leading Killer of the Oldest Adults

Cancer claims more lives among the middle aged.

The majority of deaths in any given year occur among people aged 65 or older. In 2007, nearly 73 percent of deaths occurred in the 65-or-older age group.

People aged 65 or older account for the majority of deaths for most of the 10 leading causes of death. They account for 81 percent of deaths from heart disease, for example, and 99 percent of deaths from Alzheimer's disease. Among the 10 leading causes of death, only accidents are more likely to claim people under age 65.

Accidents are the number-one cause of death among people under age 45 (except for infants). Cancer is the leading cause of death among people aged 45 to 64. Heart disease is the leading cause of death among people aged 65 or older.

■ More effective treatments for heart disease and cancer would extend the lives of middle-aged and older Americans.

Most deaths occur among people aged 65 or older

(percent of deaths occurring to people aged 65 or older, by cause, 2007)

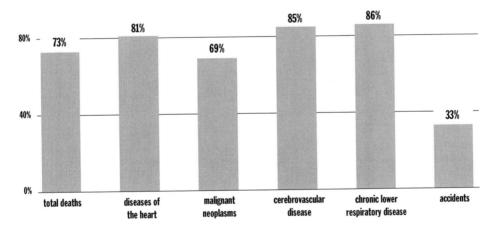

Table 4.45 Deaths from the 10 Leading Causes by Age, 2007

(total number of deaths, and number and percent occurring to people aged 65 or older, for the 10 leading causes of death, 2007; ranked by total number of deaths)

		aged 65 or older	
	total	number	percent of total
Total deaths	**2,424,059**	**1,759,472**	**72.6%**
Diseases of the heart	615,651	498,980	81.0
Malignant neoplasms (cancer)	560,187	388,548	69.4
Cerebrovascular disease	133,990	114,237	85.3
Chronic lower respiratory disease	129,311	111,087	85.9
Accidents	117,075	38,222	32.6
Alzheimer's disease	74,944	74,106	98.9
Diabetes mellitus	70,905	51,359	72.4
Influenza and pneumonia	52,847	46,135	87.3
Nephritis, nephrotic syndrome, nephrosis	46,095	38,249	83.0
Septicemia	34,851	26,388	75.7
All other causes	588,203	372,161	63.3

Source: National Center for Health Statistics, Deaths: Preliminary Data for 2007, National Vital Statistics Report, Vol. 58, No. 1, 2009, Internet site http://www.cdc.gov/nchs/products/nvsr.htm#vol58; calculations by New Strategist

Table 4.46 Leading Causes of Death for Infants, 2007

(number and percent distribution of deaths accounted for by the 10 leading causes of death for children under age 1, 2007)

	number	percent distribution
All causes	**29,241**	**100.0%**
1. Congenital malformations	5,769	19.7
2. Disorders related to short gestation and low birth weight	4,678	16.0
3. Sudden infant death syndrome	2,118	7.2
4. Newborn affected by maternal complications of pregnancy	1,770	6.1
5. Accidents (5)	1,238	4.2
6. Newborn affected by complications of placenta, cord and membranes	1,139	3.9
7. Respiratory distress of newborn	735	2.5
8. Bacterial sepsis of newborn	790	2.7
9. Neonatal hemorrhage	614	2.1
10. Diseases of circulatory system	612	2.1
All other causes	9,778	33.4

Note: Number in parentheses shows rank for all Americans if the cause of death is among top 15.
Source: National Center for Health Statistics, Deaths: Preliminary Data for 2007, National Vital Statistics Report, Vol. 58, No. 1, 2009, Internet site http://www.cdc.gov/nchs/products/nvsr.htm#vol58; calculations by New Strategist

Table 4.47 Leading Causes of Death for Children Aged 1 to 4, 2007

(number and percent distribution of deaths accounted for by the 10 leading causes of death for children aged 1 to 4, 2007)

		number	percent distribution
	All causes	**4,651**	**100.0%**
1.	Accidents (5)	1,566	33.7
2.	Congenital malformations	506	10.9
3.	Homicide (15)	365	7.8
4.	Malignant neoplasms (cancer) (2)	361	7.8
5.	Diseases of the heart (1)	163	3.5
6.	Influenza and pneumonia (8)	106	2.3
7.	Certain conditions originating in perinatal period	77	1.7
8.	Septicemia (10)	74	1.6
9.	In situ neoplasms, benign neoplasms	55	1.2
10.	Cerebrovascular diseases (3)	52	1.1
	All other causes	1,326	28.5

Note: Number in parentheses shows rank for all Americans if the cause of death is among top 15.
Source: National Center for Health Statistics, Deaths: Preliminary Data for 2007, National Vital Statistics Report, Vol. 58, No. 1, 2009, Internet site http://www.cdc.gov/nchs/products/nvsr.htm#vol58; calculations by New Strategist

Table 4.48 Leading Causes of Death for Children Aged 5 to 14, 2007

(number and percent distribution of deaths accounted for by the 10 leading causes of death for children aged 5 to 14, 2007)

		number	percent distribution
	All causes	**6,091**	**100.0%**
1.	Accidents (5)	2,157	35.4
2.	Malignant neoplasms (cancer) (2)	929	15.3
3.	Congenital malformations	356	5.8
4.	Homicide (15)	337	5.5
5.	Diseases of the heart (1)	209	3.4
6.	Suicide (11)	195	3.2
7.	Influenza and pneumonia (8)	111	1.8
8.	Chronic lower respiratory diseases (4)	98	1.6
9.	Cerebrovascular diseases (3)	85	1.4
10.	In situ neoplasms, benign neoplasms	82	1.3
	All other causes	1,532	25.2

Note: Number in parentheses shows rank for all Americans if the cause of death is among top 15.
Source: National Center for Health Statistics, Deaths: Preliminary Data for 2007, National Vital Statistics Report, Vol. 58, No. 1, 2009, Internet site http://www.cdc.gov/nchs/products/nvsr.htm#vol58; calculations by New Strategist

Table 4.49 Leading Causes of Death for People Aged 15 to 24, 2007

(number and percent distribution of deaths accounted for by the 10 leading causes of death for people aged 15 to 24, 2007)

		number	percent distribution
	All causes	**33,788**	**100.0%**
1.	Accidents (5)	15,356	45.4
2.	Homicide (15)	5,284	15.6
3.	Suicide (11)	4,030	11.9
4.	Malignant neoplasms (cancer) (2)	1,609	4.8
5.	Diseases of the heart (1)	991	2.9
6.	Congenital malformations, deformations	373	1.1
7.	Cerebrovascular diseases (3)	197	0.6
8.	Pregnancy, childbirth, and the puerperium	166	0.5
9.	Septicemia (10)	156	0.5
10.	Influenza and pneumonia (8)	154	0.5
	All other causes	5,472	16.2

Note: Number in parentheses shows rank for all Americans if the cause of death is among top 15.
Source: National Center for Health Statistics, Deaths: Preliminary Data for 2007, National Vital Statistics Report, Vol. 58, No. 1, 2009, Internet site http://www.cdc.gov/nchs/products/nvsr.htm#vol58; calculations by New Strategist

Table 4.50 Leading Causes of Death for People Aged 25 to 44, 2007

(number and percent distribution of deaths accounted for by the 10 leading causes of death for people aged 25 to 44, 2007)

		number	percent distribution
	All causes	**121,087**	**100.0%**
1.	Accidents (5)	29,085	24.0
2.	Malignant neoplasms (cancer) (2)	16,577	13.7
3.	Diseases of the heart (1)	14,110	11.7
4.	Suicide (11)	11,528	9.5
5.	Homicide (15)	7,457	6.2
6.	Human immunodeficiency virus infection	4,552	3.8
7.	Chronic liver disease and cirrhosis (12)	2,849	2.4
8.	Cerebrovascular diseases (3)	2,568	2.1
9.	Diabetes mellitus (7)	2,495	2.1
10.	Septicemia (10)	1,191	1.0
	All other causes	28,675	23.7

Note: Number in parentheses shows rank for all Americans if the cause of death is among top 15.
Source: National Center for Health Statistics, Deaths: Preliminary Data for 2007, National Vital Statistics Report, Vol. 58, No. 1, 2009, Internet site http://www.cdc.gov/nchs/products/nvsr.htm#vol58; calculations by New Strategist

Table 4.51 Leading Causes of Death for People Aged 45 to 64, 2007

(number and percent distribution of deaths accounted for by the 10 leading causes of death for people aged 45 to 64, 2007)

		number	percent distribution
	All causes	**469,491**	**100.0%**
1.	Malignant neoplasms (cancer) (2)	152,059	32.4
2.	Diseases of heart (1)	100,751	21.5
3.	Accidents (5)	29,417	6.3
4.	Chronic lower respiratory disease (4)	16,886	3.6
5.	Diabetes mellitus (7)	16,862	3.6
6.	Cerebrovascular diseases (3)	16,713	3.6
7.	Chronic liver disease and cirrhosis (12)	15,738	3.4
8.	Suicide (11)	12,138	2.6
9.	Septicemia (10)	6,698	1.4
10.	Nephritis, nephrotic syndrome, nephrosis (9)	6,604	1.4
	All other causes	95,625	20.4

Note: Number in parentheses shows rank for all Americans if the cause of death is among top 15.
Source: National Center for Health Statistics, Deaths: Preliminary Data for 2007, National Vital Statistics Report, Vol. 58, No. 1, 2009, Internet site http://www.cdc.gov/nchs/products/nvsr.htm#vol58; calculations by New Strategist

Table 4.52 Leading Causes of Death for People Aged 65 or Older, 2007

(number and percent distribution of deaths accounted for by the 10 leading causes of death for people aged 65 or older, 2007)

		number	percent distribution
	All causes	**1,759,472**	**100.0%**
1.	Diseases of the heart (1)	498,980	28.4
2.	Malignant neoplasms (cancer) (2)	388,548	22.1
3.	Cerebrovascular diseases (3)	114,237	6.5
4.	Chronic lower respiratory diseases (4)	111,087	6.3
5.	Alzheimer's disease (6)	74,106	4.2
6.	Diabetes mellitus (7)	51,359	2.9
7.	Influenza and pneumonia (8)	46,135	2.6
8.	Nephritis, nephrotic syndrome, nephrosis (9)	38,249	2.2
9.	Accidents (5)	38,222	2.2
10.	Septicemia (10)	26,388	1.5
	All other causes	372,161	21.2

Note: Number in parentheses shows rank for all Americans if the cause of death is among top 15.
Source: National Center for Health Statistics, Deaths: Preliminary Data for 2007, National Vital Statistics Report, Vol. 58, No. 1, 2009, Internet site http://www.cdc.gov/nchs/products/nvsr.htm#vol58; calculations by New Strategist

Americans Are Living Longer

Scientific advances have reduced the number of deaths from many causes.

The longer people live, the longer they can expect to live, on average. Life expectancy increases as people get older because they have managed to live through life's dangers up to that point.

Women aged 20 in 2007 could expect to live to be 81 years old (61.2 years of life remaining), on average. But a 50-year-old woman could expect to live to be 83 (32.6 years remaining.) A woman aged 80 could expect to reach the ripe old age of nearly 89 (9.3 years of life remaining).

Men have a shorter life expectancy than women, but the same pattern holds. At age 20, the average man can expect to live to age 76 (56.3 years remaining). If a man reaches age 50, his life expectancy rises to 79 (28.9 years remaining). By age 80, the life expectancy of men differs little from women—at this age men can expect to live to age 88 (7.9 years remaining).

■ The dramatic increase in life expectancy during the past century is largely the result of a sharp decline in infant and childhood mortality and some reductions in mortality at older ages.

Life expectancy is now nearly 78 years

(average number of years of life remaining at selected ages, 2007)

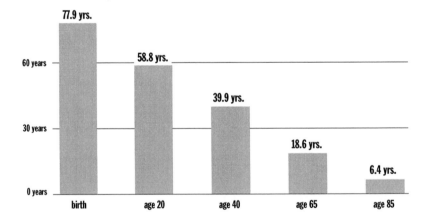

Table 4.53 Life Expectancy by Age and Sex, 2007

(average years of life remaining at selected ages, by sex, 2007)

	total	females	males
At birth	77.9	80.4	75.3
Aged 1	77.4	79.9	74.9
Aged 5	73.5	75.9	71.0
Aged 10	68.6	71.0	66.0
Aged 15	63.6	66.0	61.1
Aged 20	58.8	61.2	56.3
Aged 25	54.1	56.3	51.7
Aged 30	49.3	51.4	47.1
Aged 35	44.6	46.6	42.4
Aged 40	39.9	41.9	37.8
Aged 45	35.3	37.2	33.3
Aged 50	30.9	32.6	28.9
Aged 55	26.6	28.2	24.8
Aged 60	22.5	23.9	20.8
Aged 65	18.6	19.8	17.1
Aged 70	14.9	15.9	13.6
Aged 75	11.6	12.4	10.5
Aged 80	8.8	9.3	7.9
Aged 85	6.4	6.8	5.7
Aged 90	4.6	4.8	4.1
Aged 95	3.2	3.3	2.9
Aged 100	2.2	2.3	2.0

Source: National Center for Health Statistics, Deaths: Preliminary Data for 2007, National Vital Statistics Report, Vol. 58, No. 1, 2009, Internet site http://www.cdc.gov/nchs/products/nvsr.htm#vol58; calculations by New Strategist

Housing

The nation's homeownership rate peaked in 2004 and has fallen since then. In 2009, the homeownership rate was below the 2000 level in all but a few age groups. Young adults and the oldest Americans are the only ones who had a higher homeownership rate in 2009 than in 2000. Householders ranging in age from 30 to 54 saw their homeownership rate fall about 2 percentage points during those years.

The collapse of the housing market is affecting the generations differently. Those who entered the housing market when prices were at their peak (Generation X and some Millennials) are at risk of losing their homes. Boomers and older Americans with traditional mortgages and plenty of home equity are hanging on and waiting for better times. Buying opportunities have emerged for Millennial renters, but it will be harder for them to qualify for a mortgage.

What to expect in the future

■ The large Millennial generation will help prop up the housing market as they enter the home-buying age groups.

■ The financial well-being of Boomers in old age will be determined by their mortgage status. Those who have paid off their mortgage will have a much more comfortable retirement than those still paying off the loan.

Young Adults Are Most Likely to Move

But older people move the farthest.

People in their early twenties are most likely to move in a given year. More than one in four people aged 20 to 29 moved between March 2008 and March 2009. Most of their moves are triggered by life changes such as college graduation, marriage, or a new job.

The likelihood of moving is much smaller among people aged 30 or older. Eighteen percent of people aged 30 to 34 moved between 2008 and 2009, as did 14 percent of 35-to-39-year-olds. Among people aged 45 or older, fewer than 10 percent move in a given year. One reason for the lower mobility of middle-aged and older Americans is their higher rate of homeownership.

Most movers (67 percent) stay in the same county. Only 13 percent moved to a different state between 2008 and 2009. Older movers are most likely to cross state lines, the rate peaking at 19 percent among movers aged 62 to 64, many of them retirees moving to warmer climates.

■ The slump in the housing market pushed the mobility rate to a historic low in 2007–08 (11.9 percent), but the rate rebounded slightly to 12.5 percent in 2008–09.

Older people are least likely to move

(percent of people who moved between March 2008 and March 2009, by age)

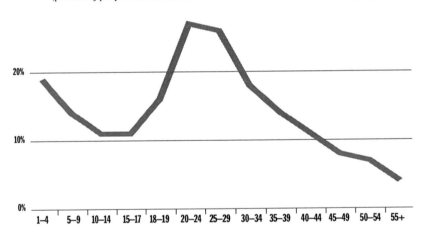

Table 5.1 Geographic Mobility by Age, 2008–09

(total number of people aged 1 or older, number and percent who moved between March 2008 and March 2009, and percent distribution by moving status, by age; numbers in thousands)

	total	same house (nonmovers)	total movers	same county	different county, same state	different state total	same region	different region	movers from abroad
Total, 1 or older	**297,182**	**260,077**	**37,105**	**24,984**	**6,374**	**4,660**	**2,190**	**2,470**	**1,087**
Aged 1 to 4	16,886	13,652	3,234	2,286	481	393	170	223	73
Aged 5 to 9	20,245	17,381	2,864	2,022	435	330	144	186	78
Aged 10 to 14	19,907	17,644	2,263	1,612	325	270	149	121	57
Aged 15 to 17	13,171	11,768	1,403	977	198	171	91	80	56
Aged 18 to 19	8,056	6,782	1,274	908	211	117	67	50	38
Aged 20 to 24	20,632	14,973	5,659	3,768	1,153	569	258	311	169
Aged 25 to 29	21,256	15,798	5,458	3,487	1,013	791	386	405	166
Aged 30 to 34	19,264	15,792	3,472	2,325	578	471	233	238	98
Aged 35 to 39	20,445	17,628	2,817	1,866	473	367	183	184	111
Aged 40 to 44	20,877	18,683	2,194	1,473	345	286	123	163	90
Aged 45 to 49	22,712	20,830	1,882	1,307	286	230	110	120	58
Aged 50 to 54	21,654	20,165	1,489	1,011	266	190	71	119	21
Aged 55 to 59	18,755	17,689	1,066	694	188	170	68	102	14
Aged 60 to 61	7,041	6,664	377	228	77	58	24	34	14
Aged 62 to 64	8,493	8,117	376	219	78	70	35	35	8
Aged 65 or older	37,787	36,513	1,274	800	268	172	75	97	36
Aged 65 to 69	11,825	11,407	418	265	77	68	29	39	8
Aged 70 to 74	8,579	8,292	287	188	54	36	14	22	10
Aged 75 to 79	7,329	7,096	233	152	49	28	15	13	4
Aged 80 to 84	5,676	5,515	161	92	39	21	10	11	10
Aged 85 or older	4,378	4,203	175	103	49	19	7	12	4

PERCENT DISTRIBUTION BY MOBILITY STATUS

Total, 1 or older	**100.0%**	**87.5%**	**12.5%**	**8.4%**	**2.1%**	**1.6%**	**0.7%**	**0.8%**	**0.4%**
Aged 1 to 4	100.0	80.8	19.2	13.5	2.8	2.3	1.0	1.3	0.4
Aged 5 to 9	100.0	85.9	14.1	10.0	2.1	1.6	0.7	0.9	0.4
Aged 10 to 14	100.0	88.6	11.4	8.1	1.6	1.4	0.7	0.6	0.3
Aged 15 to 17	100.0	89.3	10.7	7.4	1.5	1.3	0.7	0.6	0.4
Aged 18 to 19	100.0	84.2	15.8	11.3	2.6	1.5	0.8	0.6	0.5
Aged 20 to 24	100.0	72.6	27.4	18.3	5.6	2.8	1.3	1.5	0.8
Aged 25 to 29	100.0	74.3	25.7	16.4	4.8	3.7	1.8	1.9	0.8
Aged 30 to 34	100.0	82.0	18.0	12.1	3.0	2.4	1.2	1.2	0.5
Aged 35 to 39	100.0	86.2	13.8	9.1	2.3	1.8	0.9	0.9	0.5
Aged 40 to 44	100.0	89.5	10.5	7.1	1.7	1.4	0.6	0.8	0.4
Aged 45 to 49	100.0	91.7	8.3	5.8	1.3	1.0	0.5	0.5	0.3
Aged 50 to 54	100.0	93.1	6.9	4.7	1.2	0.9	0.3	0.5	0.1
Aged 55 to 59	100.0	94.3	5.7	3.7	1.0	0.9	0.4	0.5	0.1
Aged 60 to 61	100.0	94.6	5.4	3.2	1.1	0.8	0.3	0.5	0.2
Aged 62 to 64	100.0	95.6	4.4	2.6	0.9	0.8	0.4	0.4	0.1
Aged 65 or older	100.0	96.6	3.4	2.1	0.7	0.5	0.2	0.3	0.1
Aged 65 to 69	100.0	96.5	3.5	2.2	0.7	0.6	0.2	0.3	0.1
Aged 70 to 74	100.0	96.7	3.3	2.2	0.6	0.4	0.2	0.3	0.1
Aged 75 to 79	100.0	96.8	3.2	2.1	0.7	0.4	0.2	0.2	0.1
Aged 80 to 84	100.0	97.2	2.8	1.6	0.7	0.4	0.2	0.2	0.2
Aged 85 or older	100.0	96.0	4.0	2.4	1.1	0.4	0.2	0.3	0.1

Source: Bureau of the Census, Geographic Mobility: 2008 to 2009, Detailed Tables, Internet site http://www.census.gov/population/www/socdemo/migrate/cps2009.html; calculations by New Strategist

Table 5.2 Movers by Age and Destination, 2008–09

(number of people aged 1 or older who moved and percent distribution by type of move, March 2008 to March 2009; numbers in thousands)

	total movers	same county	different county, same state	different state total	different state same region	different state different region	movers from abroad
Total, 1 or older	37,105	24,984	6,374	4,660	2,190	2,470	1,087
Aged 1 to 4	3,234	2,286	481	393	170	223	73
Aged 5 to 9	2,864	2,022	435	330	144	186	78
Aged 10 to 14	2,263	1,612	325	270	149	121	57
Aged 15 to 17	1,403	977	198	171	91	80	56
Aged 18 to 19	1,274	908	211	117	67	50	38
Aged 20 to 24	5,659	3,768	1,153	569	258	311	169
Aged 25 to 29	5,458	3,487	1,013	791	386	405	166
Aged 30 to 34	3,472	2,325	578	471	233	238	98
Aged 35 to 39	2,817	1,866	473	367	183	184	111
Aged 40 to 44	2,194	1,473	345	286	123	163	90
Aged 45 to 49	1,882	1,307	286	230	110	120	58
Aged 50 to 54	1,489	1,011	266	190	71	119	21
Aged 55 to 59	1,066	694	188	170	68	102	14
Aged 60 to 61	377	228	77	58	24	34	14
Aged 62 to 64	376	219	78	70	35	35	8
Aged 65 or older	1,274	800	268	172	75	97	36
Aged 65 to 69	418	265	77	68	29	39	8
Aged 70 to 74	287	188	54	36	14	22	10
Aged 75 to 79	233	152	49	28	15	13	4
Aged 80 to 84	161	92	39	21	10	11	10
Aged 85 or older	175	103	49	19	7	12	4

PERCENT DISTRIBUTION OF MOVERS BY TYPE OF MOVE

	total movers	same county	different county, same state	different state total	different state same region	different state different region	movers from abroad
Total, 1 or older	100.0%	67.3%	17.2%	12.6%	5.9%	6.7%	2.9%
Aged 1 to 4	100.0	70.7	14.9	12.2	5.3	6.9	2.3
Aged 5 to 9	100.0	70.6	15.2	11.5	5.0	6.5	2.7
Aged 10 to 14	100.0	71.2	14.4	11.9	6.6	5.3	2.5
Aged 15 to 17	100.0	69.6	14.1	12.2	6.5	5.7	4.0
Aged 18 to 19	100.0	71.3	16.6	9.2	5.3	3.9	3.0
Aged 20 to 24	100.0	66.6	20.4	10.1	4.6	5.5	3.0
Aged 25 to 29	100.0	63.9	18.6	14.5	7.1	7.4	3.0
Aged 30 to 34	100.0	67.0	16.6	13.6	6.7	6.9	2.8
Aged 35 to 39	100.0	66.2	16.8	13.0	6.5	6.5	3.9
Aged 40 to 44	100.0	67.1	15.7	13.0	5.6	7.4	4.1
Aged 45 to 49	100.0	69.4	15.2	12.2	5.8	6.4	3.1
Aged 50 to 54	100.0	67.9	17.9	12.8	4.8	8.0	1.4
Aged 55 to 59	100.0	65.1	17.6	15.9	6.4	9.6	1.3
Aged 60 to 61	100.0	60.5	20.4	15.4	6.4	9.0	3.7
Aged 62 to 64	100.0	58.2	20.7	18.6	9.3	9.3	2.1
Aged 65 or older	100.0	62.8	21.0	13.5	5.9	7.6	2.8
Aged 65 to 69	100.0	63.4	18.4	16.3	6.9	9.3	1.9
Aged 70 to 74	100.0	65.5	18.8	12.5	4.9	7.7	3.5
Aged 75 to 79	100.0	65.2	21.0	12.0	6.4	5.6	1.7
Aged 80 to 84	100.0	57.1	24.2	13.0	6.2	6.8	6.2
Aged 85 or older	100.0	58.9	28.0	10.9	4.0	6.9	2.3

Source: Bureau of the Census, Geographic Mobility: 2008 to 2009, Detailed Tables, Internet site http://www.census.gov/ population/www/socdemo/migrate/cps2009.html; calculations by New Strategist

Homeownership Rises with Age

Most householders aged 30 or older are homeowners.

The homeownership rate peaks at more than 80 percent among Americans aged 60 to 74. Predictably, those least likely to own a home are young adults who have not yet accumulated enough savings for a down payment and are not yet earning enough to qualify for a mortgage. Only 23 percent of householders under age 25 own a home.

By age 30 to 34, more than half of householders own their home. In the 65-to-69 age group, the homeownership rate reaches 82 percent. Homeownership declines slightly after age 75, however, as some older people sell their homes to move into nursing homes or assisted living facilities. Nevertheless, 79 percent of householders aged 75 or older are homeowners.

■ Easy money during the housing bubble allowed many younger adults to buy homes, and some of those buyers are now in financial trouble.

Homeownership reaches the majority in the 30-to-34 age group

(percent of householders who own a home, by age, 2009)

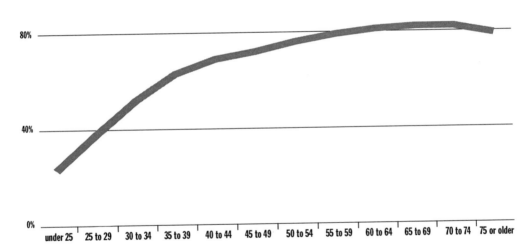

Table 5.3 Owners and Renters by Age of Householder, 2009

(number and percent distribution of householders by homeownership status, by age of householder, 2009; numbers in thousands)

		number		percent	
	total	owner	renter	owner	renter
Total households	**111,344**	**75,014**	**36,330**	**67.4%**	**32.6%**
Under age 25	6,106	1,424	4,682	23.3	76.7
Aged 25 to 29	9,076	3,421	5,655	37.7	62.3
Aged 30 to 34	9,331	4,897	4,434	52.5	47.5
Aged 35 to 39	10,185	6,462	3,723	63.4	36.6
Aged 40 to 44	10,705	7,358	3,347	68.7	31.3
Aged 45 to 49	11,861	8,578	3,283	72.3	27.7
Aged 50 to 54	11,605	8,874	2,731	76.5	23.5
Aged 55 to 59	10,226	8,038	2,188	78.6	21.4
Aged 60 to 64	8,920	7,186	1,734	80.6	19.4
Aged 65 to 69	6,822	5,592	1,230	82.0	18.0
Aged 70 to 74	5,288	4,331	957	81.9	18.1
Aged 75 or older	11,220	8,852	2,368	78.9	21.1

Source: Bureau of the Census, Housing Vacancies and Homeownership Survey, Internet site http://www.census.gov/hhes/www/ housing/hvs/hvs.html; calculations by New Strategist

Married Couples Are Most Likely to Be Homeowners

Two incomes make homes more affordable

The homeownership rate among all households was 67 percent in 2009. But among married couples, 83 percent owned their home. A much smaller 57 percent of male-headed families and 49 percent of female-headed families were homeowners. The primary reason for the higher homeownership rate of married couples is economic—most are dual earners and can afford to buy a house.

Among the youngest householders (under age 25), male-headed families are more likely than married couples to be homeowners. But among all other age groups, married couples have a higher homeownership rate than other types of households.

Homeownership rates rise with age regardless of household type. The gap in homeownership rates by household type is smallest among older householders.

■ The lax regulatory standards of the past few years allowed many more people to buy a home, but they did not narrow the gap in homeownership between married couples and other household types.

Fifty-nine percent of women who live alone own their home

(percent of households owning a home, by household type, 2009)

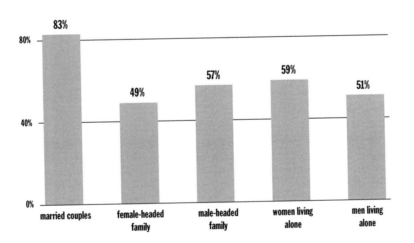

Table 5.4 Homeownership Rate by Age of Householder and Type of Household, 2009

(percent of households that own their home, by age of householder and type of household, 2009)

	total	married couples	female-headed families, no spouse present	male-headed families, no spouse present	women living alone	men living alone
Total households	**67.4%**	**82.8%**	**49.0%**	**56.9%**	**58.6%**	**50.9%**
Under age 25	23.3	36.6	24.1	43.4	10.4	15.5
Aged 25 to 29	37.7	55.1	22.9	38.1	22.6	28.1
Aged 30 to 34	52.5	68.6	29.6	44.5	36.2	37.9
Aged 35 to 39	63.4	77.9	39.7	50.5	44.5	44.5
Aged 40 to 44	68.7	83.5	47.7	58.4	45.0	46.5
Aged 45 to 49	72.3	86.5	56.9	64.3	50.0	51.3
Aged 50 to 54	76.5	88.8	62.6	70.8	57.5	57.0
Aged 55 to 59	78.6	90.4	64.5	74.2	62.8	59.3
Aged 60 to 64	80.6	91.3	68.4	76.8	66.8	61.3
Aged 65 to 69	82.0	92.5	75.1	78.3	69.6	64.9
Aged 70 to 74	81.9	92.6	78.9	77.9	72.5	63.7
Aged 75 or older	78.9	90.8	86.4	86.1	69.9	71.3

Source: Bureau of the Census, Housing Vacancies and Homeownership Survey, Internet site http://www.census.gov/hhes/www/housing/hvs/hvs.html; calculations by New Strategist

Blacks and Hispanics Have Lower Homeownership Rates

But most older blacks and Hispanics are homeowners.

In 2007, 68.3 percent of households owned their home, according to the American Housing Survey. Homeownership rates were lower for blacks (46.7 percent) and Hispanics (50.5 percent).

Homeownership rates rise with age regardless of race or Hispanic origin. Among all households, the homeownership rate surpasses 50 percent in the 30-to-34 age group. Among Hispanics, that threshold is crossed in the 35-to-44 age group. Among blacks, the homeownership rate surpasses 50 percent in the 45-to-54 age group.

■ The collapse of the housing bubble probably has reduced homeownership rates among blacks and Hispanics.

Homeownership rate varies by race and Hispanic origin

(percent of households owning their home, by race and Hispanic origin, 2007)

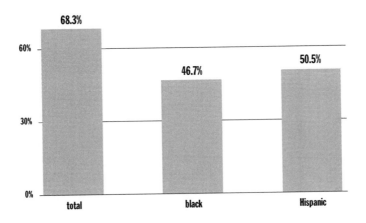

Table 5.5 Black and Hispanic Homeownership Rate by Age, 2007

(percent of total, black, and Hispanic households that own their home, by age of householder, 2007)

	total	black	Hispanic
Total households	**68.3%**	**46.7%**	**50.5%**
Under age 25	23.3	14.8	17.0
Aged 25 to 29	41.6	19.5	31.6
Aged 30 to 34	54.7	28.7	41.3
Aged 35 to 44	67.9	44.8	53.5
Aged 45 to 54	75.6	55.1	61.1
Aged 55 to 64	80.7	60.6	64.2
Aged 65 to 74	82.2	64.2	67.4
Aged 75 or older	77.5	66.4	63.7

Note: Blacks include only those who identify themselves as being black alone. Hispanics may be of any race.
Source: Bureau of the Census, American Housing Survey for the United States: 2007, Internet site http://www.census.gov/hhes/ www/housing/ahs/ahs07/ahs07.html; calculations by New Strategist

The Homeownership Rate Is Falling

The rate of homeownership has fallen in almost every age group since it peaked in 2004.

Evidence of the collapse of the housing bubble can be seen in the latest statistics on homeownership from the Census Bureau. In 2009, the nation's homeownership rate fell for the fifth year in a row since it had peaked in 2004 at 69.0 percent. In 2009, the homeownership rate stood at 67.4 percent. Homeownership declined in all but one age group since peaking in 2004. Householders aged 75 or older are the only ones who saw their homeownership climb since then, although their gain was just 0.1 percentage points.

The 2009 homeownership rate was slightly below the rate of 2000. All but the youngest and oldest age groups were less likely to own a home in 2009 than in 2000. Despite the decline in the homeownership rate, the number of homeowners grew 2 percent between 2004 and 2009 because of population growth. The number aged 60 to 64 increased by a substantial 22 percent during those years although the homeownership rate of the age group fell by nearly 2 percentage points.

■ The aging of the population will stabilize the homeownership rate over the next few years.

All but one age group is losing ground

(percentage point change in homeownership rate, by age of householder, 2004 to 2009)

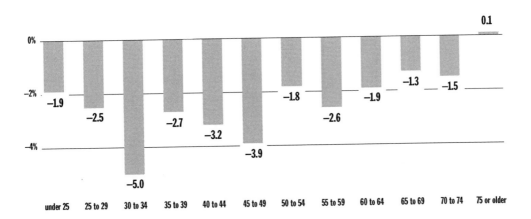

Table 5.6 Homeownership Rate by Age, 2000 to 2009

(percent of householders who own their home by age of householder, 2000 to 2009; percentage point change for selected years)

	2009	2008	2007	2006	2005	2004	2003	2002	2001	2000	percentage point change	
											2004–09	2000–09
Total households	**67.4%**	**67.8%**	**68.1%**	**68.8%**	**68.9%**	**69.0%**	**68.3%**	**67.9%**	**67.9%**	**67.5%**	**-1.7**	**-0.1**
Under age 25	23.3	23.6	24.8	24.8	25.7	25.2	22.8	22.9	22.5	21.8	-1.9	1.5
Aged 25 to 29	37.7	40.0	40.6	41.8	40.9	40.2	39.8	38.8	39.0	37.8	-2.5	-0.1
Aged 30 to 34	52.5	53.5	54.4	55.9	56.8	57.4	56.5	54.9	54.9	54.5	-5.0	-2.0
Aged 35 to 39	63.4	64.6	65.0	66.4	66.6	66.2	65.1	65.2	65.6	65.2	-2.7	-1.8
Aged 40 to 44	68.7	69.4	70.4	71.2	71.7	71.9	71.3	71.7	70.8	70.6	-3.2	-1.9
Aged 45 to 49	72.3	73.6	74.0	74.9	75.0	76.3	75.4	74.8	75.4	75.0	-3.9	-2.7
Aged 50 to 54	76.5	76.4	76.9	77.7	78.3	78.3	77.9	77.9	78.2	78.7	-1.8	-2.3
Aged 55 to 59	78.6	79.4	79.9	80.4	80.6	81.2	80.9	80.8	81.0	79.8	-2.6	-1.2
Aged 60 to 64	80.6	80.9	81.5	81.5	81.9	82.4	81.9	81.6	81.8	80.6	-1.9	-0.1
Aged 65 to 69	82.0	81.6	81.7	82.4	82.8	83.2	82.5	82.9	82.4	83.4	-1.3	-1.4
Aged 70 to 74	81.9	81.6	82.4	83.0	82.9	83.4	82.0	82.5	82.5	81.6	-1.5	0.3
Aged 75 or older	78.9	78.6	78.7	79.1	78.4	78.8	78.7	78.4	78.1	78.2	0.1	0.6

Source: Bureau of the Census, Housing Vacancies and Homeownership surveys, Internet site http://www.census.gov/hhes/www/housing/hvs/hvs.html; calculations by New Strategist

Table 5.7 Number of Homeowners by Age, 2000 to 2009

(number of householders who own their home by age of householder, selected years, 2000 to 2009; percent change for selected years; numbers in thousands)

	2009	2004	2000	percent change	
				2004–09	2000–09
Total homeowners	**75,014**	**73,846**	**69,203**	**1.6%**	**8.4%**
Under age 25	1,424	1,653	1,299	−13.9	9.6
Aged 25 to 29	3,421	3,427	3,097	−0.2	10.5
Aged 30 to 34	4,897	5,687	5,416	−13.9	−9.6
Aged 35 to 39	6,462	6,931	7,545	−6.8	−14.4
Aged 40 to 44	7,358	8,496	8,482	−13.4	−13.3
Aged 45 to 49	8,578	8,865	8,129	−3.2	5.5
Aged 50 to 54	8,874	8,102	7,411	9.5	19.7
Aged 55 to 59	8,038	7,275	5,950	10.5	35.1
Aged 60 to 64	7,186	5,882	4,847	22.2	48.3
Aged 65 to 69	5,592	4,725	4,735	18.3	18.1
Aged 70 to 74	4,331	4,240	4,421	2.1	−2.0
Aged 75 or older	8,852	8,563	7,870	3.4	12.5

Source: Bureau of the Census, Housing Vacancies and Homeownership surveys, Internet site http://www.census.gov/hhes/www/housing/hvs/hvs.html; calculations by New Strategist

Homeownership Is Highest in the Midwest

Homeownership has declined in every age group in the Midwest since 2004, however.

The homeownership rate stood at 71.0 percent in the Midwest in 2009. This compares with a rate of 69.6 percent in the South, 64.0 percent in the Northeast, and 62.6 percent in the West. Between 2000 and 2009, the overall homeownership rate increased slightly in the Northeast and West, was stable in the South, and fell in the Midwest.

During the housing bubble, homeownership rates peaked in different regions at different times. In the Midwest and South, the peak occurred in 2004. In the Northeast and West, the peak occurred in 2006. Since those homeownership peaks, the decline has been greatest in the Midwest, where the overall homeownership rate fell by 2.8 percentage points. The loss was a slightly smaller 2.1 percentage points in the West, 1.3 percentage points in the South, and 1.2 percentage points in the Northeast. Nearly every age group in every region lost ground during the past few years. The biggest losers were 30-to-34-year-olds in the Midwest. Their homeownership rate fell 5.3 percentage points between 2004 and 2009.

■ Foreclosures are turning homeowners back into renters and lowering the homeownership rate in every region.

People in their early thirties are losing ground in every region

(homeownership rate for 30-to-34-year-olds at peak of housing bubble and in 2009, by region)

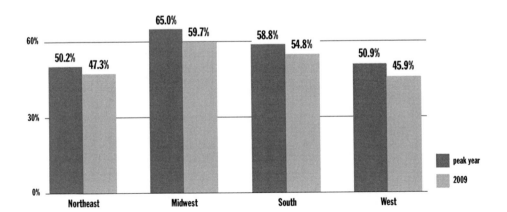

Table 5.8 Homeownership Rate by Age and Region, 2000 to 2009: Northeast

(percent of householders in the Northeast who own their home by age of householder, 2000, peak year, and 2009; percentage point change for selected years)

				percentage point change	
	2009	2006	2000	2006–09	2000–09
Total households in Northeast	**64.0%**	**65.2%**	**63.4%**	**–1.2**	**0.6**
Under age 25	19.4	23.7	17.8	–4.3	1.6
Aged 25 to 29	33.2	35.1	33.0	–1.9	0.2
Aged 30 to 34	47.3	50.2	49.6	–2.9	–2.3
Aged 35 to 39	59.9	62.4	60.5	–2.5	–0.6
Aged 40 to 44	65.4	68.5	66.6	–3.1	–1.2
Aged 45 to 49	69.6	69.9	71.2	–0.3	–1.6
Aged 50 to 54	71.4	73.3	73.3	–1.9	–1.9
Aged 55 to 59	75.0	75.4	75.0	–0.4	0.0
Aged 60 to 64	76.3	76.7	74.2	–0.4	2.1
Aged 65 to 69	74.8	76.0	75.0	–1.2	–0.2
Aged 70 to 74	74.4	74.8	74.3	–0.4	0.1
Aged 75 or older	72.0	72.0	68.5	0.0	3.5

Source: Bureau of the Census, Housing Vacancies and Homeownership surveys, Internet site http://www.census.gov/hhes/www/housing/hvs/hvs.html; calculations by New Strategist

Table 5.9 Homeownership Rate by Age and Region, 2000 to 2009: Midwest

(percent of householders in the Midwest who own their home by age of householder, 2000, peak year, and 2009; percentage point change for selected years)

				percentage point change	
	2009	2004	2000	2004–09	2000–09
Total households in Midwest	**71.0%**	**73.8%**	**72.5%**	**–2.8**	**–1.5**
Under age 25	23.6	27.8	24.8	–4.2	–1.2
Aged 25 to 29	44.6	47.9	45.7	–3.3	–1.1
Aged 30 to 34	59.7	65.0	64.3	–5.3	–4.6
Aged 35 to 39	69.9	74.2	72.6	–4.3	–2.7
Aged 40 to 44	75.2	78.5	76.9	–3.3	–1.7
Aged 45 to 49	76.3	81.4	80.4	–5.1	–4.1
Aged 50 to 54	80.1	83.8	83.4	–3.7	–3.3
Aged 55 to 59	80.5	84.7	83.6	–4.2	–3.1
Aged 60 to 64	82.7	84.8	83.2	–2.1	–0.5
Aged 65 to 69	83.6	86.6	86.6	–3.0	–3.0
Aged 70 to 74	85.3	86.0	84.6	–0.7	0.7
Aged 75 or older	77.7	79.1	78.9	–1.4	–1.2

Source: Bureau of the Census, Housing Vacancies and Homeownership surveys, Internet site http://www.census.gov/hhes/www/housing/hvs/hvs.html; calculations by New Strategist

Table 5.10 Homeownership Rate by Age and Region, 2000 to 2009: South

(percent of householders in the South who own their home by age of householder, 2000, peak year, and 2009; percentage point change for selected years)

	2009	2004	2000	percentage point change 2004–09	percentage point change 2000–09
Total households in South	**69.6%**	**70.9%**	**69.6%**	**–1.3**	**0.0**
Under age 25	25.9	26.2	23.7	–0.3	2.2
Aged 25 to 29	39.3	40.8	40.1	–1.5	–0.8
Aged 30 to 34	54.8	58.8	56.6	–4.0	–1.8
Aged 35 to 39	65.4	67.9	66.9	–2.5	–1.5
Aged 40 to 44	69.6	73.2	72.4	–3.6	–2.8
Aged 45 to 49	74.1	78.3	75.7	–4.2	–1.6
Aged 50 to 54	78.6	80.2	80.7	–1.6	–2.1
Aged 55 to 59	80.9	83.2	82.8	–2.3	–1.9
Aged 60 to 64	82.7	84.6	83.4	–1.9	–0.7
Aged 65 to 69	86.1	87.7	85.8	–1.6	0.3
Aged 70 to 74	85.8	87.7	86.4	–1.9	–0.6
Aged 75 or older	84.4	84.8	83.5	–0.4	0.9

Source: Bureau of the Census, Housing Vacancies and Homeownership surveys, Internet site http://www.census.gov/hhes/www/ housing/hvs/hvs.html; calculations by New Strategist

Table 5.11 Homeownership Rate by Age and Region, 2000 to 2009: West

(percent of householders in the West who own their home by age of householder, 2000, peak year, and 2009; percentage point change for selected years)

	2009	2006	2000	percentage point change 2006–09	percentage point change 2000–09
Total households in West	**62.6%**	**64.7%**	**61.7%**	**–2.1**	**0.9**
Under age 25	21.4	21.4	17.4	0.0	4.0
Aged 25 to 29	31.0	36.0	30.7	–5.0	0.3
Aged 30 to 34	45.9	50.9	46.1	–5.0	–0.2
Aged 35 to 39	56.7	61.2	57.8	–4.5	–1.1
Aged 40 to 44	63.7	67.0	64.8	–3.3	–1.1
Aged 45 to 49	67.2	71.5	70.1	–4.3	–2.9
Aged 50 to 54	73.3	74.6	74.4	–1.3	–1.1
Aged 55 to 59	75.9	77.3	77.7	–1.4	–1.8
Aged 60 to 64	78.4	80.2	77.7	–1.8	0.7
Aged 65 to 69	79.2	81.1	81.6	–1.9	–2.4
Aged 70 to 74	78.0	81.7	80.0	–3.7	–2.0
Aged 75 or older	77.6	76.5	76.4	1.1	1.2

Source: Bureau of the Census, Housing Vacancies and Homeownership surveys, Internet site http://www.census.gov/hhes/www/ housing/hvs/hvs.html; calculations by New Strategist

Most Americans Live in a Single-Family Home

A large share of the oldest Americans lives in an apartment building, however.

Nearly two out of three American households (65 percent) live in a detached, single-family home. Middle-aged and older householders are most likely to live in this type of house. Among householders aged 45 to 74, from 71 to 72 percent live in a detached, single-family housing unit.

The youngest adults are most likely to live in a multi-unit dwelling, 57 percent of householders under age 25 living in a building with two or more units. Apartment living declines with age to a low of 16 percent among householders aged 55 to 74. The percentage that lives in multi-unit dwellings rises in the oldest age group to 23 percent. Householders aged 75 or older are more likely than younger adults to live in the largest apartment buildings—with 50 or more units.

■ The percentage of households that live in a mobile home does not vary much by age.

The youngest householders are most likely to live in a multi-unit dwelling

(percent of householders who live in multi-unit buildings, by age of householder, 2007)

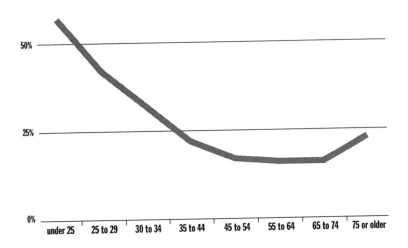

Table 5.12 Number of Units in Structure by Age of Householder, 2007

(number and percent distribution of households by age of householder and number of units in structure, 2007; numbers in thousands)

	total	one, detached	one, attached	multi-unit dwellings total	2 to 4	5 to 9	10 to 19	20 to 49	50 or more	mobile homes
Total households	**110,692**	**71,435**	**6,083**	**26,256**	**8,790**	**5,258**	**4,697**	**3,645**	**3,866**	**6,919**
Under age 25	6,273	1,971	357	3,595	1,091	900	880	476	248	349
Aged 25 to 29	8,809	4,040	594	3,690	1,228	812	733	572	344	485
Aged 30 to 34	9,571	5,263	643	3,058	1,058	677	601	459	262	607
Aged 35 to 44	21,756	14,644	1,146	4,705	1,707	986	857	684	470	1,262
Aged 45 to 54	23,208	16,683	1,153	3,906	1,440	760	724	484	497	1,467
Aged 55 to 64	18,211	13,125	1,033	2,832	1,020	499	440	351	521	1,222
Aged 65 to 74	11,700	8,359	597	1,863	605	293	236	249	480	881
Aged 75 or older	11,165	7,351	560	2,607	641	329	225	368	1,044	647
Median age (years)	49	51	48	41	41	37	37	40	57	50

PERCENT DISTRIBUTION BY AGE OF HOUSEHOLDER

	total	one, detached	one, attached	multi-unit dwellings total	2 to 4	5 to 9	10 to 19	20 to 49	50 or more	mobile homes
Total households	**100.0%**	**100.0%**	**100.0%**	**100.0%**	**100.0%**	**100.0%**	**100.0%**	**100.0%**	**100.0%**	**100.0%**
Under age 25	5.7	2.8	5.9	13.7	12.4	17.1	18.7	13.1	6.4	5.0
Aged 25 to 29	8.0	5.7	9.8	14.1	14.0	15.4	15.6	15.7	8.9	7.0
Aged 30 to 34	8.6	7.4	10.6	11.6	12.0	12.9	12.8	12.6	6.8	8.8
Aged 35 to 44	19.7	20.5	18.8	17.9	19.4	18.8	18.2	18.8	12.2	18.2
Aged 45 to 54	21.0	23.4	19.0	14.9	16.4	14.5	15.4	13.3	12.9	21.2
Aged 55 to 64	16.5	18.4	17.0	10.8	11.6	9.5	9.4	9.6	13.5	17.7
Aged 65 to 74	10.6	11.7	9.8	7.1	6.9	5.6	5.0	6.8	12.4	12.7
Aged 75 or older	10.1	10.3	9.2	9.9	7.3	6.3	4.8	10.1	27.0	9.4

PERCENT DISTRIBUTION BY UNITS IN STRUCTURE

	total	one, detached	one, attached	multi-unit dwellings total	2 to 4	5 to 9	10 to 19	20 to 49	50 or more	mobile homes
Total households	**100.0%**	**64.5%**	**5.5%**	**23.7%**	**7.9%**	**4.8%**	**4.2%**	**3.3%**	**3.5%**	**6.3%**
Under age 25	100.0	31.4	5.7	57.3	17.4	14.3	14.0	7.6	4.0	5.6
Aged 25 to 29	100.0	45.9	6.7	41.9	13.9	9.2	8.3	6.5	3.9	5.5
Aged 30 to 34	100.0	55.0	6.7	32.0	11.1	7.1	6.3	4.8	2.7	6.3
Aged 35 to 44	100.0	67.3	5.3	21.6	7.8	4.5	3.9	3.1	2.2	5.8
Aged 45 to 54	100.0	71.9	5.0	16.8	6.2	3.3	3.1	2.1	2.1	6.3
Aged 55 to 64	100.0	72.1	5.7	15.6	5.6	2.7	2.4	1.9	2.9	6.7
Aged 65 to 74	100.0	71.4	5.1	15.9	5.2	2.5	2.0	2.1	4.1	7.5
Aged 75 or older	100.0	65.8	5.0	23.3	5.7	2.9	2.0	3.3	9.4	5.8

Source: Bureau of the Census, American Housing Survey for the United States: 2007, Internet site http://www.census.gov/hhes/ www/housing/ahs/ahs07/ahs07.html; calculations by New Strategist

6

Income

Economic ups and downs influence the attitudes and financial status of every generation. After enduring the Depression and World War II, today's older generations of Americans (the Swing and World War II generations) prospered in the 1950s and 1960s thanks to a rapidly expanding postwar economy. Since 1980, the incomes of older Americans have grown faster than those of middle-aged or younger adults. The older generations had the good luck to mature during an era when men's incomes were growing, one income was sufficient to support a family, and government- and employer-provided benefits were expansive and generous.

As Boomers reached adulthood, the growth in men's incomes came to a halt. Their household incomes continued to grow, however, because women were going to work. Now the Great Recession has ended the rise in women's incomes. Consequently, Boomers' household incomes are declining and millions will be postponing retirement—not because they want to work longer than their parents did, but because they must.

What to expect in the future

■ Today's older generations are wealthier in retirement than any previous generation. Boomers will not be able to match their standard of living in retirement.

■ The older half of the Baby-Boom generation is now in the 55-to-64 age group. As Boomers are forced to postpone retirement, expect the household incomes of 55-to-64-year-olds to rise.

■ Millennials and Gen Xers will be entering their peak-earning years in a time of economic uncertainty. Many are unemployed, and incomes are stagnant or falling. Expect the younger generations to be cautious and pragmatic spenders as they struggle to achieve the American Dream.

Men's Incomes Are Falling

Most men have lower incomes today than they did in 1980.

Men under age 55 had sharply lower incomes in 2008 than they did in 1980, declines in median income ranging from 6 to 14 percent. In contrast, men aged 55 to 64 saw their median income climb by 5 percent during those years, and men aged 65 or older saw an enormous gain of 40 percent.

Since 2000, men aged 65 or older are the only ones who have seen their standard of living rise. In 1980, men aged 65 or older had a median income only 59 percent as high as that of the average man. By 2008, their median income was 77 percent of the average.

■ Today's elderly men were the beneficiaries of generous government and employer handouts that have been eliminated or sharply reduced for middle-aged and younger men.

Older men have gained ground since 1980

(percent change in median income of men aged 15 or older, by age, 1980 to 2008; in 2008 dollars)

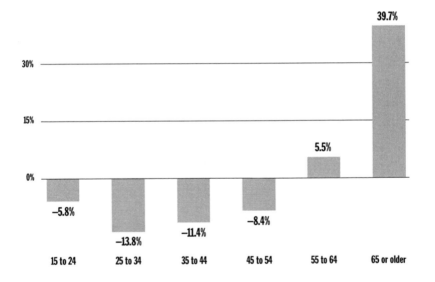

Table 6.1 Median Income of Men by Age, 1980 to 2008

(median income of men aged 15 or older with income by age, 1980 to 2008; percent change in income for selected years; in 2008 dollars)

	total men	15 to 24	25 to 34	35 to 44	45 to 54	55 to 64	aged 65 or older total	65 to 74	75 or older
2008	$33,161	$10,778	$33,415	$44,189	$45,540	$41,757	$25,503	$28,993	$21,911
2007	34,472	11,640	34,138	46,748	47,611	43,748	25,258	28,854	21,598
2006	34,455	11,708	34,312	45,531	48,795	44,293	25,095	28,056	22,040
2005	34,493	11,546	34,367	45,179	48,116	44,837	24,025	26,824	21,442
2004	34,784	11,492	35,327	46,203	47,721	44,783	24,087	27,600	21,345
2003	35,040	11,661	35,778	45,885	49,261	45,557	23,839	27,114	20,815
2002	34,993	11,540	36,715	45,350	49,033	43,417	23,261	25,482	20,954
2001	35,391	11,311	37,105	46,627	49,989	43,340	23,944	26,384	21,308
2000	35,437	11,935	37,826	47,414	51,311	42,746	24,270	26,839	21,498
1999	35,268	10,790	37,961	47,032	52,727	43,269	24,939	27,730	21,938
1998	34,947	10,804	37,091	46,404	51,344	43,236	23,964	26,032	21,738
1997	33,723	9,989	34,771	43,940	50,324	41,674	23,766	26,284	20,608
1996	32,568	9,511	34,406	43,955	49,510	40,346	22,798	25,423	19,806
1995	31,651	9,698	33,120	44,077	49,921	40,654	23,124	25,738	19,864
1994	31,203	10,125	32,476	44,114	50,185	38,896	21,908	23,846	19,623
1993	30,963	9,433	32,173	44,520	48,646	36,886	21,984	23,896	19,694
1992	30,755	9,468	32,322	44,342	48,386	38,514	21,948	23,771	19,375
1991	31,557	9,683	33,293	45,173	48,993	39,251	22,134	23,642	20,099
1990	32,407	10,091	34,164	47,547	49,517	39,611	22,650	25,500	18,654
1989	33,352	10,584	35,823	49,353	51,910	40,953	21,975	24,252	18,186
1988	33,068	10,219	36,346	49,922	51,729	39,607	21,810	24,381	17,888
1987	32,247	9,894	36,129	49,029	51,649	39,675	21,625	24,317	17,583
1986	32,077	9,902	35,916	49,055	52,024	39,425	21,637	–	–
1985	31,126	9,532	35,612	48,390	49,319	38,656	20,800	–	–
1984	30,791	9,295	35,712	48,488	48,533	38,542	20,626	–	–
1983	30,061	8,802	34,527	46,105	47,492	38,408	20,016	–	–
1982	29,885	9,484	35,168	46,378	46,151	38,193	19,683	–	–
1981	30,605	6,978	36,554	47,968	47,753	39,445	18,486	–	–
1980	31,172	11,436	38,760	49,848	49,691	39,591	18,258	–	–

Percent change

	total men	15 to 24	25 to 34	35 to 44	45 to 54	55 to 64	aged 65 or older total	65 to 74	75 or older
2000 to 2008	−6.4%	−9.7%	−11.7%	−6.8%	−11.2%	−2.3%	5.1%	8.0%	1.9%
1990 to 2008	2.3	6.8	−2.2	−7.1	−8.0	5.4	12.6	13.7	17.5
1980 to 2008	6.4	−5.8	−13.8	−11.4	−8.4	5.5	39.7	–	–

Note: "–" means data are not available.
Source: Bureau of the Census, Current Population Surveys, Annual Social and Economic Supplement, Internet site http://www
.census.gov/hhes/www/income/histinc/incpertoc.html; calculations by New Strategist

Many Women Are Losing Ground

The rapid growth in women's incomes may be coming to an end.

As better-educated and career-oriented Baby-Boom women entered the labor force, they boosted women's incomes. Generation X and Millennial women followed in their footsteps, with a growing percentage of women committed to full-time jobs. With more women working full-time, women's median income increased substantially over the years, climbing 70 percent between 1980 and 2008, to $20,867, after adjusting for inflation.

Most women experienced large income gains between 1980 and 2008, women aged 55 to 64 seeing their median income more than double during those years. In contrast, the median income of women under age 25 grew by a much smaller 15 percent, after adjusting for inflation. The slower growth among the youngest women is due largely to the increasing proportion going to college and not available for full-time work.

Between 2000 and 2008, the median income of women climbed by 4 percent, but only because of growing incomes among women aged 55 or older. Every age group under age 55 lost ground during those years. The median income of women aged 55 to 64 grew 21 percent between 2000 and 2008 as Boomers filled the age group and postponed retirement.

■ Expect to see the median income of women aged 65 or older climb substantially in the years ahead as Boomer women enter the age group.

Women's incomes have made big gains since 1980

(percent change in median income of women aged 15 or older, by age, 1980 to 2008; in 2008 dollars)

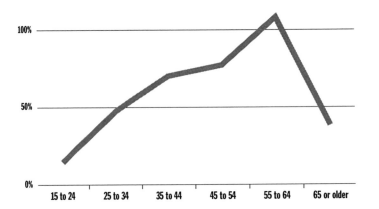

Table 6.2 Median Income of Women by Age, 1980 to 2008

(median income of women aged 15 or older with income by age, 1980 to 2008; percent change in income for selected years; in 2008 dollars)

	total women	15 to 24	25 to 34	35 to 44	45 to 54	55 to 64	aged 65 or older total	65 to 74	75 or older
2008	$20,867	$8,901	$25,553	$27,371	$28,236	$25,515	$14,559	$14,831	$14,378
2007	21,726	9,303	26,879	28,766	30,585	26,233	14,560	14,997	14,223
2006	21,373	9,240	25,820	28,158	29,734	25,828	14,526	15,035	14,205
2005	20,487	9,066	25,163	28,052	29,200	24,398	13,781	14,161	13,556
2004	20,138	8,780	25,154	27,815	29,901	23,712	13,771	14,006	13,612
2003	20,205	8,704	25,746	27,478	30,281	23,844	13,867	14,216	13,620
2002	20,121	9,074	25,910	26,715	30,118	22,937	13,651	13,499	13,767
2001	20,205	9,081	26,114	27,328	29,352	21,676	13,758	13,622	13,859
2000	20,084	9,202	26,317	27,603	29,672	21,155	13,782	13,638	13,891
1999	19,776	8,629	24,950	26,697	29,162	20,600	14,160	14,186	14,140
1998	19,035	8,619	24,084	26,759	28,478	19,359	13,856	13,789	13,910
1997	18,329	8,483	23,604	25,020	27,466	19,229	13,459	13,564	13,370
1996	17,511	8,036	22,388	25,207	26,026	18,196	13,154	13,195	13,115
1995	17,016	7,449	21,824	24,405	24,863	17,369	13,124	13,014	13,225
1994	16,472	7,913	21,383	23,257	24,496	15,612	12,858	12,680	13,019
1993	16,208	7,851	20,524	23,248	23,952	15,889	12,470	12,688	12,274
1992	16,109	7,773	20,495	23,180	23,835	15,236	12,304	12,352	12,256
1991	16,151	8,012	19,986	23,318	22,700	15,266	12,625	12,542	12,705
1990	16,081	7,828	20,104	23,162	22,725	15,012	12,846	13,079	12,602
1989	16,135	7,945	20,506	23,145	22,035	15,362	12,834	13,325	12,368
1988	15,537	7,844	20,226	21,942	21,022	14,650	12,422	12,690	12,144
1987	15,039	7,992	19,906	21,748	20,421	13,672	12,503	12,666	12,325
1986	14,264	7,580	19,324	20,738	19,456	13,827	12,043	–	–
1985	13,772	7,234	18,852	19,607	18,356	13,688	12,047	–	–
1984	13,556	7,123	18,538	18,871	17,573	13,495	11,882	–	–
1983	12,983	7,103	17,470	18,204	16,858	12,593	11,504	–	–
1982	12,612	7,181	17,078	16,819	16,071	12,654	11,493	–	–
1981	12,398	4,534	17,259	16,732	15,969	12,210	10,690	–	–
1980	12,240	7,772	17,347	16,084	15,929	12,255	10,513	–	–
Percent change									
2000 to 2008	3.9%	–3.3%	–2.9%	–0.8%	–4.8%	20.6%	5.6%	8.7%	3.5%
1990 to 2008	29.8	13.7	27.1	18.2	24.3	70.0	13.3	13.4	14.1
1980 to 2008	70.5	14.5	47.3	70.2	77.3	108.2	38.5	–	–

Note: "–" means data are not available.
Source: Bureau of the Census, Current Population Surveys, Annual Social and Economic Supplement, Internet site http://www.census.gov/hhes/www/income/histinc/incpertoc.html; calculations by New Strategist

Boomer Men Have the Highest Incomes

The median income of Boomer men is 34 percent above average.

Given the stagnation in men's earnings over the past few decades, it is no surprise that the majority of men have modest incomes. Half of men had incomes below $33,161 in 2008. It is only when husbands and wives combine their earnings that most families can achieve a middle-class standard of living.

Incomes are highest in the 35-to-54 age group—the peak-earning years—which now includes most of Generation X and the younger half of the Baby-Boom generation. The median income of men aged 35 to 44 was $44,189 in 2008. Those aged 45 to 54 had a slightly higher median income of $45,540. By generation, Boomer men have the highest incomes, a median of $44,396 in 2008.

Men's income declines in the 55-to-64 age group because many are retired. Only 56 percent work full-time, down from the 71 percent who are full-time workers among 45-to-54-year-olds. Among men who work full-time, however, median income continues to rise well into old age, peaking in the 65-to-74 age group.

■ Young men have the lowest median income because many are still in school.

Boomers are in their peak earning years

(median income of men by generation, 2008)

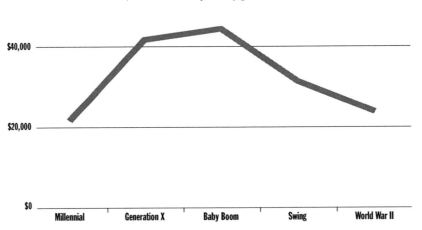

Table 6.3 Men by Income and Age, 2008

(number and percent distribution of men aged 15 or older by income and age, 2008; median income of men with income and of men working full-time, year-round; percent working full-time, year-round; men in thousands as of 2009)

	total	15 to 24	25 to 34	35 to 44	45 to 54	55 to 64	65 or older total	65 to 74	75 or older
TOTAL MEN	116,720	21,202	20,440	20,491	21,772	16,506	16,308	9,401	6,907
Without income	11,292	7,427	1,124	758	977	610	395	210	185
With income	105,428	13,775	19,316	19,733	20,795	15,896	15,913	9,191	6,722
Under $5,000	7,183	4,036	838	561	724	637	388	196	192
$5,000 to $9,999	7,445	2,480	1,110	765	1,073	877	1,139	552	587
$10,000 to $14,999	8,596	1,818	1,269	1,069	1,055	1,027	2,357	1,209	1,148
$15,000 to $19,999	8,151	1,262	1,403	1,084	1,137	1,030	2,234	1,141	1,092
$20,000 to $24,999	8,370	1,169	1,856	1,246	1,290	1,124	1,686	860	826
$25,000 to $29,999	7,220	866	1,722	1,212	1,095	931	1,393	780	613
$30,000 to $34,999	7,327	693	1,744	1,439	1,386	992	1,073	607	466
$35,000 to $39,999	6,311	463	1,491	1,300	1,287	881	890	580	310
$40,000 to $44,999	5,769	253	1,434	1,286	1,210	926	658	424	235
$45,000 to $49,999	4,417	163	990	978	1,038	686	562	375	188
$50,000 to $54,999	5,237	160	1,071	1,317	1,283	922	486	316	170
$55,000 to $59,999	3,066	93	631	703	723	544	372	242	129
$60,000 to $64,999	3,689	108	783	852	857	716	373	253	121
$65,000 to $69,999	2,447	36	399	623	644	461	282	201	82
$70,000 to $74,999	2,629	29	448	741	690	465	256	164	92
$75,000 to $79,999	2,180	16	375	559	623	373	234	169	65
$80,000 to $84,999	1,973	25	337	515	564	368	165	110	55
$85,000 to $89,999	1,184	4	162	309	374	236	99	69	29
$90,000 to $94,999	1,305	8	192	360	367	248	130	103	27
$95,000 to $99,999	903	14	120	215	271	191	91	74	17
$100,000 or more	10,028	80	947	2,595	3,103	2,259	1,045	768	277
Median income									
Men with income	$33,161	$10,778	$33,415	$44,189	$45,540	$41,757	$25,503	$28,993	$21,911
Working full-time	47,779	25,780	40,645	51,213	53,331	56,190	62,240	66,026	52,179
Percent full-time	51.3%	19.9%	67.4%	74.3%	70.6%	56.1%	12.4%	18.2%	4.5%
TOTAL MEN	100.0%	100.0%	100.0%	100.0%	100.0%	100.0%	100.0%	100.0%	100.0%
Without income	9.7	35.0	5.5	3.7	4.5	3.7	2.4	2.2	2.7
With income	90.3	65.0	94.5	96.3	95.5	96.3	97.6	97.8	97.3
Under $15,000	19.9	39.3	15.7	11.7	13.1	15.4	23.8	20.8	27.9
$15,000 to $24,999	14.2	11.5	15.9	11.4	11.1	13.0	24.0	21.3	27.8
$25,000 to $34,999	12.5	7.4	17.0	12.9	11.4	11.7	15.1	14.8	15.6
$35,000 to $49,999	14.1	4.1	19.2	17.4	16.2	15.1	12.9	14.7	10.6
$50,000 to $74,999	14.6	2.0	16.3	20.7	19.3	18.8	10.8	12.5	8.6
$75,000 to $99,999	6.5	0.3	5.8	9.6	10.1	8.6	4.4	5.6	2.8
$100,000 or more	8.6	0.4	4.6	12.7	14.3	13.7	6.4	8.2	4.0

Source: Bureau of the Census, 2009 Current Population Survey, Annual Social and Economic Supplement, Internet site http://www.census.gov/hhes/www/cpstables/032009/perinc/toc.htm; calculations by New Strategist

Table 6.4 Men by Income and Generation, 2008

(number and percent distribution of men aged 15 or older by income and generation, 2008; median income of men with income; men in thousands as of 2009)

	total	Millennial (15 to 31)	Generation X (32 to 43)	Baby Boom (44 to 62)	Swing (63 to 75)	World War II (76 or older)
TOTAL MEN	**116,720**	**35,510**	**24,574**	**37,026**	**13,255**	**6,355**
Without income	**11,292**	**8,214**	**1,019**	**1,541**	**347**	**171**
With income	**105,428**	**27,296**	**23,555**	**35,485**	**12,908**	**6,184**
Under $5,000	7,183	4,623	756	1,290	339	176
$5,000 to $9,999	7,445	3,257	1,022	1,851	774	541
$10,000 to $14,999	8,596	2,706	1,343	1,984	1,506	1,057
$15,000 to $19,999	8,151	2,244	1,397	2,069	1,434	1,007
$20,000 to $24,999	8,370	2,468	1,678	2,314	1,151	759
$25,000 to $29,999	7,220	2,071	1,607	1,961	1,015	565
$30,000 to $34,999	7,327	1,914	1,818	2,324	843	429
$35,000 to $39,999	6,311	1,507	1,617	2,122	781	284
$40,000 to $44,999	5,769	1,257	1,588	2,079	628	217
$45,000 to $49,999	4,417	856	1,177	1,685	527	172
$50,000 to $54,999	5,237	910	1,507	2,152	514	154
$55,000 to $59,999	3,066	535	822	1,229	361	120
$60,000 to $64,999	3,689	656	1,002	1,515	406	110
$65,000 to $69,999	2,447	315	680	1,075	300	76
$70,000 to $74,999	2,629	343	801	1,136	264	85
$75,000 to $79,999	2,180	279	616	977	249	60
$80,000 to $84,999	1,973	261	565	910	188	50
$85,000 to $89,999	1,184	117	327	594	119	28
$90,000 to $94,999	1,305	142	382	601	155	25
$95,000 to $99,999	903	98	230	445	114	17
$100,000 or more	10,028	743	2,620	5,170	1,242	254
Median income	$33,161	$21,657	$41,697	$44,396	$31,394	$23,834
TOTAL MEN	**100.0%**	**100.0%**	**100.0%**	**100.0%**	**100.0%**	**100.0%**
Without income	**9.7**	**23.1**	**4.1**	**4.2**	**2.6**	**2.7**
With income	**90.3**	**76.9**	**95.9**	**95.8**	**97.4**	**97.3**
Under $15,000	19.9	29.8	12.7	13.8	19.8	27.9
$15,000 to $24,999	14.2	13.3	12.5	11.8	19.5	27.8
$25,000 to $34,999	12.5	11.2	13.9	11.6	14.0	15.6
$35,000 to $49,999	14.1	10.2	17.8	15.9	14.6	10.6
$50,000 to $74,999	14.6	7.8	19.6	19.2	13.9	8.6
$75,000 to $99,999	6.5	2.5	8.6	9.5	6.2	2.8
$100,000 or more	8.6	2.1	10.7	14.0	9.4	4.0

Note: Men by generation are calculations by New Strategist.
Source: Bureau of the Census, 2009 Current Population Survey, Annual Social and Economic Supplement, Internet site http://www.census.gov/hhes/www/cpstables/032009/perinc/toc.htm; calculations by New Strategist

Gen X and Baby-Boom Women Have the Highest Incomes

Millennial women have a lower median income because many are still in school.

Women's median income was only $20,867 in 2008. The figure is far below the $33,161 median income of men in part because a larger proportion of women work part-time. Although women's incomes are well below men's, they have become a necessity to achieving a middle-class lifestyle because men's incomes are not keeping up with the cost of living.

Incomes are highest for Generation X and Boomer women, with a median income of more than $27,000 in 2008. Income drops sharply for the Swing and World War II generations because many women are retired.

■ By age group, women aged 15 to 24 have the lowest median income because many are still in school.

Generation X and Boomer women are in their peak earning years

(median income of women by generation, 2008)

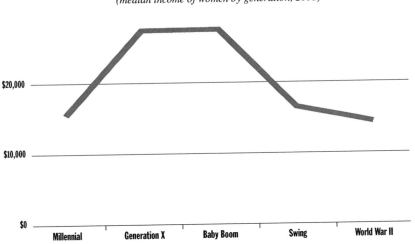

Table 6.5 Women by Income and Age, 2008

(number and percent distribution of women aged 15 or older by income and age, 2008; median income of women with income and of women working full-time, year-round; percent working full-time, year-round; women in thousands as of 2009)

	total	15 to 24	25 to 34	35 to 44	45 to 54	55 to 64	65 or older total	65 to 74	75 or older
TOTAL WOMEN	123,424	20,657	20,079	20,831	22,594	17,783	21,480	11,003	10,477
Without income	17,021	7,397	2,634	2,354	2,104	1,645	887	489	398
With income	106,403	13,260	17,445	18,477	20,490	16,138	20,593	10,514	10,079
Under $5,000	13,170	4,434	1,976	2,123	1,916	1,663	1,057	599	458
$5,000 to $9,999	14,031	2,687	1,520	1,428	1,766	1,807	4,821	2,556	2,265
$10,000 to $14,999	13,385	1,810	1,638	1,648	1,769	1,714	4,807	2,162	2,644
$15,000 to $19,999	10,650	1,329	1,679	1,602	1,676	1,411	2,952	1,230	1,722
$20,000 to $24,999	9,372	1,007	1,705	1,618	1,927	1,315	1,798	882	916
$25,000 to $29,999	7,722	668	1,492	1,346	1,628	1,314	1,273	656	617
$30,000 to $34,999	6,751	387	1,534	1,434	1,518	1,043	835	464	372
$35,000 to $39,999	5,583	319	1,214	1,173	1,274	951	654	342	311
$40,000 to $44,999	4,677	199	1,055	1,051	1,151	738	485	293	192
$45,000 to $49,999	3,577	133	813	844	873	602	313	209	103
$50,000 to $54,999	3,726	121	696	826	990	715	379	244	134
$55,000 to $59,999	2,070	55	393	461	567	388	206	148	57
$60,000 to $64,999	2,233	24	410	498	680	449	170	123	47
$65,000 to $69,999	1,462	8	298	332	441	281	102	77	24
$70,000 to $74,999	1,333	16	224	393	356	253	91	62	29
$75,000 to $79,999	959	3	146	254	259	214	83	70	13
$80,000 to $84,999	912	7	118	235	248	213	92	67	25
$85,000 to $89,999	622	2	77	161	182	146	53	34	19
$90,000 to $94,999	605	8	78	162	173	121	63	45	18
$95,000 to $99,999	375	0	40	86	106	113	30	28	2
$100,000 or more	3,187	42	338	798	989	689	331	221	110
Median income									
Women with income	$20,867	$8,901	$25,553	$27,371	$28,236	$25,515	$14,559	$14,831	$14,378
Working full-time	36,688	22,731	35,164	38,950	39,267	40,796	43,027	43,814	40,026
Percent full-time	35.8%	15.4%	48.8%	51.1%	53.2%	40.7%	5.9%	10.0%	1.7%
TOTAL WOMEN	100.0%	100.0%	100.0%	100.0%	100.0%	100.0%	100.0%	100.0%	100.0%
Without income	13.8	35.8	13.1	11.3	9.3	9.3	4.1	4.4	3.8
With income	86.2	64.2	86.9	88.7	90.7	90.7	95.9	95.6	96.2
Under $15,000	32.9	43.2	25.6	25.0	24.1	29.2	49.7	48.3	51.2
$15,000 to $24,999	16.2	11.3	16.9	15.5	15.9	15.3	22.1	19.2	25.2
$25,000 to $34,999	11.7	5.1	15.1	13.3	13.9	13.3	9.8	10.2	9.4
$35,000 to $49,999	11.2	3.2	15.3	14.7	14.6	12.9	6.8	7.7	5.8
$50,000 to $74,999	8.8	1.1	10.1	12.0	13.4	11.7	4.4	5.9	2.8
$75,000 to $99,999	2.8	0.1	2.3	4.3	4.3	4.5	1.5	2.2	0.7
$100,000 or more	2.6	0.2	1.7	3.8	4.4	3.9	1.5	2.0	1.0

Source: Bureau of the Census, 2009 Current Population Survey, Annual Social and Economic Supplement, Internet site http:// www.census.gov/hhes/www/cpstables/032009/perinc/toc.htm; calculations by New Strategist

Table 6.6 Women by Income and Generation, 2008

(number and percent distribution of women aged 15 or older by income and generation, 2008; median income of women with income; women in thousands as of 2009)

	total	Millennial (15 to 31)	Generation X (32 to 43)	Baby Boom (44 to 62)	Swing (63 to 75)	World War II (76 or older)
TOTAL WOMEN	**123,424**	**34,712**	**24,772**	**38,904**	**15,398**	**9,639**
Without income	**17,021**	**9,241**	**2,909**	**3,655**	**850**	**366**
With income	**106,403**	**25,472**	**21,863**	**35,248**	**14,548**	**9,273**
Under $5,000	13,170	5,817	2,504	3,459	968	422
$5,000 to $9,999	14,031	3,751	1,741	3,354	3,099	2,086
$10,000 to $14,999	13,385	2,957	1,975	3,305	2,716	2,432
$15,000 to $19,999	10,650	2,504	1,946	2,965	1,650	1,585
$20,000 to $24,999	9,372	2,201	1,968	3,141	1,218	845
$25,000 to $29,999	7,722	1,712	1,659	2,814	968	569
$30,000 to $34,999	6,751	1,461	1,751	2,496	702	341
$35,000 to $39,999	5,583	1,169	1,420	2,152	557	285
$40,000 to $44,999	4,677	938	1,262	1,847	456	175
$45,000 to $49,999	3,577	702	1,004	1,439	338	95
$50,000 to $54,999	3,726	608	952	1,645	398	123
$55,000 to $59,999	2,070	330	533	924	230	53
$60,000 to $64,999	2,233	311	571	1,089	217	45
$65,000 to $69,999	1,462	217	388	699	135	23
$70,000 to $74,999	1,333	173	421	598	115	27
$75,000 to $79,999	959	105	272	456	114	12
$80,000 to $84,999	912	90	247	442	112	22
$85,000 to $89,999	622	56	168	315	65	18
$90,000 to $94,999	605	63	169	286	71	17
$95,000 to $99,999	375	28	89	205	51	2
$100,000 or more	3,187	279	820	1,620	368	101
Median income	$20,867	$15,421	$27,405	$27,488	$16,488	$14,375
TOTAL WOMEN	**100.0%**	**100.0%**	**100.0%**	**100.0%**	**100.0%**	**100.0%**
Without income	**13.8**	**26.6**	**11.7**	**9.4**	**5.5**	**3.8**
With income	**86.2**	**73.4**	**88.3**	**90.6**	**94.5**	**96.2**
Under $15,000	32.9	36.1	25.1	26.0	44.1	51.3
$15,000 to $24,999	16.2	13.6	15.8	15.7	18.6	25.2
$25,000 to $34,999	11.7	9.1	13.8	13.6	10.8	9.4
$35,000 to $49,999	11.2	8.1	14.9	14.0	8.8	5.8
$50,000 to $74,999	8.8	4.7	11.6	12.7	7.1	2.8
$75,000 to $99,999	2.8	1.0	3.8	4.4	2.7	0.7
$100,000 or more	2.6	0.8	3.3	4.2	2.4	1.0

Note: Women by generation are calculations by New Strategist.
Source: Bureau of the Census, 2009 Current Population Survey Annual Social and Economic Supplement, Internet site http:// www.census.gov/hhes/www/cpstables/032009/perinc/toc.htm; calculations by New Strategist

Incomes of Young Women Nearly Match Those of Young Men

A wide gap in the incomes of older women and men remains, however.

In 1960, women working full-time made about 60 cents for every dollar made by a man. Since then, the ratio of women's to men's incomes has increased to 77 cents for every dollar earned by a man.

The income gap between women and men varies by age. The median income of women aged 65 or older who work full-time is only 69 percent as high as that of their male counterparts. But among full-time workers aged 45 to 54, the median income of women is 74 percent as high as that of men. The youngest full-time workers come closest to income parity. Among full-time workers under age 35, women earn 87 to 88 percent as much as men.

Does this mean younger women are achieving income equality? Not really. With each generation, the educational level of women has increased, and women now spend more years in the labor force—two factors that contribute to the narrowing gap between men's and women's incomes. But the relatively low incomes of young workers also play a role. The real test will be whether or not the gap narrows in the older age groups in the years ahead.

■ As well-educated younger women move into jobs at the highest levels of business and government, their progress will help close the income gap.

Earnings gap is narrower among the young

(income of women who work full-time as a percent of the income of men who work full-time, by age, 2008)

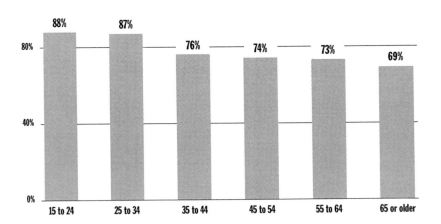

Table 6.7 Median Income of Full-Time Workers by Age and Sex, 2008

(median income of year-round, full-time workers by age and sex, and women's income as a percent of men's, 2008)

	men	women	women's income as a percent of men's
Total people	**$47,779**	**$36,688**	**76.8%**
Aged 15 to 24	25,780	22,731	88.2
Aged 25 to 34	40,645	35,164	86.5
Aged 35 to 44	51,213	38,950	76.1
Aged 45 to 54	53,331	39,267	73.6
Aged 55 to 64	56,190	40,796	72.6
Aged 65 or older	62,240	43,027	69.1

Source: Bureau of the Census, 2009 Current Population Survey, Internet site http://www.census.gov/hhes/www/cpstables/032009/hhinc/toc.htm

Since 1980, Older Householders Have Seen Biggest Gains

Householders aged 65 or older have made the largest gains since 2000.

Between 1980 and 2008, the median income of households headed by people aged 65 or older rose from $21,845 to $29,744, an increase of 36 percent, after adjusting for inflation. Younger households also saw their incomes rise, but by much less. The median income of householders under age 25 rose only 2 percent between 1980 and 2008, in large part because a growing proportion are in school and not yet working full-time.

Since 2000, householders under age 55 have seen their incomes decline sharply. In contrast, householders aged 55 to 64 saw their median income rise 2 percent between 2000 and 2008, and householders aged 65 or older experienced a 3 percent gain. Behind the gains for householders aged 55 or older is rising labor force participation as early retirement becomes less common.

■ The median income of householders aged 55 or older should continue to grow as labor force participation in the older age groups increases.

Since 2000, householders aged 45 to 54 have lost the most

(percent change in median household income, by age of householder, 2000 to 2008)

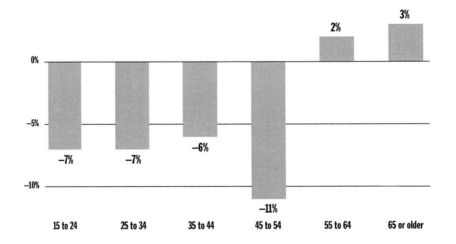

Table 6.8 Median Income of Households by Age of Householder, 1980 to 2008

(median household income by age of householder, 1980 to 2008; percent change for selected years; in 2008 dollars)

	total households	under 25	25 to 34	35 to 44	45 to 54	55 to 64	65 or older
2008	$50,303	$32,270	$51,400	$62,954	$64,349	$57,265	$29,744
2007	52,163	33,011	52,976	64,511	67,992	59,591	29,393
2006	51,473	33,037	52,501	64,505	69,278	58,298	29,685
2005	51,093	31,730	52,254	64,061	68,847	57,637	28,715
2004	50,535	31,432	51,824	64,610	69,563	57,440	27,945
2003	50,711	31,670	52,422	64,439	70,524	57,615	27,847
2002	50,756	33,305	54,252	64,055	70,638	56,494	27,709
2001	51,356	34,291	54,824	64,845	70,592	55,778	28,115
2000	52,500	34,817	55,531	67,218	72,070	56,080	28,861
1999	52,587	32,496	54,388	65,655	73,527	57,715	29,458
1998	51,295	31,084	52,857	63,914	71,429	56,944	28,664
1997	49,497	30,206	51,060	62,008	69,386	55,316	27,769
1996	48,499	29,294	49,040	60,698	68,968	54,406	26,575
1995	47,803	29,430	48,680	60,974	67,418	53,416	26,789
1994	46,351	27,784	47,625	59,860	67,896	50,615	25,996
1993	45,839	28,367	45,898	59,956	67,799	49,116	26,046
1992	46,063	26,557	46,970	59,922	66,812	51,111	25,764
1991	46,445	28,233	47,549	60,664	67,450	51,344	26,170
1990	47,818	28,749	48,482	61,581	66,948	51,686	26,917
1989	48,463	31,290	50,000	63,097	69,616	51,670	26,441
1988	47,614	29,801	49,683	63,929	66,830	50,548	26,099
1987	47,251	29,820	48,891	63,793	67,455	49,968	26,186
1986	46,665	28,696	48,541	61,454	66,839	50,187	25,950
1985	45,069	28,718	47,869	59,282	63,398	48,770	25,292
1984	44,242	27,688	46,848	58,787	62,206	47,556	25,262
1983	42,910	27,535	44,679	56,869	62,361	46,799	24,076
1982	43,212	29,598	45,590	56,492	59,952	47,291	23,653
1981	43,328	30,080	46,596	57,661	61,432	47,796	22,495
1980	44,059	31,622	48,107	58,779	62,496	48,629	21,845

Percent change

	total households	under 25	25 to 34	35 to 44	45 to 54	55 to 64	65 or older
2000 to 2008	–4.2%	–7.3%	–7.4%	–6.3%	–10.7%	2.1%	3.1%
1990 to 2008	5.2	12.2	6.0	2.2	–3.9	10.8	10.5
1980 to 2008	14.2	2.0	6.8	7.1	3.0	17.8	36.2

*Source: Bureau of the Census, Current Population Surveys, Annual Social and Economic Supplement, Internet site http://www
.census.gov/hhes/www/income/histinc/inchhtoc.html; calculations by New Strategist*

Americans Aged 45 to 54 Are Most Likely to Be Affluent

The age group accounts for nearly 30 percent of the richest 20 percent of households.

One way of examining the characteristics of households by income is to divide households into fifths, or quintiles, and examine the characteristics of households within each quintile. This exercise shows how the middle aged dominate the nation's affluent. Householders aged 45 to 54 account for the largest share of the most affluent households. Together with householders aged 35 to 44 and 55 to 64, the three age groups account for 80 percent of the richest 5 percent of households (with incomes of $174,000 or higher). Among householders aged 45 to 54, nearly 28 percent are in the top 20 percent of households, as are 26 percent of householders aged 35 to 44 and 25 percent of those aged 55 to 64.

At the other end of the income spectrum, householders aged 65 or older account for 36 percent of the poorest 20 percent of households, with incomes below $20,712. More than one-third of householders in the age group are in the bottom income quintile.

■ As Boomers postpone retirement in the years ahead, the share of householders aged 55 or older in the top income quintile will expand.

Few of the affluent are aged 65 or older

(percent of households in the top income quintile, by age, 2008)

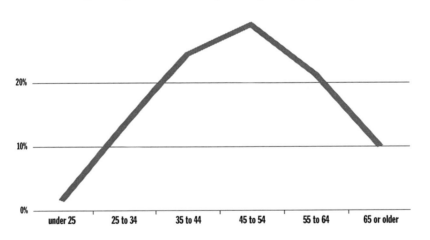

Table 6.9 Households by Age of Householder and Income Quintile, 2008

(number and percent distribution of households by age of householder, income quintile, and top 5 percent, 2008; households in thousands as of 2009)

	total	bottom fifth	second fifth	middle fifth	fourth fifth	top fifth	top five percent
Total households	117,181	23,436	23,436	23,436	23,436	5,861	5,803
Lower income limit	–	$20,712	$39,000	$62,750	$100,250	$180,000	$174,000

DISTRIBUTION BY INCOME QUINTILE AND TOP 5 PERCENT

	total	bottom fifth	second fifth	middle fifth	fourth fifth	top fifth	top five percent
Total households	100.0%	20.0%	20.0%	20.0%	20.0%	20.0%	5.0%
Aged 15 to 24	100.0	30.9	28.7	21.4	13.1	5.9	0.8
Aged 25 to 34	100.0	16.7	20.6	23.3	23.0	16.3	2.9
Aged 35 to 44	100.0	13.1	16.2	20.5	24.2	25.9	6.5
Aged 45 to 54	100.0	13.7	15.2	20.1	23.3	27.7	7.4
Aged 55 to 64	100.0	17.3	17.3	19.4	20.8	25.1	7.0
Aged 65 or older	100.0	34.3	27.6	16.9	11.7	9.5	2.3
Aged 65 to 74	100.0	25.9	26.0	19.4	15.4	13.3	3.4
Aged 75 or older	100.0	43.4	29.3	14.3	7.6	5.4	1.2

DISTRIBUTION BY AGE OF HOUSEHOLDER

	total	bottom fifth	second fifth	middle fifth	fourth fifth	top fifth	top five percent
Total households	100.0%	100.0%	100.0%	100.0%	100.0%	100.0%	100.0%
Aged 15 to 24	5.4	8.4	7.8	5.8	3.5	1.6	0.9
Aged 25 to 34	16.5	13.8	17.0	19.2	19.0	13.4	9.7
Aged 35 to 44	18.9	12.4	15.3	19.4	22.9	24.5	24.6
Aged 45 to 54	21.0	14.4	16.0	21.1	24.5	29.1	31.3
Aged 55 to 64	17.0	14.7	14.7	16.5	17.7	21.3	23.7
Aged 65 or older	21.2	36.4	29.2	18.0	12.4	10.0	9.8
Aged 65 to 74	11.0	14.2	14.2	10.6	8.5	7.3	7.4
Aged 75 or older	10.2	22.2	15.0	7.3	3.9	2.8	2.5

Note: "–" means not applicable.
Source: Bureau of the Census, 2009 Current Population Survey, Internet site http://www.census.gov/hhes/www/ cpstables/032009/hhinc/toc.htm

The Oldest Americans Have the Lowest Incomes

Incomes peak among Boomers.

The median income of the World War II generation was a modest $24,127 in 2008, well below the median income of younger age groups, because many are elderly widows who live alone. Households headed by Millennials had a much larger median income of $44,320 although many are in school.

Income peaks among householders aged 45 to 54 at $64,349—28 percent higher than the $50,303 median for all households. Not only are 45-to-54-year-olds in their peak earning years, but many of these households have at least two earners. The median income of 35-to-44-year-olds (most of them Gen Xers) is close to the peak at $62,954. Median income drops in the 55-to-64 age group because many people retire before age 65.

■ Expect to see the household incomes of 55-to-64-year-olds rise as older Boomers postpone retirement.

Generation Xers are entering peak earning years

(median income of households by generation, 2008)

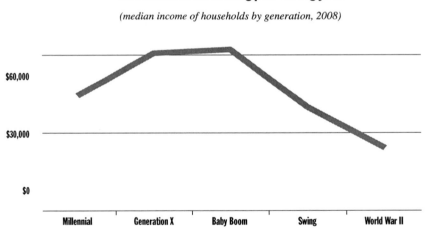

Table 6.10 Households by Income and Age of Householder, 2008

(number and percent distribution of households by household income and age of householder, 2008; households in thousands as of 2009)

	total	15 to 24	25 to 34	35 to 44	45 to 54	55 to 64	65 or older total	65 to 74	75 or older
Total households	**117,181**	**6,357**	**19,302**	**22,171**	**24,633**	**19,883**	**24,834**	**12,842**	**11,992**
Under $5,000	3,559	541	652	500	660	623	583	252	330
$5,000 to $9,999	4,818	363	625	557	800	830	1,641	716	926
$10,000 to $14,999	6,847	463	769	737	805	928	3,147	1,167	1,980
$15,000 to $19,999	6,716	498	930	837	869	842	2,738	1,008	1,730
$20,000 to $24,999	7,084	504	1,050	987	1,069	1,071	2,405	1,157	1,247
$25,000 to $29,999	6,428	528	1,069	967	936	927	2,000	929	1,071
$30,000 to $34,999	6,305	507	1,053	1,056	1,083	943	1,662	839	822
$35,000 to $39,999	6,000	434	1,191	997	1,056	865	1,458	727	730
$40,000 to $44,999	5,593	385	1,036	1,011	1,105	943	1,112	628	485
$45,000 to $49,999	4,839	301	958	861	1,033	754	932	524	407
$50,000 to $54,999	5,147	260	927	1,079	1,126	870	885	547	337
$55,000 to $59,999	4,087	224	839	854	858	676	634	413	221
$60,000 to $64,999	4,450	230	878	908	1,011	773	650	415	236
$65,000 to $69,999	3,598	154	717	789	858	607	472	310	163
$70,000 to $74,999	3,695	110	675	894	847	704	464	317	146
$75,000 to $79,999	3,388	130	659	769	809	549	473	314	160
$80,000 to $84,999	3,077	107	664	696	758	523	330	224	105
$85,000 to $89,999	2,775	101	501	641	697	503	331	224	107
$90,000 to $94,999	2,585	68	462	599	684	476	296	211	85
$95,000 to $99,999	2,179	69	373	511	591	401	233	182	51
$100,000 or more	24,013	382	3,275	5,919	6,975	5,073	2,388	1,736	652
Median income	$50,303	$32,270	$51,400	$62,954	$64,349	$57,265	$29,744	$37,373	$24,052

PERCENT DISTRIBUTION

	total	15 to 24	25 to 34	35 to 44	45 to 54	55 to 64	65 or older total	65 to 74	75 or older
Total households	**100.0%**	**100.0%**	**100.0%**	**100.0%**	**100.0%**	**100.0%**	**100.0%**	**100.0%**	**100.0%**
Under $25,000	24.8	37.3	20.9	16.3	17.1	21.6	42.3	33.5	51.8
$25,000 to $49,999	24.9	33.9	27.5	22.1	21.2	22.3	28.8	28.4	29.3
$50,000 to $74,999	17.9	15.4	20.9	20.4	19.1	18.3	12.5	15.6	9.2
$75,000 to $99,999	12.0	7.5	13.8	14.5	14.4	12.3	6.7	9.0	4.2
$100,000 or more	20.5	6.0	17.0	26.7	28.3	25.5	9.6	13.5	5.4

Source: Bureau of the Census, 2009 Current Population Survey, Internet site http://www.census.gov/hhes/www/cpstables/032009/hhinc/toc.htm; calculations by New Strategist

Table 6.11 Households by Income and Generation of Householder, 2008

(number and percent distribution of households by household income and generation of householder, 2008; households in thousands as of 2009)

	total	Millennial (15 to 31)	Generation X (32 to 43)	Baby Boom (44 to 62)	Swing (63 to 75)	World War II (76 or older)
Total households	**117,181**	**19,868**	**25,745**	**42,757**	**17,778**	**11,034**
Under $5,000	3,559	997	646	1,208	403	305
$5,000 to $9,999	4,818	801	689	1,520	956	853
$10,000 to $14,999	6,847	1,001	894	1,621	1,511	1,820
$15,000 to $19,999	6,716	1,149	1,032	1,626	1,315	1,594
$20,000 to $24,999	7,084	1,239	1,203	2,025	1,471	1,146
$25,000 to $29,999	6,428	1,276	1,191	1,774	1,200	986
$30,000 to $34,999	6,305	1,244	1,266	1,943	1,093	758
$35,000 to $39,999	6,000	1,268	1,255	1,848	958	672
$40,000 to $44,999	5,593	1,110	1,221	1,961	855	446
$45,000 to $49,999	4,839	972	1,062	1,722	707	375
$50,000 to $54,999	5,147	909	1,249	1,930	748	311
$55,000 to $59,999	4,087	811	1,020	1,484	566	205
$60,000 to $64,999	4,450	845	1,081	1,720	588	216
$65,000 to $69,999	3,598	656	925	1,423	444	150
$70,000 to $74,999	3,695	583	1,007	1,500	469	136
$75,000 to $79,999	3,388	591	890	1,325	437	145
$80,000 to $84,999	3,077	572	826	1,246	337	97
$85,000 to $89,999	2,775	452	727	1,164	333	99
$90,000 to $94,999	2,585	391	678	1,125	313	78
$95,000 to $99,999	2,179	330	572	963	266	48
$100,000 or more	24,013	2,675	6,310	11,625	2,803	601
Median income	$50,303	$44,320	$60,666	$62,081	$39,906	$24,127

PERCENT DISTRIBUTION

	total	Millennial (15 to 31)	Generation X (32 to 43)	Baby Boom (44 to 62)	Swing (63 to 75)	World War II (76 or older)
Total households	**100.0%**	**100.0%**	**100.0%**	**100.0%**	**100.0%**	**100.0%**
Under $25,000	24.8	26.1	17.3	18.7	31.8	51.8
$25,000 to $49,999	24.9	29.5	23.3	21.6	27.1	29.3
$50,000 to $74,999	17.9	19.1	20.5	18.8	15.8	9.2
$75,000 to $99,999	12.0	11.8	14.3	13.6	9.5	4.2
$100,000 or more	20.5	13.5	24.5	27.2	15.8	5.4

Note: Households by generation are calculations by New Strategist.
Source: Bureau of the Census, 2009 Current Population Survey, Internet site http://www.census.gov/hhes/www/ cpstables/032009/hhinc/toc.htm; calculations by New Strategist

Two Earners Mean Higher Incomes

Middle-aged married couples have the highest incomes.

The key to economic security is two incomes. Married couples have far higher incomes than any other household type because most couples are dual earners.

In 2008, married couples had a median income of $73,010, 45 percent above the all-household median. Married couples with a householder aged 45 to 54 had the highest median income of all, $87,331 in 2008.

In nearly every age group, the median income of married couples exceeds that of other household types. The only exceptions are among the youngest and the oldest householders, where the incomes of married couples are second to those of families headed by men. Behind this pattern is the greater number of earners in younger and older households headed by men.

Women living alone have the lowest incomes, the median bottoming out at $16,186 among women aged 75 or older who live alone. Women aged 15 to 24 who live alone had a median income of only $17,115.

■ Because the early retirement trend has come to an end, the incomes of older couples should rise in the years ahead.

Among married couples, the oldest have the lowest incomes

(median income of married couples, by age of householder, 2008)

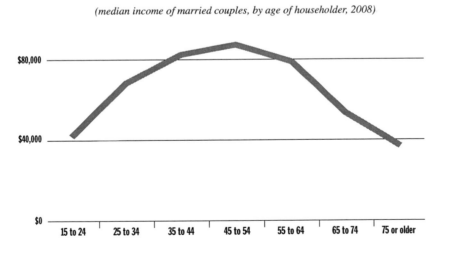

Table 6.12 Median Household Income by Age of Householder and Household Type, 2008

(median income of households by age of householder and type of household, and index of median to average, 2008)

| | | family households | | | nonfamily households | | | |
| | | | | | female householder | | male householder | |
	total	married couples	female hh, no spouse present	male hh, no spouse present	total	living alone	total	living alone
Total households	**$50,303**	**$73,010**	**$33,073**	**$49,186**	**$25,014**	**$22,018**	**$36,006**	**$30,726**
Aged 15 to 24	32,270	41,887	25,230	43,537	28,068	17,115	30,718	23,368
Aged 25 to 34	51,400	68,263	25,120	49,117	43,453	36,308	45,698	35,542
Aged 35 to 44	62,954	82,432	33,233	50,356	40,953	36,061	44,124	40,223
Aged 45 to 54	64,349	87,331	41,393	51,614	33,944	31,019	40,102	35,007
Aged 55 to 64	57,265	78,975	42,203	56,982	30,483	28,514	31,775	30,122
Aged 65 or older	29,744	46,181	36,896	43,407	17,244	16,987	23,622	22,219
Aged 65 to 74	37,373	53,425	37,757	43,163	20,063	19,500	25,824	23,741
Aged 75 or older	24,052	36,873	36,276	43,460	16,373	16,186	22,011	21,315

INDEX OF MEDIAN INCOME TO AVERAGE BY AGE

Total households	**100**	**145**	**66**	**98**	**50**	**44**	**72**	**61**
Aged 15 to 24	64	83	50	87	56	34	61	46
Aged 25 to 34	102	136	50	98	86	72	91	71
Aged 35 to 44	125	164	66	100	81	72	88	80
Aged 45 to 54	128	174	82	103	67	62	80	70
Aged 55 to 64	114	157	84	113	61	57	63	60
Aged 65 or older	59	92	73	86	34	34	47	44
Aged 65 to 74	74	106	75	86	40	39	51	47
Aged 75 or older	48	73	72	86	33	32	44	42

Note: "hh" stands for householder.
Source: Bureau of the Census, 2009 Current Population Survey, Internet site http://www.census.gov/hhes/www/cpstables/032009/hhinc/toc.htm

Table 6.13 Household Income by Household Type, 2008: Householders Aged 15 to 24

(number and percent distribution of households headed by people aged 15 to 24, by household income and household type, 2008; households in thousands as of 2009)

| | total | family households | | | nonfamily households | | | |
| | | | | | female householder | | male householder | |
		married couples	female hh, no spouse present	male hh, no spouse present	total	living alone	total	living alone
Total households	**6,357**	**1,203**	**1,356**	**835**	**1,366**	**667**	**1,597**	**871**
Under $25,000	2,369	269	672	184	623	444	621	461
$25,000 to $49,999	2,155	447	383	294	423	191	603	310
$50,000 to $74,999	978	303	156	126	165	23	228	74
$75,000 to $99,999	475	110	88	115	94	5	71	10
$100,000 or more	382	75	57	116	60	2	75	15
Median income	$32,270	$41,887	$25,230	$43,537	$28,068	$17,115	$30,718	$23,368

PERCENT DISTRIBUTION BY INCOME

Total households	**100.0%**	**100.0%**	**100.0%**	**100.0%**	**100.0%**	**100.0%**	**100.0%**	**100.0%**
Under $25,000	37.3	22.4	49.6	22.0	45.6	66.6	38.9	52.9
$25,000 to $49,999	33.9	37.2	28.2	35.2	31.0	28.6	37.8	35.6
$50,000 to $74,999	15.4	25.2	11.5	15.1	12.1	3.4	14.3	8.5
$75,000 to $99,999	7.5	9.1	6.5	13.8	6.9	0.7	4.4	1.1
$100,000 or more	6.0	6.2	4.2	13.9	4.4	0.3	4.7	1.7

Note: "hh" stands for householder.
Source: Bureau of the Census, 2009 Current Population Survey, Internet site http://www.census.gov/hhes/www/cpstables/032009/hhinc/toc.htm; calculations by New Strategist

Table 6.14 Household Income by Household Type, 2008: Householders Aged 25 to 34

(number and percent distribution of households headed by people aged 25 to 34, by household income and household type, 2008; households in thousands as of 2009)

| | | family households | | | nonfamily households | | | |
| | | | | | female householder | | male householder | |
	total	married couples	female hh, no spouse present	male hh, no spouse present	total	living alone	total	living alone
Total households	**19,302**	**9,022**	**3,137**	**1,188**	**2,261**	**1,486**	**3,693**	**2,309**
Under $25,000	4,026	907	1,561	242	533	456	783	685
$25,000 to $49,999	5,307	1,959	947	367	789	645	1,246	956
$50,000 to $74,999	4,036	2,182	336	259	476	260	785	424
$75,000 to $99,999	2,659	1,714	156	152	204	60	430	133
$100,000 or more	3,275	2,260	138	168	259	62	450	112
Median income	$51,400	$68,263	$25,120	$49,117	$43,453	$36,308	$45,698	$35,542

PERCENT DISTRIBUTION BY INCOME

Total households	**100.0%**	**100.0%**	**100.0%**	**100.0%**	**100.0%**	**100.0%**	**100.0%**	**100.0%**
Under $25,000	20.9	10.1	49.8	20.4	23.6	30.7	21.2	29.7
$25,000 to $49,999	27.5	21.7	30.2	30.9	34.9	43.4	33.7	41.4
$50,000 to $74,999	20.9	24.2	10.7	21.8	21.1	17.5	21.3	18.4
$75,000 to $99,999	13.8	19.0	5.0	12.8	9.0	4.0	11.6	5.8
$100,000 or more	17.0	25.0	4.4	14.1	11.5	4.2	12.2	4.9

Note: "hh" stands for householder.
Source: Bureau of the Census, 2009 Current Population Survey, Internet site http://www.census.gov/hhes/www/cpstables/032009/hhinc/toc.htm; calculations by New Strategist

Table 6.15 Household Income by Household Type, 2008: Householders Aged 35 to 44

(number and percent distribution of households headed by people aged 35 to 44, by household income and household type, 2008; households in thousands as of 2009)

| | | family households | | | nonfamily households | | | |
| | | | female hh, no spouse present | male hh, no spouse present | female householder | | male householder | |
	total	married couples			total	living alone	total	living alone
Total households	**22,171**	**12,914**	**3,484**	**1,149**	**1,756**	**1,439**	**2,868**	**2,259**
Under $25,000	3,618	889	1,284	221	506	471	719	650
$25,000 to $49,999	4,892	1,968	1,183	350	527	456	867	717
$50,000 to $74,999	4,524	2,746	558	254	356	282	611	471
$75,000 to $99,999	3,216	2,415	218	133	150	106	301	213
$100,000 or more	5,919	4,899	240	190	218	123	371	207
Median income	$62,954	$82,432	$33,233	$50,356	$40,953	$36,061	$44,124	$40,223

PERCENT DISTRIBUTION BY INCOME

Total households	**100.0%**	**100.0%**	**100.0%**	**100.0%**	**100.0%**	**100.0%**	**100.0%**	**100.0%**
Under $25,000	16.3	6.9	36.9	19.2	28.8	32.7	25.1	28.8
$25,000 to $49,999	22.1	15.2	34.0	30.5	30.0	31.7	30.2	31.7
$50,000 to $74,999	20.4	21.3	16.0	22.1	20.3	19.6	21.3	20.8
$75,000 to $99,999	14.5	18.7	6.3	11.6	8.5	7.4	10.5	9.4
$100,000 or more	26.7	37.9	6.9	16.5	12.4	8.5	12.9	9.2

Note: "hh" stands for householder.
Source: Bureau of the Census, 2009 Current Population Survey, Internet site http://www.census.gov/hhes/www/cpstables/032009/hhinc/toc.htm; calculations by New Strategist

Table 6.16 Household Income by Household Type, 2008: Householders Aged 45 to 54

(number and percent distribution of households headed by people aged 45 to 54, by household income and household type, 2008; households in thousands as of 2009)

| | | family households | | | nonfamily households | | | |
| | | | | | female householder | | male householder | |
	total	married couples	female hh, no spouse present	male hh, no spouse present	total	living alone	total	living alone
Total households	**24,633**	**13,981**	**3,063**	**1,075**	**2,986**	**2,570**	**3,528**	**2,929**
Under $25,000	4,203	858	842	218	1,122	1,064	1,163	1,086
$25,000 to $49,999	5,213	2,044	983	288	912	783	987	847
$50,000 to $74,999	4,700	2,732	590	244	531	444	603	464
$75,000 to $99,999	3,539	2,560	312	129	193	144	345	245
$100,000 or more	6,975	5,788	334	195	228	134	431	286
Median income	$64,349	$87,331	$41,393	$51,614	$33,944	$31,019	$40,102	$35,007

PERCENT DISTRIBUTION BY INCOME

Total households	**100.0%**	**100.0%**	**100.0%**	**100.0%**	**100.0%**	**100.0%**	**100.0%**	**100.0%**
Under $25,000	17.1	6.1	27.5	20.3	37.6	41.4	33.0	37.1
$25,000 to $49,999	21.2	14.6	32.1	26.8	30.5	30.5	28.0	28.9
$50,000 to $74,999	19.1	19.5	19.3	22.7	17.8	17.3	17.1	15.8
$75,000 to $99,999	14.4	18.3	10.2	12.0	6.5	5.6	9.8	8.4
$100,000 or more	28.3	41.4	10.9	18.1	7.6	5.2	12.2	9.8

Note: "hh" stands for householder.
Source: Bureau of the Census, 2009 Current Population Survey, Internet site http://www.census.gov/hhes/www/cpstables/032009/hhinc/toc.htm; calculations by New Strategist

Table 6.17 Household Income by Household Type, 2008: Householders Aged 55 to 64

(number and percent distribution of households headed by people aged 55 to 64, by household income and house-hold type, 2008; households in thousands as of 2009)

| | | family households | | | nonfamily households | | | |
| | | | | | female householder | | male householder | |
	total	married couples	female hh, no spouse present	male hh, no spouse present	total	living alone	total	living alone
Total households	**19,883**	**11,417**	**1,493**	**552**	**3,701**	**3,406**	**2,720**	**2,344**
Under $25,000	4,294	1,097	414	112	1,570	1,521	1,100	1,017
$25,000 to $49,999	4,432	2,064	464	133	1,077	1,022	697	626
$50,000 to $74,999	3,630	2,219	269	122	557	473	463	387
$75,000 to $99,999	2,452	1,850	166	60	220	172	156	103
$100,000 or more	5,073	4,186	180	127	276	218	305	209
Median income	$57,265	$78,975	$42,203	$56,982	$30,483	$28,514	$31,775	$30,122

PERCENT DISTRIBUTION BY INCOME

Total households	**100.0%**	**100.0%**	**100.0%**	**100.0%**	**100.0%**	**100.0%**	**100.0%**	**100.0%**
Under $25,000	21.6	9.6	27.7	20.3	42.4	44.7	40.4	43.4
$25,000 to $49,999	22.3	18.1	31.1	24.1	29.1	30.0	25.6	26.7
$50,000 to $74,999	18.3	19.4	18.0	22.1	15.0	13.9	17.0	16.5
$75,000 to $99,999	12.3	16.2	11.1	10.9	5.9	5.0	5.7	4.4
$100,000 or more	25.5	36.7	12.1	23.0	7.5	6.4	11.2	8.9

Note: "hh" stands for householder.
Source: Bureau of the Census, 2009 Current Population Survey, Internet site http://www.census.gov/hhes/www/cpstables/032009/hhinc/toc.htm; calculations by New Strategist

Table 6.18 Household Income by Household Type, 2008: Householders Aged 65 or Older

(number and percent distribution of households headed by people aged 65 or older, by household income and household type, 2008; households in thousands as of 2009)

| | | family households | | | nonfamily households | | | |
| | | | female hh, no spouse present | male hh, no spouse present | female householder | | male householder | |
	total	married couples			total	living alone	total	living alone
Total households	**24,834**	**10,580**	**1,947**	**452**	**8,566**	**8,331**	**3,289**	**3,047**
Under $25,000	10,514	2,090	618	109	5,961	5,900	1,739	1,701
$25,000 to $49,999	7,164	3,604	674	155	1,853	1,777	876	803
$50,000 to $74,999	3,105	1,972	317	74	422	383	322	267
$75,000 to $99,999	1,663	1,142	190	68	141	129	121	94
$100,000 or more	2,388	1,774	151	45	191	144	228	182
Median income	$29,744	$46,181	$36,896	$43,407	$17,244	$16,987	$23,622	$22,219

PERCENT DISTRIBUTION BY INCOME

Total households	**100.0%**	**100.0%**	**100.0%**	**100.0%**	**100.0%**	**100.0%**	**100.0%**	**100.0%**
Under $25,000	42.3	19.8	31.7	24.1	69.6	70.8	52.9	55.8
$25,000 to $49,999	28.8	34.1	34.6	34.3	21.6	21.3	26.6	26.4
$50,000 to $74,999	12.5	18.6	16.3	16.4	4.9	4.6	9.8	8.8
$75,000 to $99,999	6.7	10.8	9.8	15.0	1.6	1.5	3.7	3.1
$100,000 or more	9.6	16.8	7.8	10.0	2.2	1.7	6.9	6.0

Note: "hh" stands for householder.
Source: Bureau of the Census, 2009 Current Population Survey, Internet site http://www.census.gov/hhes/www/cpstables/032009/hhinc/toc.htm; calculations by New Strategist

Table 6.19 Household Income by Household Type, 2008: Householders Aged 65 to 74

(number and percent distribution of households headed by people aged 65 to 74, by household income and household type, 2008; households in thousands as of 2009)

| | | family households | | | nonfamily households | | | |
| | | | | | female householder | | male householder | |
	total	married couples	female hh, no spouse present	male hh, no spouse present	total	living alone	total	living alone
Total households	**12,842**	**6,716**	**984**	**204**	**3,331**	**3,203**	**1,608**	**1,454**
Under $25,000	4,300	1,088	325	50	2,058	2,028	782	761
$25,000 to $49,999	3,647	2,029	305	63	820	779	429	386
$50,000 to $74,999	2,002	1,377	171	34	252	230	172	131
$75,000 to $99,999	1,155	847	104	34	101	88	70	52
$100,000 or more	1,736	1,375	80	21	104	79	157	122
Median income	$37,373	$53,425	$37,757	$43,163	$20,063	$19,500	$25,824	$23,741

PERCENT DISTRIBUTION BY INCOME

Total households	**100.0%**	**100.0%**	**100.0%**	**100.0%**	**100.0%**	**100.0%**	**100.0%**	**100.0%**
Under $25,000	33.5	16.2	33.0	24.5	61.8	63.3	48.6	52.3
$25,000 to $49,999	28.4	30.2	31.0	30.9	24.6	24.3	26.7	26.5
$50,000 to $74,999	15.6	20.5	17.4	16.7	7.6	7.2	10.7	9.0
$75,000 to $99,999	9.0	12.6	10.6	16.7	3.0	2.7	4.4	3.6
$100,000 or more	13.5	20.5	8.1	10.3	3.1	2.5	9.8	8.4

Note: "hh" stands for householder.
Source: Bureau of the Census, 2009 Current Population Survey, Internet site http://www.census.gov/hhes/www/cpstables/032009/hhinc/toc.htm; calculations by New Strategist

Table 6.20 Household Income by Household Type, 2008: Householders Aged 75 or Older

(number and percent distribution of households headed by people aged 75 or older, by household income and household type, 2008; households in thousands as of 2009)

| | | family households | | | nonfamily households | | | |
| | | | | | female householder | | male householder | |
	total	married couples	female hh, no spouse present	male hh, no spouse present	total	living alone	total	living alone
Total households	**11,992**	**3,864**	**963**	**248**	**5,236**	**5,128**	**1,681**	**1,593**
Under $25,000	6,213	1,002	292	60	3,903	3,873	959	942
$25,000 to $49,999	3,515	1,575	367	91	1,032	997	446	415
$50,000 to $74,999	1,103	592	145	39	171	153	152	135
$75,000 to $99,999	508	295	87	31	41	39	52	42
$100,000 or more	652	399	71	24	87	65	71	60
Median income	$24,052	$36,873	$36,276	$43,460	$16,373	$16,186	$22,011	$21,315

PERCENT DISTRIBUTION BY INCOME

Total households	**100.0%**	**100.0%**	**100.0%**	**100.0%**	**100.0%**	**100.0%**	**100.0%**	**100.0%**
Under $25,000	51.8	25.9	30.3	24.2	74.5	75.5	57.0	59.1
$25,000 to $49,999	29.3	40.8	38.1	36.7	19.7	19.4	26.5	26.1
$50,000 to $74,999	9.2	15.3	15.1	15.7	3.3	3.0	9.0	8.5
$75,000 to $99,999	4.2	7.6	9.0	12.5	0.8	0.8	3.1	2.6
$100,000 or more	5.4	10.3	7.4	9.7	1.7	1.3	4.2	3.8

Note: "hh" stands for householder.
Source: Bureau of the Census, 2009 Current Population Survey, Internet site http://www.census.gov/hhes/www/cpstables/032009/hhinc/toc.htm; calculations by New Strategist

Regardless of Race or Hispanic Origin, Incomes Peak in Middle Age

But the income peak of black and Hispanic households is much lower than that of Asians or non-Hispanic whites.

Asians have the highest household incomes, a median of $65,567 in 2008. This figure is substantially higher than the $55,530 median of non-Hispanic whites and well above the $37,913 median of Hispanics and $34,345 median of blacks.

Despite these differences, household income in every racial and ethnic group rises through adulthood, peaks in middle age, then declines. This income trajectory follows a predictable life pattern: more years in the labor force translate into higher incomes. Once people reach their sixties, most retire. Health also begins to decline, forcing some people to leave the workforce because of disability. With fewer household members working, household income falls.

Among Asians, median household income peaks in the 35-to-44 age group, at $82,200, or 63 percent above the national median. Black and Hispanic median household incomes also peak in the 45-to-54 age group, but at much lower levels. For Hispanics, the income peak is $45,181, and for blacks an even lower $43,616. Among non-Hispanic whites, householders aged 35 to 44 have a slightly higher median income than those aged 45 to 54, at $72,520 versus $71,923 for the older age group.

■ Black incomes are low because relatively few black households are headed by married couples. Hispanic incomes are low because many are recent immigrants with little education.

Asian households have the highest incomes

(median household income by race and Hispanic origin, 2008)

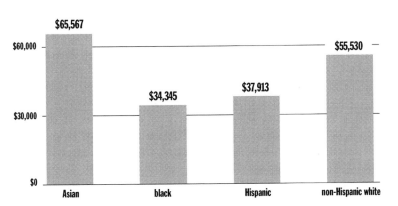

Table 6.21 Median Household Income by Age, Race, and Hispanic Origin of Householder, 2008

(median income of households by age, race, and Hispanic origin of householder, and index of age/race/Hispanic median to national median by age, 2008)

	total	Asian	black	Hispanic	non-Hispanic white
Total households	**$50,303**	**$65,567**	**$34,345**	**$37,913**	**$55,530**
Aged 15 to 24	32,270	36,424	24,601	30,907	34,800
Aged 25 to 34	51,400	71,947	32,096	38,618	59,566
Aged 35 to 44	62,954	82,200	40,737	41,938	72,520
Aged 45 to 54	64,349	72,251	43,616	45,181	71,923
Aged 55 to 64	57,265	66,740	34,976	41,035	63,196
Aged 65 or older	29,744	30,569	22,167	22,116	31,162
Aged 65 to 74	37,373	38,329	24,680	25,426	40,633
Aged 75 or older	24,052	22,199	17,790	18,409	24,739

INDEX OF MEDIAN INCOME BY RACE AND HISPANIC ORIGIN TO AVERAGE BY AGE

	total	Asian	black	Hispanic	non-Hispanic white
Total households	**100**	**130**	**68**	**75**	**110**
Aged 15 to 24	64	72	49	61	69
Aged 25 to 34	102	143	64	77	118
Aged 35 to 44	125	163	81	83	144
Aged 45 to 54	128	144	87	90	143
Aged 55 to 64	114	133	70	82	126
Aged 65 or older	59	61	44	44	62
Aged 65 to 74	74	76	49	51	81
Aged 75 or older	48	44	35	37	49

Note: Data for Asians and blacks are for those who identified themselves as being of the race alone or in combination with other races. Data for non-Hispanic whites are for those who identified themselves as being white alone and not Hispanic. Hispanics may be of any race.
Source: Bureau of the Census, 2009 Current Population Survey, Internet site http://www.census.gov/hhes/www/cpstables/032009/hhinc/toc.htm

Table 6.22 Households by Income and Age of Householder, 2008: Asian Households

(number and percent distribution of Asian households by household income and age of householder, 2008; households in thousands as of 2009)

	total	15 to 24	25 to 34	35 to 44	45 to 54	55 to 64	65 or older total	65 to 74	75 or older
Asian households	**4,805**	**281**	**1,043**	**1,188**	**994**	**700**	**600**	**373**	**227**
Under $5,000	205	31	49	40	29	34	23	11	12
$5,000 to $9,999	121	9	12	5	20	25	50	28	22
$10,000 to $14,999	231	22	29	25	36	29	88	41	47
$15,000 to $19,999	178	12	36	41	21	30	39	25	14
$20,000 to $24,999	240	29	33	47	32	33	65	39	27
$25,000 to $29,999	159	10	34	25	42	18	30	20	11
$30,000 to $34,999	207	20	43	48	43	29	24	17	8
$35,000 to $39,999	210	16	47	51	43	25	27	12	16
$40,000 to $44,999	197	19	43	52	36	28	19	16	3
$45,000 to $49,999	166	20	43	44	27	23	8	6	2
$50,000 to $54,999	183	5	42	54	35	25	23	13	10
$55,000 to $59,999	129	10	26	22	33	19	19	13	6
$60,000 to $64,999	159	8	42	35	44	21	10	6	4
$65,000 to $69,999	126	5	23	25	33	20	19	11	8
$70,000 to $74,999	155	8	37	35	31	23	21	16	5
$75,000 to $79,999	134	2	39	32	26	23	11	6	5
$80,000 to $84,999	123	3	42	26	15	22	15	9	6
$85,000 to $89,999	125	14	29	39	20	11	11	10	2
$90,000 to $94,999	116	0	40	37	14	19	6	6	1
$95,000 to $99,999	97	5	27	22	23	16	5	5	0
$100,000 or more	1,544	32	329	481	391	227	83	65	18
Median income	$65,567	$36,424	$71,947	$82,200	$72,251	$66,740	$30,569	$38,329	$22,199

PERCENT DISTRIBUTION

	total	15 to 24	25 to 34	35 to 44	45 to 54	55 to 64	65 or older total	65 to 74	75 or older
Asian households	**100.0%**	**100.0%**	**100.0%**	**100.0%**	**100.0%**	**100.0%**	**100.0%**	**100.0%**	**100.0%**
Under $25,000	20.3	36.7	15.2	13.3	13.9	21.6	44.2	38.6	53.7
$25,000 to $49,999	19.5	30.2	20.1	18.5	19.2	17.6	18.0	19.0	17.6
$50,000 to $74,999	15.7	12.8	16.3	14.4	17.7	15.4	15.3	15.8	14.5
$75,000 to $99,999	12.4	8.5	17.0	13.1	9.9	13.0	8.0	9.7	6.2
$100,000 or more	32.1	11.4	31.5	40.5	39.3	32.4	13.8	17.4	7.9

Note: Asians are those who identify themselves as being of the race alone and those who identify themselves as being of the race in combination with other races.
Source: Bureau of the Census, 2009 Current Population Survey, Internet site http://www.census.gov/hhes/www/cpstables/032009/hhinc/toc.htm; calculations by New Strategist

Table 6.23 Households by Income and Age of Householder, 2008: Black Households

(number and percent distribution of black households by household income and age of householder, 2008; households in thousands as of 2009)

	total	15 to 24	25 to 34	35 to 44	45 to 54	55 to 64	65 or older total	65 to 74	75 or older
Black households	**15,056**	**1,019**	**2,865**	**3,240**	**3,212**	**2,365**	**2,356**	**1,354**	**1,002**
Under $5,000	899	161	195	153	153	131	106	55	51
$5,000 to $9,999	1,280	90	214	186	232	223	334	167	167
$10,000 to $14,999	1,254	114	198	182	163	220	379	178	200
$15,000 to $19,999	1,064	75	213	186	173	159	258	137	121
$20,000 to $24,999	1,115	76	230	232	208	156	213	149	65
$25,000 to $29,999	1,051	67	265	221	161	165	172	103	68
$30,000 to $34,999	967	81	211	231	186	127	130	78	52
$35,000 to $39,999	879	46	191	197	199	133	112	71	42
$40,000 to $44,999	832	55	164	175	164	141	133	87	45
$45,000 to $49,999	638	42	144	141	154	77	80	50	29
$50,000 to $54,999	697	38	112	178	183	105	80	51	29
$55,000 to $59,999	406	18	56	130	103	60	40	22	19
$60,000 to $64,999	528	27	90	123	140	91	55	27	28
$65,000 to $69,999	323	22	49	85	89	51	26	13	13
$70,000 to $74,999	367	12	73	95	96	57	36	21	15
$75,000 to $79,999	329	12	58	83	96	52	27	20	7
$80,000 to $84,999	283	16	49	66	97	38	17	10	7
$85,000 to $89,999	233	15	58	65	53	24	18	12	6
$90,000 to $94,999	209	11	52	60	40	33	14	11	3
$95,000 to $99,999	175	7	32	51	47	23	15	15	0
$100,000 or more	1,526	37	211	399	475	295	109	74	35
Median income	$34,345	$24,601	$32,096	$40,737	$43,616	$34,976	$22,167	$24,680	$17,790

PERCENT DISTRIBUTION

	total	15 to 24	25 to 34	35 to 44	45 to 54	55 to 64	65 or older total	65 to 74	75 or older
Black households	**100.0%**	**100.0%**	**100.0%**	**100.0%**	**100.0%**	**100.0%**	**100.0%**	**100.0%**	**100.0%**
Under $25,000	37.3	50.6	36.6	29.0	28.9	37.6	54.8	50.7	60.3
$25,000 to $49,999	29.0	28.6	34.0	29.8	26.9	27.2	26.6	28.7	23.6
$50,000 to $74,999	15.4	11.5	13.3	18.9	19.0	15.4	10.1	9.9	10.4
$75,000 to $99,999	8.2	6.0	8.7	10.0	10.4	7.2	3.9	5.0	2.3
$100,000 or more	10.1	3.6	7.4	12.3	14.8	12.5	4.6	5.5	3.5

Note: Blacks are those who identify themselves as being of the race alone and those who identify themselves as being of the race in combination with other races.
Source: Bureau of the Census, 2009 Current Population Survey, Internet site http://www.census.gov/hhes/www/cpstables/032009/hhinc/toc.htm; calculations by New Strategist

Table 6.24 Households by Income and Age of Householder, 2008: Hispanic Households

(number and percent distribution of Hispanic households by household income and age of householder, 2008; households in thousands as of 2009)

	total	15 to 24	25 to 34	35 to 44	45 to 54	55 to 64	65 or older total	65 to 74	75 or older
Hispanic households	**13,425**	**1,166**	**3,282**	**3,392**	**2,548**	**1,561**	**1,476**	**912**	**563**
Under $5,000	540	87	121	109	93	62	69	37	32
$5,000 to $9,999	714	60	141	115	101	100	196	106	89
$10,000 to $14,999	1,006	97	208	189	136	107	270	151	118
$15,000 to $19,999	949	110	252	213	137	90	148	85	63
$20,000 to $24,999	1,008	91	274	245	176	127	95	71	26
$25,000 to $29,999	915	112	223	217	155	88	121	70	51
$30,000 to $34,999	1,028	100	269	281	185	98	95	49	46
$35,000 to $39,999	821	92	206	228	135	84	75	54	22
$40,000 to $44,999	789	64	206	226	153	96	42	34	8
$45,000 to $49,999	592	38	161	139	140	58	55	34	22
$50,000 to $54,999	571	42	157	162	112	55	41	33	9
$55,000 to $59,999	474	53	119	116	87	60	41	28	13
$60,000 to $64,999	498	40	137	125	111	57	29	12	16
$65,000 to $69,999	376	33	96	100	83	42	22	18	4
$70,000 to $74,999	346	22	85	98	78	42	20	13	7
$75,000 to $79,999	319	25	75	93	71	37	19	17	2
$80,000 to $84,999	252	10	77	70	54	29	11	9	2
$85,000 to $89,999	235	11	44	84	50	33	12	6	5
$90,000 to $94,999	225	16	54	59	49	35	12	8	3
$95,000 to $99,999	201	12	54	53	34	32	15	9	6
$100,000 or more	1,566	51	321	471	409	229	85	67	18
Median income	$37,913	$30,907	$38,618	$41,938	$45,181	$41,035	$22,116	$25,426	$18,409

PERCENT DISTRIBUTION

	total	15 to 24	25 to 34	35 to 44	45 to 54	55 to 64	65 or older total	65 to 74	75 or older
Hispanic households	**100.0%**	**100.0%**	**100.0%**	**100.0%**	**100.0%**	**100.0%**	**100.0%**	**100.0%**	**100.0%**
Under $25,000	31.4	38.2	30.3	25.7	25.2	31.1	52.7	49.3	58.3
$25,000 to $49,999	30.9	34.8	32.4	32.2	30.1	27.2	26.3	26.4	26.5
$50,000 to $74,999	16.9	16.3	18.1	17.7	18.5	16.4	10.4	11.4	8.7
$75,000 to $99,999	9.2	6.3	9.3	10.6	10.1	10.6	4.7	5.4	3.2
$100,000 or more	11.7	4.4	9.8	13.9	16.1	14.7	5.8	7.3	3.2

Source: Bureau of the Census, 2009 Current Population Survey, Internet site http://www.census.gov/hhes/www/cpstables/032009/hhinc/toc.htm; calculations by New Strategist

Table 6.25 Households by Income and Age of Householder, 2008: Non-Hispanic White Households

(number and percent distribution of non-Hispanic white households by household income and age of householder, 2008; households in thousands as of 2009)

	total	15 to 24	25 to 34	35 to 44	45 to 54	55 to 64	65 or older total	65 to 74	75 or older
Non-Hispanic white households	**82,884**	**3,869**	**11,970**	**14,173**	**17,636**	**15,039**	**20,197**	**10,057**	**10,140**
Under $5,000	1,863	252	270	195	379	389	379	146	232
$5,000 to $9,999	2,631	194	243	248	426	467	1,053	406	646
$10,000 to $14,999	4,322	238	335	337	464	564	2,383	781	1,601
$15,000 to $19,999	4,484	307	427	398	534	554	2,265	748	1,516
$20,000 to $24,999	4,645	305	505	452	636	734	2,013	885	1,129
$25,000 to $29,999	4,257	342	548	491	571	649	1,656	727	930
$30,000 to $34,999	4,063	307	522	502	654	678	1,401	686	714
$35,000 to $39,999	4,049	282	731	518	671	613	1,232	583	649
$40,000 to $44,999	3,719	251	616	540	738	664	910	482	428
$45,000 to $49,999	3,403	193	603	532	711	582	781	430	352
$50,000 to $54,999	3,644	174	607	673	779	682	728	442	286
$55,000 to $59,999	3,028	142	622	584	634	525	521	339	182
$60,000 to $64,999	3,233	155	603	622	709	593	551	363	187
$65,000 to $69,999	2,721	91	533	573	636	488	401	264	137
$70,000 to $74,999	2,787	67	481	655	626	574	383	263	121
$75,000 to $79,999	2,565	84	481	553	606	427	414	267	147
$80,000 to $84,999	2,377	78	484	522	589	422	284	195	90
$85,000 to $89,999	2,152	62	364	451	561	425	289	196	93
$90,000 to $94,999	2,016	40	315	437	579	386	259	184	75
$95,000 to $99,999	1,689	45	261	380	479	330	194	149	44
$100,000 or more	19,235	259	2,418	4,509	5,656	4,294	2,099	1,519	579
Median income	$55,530	$34,800	$59,566	$72,520	$71,923	$63,196	$31,162	$40,633	$24,739

PERCENT DISTRIBUTION

	total	15 to 24	25 to 34	35 to 44	45 to 54	55 to 64	65 or older total	65 to 74	75 or older
Non-Hispanic white households	**100.0%**	**100.0%**	**100.0%**	**100.0%**	**100.0%**	**100.0%**	**100.0%**	**100.0%**	**100.0%**
Under $25,000	21.7	33.5	14.9	11.5	13.8	18.0	40.1	29.5	50.5
$25,000 to $49,999	23.5	35.5	25.2	18.2	19.0	21.2	29.6	28.9	30.3
$50,000 to $74,999	18.6	16.3	23.8	21.9	19.2	19.0	12.8	16.6	9.0
$75,000 to $99,999	13.0	8.0	15.9	16.5	16.0	13.2	7.1	9.9	4.4
$100,000 or more	23.2	6.7	20.2	31.8	32.1	28.6	10.4	15.1	5.7

Note: Non-Hispanic whites are those who identify themselves as being white alone and not Hispanic.
Source: Bureau of the Census, 2009 Current Population Survey, Internet site http://www.census.gov/hhes/www/ cpstables/032009/hhinc/toc.htm; calculations by New Strategist

Nearly One-Third of the Elderly Receive Pension Income

For younger Americans, most income is from wages or salaries.

The proportion of people with wage or salary income is as high as 89 percent in the 25-to-34 age group. It falls slowly with age to 67 percent in the 55-to-64 age group, then drops sharply to 18 percent among people aged 65 or older as labor force participation declines with retirement.

The proportion of Americans who receive property income (interest, dividends, rents, or royalties) rises with age to a peak of 58 percent in the 55-to-64 age group, reflecting the accumulation of assets. Thirty-one percent of people aged 65 or older receive pension income, and 89 percent receive Social Security.

Social security is by far the most important source of income for people aged 65 or older. It accounts for 65 percent of the total income received by the population aged 65 or older. For the 57 percent majority of the elderly, Social Security accounts for half or more of their income. Private pensions account for only 8 percent of the total income of the population aged 65 or older.

■ A growing share of the elderly will receive income from wages and salaries in the years ahead as labor force participation climbs in the older age groups.

The percentage of people who receive wage and salary income falls sharply in the older age groups

(percent of people who receive wage and salary income, by age, 2008)

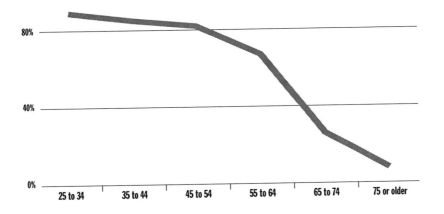

Table 6.26 Sources of Income by Age, 2008

(number and percent of total people aged 25 or older receiving income from specified source and median amount received, and percent receiving income by source and age, 2008; people in thousands as of 2009)

	total			percent receiving income by age				aged 65 or older		
	number receiving	percent receiving	median amount	25 to 34	35 to 44	45 to 54	55 to 64	total	65 to 74	75 or older
Total people	**184,796**	**100.0%**	**$30,186**	**100.0%**	**100.0%**	**100.0%**	**100.0%**	**100.0%**	**100.0%**	**100.0%**
Earnings	135,895	73.5	35,381	92.6	90.6	87.8	72.8	20.8	30.5	9.5
Wages and salary	127,028	68.7	35,805	89.3	85.4	81.7	66.5	17.9	26.2	8.1
Nonfarm self-employment	11,661	6.3	16,301	5.1	7.5	8.1	7.8	3.0	4.5	1.4
Farm self-employment	1,833	1.0	2,235	0.9	1.0	1.2	1.3	0.7	0.9	0.4
Social Security	42,079	22.8	11,992	1.9	3.3	5.1	17.4	88.8	85.1	93.1
SSI (Supplemental Security Income)	4,993	2.7	7,290	1.9	2.1	3.0	3.5	3.1	3.1	3.1
Public assistance	1,499	0.8	2,316	1.6	1.0	0.7	0.5	0.2	0.2	0.1
Veterans' benefits	2,698	1.5	8,946	0.4	0.6	1.0	2.5	2.9	2.3	3.7
Survivors' benefits	2,797	1.5	7,197	0.1	0.2	0.6	1.4	5.3	3.5	7.4
Disability benefits	1,489	0.8	9,082	0.4	0.5	1.0	1.7	0.5	0.7	0.3
Unemployment compensation	7,439	4.0	3,451	5.2	5.0	5.2	3.7	0.8	1.1	0.4
Workers' compensation	1,532	0.8	3,973	0.7	0.9	1.1	1.1	0.4	0.5	0.3
Property income	92,457	50.0	1,609	38.5	47.3	52.3	57.6	55.3	55.9	54.6
Interest	87,543	47.4	1,467	36.7	44.7	49.4	54.3	52.6	53.5	51.6
Dividends	27,582	14.9	1,619	8.1	13.4	16.1	19.5	18.0	18.6	17.4
Rents, royalties, estates, trusts	10,285	5.6	2,224	2.5	4.4	5.9	8.1	7.2	7.5	6.8
Retirement income	20,332	11.0	11,848	0.8	1.2	3.1	15.9	36.2	34.5	38.1
Pension income	16,794	9.1	12,458	0.2	0.7	1.9	13.2	31.3	31.0	31.7
Alimony	430	0.2	7,370	0.0	0.3	0.4	0.3	0.2	0.2	0.1
Child support	4,417	2.4	3,956	4.1	4.8	2.2	0.4	0.1	0.2	0.0
Educational assistance	3,073	1.7	3,526	5.2	1.7	0.9	0.3	0.1	0.1	0.0
Financial assistance from other household	1,555	0.8	3,062	1.4	0.9	0.8	0.7	0.5	0.4	0.7
Other income	903	0.5	2,790	0.4	0.3	0.6	0.6	0.6	0.6	0.5

Source: Bureau of the Census, 2009 Current Population Survey, Internet site http://www.census.gov/hhes/www/cpstables/032009/hhinc/toc.htm

Table 6.27 Relative Importance of Income Sources among the Population Aged 55 or Older, 2008

(total number of units aged 55 or older, percent of units' total income accounted for by source, percent of units for which source accounts for 50 percent or more of total income, and median income for recipients, by age, 2008; units in thousands as of 2009)

	55 to 61	62 to 64	aged 65 or older total	65 to 69	70 to 74	75 to 79	80+
Number of units	17,452	5,603	27,966	8,075	6,002	5,496	8,393
EARNINGS							
Proportion of total income, all units	74.1%	53.7%	14.6%	29.6%	15.4%	8.1%	3.8%
Proportion of total income, recipient units	88.6	77.9	54.5	60.9	49.6	43.4	47.6
Percent receiving at least half of total income from source	77.5	56.1	14.9	31.4	15.4	7.3	3.5
Median income from source, recipient units	$52,100	$45,000	$25,000	$33,000	$22,000	$14,360	$16,000
SOCIAL SECURITY							
Proportion of total income, all units	7.6%	22.5%	58.1%	44.9%	57.7%	63.1%	67.7%
Proportion of total income, recipient units	59.4	51.2	64.8	55.0	63.2	67.9	72.2
Percent receiving at least half of total income from source	7.1	19.7	57.2	41.0	56.1	63.5	69.5
Median income from source, recipient units	$12,425	$12,157	$14,966	$15,600	$15,557	$14,957	$14,045
GOVERNMENT EMPLOYEE PENSIONS							
Proportion of total income, all units	3.0%	6.0%	6.6%	6.3%	6.7%	6.8%	6.7%
Proportion of total income, recipient units	41.6	44.9	45.4	44.1	43.9	45.7	47.7
Percent receiving at least half of total income from source	2.3	5.0	6.1	5.8	5.7	6.3	6.6
Median income from source, recipient units	$22,884	$25,000	$19,044	$24,000	$19,200	$16,800	$15,915
PRIVATE PENSIONS AND ANNUITIES							
Proportion of total income, all units	3.3%	5.8%	8.2%	7.8%	8.4%	8.5%	8.4%
Proportion of total income, recipient units	39.8	33.6	28.3	28.1	28.4	27.9	28.8
Percent receiving at least half of total income from source	2.6	4.2	4.4	4.7	4.3	4.3	4.1
Median income from source, recipient units	$12,732	$13,200	$8,292	$10,800	$8,500	$7,260	$7,056
INCOME FROM ASSETS							
Proportion of total income, all units	4.6%	5.6%	7.9%	7.2%	7.4%	8.6%	8.4%
Proportion of total income, recipient units	8.1	9.6	14.2	12.3	13.4	15.6	15.7
Percent receiving at least half of total income from source	2.4	3.3	4.4	3.8	3.9	5.0	4.8
Median income from source, recipient units	$674	$762	$1,500	$1,500	$1,496	$1,500	$1,461

Note: "Units" are defined as married couples with at least one spouse aged 55 or older and nonmarried people aged 55 or older. Social Security includes retirement, survivor's, and disability benefits. Government pensions include federal, state, and local governments and military. Private pensions include company or union pensions, IRAs, and 401(k)s.
Source: Social Security Administration, Income of the Population 55 or Older, 2008, April 2010, Internet site http://www.ssa .gov/policy/docs/statcomps/income_pop55/

Poverty Has Grown among Adults of Working Age

The poverty rate has increased since 2000 in all but the oldest age group.

Between 1980 and 2008, the percentage of people who live below the poverty level remained essentially unchanged, inching up from 13.0 to 13.2 percent. The poverty rate of 2008, however, was well above the low of 11.3 percent reached in 2000.

The proportion of children who live in poverty climbed from a low of 16.2 percent in 2000 to 18.5 percent in 2008. The poverty rate among children in 2008 was slightly greater than their rate in 1980. Among Americans aged 65 or older, the poverty rate of 9.7 percent in 2008 was close to the record low of 9.4 percent achieved in 2006, and well below the 15.7 percent of 1980. Among the working-age population, the poverty rate of 11.7 percent in 2008 was substantially higher than the low of 9.6 percent reached in 2000 and above the 10.1 percent of 1980.

Females are more likely to be poor than males. In 2008, 14.4 percent of the nation's females were poor versus 12.0 percent of males. Among females, those aged 18 to 24 are most likely to be poor (21.2 percent). Among males, children have the highest poverty rate (18.8 percent).

■ The overall poverty rate rises and falls with the economy, but poverty within age groups also depends on social conditions such as the prevalence of single-parent families.

Poverty has increased among people aged 18 to 64 since 2000

(percent of people aged 18 to 64 who live below the poverty level, selected years 1980 to 2008)

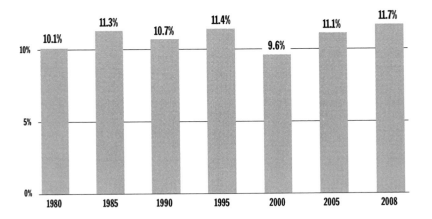

Table 6.28 Number and Percent of People below Poverty Level by Age, 1980 to 2008

(number and percent of people below poverty level by age, 1980 to 2008; people in thousands as of the following year)

	total people in poverty		under age 18		aged 18 to 64		aged 65 or older	
	number	percent	number	percent	number	percent	number	percent
2008	39,829	13.2%	13,507	18.5%	22,105	11.7%	3,656	9.7%
2007	37,276	12.5	12,802	17.6	20,396	10.9	3,556	9.7
2006	36,460	12.3	12,299	16.9	20,239	10.8	3,394	9.4
2005	36,950	12.6	12,896	17.6	20,450	11.1	3,603	10.1
2004	37,040	12.7	13,041	17.8	20,545	11.3	3,453	9.8
2003	35,861	12.5	12,866	17.6	19,443	10.8	3,552	10.2
2002	34,570	12.1	12,133	16.7	18,861	10.6	3,576	10.4
2001	32,907	11.7	11,733	16.3	17,760	10.1	3,414	10.1
2000	31,581	11.3	11,587	16.2	16,671	9.6	3,323	9.9
1999	32,791	11.9	12,280	17.1	17,289	10.1	3,222	9.7
1998	34,476	12.7	13,467	18.9	17,623	10.5	3,386	10.5
1997	35,574	13.3	14,113	19.9	18,085	10.9	3,376	10.5
1996	36,529	13.7	14,463	20.5	18,638	11.4	3,428	10.8
1995	36,425	13.8	14,665	20.8	18,442	11.4	3,318	10.5
1994	38,059	14.5	15,289	21.8	19,107	11.9	3,663	11.7
1993	39,265	15.1	15,727	22.7	19,781	12.4	3,755	12.2
1992	38,014	14.8	15,294	22.3	18,793	11.9	3,928	12.9
1991	35,708	14.2	14,341	21.8	17,586	11.4	3,781	12.4
1990	33,585	13.5	13,431	20.6	16,496	10.7	3,658	12.2
1989	31,528	12.8	12,590	19.6	15,575	10.2	3,363	11.4
1988	31,745	13.0	12,455	19.5	15,809	10.5	3,481	12.0
1987	32,221	13.4	12,843	20.3	15,815	10.6	3,563	12.5
1986	32,370	13.6	12,876	20.5	16,017	10.8	3,477	12.4
1985	33,064	14.0	13,010	20.7	16,598	11.3	3,456	12.6
1984	33,700	14.4	13,420	21.5	16,952	11.7	3,330	12.4
1983	35,303	15.2	13,911	22.3	17,767	12.4	3,625	13.8
1982	34,398	15.0	13,647	21.9	17,000	12.0	3,751	14.6
1981	31,822	14.0	12,505	20.0	15,464	11.1	3,853	15.3
1980	29,272	13.0	11,543	18.3	13,858	10.1	3,871	15.7

Source: Bureau of the Census, Current Population Surveys, Annual Social and Economic Supplement, Internet site http://www.census.gov/hhes/www/poverty/histpov/histpovtb.html

Table 6.29 People below Poverty Level by Age and Sex, 2008

(number and percent of people below poverty level by age and sex, 2008; numbers in thousands)

	total	females	males
Total people in poverty	**39,829**	**22,131**	**17,698**
Under age 18	14,068	6,941	7,127
Aged 18 to 64	22,105	12,626	9,479
Aged 18 to 24	5,283	3,007	2,276
Aged 25 to 34	5,351	3,286	2,065
Aged 35 to 44	4,277	2,470	1,807
Aged 45 to 54	4,047	2,167	1,880
Aged 55 to 59	1,642	888	754
Aged 60 to 64	1,504	807	697
Aged 65 or older	3,656	2,564	1,092
Aged 65 to 74	1,710	1,171	540
Aged 75 or older	1,945	1,393	552
PERCENT IN POVERTY			
Total people	**13.2%**	**14.4%**	**12.0%**
Under age 18	19.0	19.2	18.8
Aged 18 to 64	11.7	13.2	10.1
Aged 18 to 24	18.4	21.2	15.7
Aged 25 to 34	13.2	16.4	10.1
Aged 35 to 44	10.4	11.9	8.8
Aged 45 to 54	9.1	9.6	8.6
Aged 55 to 59	8.8	9.2	8.3
Aged 60 to 64	9.7	10.0	9.4
Aged 65 or older	9.7	11.9	6.7
Aged 65 to 74	8.4	10.6	5.7
Aged 75 or older	11.2	13.3	8.0

Source: Bureau of the Census, 2009 Current Population Survey, Annual Social and Economic Supplement, Internet site http://www.census.gov/hhes/www/cpstables/032009/pov/toc.htm; calculations by New Strategist

Black and Hispanic Children Are Most Likely to Be Poor

Middle-aged and older non-Hispanic whites are least likely to be poor.

Social Security benefits have substantially reduced poverty among the elderly, but the nation's young have no similar program to improve their socioeconomic condition. Overall, 19.0 percent of the nation's children are poor. The figure ranges from a low of 10.6 percent among non-Hispanic white children to a high of 33.9 percent among black children. Hispanic children are slightly less likely than black children to be poor, with a poverty rate of 30.6 percent.

Poverty bottoms out among non-Hispanic whites aged 65 to 74, at 6.2 percent in 2008. Among blacks and Hispanics in the age group, 17.7 percent are poor. Among Asians, the figure is 11.0 percent.

■ Lower educational attainment is one factor that contributes to the higher poverty rates among blacks and Hispanics.

Poverty is higher for black and Hispanic children

(percent of people under age 18 who live below poverty level, by race and Hispanic origin, 2008)

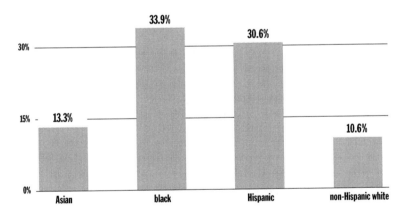

Table 6.30 People below Poverty Level by Age, Race, and Hispanic Origin, 2008

(number and percent of people below poverty level by age, race, and Hispanic origin, 2008; numbers in thousands)

	total	Asian	black	Hispanic	non-Hispanic white
Total in poverty	**39,829**	**1,686**	**9,882**	**10,987**	**17,024**
Under age 18	14,068	494	4,202	5,010	4,364
Aged 18 to 64	22,105	1,031	5,017	5,452	10,380
Aged 18 to 24	5,283	228	1,231	1,172	2,621
Aged 25 to 34	5,351	235	1,266	1,672	2,128
Aged 35 to 44	4,277	232	937	1,347	1,729
Aged 45 to 54	4,047	173	905	802	2,097
Aged 55 to 59	1,642	90	394	245	893
Aged 60 to 64	1,504	74	283	214	913
Aged 65 or older	3,656	162	663	525	2,280
Aged 65 to 74	1,710	85	337	288	978
Aged 75 or older	1,945	77	325	238	1,303
PERCENT IN POVERTY					
Total in poverty	**13.2%**	**11.6%**	**24.6%**	**23.2%**	**8.6%**
Under age 18	19.0	13.3	33.9	30.6	10.6
Aged 18 to 64	11.7	10.8	20.6	19.3	8.3
Aged 18 to 24	18.4	17.4	27.8	23.1	14.8
Aged 25 to 34	13.2	10.1	22.6	20.6	8.8
Aged 35 to 44	10.4	9.5	17.6	19.2	6.6
Aged 45 to 54	9.1	8.5	16.7	15.6	6.7
Aged 55 to 59	8.8	11.1	19.1	13.9	6.4
Aged 60 to 64	9.7	12.4	18.2	17.8	7.6
Aged 65 or older	9.7	12.3	20.0	19.3	7.6
Aged 65 to 74	8.4	11.0	17.7	17.7	6.2
Aged 75 or older	11.2	14.0	23.3	21.8	9.1

Note: Asians and blacks include those who identify themselves as being of the race alone and those who identify themselves as being of the race in combination with other races. Non-Hispanic whites are those who identify themselves as white alone and not Hispanic. Numbers do not add to total because not all races are shown and Hispanics may be of any race.
Source: Bureau of the Census, 2009 Current Population Survey Annual Social and Economic Supplement, Internet site http://www.census.gov/hhes/www/cpstables/032009/pov/toc.htm; calculations by New Strategist

Many Workers Cannot Keep Their Families Out of Poverty

The proportion is highest among the youngest and the oldest workers.

Among all workers aged 18 or older, 32 million—or 20 percent—do not earn enough to keep a family of four above the poverty level. The percentage of workers who earn wages below poverty level for a family of four is highest among young adults and the elderly. Thirty-one percent of workers aged 18 to 24 do not earn enough to keep a family of four out of poverty. The figure bottoms out at 14 percent among workers aged 45 to 54, then rises to 44 percent among workers aged 65 or older.

Among full-time workers, more than 12 million do not earn enough to keep a family of four above poverty level. The proportion is highest among 18-to-24-year-olds at 26 percent. The figure falls to a low of 9 percent among 45-to-54-year-olds, then rises in the older age groups. Among men who work full-time, 10 percent have earnings below the poverty level for a family of four.

■ For many families, it takes more than one full-time worker to stay out of poverty.

Many men who work full-time cannot support a family of four

(percent of men who work full-time and have earnings below poverty level for a family of four, by age, 2008)

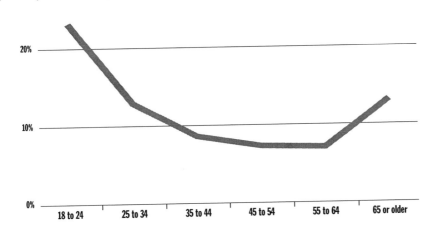

Table 6.31 Number and Percent of Workers below Poverty Level by Sex, Age, and Work Status, 2008

(number and percent of workers aged 18 or older below poverty threshold for a four-person family, by sex, age, and work status, 2008; numbers in thousands)

	all workers			full-time workers		
		earnings below poverty threshold for four-person family			earnings below poverty threshold for four-person family	
	total	number	percent	total	number	percent
Total workers	**158,317**	**31,774**	**20.1%**	**104,023**	**12,219**	**11.7%**
Aged 18 to 64	148,463	28,061	18.9	100,626	11,651	11.6
Aged 18 to 24	20,123	6,253	31.1	7,284	1,870	25.7
Aged 25 to 34	34,065	7,380	21.7	23,580	3,300	14.0
Aged 35 to 54	34,650	5,194	15.0	25,859	2,489	9.6
Aged 45 to 54	36,275	5,210	14.4	27,399	2,417	8.8
Aged 55 to 64	23,350	4,025	17.2	16,504	1,574	9.5
Aged 65 or older	7,625	3,364	44.1	3,298	549	16.6
Male workers	**83,889**	**15,090**	**18.0**	**59,869**	**6,096**	**10.2**
Aged 18 to 64	78,581	13,358	17.0	57,792	5,821	10.1
Aged 18 to 24	10,451	2,925	28.0	4,158	964	23.2
Aged 25 to 34	18,537	3,770	20.3	13,780	1,774	12.9
Aged 35 to 54	18,667	2,615	14.0	15,221	1,312	8.6
Aged 45 to 54	18,818	2,443	13.0	15,372	1,115	7.3
Aged 55 to 64	12,108	1,605	13.3	9,261	655	7.1
Aged 65 or older	4,185	1,552	37.1	2,023	266	13.2
Female workers	**74,428**	**16,684**	**22.4**	**44,154**	**6,123**	**13.9**
Aged 18 to 64	69,882	14,704	21.0	42,834	5,830	13.6
Aged 18 to 24	9,672	3,328	34.4	3,127	906	29.0
Aged 25 to 34	15,528	3,610	23.3	9,800	1,526	15.6
Aged 35 to 54	15,983	2,579	16.1	10,638	1,176	11.1
Aged 45 to 54	17,457	2,767	15.8	12,027	1,302	10.8
Aged 55 to 64	11,242	2,420	21.5	7,243	920	12.7
Aged 65 or older	3,440	1,811	52.6	1,275	283	22.2

Source: Bureau of the Census, 2009 Current Population Survey Annual Social and Economic Supplement, Internet site http://www.census.gov/hhes/www/cpstables/032009/pov/toc.htm; calculations by New Strategist

7

Labor Force

The labor force is changing rapidly as the Baby-Boom generation ages. The number of older workers will soar during the next decade, and labor force participation rates among people aged 55 or older will continue to climb.

As Boomers postpone retirement—thanks to the disappearance of defined-benefit pension plans and the Great Recession—it will be harder for Gen Xers and Millennials to move up the corporate ladder. The increase in job tenure and long-term employment among older men and women portends the struggle that lies ahead for younger generations as they try to achieve economic security.

What to expect in the future

■ The workforce will age rapidly during the next decade, creating competition between older and younger workers for the best jobs.

■ Older workers will cling to their jobs until they have replenished their retirement savings, slowing turnover in the labor force.

Men's Labor Force Participation Has Declined

Labor force participation has increased among older men, however.

The percentage of men in the labor force has declined substantially in every age group since 1950. The largest drop has been among men aged 65 or older, falling from 46 percent in 1950 to a low of 16 percent in 1990. Since 1990, however, the labor force participation of men aged 65 or older has increased, rising to 22 percent in 2009. Among men aged 55 to 64, labor force participation climbed from 67 to 70 percent between 2000 and 2009 as early retirement became less common.

Women's labor force participation increased in every age group between 1950 and 2009. Women ranging in age from 25 to 64 saw their labor force participation rate rise by more than 30 percentage points between 1950 and 2009 as working wives (and mothers) became the norm. Since 2000, however, the percentage of women in the labor force has fallen among those younger than age 55, in large part because of the recession. Rates are continuing to rise for older women, however.

■ The labor force participation rate of men and women aged 55 or older will continue to rise as Boomers postpone retirement.

The labor force participation rate of older men has increased

(percentage point change in labor force participation rate of men, by age, 2000 to 2009)

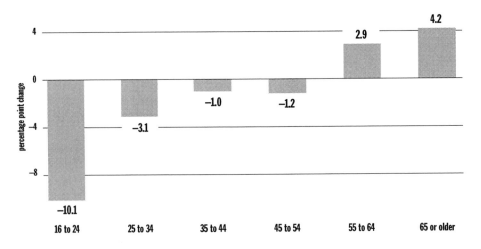

Table 7.1 Labor Force Participation Rate by Sex and Age, 1950 to 2009

(percent of people aged 16 or older in the civilian labor force by sex and age, and percentage point change, 1950–2009 and 2000–09)

| | | | | | | | | percentage point change | |
	2009	2000	1990	1980	1970	1960	1950	2000–09	1950–09
Total people	**65.4%**	**67.1%**	**66.4%**	**63.8%**	**60.4%**	**59.4%**	**59.2%**	**−1.7**	**6.2**
Aged 16 to 24	56.9	65.8	67.3	68.1	59.8	56.4	59.9	−8.9	−3.0
Aged 25 to 34	82.7	84.6	83.6	79.9	69.7	65.4	63.5	−1.9	19.2
Aged 35 to 44	83.7	84.8	85.2	80.0	73.1	69.4	67.5	−1.1	16.2
Aged 45 to 54	81.6	82.5	80.7	74.9	73.5	72.2	66.4	−0.9	15.2
Aged 55 to 64	64.9	59.2	55.9	55.7	61.8	60.9	56.7	5.7	8.2
Aged 65 or older	17.2	12.9	11.8	12.5	17.0	20.8	26.7	4.3	−9.5
Total men	**72.0**	**74.8**	**76.1**	**77.4**	**79.7**	**83.3**	**86.4**	**−2.8**	**−14.4**
Aged 16 to 24	58.5	68.6	71.5	74.4	69.4	71.7	77.3	−10.1	−18.8
Aged 25 to 34	90.3	93.4	94.2	95.2	96.4	97.5	96.0	−3.1	−5.7
Aged 35 to 44	91.7	92.7	94.4	95.5	96.8	97.7	97.6	−1.0	−5.9
Aged 45 to 54	87.4	88.6	90.7	91.2	94.3	95.7	95.8	−1.2	−8.4
Aged 55 to 64	70.2	67.3	67.7	72.1	83.0	87.3	86.9	2.9	−16.7
Aged 65 or older	21.9	17.7	16.4	19.0	26.8	33.1	45.8	4.2	−23.9
Total women	**59.2**	**59.9**	**57.5**	**51.5**	**43.3**	**37.7**	**33.9**	**−0.7**	**25.3**
Aged 16 to 24	55.2	63.0	63.1	61.9	51.3	42.8	43.9	−7.8	11.3
Aged 25 to 34	75.0	76.1	73.6	65.5	45.0	36.0	34.0	−1.1	41.0
Aged 35 to 44	75.9	77.2	76.5	65.5	51.1	43.4	39.1	−1.3	36.8
Aged 45 to 54	76.0	76.8	71.2	59.9	54.4	49.9	37.9	−0.8	38.1
Aged 55 to 64	60.0	51.9	45.3	41.3	43.0	37.2	27.0	8.1	33.0
Aged 65 or older	13.6	9.4	8.7	8.1	9.7	10.8	9.7	4.2	3.9

Source: Bureau of Labor Statistics, Labor Force Statistics from the Current Population Survey, Internet site http://www.bls .gov/cps/tables.htm#empstat; and Monthly Labor Review, December 1999; calculations by New Strategist

Men in Their Thirties Are Most Likely to Work

Among women, those in their forties have the highest labor force participation.

Between the ages of 30 and 44, more than 90 percent of men are in the labor force. Labor force participation peaks among men in their thirties at 92 percent. Labor force participation peaks among women in the 40-to-49 age group at 77 percent.

For men, labor force participation begins to fall rapidly after age 55. Many older men opt for early retirement, if they can afford it, although some leave the labor force because they are disabled or after a layoff. Only 78 percent of men aged 55 to 59 are working or looking for work—8 percentage points less than the rate among men aged 50 to 54. Among men aged 60 to 64, only 61 percent are still in the labor force.

Women's labor force participation also declines after age 55. Sixty-eight percent of women aged 55 to 59 are in the labor force, a figure that drops to 50 percent among women aged 60 to 64.

■ Many Boomers will work longer than their parents because they lost a large portion of their retirement savings during the Great Recession.

Women's labor force participation peaks in the 40-to-49 age group

(labor force participation rate of women, by age, 2009)

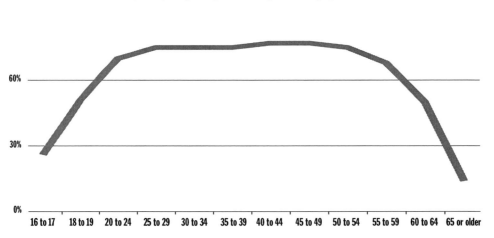

Table 7.2 Employment Status by Sex and Age, 2009

(number and percent of people aged 16 or older in the civilian labor force by sex, age, and employment status, 2009; numbers in thousands)

	civilian noninstitutional population	civilian labor force			unemployed	
		total	percent of population	employed	number	percent of labor force
Total people	**235,801**	**154,142**	**65.4%**	**139,877**	**14,265**	**9.3%**
Aged 16 to 17	8,944	2,227	24.9	1,651	576	25.9
Aged 18 to 19	8,100	4,163	51.4	3,187	976	23.4
Aged 20 to 24	20,524	14,971	72.9	12,764	2,207	14.7
Aged 25 to 29	20,872	17,138	82.1	15,315	1,822	10.6
Aged 30 to 34	19,408	16,160	83.3	14,699	1,461	9.0
Aged 35 to 39	20,174	16,868	83.6	15,486	1,382	8.2
Aged 40 to 44	20,746	17,370	83.7	16,031	1,340	7.7
Aged 45 to 49	22,683	18,803	82.9	17,455	1,347	7.2
Aged 50 to 54	21,682	17,402	80.3	16,158	1,245	7.2
Aged 55 to 59	18,882	13,799	73.1	12,887	913	6.6
Aged 60 to 64	15,789	8,706	55.1	8,132	574	6.6
Aged 65 or older	37,998	6,534	17.2	6,114	421	6.4
Aged 65 to 69	11,657	3,629	31.1	3,380	249	6.8
Aged 70 to 74	8,875	1,635	18.4	1,535	100	6.1
Aged 75 or older	17,466	1,271	7.3	1,199	72	5.7
Total men	**114,136**	**82,123**	**72.0**	**73,670**	**8,453**	**10.3**
Aged 16 to 17	4,548	1,103	24.3	786	317	28.7
Aged 18 to 19	4,095	2,123	51.9	1,543	581	27.4
Aged 20 to 24	10,284	7,839	76.2	6,510	1,329	17.0
Aged 25 to 29	10,492	9,328	88.9	8,218	1,110	11.9
Aged 30 to 34	9,675	8,883	91.8	8,005	878	9.9
Aged 35 to 39	9,963	9,215	92.5	8,414	802	8.7
Aged 40 to 44	10,235	9,303	90.9	8,504	799	8.6
Aged 45 to 49	11,136	9,879	88.7	9,071	808	8.2
Aged 50 to 54	10,596	9,121	86.1	8,371	750	8.2
Aged 55 to 59	9,125	7,121	78.0	6,608	514	7.2
Aged 60 to 64	7,572	4,608	60.9	4,283	326	7.1
Aged 65 or older	16,414	3,598	21.9	3,357	241	6.7
Aged 65 to 69	5,448	1,975	36.3	1,829	147	7.4
Aged 70 to 74	4,022	907	22.5	849	57	6.3
Aged 75 or older	6,944	716	10.3	679	37	5.1

	civilian noninstitutional population	civilian labor force			unemployed	
		total	percent of population	employed	number	percent of labor force
Total women	**121,665**	**72,019**	**59.2%**	**66,208**	**5,811**	**8.1%**
Aged 16 to 17	4,396	1,124	25.6	865	259	23.1
Aged 18 to 19	4,004	2,039	50.9	1,644	395	19.4
Aged 20 to 24	10,240	7,132	69.6	6,254	878	12.3
Aged 25 to 29	10,381	7,810	75.2	7,097	713	9.1
Aged 30 to 34	9,733	7,277	74.8	6,694	583	8.0
Aged 35 to 39	10,210	7,653	75.0	7,072	581	7.6
Aged 40 to 44	10,510	8,067	76.8	7,527	541	6.7
Aged 45 to 49	11,547	8,923	77.3	8,384	539	6.0
Aged 50 to 54	11,087	8,281	74.7	7,786	495	6.0
Aged 55 to 59	9,756	6,678	68.4	6,279	399	6.0
Aged 60 to 64	8,217	4,098	49.9	3,849	249	6.1
Aged 65 or older	21,584	2,937	13.6	2,757	180	6.1
Aged 65 to 69	6,209	1,654	26.6	1,552	102	6.2
Aged 70 to 74	4,853	728	15.0	685	43	5.8
Aged 75 or older	10,522	555	5.3	520	35	6.4

Note: The civilian labor force equals the number of the employed plus the number of the unemployed. The civilian population equals the number in the labor force plus the number not in the labor force.
Source: Bureau of Labor Statistics, Labor Force Statistics from the Current Population Survey, Internet site http://www.bls .gov/cps/tables.htm#empstat

Boomers Are the Largest Share of the Workforce

But the dominance of Boomers is on the wane as they approach retirement age.

More than one-third (37 percent) of today's workers are Baby Boomers, aged 45 to 63 in 2009. Millennials (under age 33) make up 31 percent of the labor force and are the second-largest generation at work. Generation X (aged 33 to 44) accounts for a smaller 26 percent share of workers. Americans aged 64 or older (the Swing and World War II generations) make up only 5 percent of workers. The age distribution of men and women in the labor force is nearly identical.

The Baby Boom's share of workers is declining as the oldest members of the generation reach the age of early retirement. The Millennial generation's share of the workforce is rising rapidly and will surpass the Boomer share in a few years.

■ Generation X may find promotions more plentiful when Boomers retire.

Swing and World War II generations account for few workers

(percent distribution of the labor force by generation, 2009)

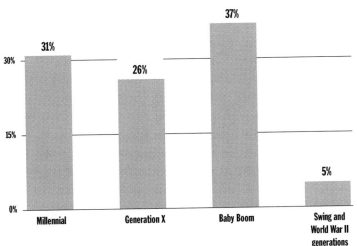

Table 7.3 Distribution of the Labor Force by Age, Generation, and Sex, 2009

(number and percent distribution of people aged 16 or older in the civilian labor force by age, generation, and sex, 2009; numbers in thousands)

	total in labor force		men in labor force		women in labor force	
	number	percent distribution	number	percent distribution	number	percent distribution
Total people	**154,142**	**100.0%**	**82,123**	**100.0%**	**72,019**	**100.0%**
Aged 16 to 17	2,227	1.4	1,103	1.3	1,124	1.6
Aged 18 to 19	4,163	2.7	2,123	2.6	2,039	2.8
Aged 20 to 24	14,971	9.7	7,839	9.5	7,132	9.9
Aged 25 to 29	17,138	11.1	9,328	11.4	7,810	10.8
Aged 30 to 34	16,160	10.5	8,883	10.8	7,277	10.1
Aged 35 to 39	16,868	10.9	9,215	11.2	7,653	10.6
Aged 40 to 44	17,370	11.3	9,303	11.3	8,067	11.2
Aged 45 to 49	18,803	12.2	9,879	12.0	8,923	12.4
Aged 50 to 54	17,402	11.3	9,121	11.1	8,281	11.5
Aged 55 to 59	13,799	9.0	7,121	8.7	6,678	9.3
Aged 60 to 64	8,706	5.6	4,608	5.6	4,098	5.7
Aged 65 or older	6,534	4.2	3,598	4.4	2,937	4.1
LABOR FORCE BY GENERATION						
Total people	**154,142**	**100.0**	**82,123**	**100.0**	**72,019**	**100.0**
Millennial (16 to 32)	48,195	31.3	25,723	31.3	22,471	31.2
Generation X (33 to 44)	40,702	26.4	22,071	26.9	18,631	25.9
Baby Boom (45 to 63)	56,969	37.0	29,807	36.3	27,160	37.7
Swing and World War II (64 or older)	8,275	5.4	4,520	5.5	3,757	5.2

Note: Labor force by generation are estimates by New Strategist.
*Source: Bureau of Labor Statistics, Labor Force Statistics from the Current Population Survey, Internet site http://www.bls
.gov/cps/tables.htm#empstat*

Millennials Are Most Likely to Be Unemployed

Unemployment rate exceeds 20 percent among teenagers.

Unemployment has increased sharply because of the Great Recession, peaking among teenagers aged 16 to 17 at 25.9 percent in 2009. By generation, Millennials are most likely to be unemployed, with an unemployment rate of 13.4 percent. Unemployment falls with advancing age. Only 7.0 percent of Boomers and an even smaller 6.5 percent of the Swing and World War II generations are unemployed.

Millennials account for the largest share (45 percent) of the 14 million unemployed in 2009. Boomers and Gen Xers together account for the 51 percent majority of those who are looking for a job.

■ The high unemployment rate among young adults is forcing many to live in their parents' home while they look for work.

Unemployment falls with advancing age

(percent unemployed by generation, 2009)

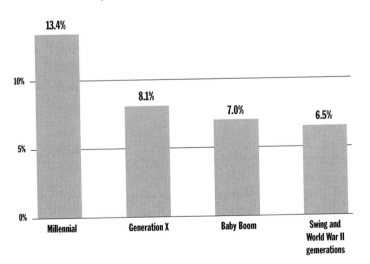

Table 7.4 Unemployment Rate by Age and Generation, 2009

(total number of people in the civilian labor force, and number and percent who are unemployed, by age and generation, 2009; numbers in thousands)

	total labor force	unemployed number	unemployed percent
Total	**154,142**	**14,265**	**9.3%**
Aged 16 to 17	2,227	576	25.9
Aged 18 to 19	4,163	976	23.4
Aged 20 to 24	14,971	2,207	14.7
Aged 25 to 29	17,138	1,822	10.6
Aged 30 to 34	16,160	1,461	9.0
Aged 35 to 39	16,868	1,382	8.2
Aged 40 to 44	17,370	1,340	7.7
Aged 45 to 49	18,803	1,347	7.2
Aged 50 to 54	17,402	1,245	7.2
Aged 55 to 59	13,799	913	6.6
Aged 60 to 64	8,706	574	6.6
Aged 65 or older	6,534	421	6.4
UNEMPLOYED BY GENERATION			
Total people	**154,142**	**14,265**	**9.3**
Millennial (16 to 32)	48,195	6,458	13.4
Generation X (33 to 44)	40,702	3,306	8.1
Baby Boom (45 to 63)	56,969	3,964	7.0
Swing and World War II (64 or older)	8,275	536	6.5

Note: Unemployed by generation are estimates by New Strategist.
*Source: Bureau of Labor Statistics, Labor Force Statistics from the Current Population Survey, Internet site http://www.bls
.gov/cps/tables.htm#empstat*

Table 7.5 Distribution of the Unemployed by Age and Generation, 2009

(number and percent distribution of unemployed people aged 16 or older by age and generation, 2009; numbers in thousands)

	number	percent distribution
Total unemployed	**14,265**	**100.0%**
Aged 16 to 17	576	4.0
Aged 18 to 19	976	6.8
Aged 20 to 24	2,207	15.5
Aged 25 to 29	1,822	12.8
Aged 30 to 34	1,461	10.2
Aged 35 to 39	1,382	9.7
Aged 40 to 44	1,340	9.4
Aged 45 to 49	1,347	9.4
Aged 50 to 54	1,245	8.7
Aged 55 to 59	913	6.4
Aged 60 to 64	574	4.0
Aged 65 or older	421	3.0
UNEMPLOYED BY GENERATION		
Total people	**14,265**	**100.0**
Millennial (16 to 32)	6,458	45.3
Generation X (33 to 44)	3,306	23.2
Baby Boom (45 to 63)	3,964	27.8
Swing and World War II (64 or older)	536	3.8

Note: Unemployed by generation are estimates by New Strategist.
Source: Bureau of Labor Statistics, Labor Force Statistics from the Current Population Survey, Internet site http://www.bls .gov/cps/tables.htm#empstat

Hispanic Women Are Least Likely to Work

Hispanic men have the highest labor force participation rate.

Women are less likely than men to be in the labor force, but the gap between men's and women's labor force participation rate varies by age, race, and Hispanic origin. The largest gap by gender is found between Hispanic men and women, with 79 percent of men and only 57 percent of women in the labor force.

Hispanic men have a higher overall labor force participation rate than Asian, black, or white men (79 percent versus 75, 65, and 73 percent, respectively). Hispanic men have a higher labor force participation rate than white men because the Hispanic population is younger and less likely to be retired. They have a higher participation rate than Asian men because young Hispanic men are much less likely to be in school.

Unemployment is highest among young black men, with a stunning 46.0 percent of those aged 16 to 19 looking for work. Among men in their peak-earning years (aged 45 to 54), the unemployment rate ranges from lows of 7.6 and 7.7 percent among Asians and whites, respectively, to highs of 10.5 and 12.4 percent among Hispanics and blacks.

■ The Great Recession has hurt blacks and Hispanics more than Asians and whites.

In most age groups, unemployment is highest among black men

(percent of men aged 45 to 54 who are unemployed, by race and Hispanic origin, 2009)

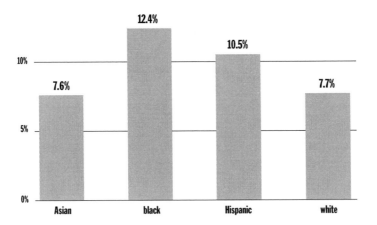

Table 7.6 Labor Force Participation Rate by Race, Hispanic Origin, Age, and Sex, 2009

(percent of people aged 16 or older in the civilian labor force, by race, Hispanic origin, age, and sex, 2009)

	percent in labor force		
	total	men	women
Total Asians	**66.0%**	**74.6%**	**58.2%**
Aged 16 to 19	20.8	23.8	17.4
Aged 20 to 24	56.7	60.2	53.4
Aged 25 to 34	78.4	88.3	69.0
Aged 35 to 44	82.4	93.6	71.9
Aged 45 to 54	83.6	92.3	75.7
Aged 55 to 64	66.7	74.3	60.2
Aged 65 or older	17.0	22.4	12.9
Total blacks	**62.4**	**65.0**	**60.3**
Aged 16 to 19	27.2	26.4	27.9
Aged 20 to 24	66.0	67.6	64.5
Aged 25 to 34	80.4	83.2	78.0
Aged 35 to 44	81.7	85.1	79.0
Aged 45 to 54	75.2	77.4	73.3
Aged 55 to 64	55.5	56.8	54.4
Aged 65 or older	15.3	18.3	13.3
Total Hispanics	**68.0**	**78.8**	**56.5**
Aged 16 to 19	34.0	36.4	31.6
Aged 20 to 24	73.1	82.3	63.2
Aged 25 to 34	79.5	91.9	64.7
Aged 35 to 44	81.3	93.0	68.2
Aged 45 to 54	79.3	88.8	69.4
Aged 55 to 64	61.9	71.7	52.6
Aged 65 or older	17.1	23.0	12.7
Total whites	**65.8**	**72.8**	**59.1**
Aged 16 to 19	40.6	40.3	40.9
Aged 20 to 24	75.1	78.6	71.6
Aged 25 to 34	83.5	91.6	75.1
Aged 35 to 44	84.2	92.7	75.7
Aged 45 to 54	82.7	88.8	76.7
Aged 55 to 64	66.2	71.8	60.8
Aged 65 or older	17.4	22.2	13.6

Source: Bureau of Labor Statistics, Labor Force Statistics from the Current Population Survey, Internet site http://www.bls .gov/cps/tables.htm#empstat

Table 7.7 Unemployment Rate by Race, Hispanic Origin, Age, and Sex, 2009

(percent of people aged 16 or older who are unemployed, by race, Hispanic origin, age, and sex, 2009)

	percent unemployed		
	total	men	women
Total Asians	**7.3%**	**7.9%**	**6.6%**
Aged 16 to 19	26.4	26.8	25.8
Aged 20 to 24	11.8	12.3	11.3
Aged 25 to 34	6.8	7.0	6.6
Aged 35 to 44	6.6	7.0	6.2
Aged 45 to 54	6.3	7.6	4.9
Aged 55 to 64	6.7	7.3	6.1
Aged 65 or older	5.5	7.1	3.3
Total blacks	**14.8**	**17.5**	**12.4**
Aged 16 to 19	39.5	46.0	33.4
Aged 20 to 24	24.9	27.7	22.2
Aged 25 to 34	16.7	19.9	13.8
Aged 35 to 44	11.7	14.0	9.7
Aged 45 to 54	10.4	12.4	8.7
Aged 55 to 64	8.4	10.1	7.1
Aged 65 or older	8.5	10.6	6.6
Total Hispanics	**12.1**	**12.5**	**11.5**
Aged 16 to 19	30.2	33.8	25.8
Aged 20 to 24	16.2	16.6	15.7
Aged 25 to 34	11.4	11.6	10.9
Aged 35 to 44	10.2	10.5	9.7
Aged 45 to 54	10.1	10.5	9.6
Aged 55 to 64	10.0	11.2	8.5
Aged 65 or older	8.0	7.8	8.3
Total whites	**8.5**	**9.4**	**7.3**
Aged 16 to 19	21.8	25.2	18.4
Aged 20 to 24	13.0	15.3	10.4
Aged 25 to 34	8.8	9.8	7.6
Aged 35 to 44	7.4	8.0	6.7
Aged 45 to 54	6.7	7.7	5.6
Aged 55 to 64	6.4	6.8	5.8
Aged 65 or older	6.2	6.3	6.0

Source: Bureau of Labor Statistics, Labor Force Statistics from the Current Population Survey, Internet site http://www.bls
.gov/cps/tables.htm#empstat

The Middle Aged Are Professionals, Managers

Young workers are most often in sales or service jobs.

Thirty-seven percent of American workers are in management or professional occupations. This category includes the highest-paying jobs in the country such as physician, lawyer, accountant, and corporate vice president.

Young adults start out in entry-level jobs—selling hamburgers at a fast-food restaurant or working at a construction site, for example. As they gain more experience with age, many move into professional or management positions. Among 16-to-19-year-olds in the labor force, 41 percent are employed in a service occupation, according to the Bureau of Labor Statistics. The proportion of Americans employed in service occupations falls with age to a low of 13 percent among 55-to-64-year-olds. Forty-one to 43 percent of workers aged 35 to 64 are employed as managers or professionals versus just 6 percent of 16-to-19-year-olds and 21 percent of 20-to-24-year-olds.

Although only 13 percent of the nation's workers are under age 25, a much larger 39 percent of food service workers are in the under-25 age group. Only 23 percent of food service workers are aged 45 or older.

■ Among workers employed in computer and mathematical jobs, a substantial 30 percent are in the youthful 25-to-34 age group.

Most managers and professionals are aged 35 to 54

(percent distribution of workers in management and professional occupations, by age, 2009)

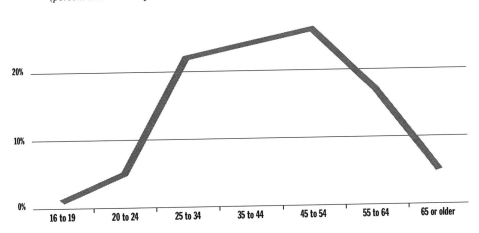

Table 7.8 Occupations by Age, 2009

(number of employed people aged 16 or older by occupation and age, 2009; numbers in thousands)

	total	16 to 19	20 to 24	25 to 34	35 to 44	45 to 54	55 to 64	65 or older
TOTAL EMPLOYED	139,877	4,837	12,764	30,014	31,517	33,613	21,019	6,114
Management and professional occupations	**52,219**	**303**	**2,679**	**11,407**	**12,773**	**13,625**	**8,954**	**2,477**
Management, business and financial operations	21,529	58	789	3,976	5,398	6,123	3,974	1,211
Management	15,447	43	465	2,519	3,918	4,573	2,985	946
Business and financial operations	6,082	16	325	1,457	1,480	1,550	988	266
Professional and related occupations	30,690	245	1,890	7,431	7,375	7,502	4,980	1,266
Computer and mathematical	3,481	15	194	1,045	997	835	339	54
Architecture and engineering	2,740	6	155	635	652	777	418	98
Life, physical, and social sciences	1,328	5	87	358	320	290	207	60
Community and social services	2,341	22	121	547	544	542	421	144
Legal	1,710	4	51	366	432	421	329	108
Education, training, and library	8,627	95	632	2,018	1,910	1,977	1,645	350
Art, design, entertainment, sports, and media	2,724	68	246	672	620	588	379	150
Health care practitioner, technical occupations	7,738	30	402	1,790	1,901	2,071	1,242	302
Service occupations	**24,598**	**2,005**	**3,629**	**5,400**	**4,916**	**4,816**	**2,832**	**1,000**
Health care support	3,309	83	455	827	729	678	428	110
Protective service	3,164	117	293	726	837	674	381	135
Food preparation and serving related	7,733	1,296	1,735	1,754	1,183	1,081	482	200
Building and grounds cleaning and maintenance	5,349	213	447	1,029	1,146	1,367	861	286
Personal care and service	5,043	295	700	1,063	1,020	1,016	681	269
Sales and office occupations	**33,787**	**1,716**	**3,912**	**6,809**	**6,851**	**7,654**	**5,222**	**1,623**
Sales and related	15,641	1,150	1,938	3,091	3,085	3,324	2,229	824
Office and administrative support	18,146	566	1,974	3,718	3,766	4,330	2,993	799
Natural resources, construction, and maintenance occupations	**13,323**	**336**	**1,188**	**3,229**	**3,223**	**3,344**	**1,649**	**354**
Farming, fishing, and forestry	926	106	116	203	171	183	115	32
Construction and extraction	7,439	143	641	1,955	1,861	1,801	867	171
Installation, maintenance, and repair	4,957	87	431	1,071	1,190	1,360	667	151
Production, transportation, and material-moving occupations	**15,951**	**477**	**1,356**	**3,169**	**3,754**	**4,174**	**2,361**	**660**
Production	7,654	134	612	1,522	1,873	2,124	1,149	240
Transportation and material moving	8,297	343	744	1,648	1,881	2,050	1,212	420

Source: Bureau of Labor Statistics, unpublished data from the 2009 Current Population Survey

Table 7.9 Distribution of Workers by Occupation and Age, 2009

(percent distribution of employed people aged 16 or older by occupation, by age, 2009)

	total	16 to 19	20 to 24	25 to 34	35 to 44	45 to 54	55 to 64	65 or older
TOTAL EMPLOYED	100.0%	100.0%	100.0%	100.0%	100.0%	100.0%	100.0%	100.0%
Management and professional occupations	**37.3**	**6.3**	**21.0**	**38.0**	**40.5**	**40.5**	**42.6**	**40.5**
Management, business and financial operations	15.4	1.2	6.2	13.2	17.1	18.2	18.9	19.8
Management	11.0	0.9	3.6	8.4	12.4	13.6	14.2	15.5
Business and financial operations	4.3	0.3	2.5	4.9	4.7	4.6	4.7	4.4
Professional and related occupations	21.9	5.1	14.8	24.8	23.4	22.3	23.7	20.7
Computer and mathematical	2.5	0.3	1.5	3.5	3.2	2.5	1.6	0.9
Architecture and engineering	2.0	0.1	1.2	2.1	2.1	2.3	2.0	1.6
Life, physical, and social sciences	0.9	0.1	0.7	1.2	1.0	0.9	1.0	1.0
Community and social services	1.7	0.5	0.9	1.8	1.7	1.6	2.0	2.4
Legal	1.2	0.1	0.4	1.2	1.4	1.3	1.6	1.8
Education, training, and library	6.2	2.0	5.0	6.7	6.1	5.9	7.8	5.7
Art, design, entertainment, sports, and media	1.9	1.4	1.9	2.2	2.0	1.7	1.8	2.5
Health care practitioner, technical occupations	5.5	0.6	3.1	6.0	6.0	6.2	5.9	4.9
Service occupations	**17.6**	**41.5**	**28.4**	**18.0**	**15.6**	**14.3**	**13.5**	**16.4**
Health care support	2.4	1.7	3.6	2.8	2.3	2.0	2.0	1.8
Protective service	2.3	2.4	2.3	2.4	2.7	2.0	1.8	2.2
Food preparation and serving related	5.5	26.8	13.6	5.8	3.8	3.2	2.3	3.3
Building and grounds cleaning and maintenance	3.8	4.4	3.5	3.4	3.6	4.1	4.1	4.7
Personal care and service	3.6	6.1	5.5	3.5	3.2	3.0	3.2	4.4
Sales and office occupations	**24.2**	**35.5**	**30.6**	**22.7**	**21.7**	**22.8**	**24.8**	**26.5**
Sales and related	11.2	23.8	15.2	10.3	9.8	9.9	10.6	13.5
Office and administrative support	13.0	11.7	15.5	12.4	11.9	12.9	14.2	13.1
Natural resources, construction, and maintenance occupations	**9.5**	**6.9**	**9.3**	**10.8**	**10.2**	**9.9**	**7.8**	**5.8**
Farming, fishing, and forestry	0.7	2.2	0.9	0.7	0.5	0.5	0.5	0.5
Construction and extraction	5.3	3.0	5.0	6.5	5.9	5.4	4.1	2.8
Installation, maintenance, and repair	3.5	1.8	3.4	3.6	3.8	4.0	3.2	2.5
Production, transportation, and material-moving occupations	**11.4**	**9.9**	**10.6**	**10.6**	**11.9**	**12.4**	**11.2**	**10.8**
Production	5.5	2.8	4.8	5.1	5.9	6.3	5.5	3.9
Transportation and material moving	5.9	7.1	5.8	5.5	6.0	6.1	5.8	6.9

Source: Bureau of Labor Statistics, unpublished data from the 2009 Current Population Survey; calculations by New Strategist

Table 7.10 Age Distribution of Workers by Occupation, 2009

(percent distribution of employed people aged 16 or older by age, by occupation, 2009)

	total	16 to 19	20 to 24	25 to 34	35 to 44	45 to 54	55 to 64	65 or older
TOTAL EMPLOYED	**100.0%**	**3.5%**	**9.1%**	**21.5%**	**22.5%**	**24.0%**	**15.0%**	**4.4%**
Management and professional occupations	**100.0**	**0.6**	**5.1**	**21.8**	**24.5**	**26.1**	**17.1**	**4.7**
Management, business and financial operations	100.0	0.3	3.7	18.5	25.1	28.4	18.5	5.6
Management	100.0	0.3	3.0	16.3	25.4	29.6	19.3	6.1
Business and financial operations	100.0	0.3	5.3	24.0	24.3	25.5	16.2	4.4
Professional and related occupations	100.0	0.8	6.2	24.2	24.0	24.4	16.2	4.1
Computer and mathematical	100.0	0.4	5.6	30.0	28.6	24.0	9.7	1.6
Architecture and engineering	100.0	0.2	5.7	23.2	23.8	28.4	15.3	3.6
Life, physical, and social sciences	100.0	0.4	6.6	27.0	24.1	21.8	15.6	4.5
Community and social services	100.0	0.9	5.2	23.4	23.2	23.2	18.0	6.2
Legal	100.0	0.2	3.0	21.4	25.3	24.6	19.2	6.3
Education, training, and library	100.0	1.1	7.3	23.4	22.1	22.9	19.1	4.1
Art, design, entertainment, sports, and media	100.0	2.5	9.0	24.7	22.8	21.6	13.9	5.5
Health care practitioner, technical occupations	100.0	0.4	5.2	23.1	24.6	26.8	16.1	3.9
Service occupations	**100.0**	**8.2**	**14.8**	**22.0**	**20.0**	**19.6**	**11.5**	**4.1**
Health care support	100.0	2.5	13.8	25.0	22.0	20.5	12.9	3.3
Protective service	100.0	3.7	9.3	22.9	26.5	21.3	12.0	4.3
Food preparation and serving related	100.0	16.8	22.4	22.7	15.3	14.0	6.2	2.6
Building and grounds cleaning and maintenance	100.0	4.0	8.4	19.2	21.4	25.6	16.1	5.3
Personal care and service	100.0	5.8	13.9	21.1	20.2	20.1	13.5	5.3
Sales and office occupations	**100.0**	**5.1**	**11.6**	**20.2**	**20.3**	**22.7**	**15.5**	**4.8**
Sales and related	100.0	7.4	12.4	19.8	19.7	21.3	14.3	5.3
Office and administrative support	100.0	3.1	10.9	20.5	20.8	23.9	16.5	4.4
Natural resources, construction, and maintenance occupations	**100.0**	**2.5**	**8.9**	**24.2**	**24.2**	**25.1**	**12.4**	**2.7**
Farming, fishing, and forestry	100.0	11.4	12.5	21.9	18.5	19.8	12.4	3.5
Construction and extraction	100.0	1.9	8.6	26.3	25.0	24.2	11.7	2.3
Installation, maintenance, and repair	100.0	1.8	8.7	21.6	24.0	27.4	13.5	3.0
Production, transportation, and material-moving occupations	**100.0**	**3.0**	**8.5**	**19.9**	**23.5**	**26.2**	**14.8**	**4.1**
Production	100.0	1.8	8.0	19.9	24.5	27.8	15.0	3.1
Transportation and material moving	100.0	4.1	9.0	19.9	22.7	24.7	14.6	5.1

Source: Bureau of Labor Statistics, unpublished data from the 2009 Current Population Survey; calculations by New Strategist

Most of the Middle Aged Work Full-Time

Part-time employment is more common among young and old.

There are sharp differences in who works part-time by age. While the majority of all workers have full-time schedules, a substantial 36 percent of workers in their early twenties and 23 percent of those aged 55 or older work part-time. The smallest share of part-time workers is found among 25-to-54-year-olds, only 13 percent of whom work part-time.

Reasons for working part-time vary by age. For those under age 25, school attendance and the fact that many still live at home with their parents influence their decision to take part-time jobs. For older Americans, part-time work provides a transition between full-time careers and full-time retirement. Many people today work part-time because they cannot find full-time jobs. Nearly one in four part-time workers is working part-time for economic reasons—including half of men aged 25 to 54 who work part-time.

Women of all ages are more likely than men to have part-time jobs. Nearly two-thirds of the nation's part-time workers are women. But most women work full-time.

■ More than 6 million part-time workers would rather have full-time jobs.

Teenagers are most likely to work part-time

(percent of employed people who work part-time, by age, 2009)

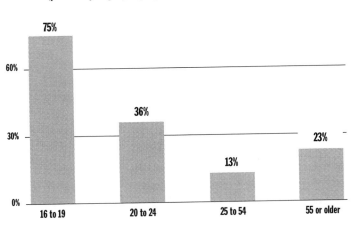

Table 7.11 Full-Time and Part-Time Workers by Age and Sex, 2009

(number and percent distribution of employed people aged 16 or older by age, employment status, and sex, 2009; numbers in thousands)

| | | total | | | men | | | women | |
	total	full-time	part-time	total	full-time	part-time	total	full-time	part-time
Total employed	139,878	112,634	27,244	73,670	63,951	9,719	66,208	48,683	17,525
Aged 16 to 19	4,837	1,220	3,617	2,328	709	1,619	2,509	511	1,998
Aged 20 to 24	12,763	8,219	4,544	6,510	4,541	1,969	6,253	3,678	2,575
Aged 25 to 54	95,145	82,314	12,831	50,584	46,914	3,670	44,560	35,400	9,160
Aged 55 or older	27,132	20,881	6,251	14,247	11,788	2,459	12,885	9,093	3,792

PERCENT DISTRIBUTION BY EMPLOYMENT STATUS

Total employed	100.0%	80.5%	19.5%	100.0%	86.8%	13.2%	100.0%	73.5%	26.5%
Aged 16 to 19	100.0	25.2	74.8	100.0	30.5	69.5	100.0	20.4	79.6
Aged 20 to 24	100.0	64.4	35.6	100.0	69.8	30.2	100.0	58.8	41.2
Aged 25 to 54	100.0	86.5	13.5	100.0	92.7	7.3	100.0	79.4	20.6
Aged 55 or older	100.0	77.0	23.0	100.0	82.7	17.3	100.0	70.6	29.4

PERCENT DISTRIBUTION BY AGE

Total employed	100.0%	100.0%	100.0%	100.0%	100.0%	100.0%	100.0%	100.0%	100.0%
Aged 16 to 19	3.5	1.1	13.3	3.2	1.1	16.7	3.8	1.0	11.4
Aged 20 to 24	9.1	7.3	16.7	8.8	7.1	20.3	9.4	7.6	14.7
Aged 25 to 54	68.0	73.1	47.1	68.7	73.4	37.8	67.3	72.7	52.3
Aged 55 or older	19.4	18.5	22.9	19.3	18.4	25.3	19.5	18.7	21.6

Source: Bureau of Labor Statistics, Current Population Survey, Internet site http://www.bls.gov/cps/home.htm; calculations by New Strategist

Table 7.12 Part-Time Work for Economic Reasons by Age and Sex, 2009

(number and percent distribution of total employed people aged 16 or older who work part-time and those who work part-time for economic reasons, by age and sex, 2009; numbers in thousands)

	total part-time workers		men who work part-time		women who work part-time	
	total	for economic reasons	total	for economic reasons	total	for economic reasons
Total employed part-time	**27,244**	**6,353**	**9,719**	**3,035**	**17,525**	**3,318**
Aged 16 to 19	3,617	419	1,619	208	1,998	211
Aged 20 to 24	4,544	1,146	1,969	600	2,575	546
Aged 25 to 54	12,831	3,945	3,670	1,837	9,160	2,108
Aged 55 or older	6,251	843	2,459	390	3,792	453
PERCENT DISTRIBUTION BY EMPLOYMENT STATUS						
Total employed part-time	**100.0%**	**23.3%**	**100.0%**	**31.2%**	**100.0%**	**18.9%**
Aged 16 to 19	100.0	11.6	100.0	12.8	100.0	10.6
Aged 20 to 24	100.0	25.2	100.0	30.5	100.0	21.2
Aged 25 to 54	100.0	30.7	100.0	50.1	100.0	23.0
Aged 55 or older	100.0	13.5	100.0	15.9	100.0	11.9
PERCENT DISTRIBUTION BY AGE						
Total employed part-time	**100.0%**	**100.0%**	**100.0%**	**100.0%**	**100.0%**	**100.0%**
Aged 16 to 19	13.3	6.6	16.7	6.9	11.4	6.4
Aged 20 to 24	16.7	18.0	20.3	19.8	14.7	16.5
Aged 25 to 54	47.1	62.1	37.8	60.5	52.3	63.5
Aged 55 or older	22.9	13.3	25.3	12.9	21.6	13.7

Note: "Economic reasons" includes people who work part-time because of slack work or poor business conditions, people who cannot find full-time jobs, and people who have seasonal jobs.
Source: Bureau of Labor Statistics, Current Population Survey, Internet site http://www.bls.gov/cps/home.htm; calculations by New Strategist

Dual Earners Are in the Majority

Working wives help families maintain financial security.

The majority of married couples are dual earners. Both husband and wife were in the labor force in 55 percent of married couples in 2009. Only 22 percent of today's couples follow traditional sex roles in which only the husband works while the wife stays home.

The largest share of two-income couples is found among people ranging in age from 40 to 54—70 percent of whom are dual earners. For the majority of couples aged 65 or older, both husband and wife no longer work. Married couples aged 55 to 74 are most likely to have a working wife and a nonworking husband. In most of these cases, a slightly younger wife is continuing to work after her husband has retired.

■ Two incomes are needed to maintain a middle-class standard of living.

Most couples under age 55 are dual earners

(percent of married couples in which both husband and wife are in the labor force, by age, 2009)

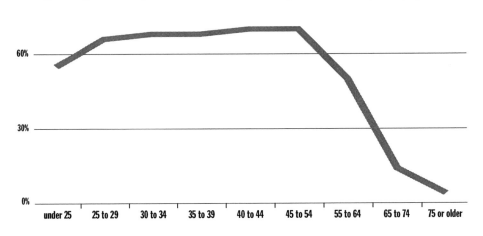

Table 7.13 Labor Force Status of Married-Couple Family Groups, 2009

(number and percent distribution of married-couple family groups aged 20 or older by age of householder and labor force status of husband and wife, 2009; numbers in thousands)

	total	husband and/or wife in labor force			neither husband nor wife in labor force
		husband and wife	husband only	wife only	
Married couples	**60,844**	**33,249**	**13,207**	**4,314**	**10,074**
Under age 25	1,437	787	528	81	40
Aged 25 to 29	3,930	2,597	1,145	104	86
Aged 30 to 34	5,450	3,710	1,465	163	110
Aged 35 to 39	6,408	4,356	1,750	170	131
Aged 40 to 44	6,815	4,771	1,617	272	154
Aged 45 to 54	14,346	10,113	2,890	854	489
Aged 55 to 64	11,668	5,801	2,427	1,513	1,927
Aged 65 to 74	6,853	969	1,130	910	3,844
Aged 75 or older	3,937	144	254	247	3,293
Married couples	**100.0%**	**54.6%**	**21.7%**	**7.1%**	**16.6%**
Under age 25	100.0	54.8	36.7	5.6	2.8
Aged 25 to 29	100.0	66.1	29.1	2.6	2.2
Aged 30 to 34	100.0	68.1	26.9	3.0	2.0
Aged 35 to 39	100.0	68.0	27.3	2.7	2.0
Aged 40 to 44	100.0	70.0	23.7	4.0	2.3
Aged 45 to 54	100.0	70.5	20.1	6.0	3.4
Aged 55 to 64	100.0	49.7	20.8	13.0	16.5
Aged 65 to 74	100.0	14.1	16.5	13.3	56.1
Aged 75 or older	100.0	3.7	6.5	6.3	83.6

Source: Bureau of the Census, America's Families and Living Arrangements: 2009, detailed tables, Internet site http://www .census.gov/population/www/socdemo/hh-fam/cps2009.html; calculations by New Strategist

Most Mothers Work

Single mothers are most likely to work.

The statistic that says the most about the revolutionary changes in sex roles over the past few decades is the labor force participation rate of mothers with young children. As younger generations of Americans have matured, new mothers have been increasingly likely to work. Fewer than one-third of mothers with children under age 1 were working in 1976, according to the Census Bureau. In 2008, 56 percent were in the labor force, most of them working full-time. Mothers with school-aged children are most likely to work, with a labor force participation rate of 77 percent in 2008.

Among married women with children under age 18, the 71 percent majority is in the labor force and 51 percent work full-time. Among single mothers, 76 percent are in the labor force and 55 percent work full-time.

■ Because of the decline in men's incomes, most of today's young women do not have the luxury of being a stay-at-home mom.

Most mothers with infants are in the labor force

(labor force status of mothers with children under age 1, 2008)

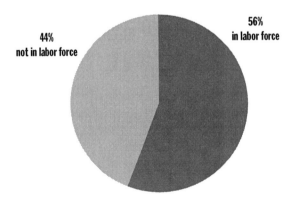

44%
not in labor force

56%
in labor force

Table 7.14 Labor Force Status of Women by Presence of Children, 2008

(number and percent distribution of women by labor force status and presence and age of own children under age 18 at home, 2008; numbers in thousands)

| | civilian population | civilian labor force | | | |
| | | total | employed | | |
			total	full-time	part-time
Total women	**120,675**	**71,767**	**67,876**	**51,178**	**16,698**
No children under age 18	84,162	45,682	43,239	32,549	10,690
With children under age 18	36,513	26,085	24,637	18,629	6,008
Children aged 6 to 17, none younger	20,325	15,718	15,003	11,679	3,324
Children under age 6	16,188	10,367	9,634	6,950	2,684
Children under age 3	9,595	5,792	5,354	3,782	1,573
Children under age 1	3,319	1,871	1,715	1,180	535
Total women	**100.0%**	**59.5%**	**56.2%**	**42.4%**	**13.8%**
No children under age 18	100.0	54.3	51.4	38.7	12.7
With children under age 18	100.0	71.4	67.5	51.0	16.5
Children aged 6 to 17, none younger	100.0	77.3	73.8	57.5	16.4
Children under age 6	100.0	64.0	59.5	42.9	16.6
Children under age 3	100.0	60.4	55.8	39.4	16.4
Children under age 1	100.0	56.4	51.7	35.6	16.1

Source: Bureau of Labor Statistics, Employment Characteristics of Families, Internet site http://www.bls.gov/news.release/famee.toc.htm

Table 7.15 Employed Parents by Age of Child, 2008

(number and percent distribution of parents with own children under age 18 at home, and percent in the labor force by age of youngest child, marital status, and sex, 2008; numbers in thousands)

	number			percent distribution		
	total parents	fathers	mothers	total parents	fathers	mothers
WITH CHILDREN UNDER AGE 18						
Total	**65,655**	**29,142**	**36,513**	**100.0%**	**100.0%**	**100.0%**
In labor force	53,506	27,422	26,085	81.5	94.1	71.4
Employed	51,017	26,380	24,637	77.7	90.5	67.5
Full-time	43,967	25,338	18,629	67.0	86.9	51.0
Part-time	7,050	1,042	6,008	10.7	3.6	16.5
Unemployed	2,490	1,041	1,448	4.7	3.8	5.6
MARRIED						
Total	**52,433**	**26,647**	**25,786**	**100.0**	**100.0**	**100.0**
In labor force	43,137	25,205	17,933	82.3	94.6	69.5
Employed	41,611	24,353	17,258	79.4	91.4	66.9
Full-time	36,128	23,444	12,685	68.9	88.0	49.2
Part-time	5,482	909	4,573	10.5	3.4	17.7
Unemployed	1,527	852	675	3.5	3.4	3.8
NOT MARRIED						
Total	**13,222**	**2,495**	**10,727**	**100.0**	**100.0**	**100.0**
In labor force	10,369	2,217	8,152	78.4	88.9	76.0
Employed	9,406	2,027	7,379	71.1	81.2	68.8
Full-time	7,838	1,894	5,944	59.3	75.9	55.4
Part-time	1,568	133	1,435	11.9	5.3	13.4
Unemployed	963	190	773	9.3	8.6	9.5
WITH YOUNGEST CHILD AGED 6 TO 17						
Total	**36,581**	**16,256**	**20,325**	**100.0**	**100.0**	**100.0**
In labor force	30,846	15,128	15,718	84.3	93.1	77.3
Employed	29,590	14,588	15,003	80.9	89.7	73.8
Full-time	25,733	14,054	11,679	70.3	86.5	57.5
Part-time	3,858	534	3,324	10.5	3.3	16.4
Unemployed	1,255	541	715	4.1	3.6	4.5
WITH YOUNGEST CHILD UNDER AGE 6						
Total	**29,074**	**12,886**	**16,188**	**100.0**	**100.0**	**100.0**
In labor force	22,661	12,293	10,367	77.9	95.4	64.0
Employed	21,426	11,792	9,634	73.7	91.5	59.5
Full-time	18,234	11,284	6,950	62.7	87.6	42.9
Part-time	3,193	508	2,684	11.0	3.9	16.6
Unemployed	1,234	501	733	4.2	3.9	4.5

Note: "Not married" includes never married, divorced, separated, and widowed.
Source: Bureau of Labor Statistics, Employment Characteristics of Families, Internet site http://www.bls.gov/news.release/ famee.toc.htm

Job Tenure Has Increased

Among older workers, a growing share has been with their current employer for 10 or more years.

The number of years the average worker has been with his or her current employer has increased. Overall, workers aged 25 or older had been with their current employer for a median of 5.1 years in 2008, up from 4.7 years in 2000. The biggest factor behind the rise is the increase in job tenure among elderly men as they postpone retirement. Median job tenure for men aged 65 or older climbed from 9.0 to 10.4 years between 2000 and 2008.

Long-term employment has dropped among middle-aged men and women, but has soared in the older age groups as they postpone retirement. Among men ranging in age from 30 to 49, the percentage with long-term jobs fell by 4 to 5 percentage points between 2000 and 2008. But among men aged 65 or older, the percentage with long-term jobs climbed sharply, rising from 49 to 59 percent. Long-term employment also climbed among women aged 60 or older.

■ The rise in long-term employment among older Americans is evidence that the early retirement trend has come to an abrupt end.

Long-term employment has increased sharply among men aged 65 or older

(percent of men aged 65 or older who have been with their current employer for 10 or more years, 2000 and 2008)

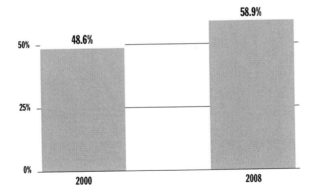

Table 7.16 Tenure with Current Employer by Sex and Age, 2000 to 2008

(median number of years workers aged 25 or older have been with their current employer by sex and age, and change in years, 2000 to 2008)

	2008	2000	change in years 2000–08
Total, aged 25 or older	**5.1**	**4.7**	**0.4**
Aged 25 to 34	2.7	2.6	0.1
Aged 35 to 44	4.9	4.8	0.1
Aged 45 to 54	7.6	8.2	−0.6
Aged 55 to 64	9.9	10.0	−0.1
Aged 65 or older	10.2	9.4	0.8
Men, aged 25 or older	**5.2**	**4.9**	**0.3**
Aged 25 to 34	2.8	2.7	0.1
Aged 35 to 44	5.2	5.3	−0.1
Aged 45 to 54	8.2	9.5	−1.3
Aged 55 to 64	10.1	10.2	−0.1
Aged 65 or older	10.4	9.0	1.4
Women, aged 25 or older	**4.9**	**4.4**	**0.5**
Aged 25 to 34	2.6	2.5	0.1
Aged 35 to 44	4.7	4.3	0.4
Aged 45 to 54	7.0	7.3	−0.3
Aged 55 to 64	9.8	9.9	−0.1
Aged 65 or older	9.9	9.7	0.2

Source: Bureau of Labor Statistics, Employee Tenure, Internet site http://www.bls.gov/news.release/tenure.toc.htm; calculations by New Strategist

Table 7.17 Long-Term Employment by Sex and Age, 2000 to 2008

(percent of workers aged 25 or older who have worked for their current employer 10 or more years by sex and age, and percentage point change, 2000 to 2008)

	2008	2000	percentage point change 2000–08
Total, aged 25 or older	**31.5%**	**31.5%**	**0.0**
Aged 25 to 29	2.3	2.5	–0.2
Aged 30 to 34	10.1	13.9	–3.8
Aged 35 to 39	23.0	26.1	–3.1
Aged 40 to 44	32.9	35.8	–2.9
Aged 45 to 49	40.2	45.2	–5.0
Aged 50 to 54	47.7	48.7	–1.0
Aged 55 to 59	52.4	53.1	–0.7
Aged 60 to 64	53.6	53.0	0.6
Aged 65 or older	56.3	49.8	6.5
Men, aged 25 or older	**32.9**	**33.4**	**–0.5**
Aged 25 to 29	2.4	3.0	–0.6
Aged 30 to 34	11.3	15.1	–3.8
Aged 35 to 39	25.4	29.4	–4.0
Aged 40 to 44	35.8	40.2	–4.4
Aged 45 to 49	43.5	49.0	–5.5
Aged 50 to 54	50.4	51.6	–1.2
Aged 55 to 59	54.9	53.7	1.2
Aged 60 to 64	52.4	52.4	0.0
Aged 65 or older	58.9	48.6	10.3
Women, aged 25 or older	**30.0**	**29.5**	**0.5**
Aged 25 to 29	2.1	1.9	0.2
Aged 30 to 34	8.7	12.5	–3.8
Aged 35 to 39	20.3	22.3	–2.0
Aged 40 to 44	29.9	31.2	–1.3
Aged 45 to 49	36.7	41.4	–4.7
Aged 50 to 54	45.0	45.8	–0.8
Aged 55 to 59	50.0	52.5	–2.5
Aged 60 to 64	54.8	53.6	1.2
Aged 65 or older	53.8	51.0	2.8

Source: Bureau of Labor Statistics, Employee Tenure, Internet site http://www.bls.gov/news.release/tenure.toc.htm; calculations by New Strategist

Union Representation Peaks among Workers Aged 45 to 64

Men are more likely than women to be represented by unions.

Union representation is lower in every age group today than it was 30 years ago. In 1970, 30 percent of nonagricultural workers were represented by labor unions. In 2009, the figure had fallen to 14 percent—although this figure is slightly higher than it had been a few years earlier.

Union representation peaks in the 45-to-64 age group at 18 percent. Men are more likely than women to be represented by a union, largely because they are more likely to work in jobs that are the traditional strongholds of labor unions. Among men, union representation peaks at 19 percent in the 45-to-64 age groups. Among women, representation peaks at 17 percent in the 55-to-64 age group.

■ Union representation is unlikely to rise much in the years ahead because today's workers are in a weak bargaining position because of high rates of unemployment.

Few workers are represented by unions

(percent of employed wage and salary workers who are represented by unions, by age, 2009)

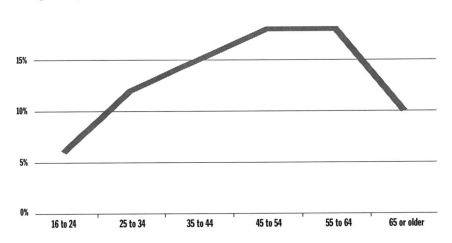

Table 7.18 Union Representation by Sex and Age, 2009

(number of employed wage and salary workers aged 16 or older, and number and percent who are represented by unions, by sex and age, 2009; numbers in thousands)

	total employed	represented by union	
		number	percent
Total people	**129,377**	**17,761**	**13.7%**
Aged 16 to 24	18,705	1,062	5.7
Aged 25 to 34	29,276	3,443	11.8
Aged 35 to 44	29,708	4,365	14.7
Aged 45 to 54	29,787	5,228	17.6
Aged 55 to 64	17,430	3,209	18.4
Aged 65 or older	4,471	454	10.2
Total men	**66,846**	**9,724**	**14.5**
Aged 16 to 24	9,537	617	6.5
Aged 25 to 34	15,780	1,909	12.1
Aged 35 to 44	15,653	2,491	15.9
Aged 45 to 54	14,988	2,812	18.8
Aged 55 to 64	8657	1,682	19.4
Aged 65 or older	2,230	213	9.6
Total women	**62,532**	**8,036**	**12.9**
Aged 16 to 24	9,168	445	4.8
Aged 25 to 34	13,496	1,534	11.4
Aged 35 to 44	14,055	1,874	13.3
Aged 45 to 54	14,799	2,416	16.3
Aged 55 to 64	8,773	1,527	17.4
Aged 65 or older	2,241	241	10.7

Source: Bureau of Labor Statistics, Current Population Survey, Internet site http://www.bls.gov/cps/tables.htm#empstat

Self-Employment Rises with Age

Few people under age 65 are self-employed.

Many Americans say they would like to be their own boss. But few people actually attain this goal—only 7 percent of workers are self-employed.

The self-employment rate rises with age. Only 2 percent of workers under age 25 are self-employed. Among workers aged 25 to 54, only 5 to 8 percent are self-employed. The rate rises slightly to 10 percent among workers aged 55 to 64 as some people begin to make the transition from work to retirement. A much larger 18 percent of workers aged 65 or older are self-employed as the Medicare health insurance program frees them from the need to find a job with health insurance coverage.

Men are more likely than women to be self-employed, especially among older workers. Twenty-one percent of working men aged 65 or older are self-employed compared with 14 percent of their female counterparts.

■ The self-employment rate among older Americans is likely to grow as Boomers reach their 65th birthday and look for ways to earn money while they postpone retirement.

Older workers are most likely to be self-employed

(percent of workers who are self-employed, by age, 2009)

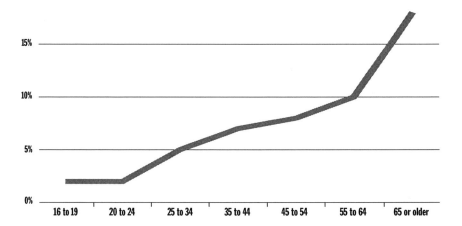

Table 7.19 Self-Employed Workers by Sex and Age, 2009

(number of people aged 16 or older in the labor force, number and percent who are self-employed, and percent distribution of self-employed, by sex and age, 2009; numbers in thousands)

	total employed	self-employed number	self-employed percent of total	self-employed percent distribution
Total people	**139,877**	**9,831**	**7.0%**	**100.0%**
Aged 16 to 19	4,838	76	1.6	0.8
Aged 20 to 24	12,764	267	2.1	2.7
Aged 25 to 34	30,014	1,367	4.6	13.9
Aged 35 to 44	31,517	2,154	6.8	21.9
Aged 45 to 54	33,613	2,753	8.2	28.0
Aged 55 to 64	21,018	2,107	10.0	21.4
Aged 65 or older	6,114	1,108	18.1	11.3
Total men	**73,669**	**6,140**	**8.3**	**100.0**
Aged 16 to 19	2,329	52	2.2	0.8
Aged 20 to 24	6,510	167	2.6	2.7
Aged 25 to 34	16,223	864	5.3	14.1
Aged 35 to 44	16,918	1,309	7.7	21.3
Aged 45 to 54	17,443	1,731	9.9	28.2
Aged 55 to 64	10,890	1,297	11.9	21.1
Aged 65 or older	3,357	720	21.4	11.7
Total women	**66,208**	**3,691**	**5.6**	**100.0**
Aged 16 to 19	2,509	24	1.0	0.7
Aged 20 to 24	6,253	100	1.6	2.7
Aged 25 to 34	13,791	503	3.6	13.6
Aged 35 to 44	14,599	845	5.8	22.9
Aged 45 to 54	16,170	1,022	6.3	27.7
Aged 55 to 64	10,128	811	8.0	22.0
Aged 65 or older	2,756	387	14.0	10.5

Source: Bureau of Labor Statistics, Current Population Survey, Internet site http://www.bls.gov/cps/home.htm

Most Minimum-Wage Workers Are Teens or Young Adults

Even among teenagers, however, minimum-wage pay is not the norm.

Among the nation's 73 million workers who are paid hourly rates, fewer than 4 million (5 percent) made minimum wage or less in 2009, according to the Bureau of Labor Statistics. Of the minimum-wage workers, 49 percent were under age 25.

Among workers paid hourly rates in the 16-to-19 age group, 19 percent earn minimum wage or less. Among those in the 20-to-24 age group, 9 percent are minimum-wage workers. The proportion falls with age to 2 percent of workers in the 45-to-64 age group. Among workers aged 65 or older, a larger 4.5 percent earn minimum wage or less.

■ The number of workers who earn minimum wage or less increased over the past few years along with the rise in the minimum wage threshold.

Teens and young adults are most likely to be minimum wage workers

(percent of workers who make minimum wage or less, by age, 2009)

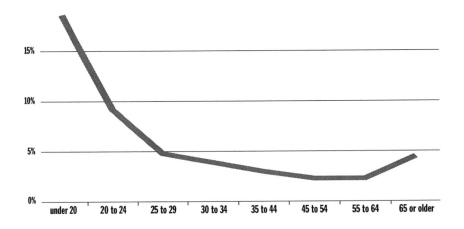

Table 7.20 Minimum Wage Workers, 2009

(number and percent distribution of total workers paid hourly rates and those paid at or below the prevailing federal minimum wage, by age, 2009; numbers in thousands)

	total paid hourly rates	at or below minimum wage
Total aged 16 or older	**72,611**	**3,572**
Aged 16 to 19	4,397	818
Aged 20 to 24	9,991	919
Aged 25 to 29	8,917	424
Aged 30 to 34	7,446	292
Aged 35 to 44	14,575	440
Aged 45 to 54	15,468	350
Aged 55 to 64	9,151	209
Aged 65 or older	2,665	120
PERCENT DISTRIBUTION BY AGE		
Total aged 16 or older	**100.0%**	**100.0%**
Aged 16 to 19	6.1	22.9
Aged 20 to 24	13.8	25.7
Aged 25 to 29	12.3	11.9
Aged 30 to 34	10.3	8.2
Aged 35 to 44	20.1	12.3
Aged 45 to 54	21.3	9.8
Aged 55 to 64	12.6	5.9
Aged 65 or older	3.7	3.4
PERCENT DISTRIBUTION BY WAGE STATUS		
Total aged 16 or older	**100.0%**	**4.9%**
Aged 16 to 19	100.0	18.6
Aged 20 to 24	100.0	9.2
Aged 25 to 29	100.0	4.8
Aged 30 to 34	100.0	3.9
Aged 35 to 44	100.0	3.0
Aged 45 to 54	100.0	2.3
Aged 55 to 64	100.0	2.3
Aged 65 or older	100.0	4.5

Note: The prevailing Federal minimum wage had been $5.15/hour from September 1, 1997, through July 23, 2007. It increased to $5.85 on July 24, 2007, to $6.55 on July 24, 2008, and to $7.25 on July 24, 2009.
Source: Bureau of Labor Statistics, Characteristics of Minimum Wage Workers: 2009, Internet site http://www.bls.gov/cps/minwage2009.htm; calculations by New Strategist

More Older Workers Will Be in the Labor Force

Participation rates are projected to climb in the older age groups.

Early retirement has come to an end. Labor force participation rates among older men and women are projected to climb, according to the Bureau of Labor Statistics. Men's overall labor force participation rate should fall by 2 percentage points between 2008 and 2018, but only because of a decline in participation among younger men and the aging of the population. Labor force participation among men aged 65 or older is projected to climb by 5 percentage points between 2008 and 2018, to 26.7 percent. Women's labor force participation rate also will rise in the older age groups.

As Boomers enter their late sixties, the number of older workers will soar. The number of workers aged 65 or older is projected to increase by 78 percent between 2008 and 2018.

■ Many Baby Boomers will have to stay in the labor force well into their sixties as they try to save for retirement.

The number of workers aged 65 or older will grow rapidly

(percent change in number of workers, by age, 2008 to 2018)

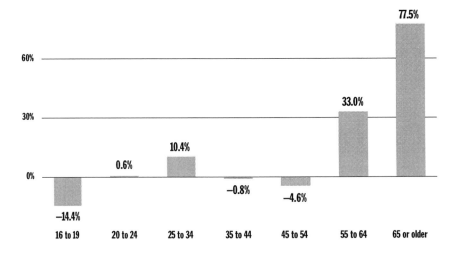

Table 7.21 Labor Force Projections by Sex and Age, 2008 and 2018

(projected number and percent of people aged 16 or older in the civilian labor force by sex and age, 2008 and 2018; percent change in number and percentage point change in rate 2008–18; numbers in thousands)

	number			participation rate		
	2008	2018	percent change 2008–18	2008	2018	percentage point change 2008–18
Total labor force	**154,287**	**166,911**	**8.2%**	**66.0%**	**64.5%**	**–1.5**
Aged 16 to 19	6,858	5,868	–14.4	40.2	33.8	–6.4
Aged 20 to 24	15,174	15,263	0.6	74.4	71.3	–3.1
Aged 25 to 34	33,332	36,814	10.4	83.3	82.4	–0.9
Aged 35 to 44	35,061	34,787	–0.8	84.1	83.2	–0.9
Aged 45 to 54	36,003	34,343	–4.6	81.9	81.7	–0.2
Aged 55 to 64	21,615	28,754	33.0	64.5	68.1	3.6
Aged 65 or older	6,243	11,082	77.5	16.8	22.4	5.6
Aged 65 to 74	4,985	9,045	81.4	25.1	30.5	5.4
Aged 75 or older	1,258	2,037	61.9	7.3	10.3	3.0
Men in labor force	**82,520**	**86,682**	**5.0**	**73.0**	**70.6**	**–2.4**
Aged 16 to 19	3,472	2,923	–15.8	40.1	33.2	–6.9
Aged 20 to 24	8,065	8,064	0.0	78.7	75.2	–3.5
Aged 25 to 34	18,302	20,173	10.2	91.5	90.6	–0.9
Aged 35 to 44	18,972	19,109	0.7	92.2	92.0	–0.2
Aged 45 to 54	18,928	18,027	–4.8	88.0	87.1	–0.9
Aged 55 to 64	11,345	14,479	27.6	70.4	71.2	0.8
Aged 65 or older	3,435	5,907	72.0	21.5	26.7	5.2
Aged 65 to 74	2,724	4,753	74.5	29.7	34.4	4.7
Aged 75 or older	711	1,154	62.3	10.4	13.9	3.5
Women in labor force	**71,767**	**78,229**	**9.0**	**59.5**	**58.7**	**–0.8**
Aged 16 to 19	3,385	2,946	–13.0	40.2	34.4	–5.8
Aged 20 to 24	7,109	7,198	1.3	70.0	67.3	–2.7
Aged 25 to 34	15,030	16,641	10.7	75.2	74.2	–1.0
Aged 35 to 44	16,089	15,678	–2.6	76.1	74.6	–1.5
Aged 45 to 54	17,075	16,316	–4.4	76.1	76.6	0.5
Aged 55 to 64	10,270	14,275	39.0	59.1	65.3	6.2
Aged 65 or older	2,808	5,174	84.3	13.3	18.9	5.6
Aged 65 to 74	2,261	4,291	89.8	21.1	27.1	6.0
Aged 75 or older	547	883	61.4	5.2	7.7	2.5

Source: Bureau of Labor Statistics, Labor force projections to 2018: older workers staying more active, Monthly Labor Review, November 2009, Internet site http://www.bls.gov/opub/mlr/2009/11/home.htm; calculations by New Strategist

Living Arrangements

Baby Boomers and younger generations have changed American family life. By their delaying marriage and childbearing, the proportion of households with children has been shrinking, reaching a low of 30 percent in 2009. As Boomers and Generation Xers divorced, the nuclear family became less common. Mom, dad, and the kids are found in less than one-quarter of the nation's households today.

Among older Americans, greater affluence and improved health has allowed more people to live alone following the death of a spouse. Men and women who live alone now head 27 percent of the nation's households, outnumbering married couples with children under age 18.

What to expect in the future

■ The number of households headed by people aged 65 or older will grow rapidly as Boomers fill the age group.

■ Older married couples without children at home will become an increasingly important household segment as Boomers age.

■ As Millennials enter their thirties and have children, expect the number of households with children under age 18 to expand.

Boomers Head the Largest Share of Households

Households headed by Generation Xers rank second in importance.

The middle aged dominate the nation's 117 million households because the large Baby-Boom generation is now in its forties, fifties, and sixties. Householders aged 45 to 63, the ages of the Baby-Boom in 2009, head 36 percent of households. The number of households headed by 55-to-64-year-olds grew by a substantial 46 percent between 2000 and 2009.

Generation Xers, aged 33 to 44 in 2009, account for 22 percent of households. As Generation X replaced the larger Baby-Boom generation in the 35-to-44 age group, the number of households headed by 35-to-44-year-olds fell 7 percent between 2000 and 2009.

The Millennial generation, the oldest members of which turned 32 in 2009, head nearly 19 percent of households. Although the Millennial generation is second only to Boomers in population size, they head fewer households than Generation X because many still live with mom and dad. In a few years, however, the number of households headed by Millennials will surpass the number headed by Generation Xers.

The Swing and World War II generations (people aged 64 or older in 2009) headed 23 percent of the nation's households. The percentage of households headed by the two older generations is shrinking.

■ The nation's households are dominated by older Americans, with people aged 50 or older heading nearly half (49 percent).

The Swing and WW II generations head the smallest share of households

(percent distribution of households by generation of householder, 2009)

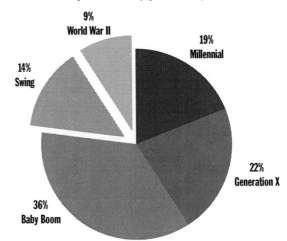

Table 8.1 Households by Age of Householder, 2000 and 2009

(number and percent distribution of households by age of householder, 2000 and 2009; percent change in number, 2000–09; numbers in thousands)

	2009		2000		percent change in number 2000–09
	number	percent distribution	number	percent distribution	
Total households	**117,181**	**100.0%**	**104,705**	**100.0%**	**11.9%**
Under age 25	6,357	5.4	5,860	5.6	8.5
Aged 25 to 34	19,302	16.5	18,627	17.8	3.6
Aged 35 to 44	22,171	18.9	23,955	22.9	–7.4
Aged 45 to 54	24,633	21.0	20,927	20.0	17.7
Aged 55 to 64	19,883	17.0	13,592	13.0	46.3
Aged 65 or older	24,834	21.2	21,745	20.8	14.2
Aged 65 to 74	12,842	11.0	11,325	10.8	13.4
Aged 75 or older	11,992	10.2	10,419	10.0	15.1

Source: Bureau of the Census, 2009 Current Population Survey Annual Social and Economic Supplement, Internet site http://www.census.gov/hhes/www/cpstables/032009/hhinc/toc.htm; calculations by New Strategist

Table 8.2 Households by Age and Generation of Householder, 2009

(number and percent distribution of households by age and generation of householder, 2009; numbers in thousands)

	number	percent distribution
Total households	**117,181**	**100.0%**
Aged 15 to 24	6,357	5.4
Aged 25 to 29	9,463	8.1
Aged 30 to 34	9,839	8.4
Aged 35 to 39	10,711	9.1
Aged 40 to 44	11,460	9.8
Aged 45 to 49	12,437	10.6
Aged 50 to 54	12,196	10.4
Aged 55 to 59	10,596	9.0
Aged 60 to 64	9,287	7.9
Aged 65 to 69	7,446	6.4
Aged 70 to 74	5,396	4.6
Aged 75 or older	11,992	10.2
Households by generation		
Millennial (15 to 32)	21,723	18.5
Generation X (33 to 44)	26,107	22.3
Baby Boom (45 to 63)	42,659	36.4
Swing (64 to 76)	16,618	14.2
World War II (77 or older)	10,074	8.6

Note: Households by generation are estimates by New Strategist.
Source: Bureau of the Census, 2009 Current Population Survey Annual Social and Economic Supplement, Internet site http://www.census.gov/hhes/www/cpstables/032009/hhinc/toc.htm; calculations by New Strategist

Young and Old Have the Most Diverse Households

The majority of middle-aged households are married couples.

Households are most diverse among the youngest and the oldest adults. They are most alike among the middle aged.

Many Millennials still live with their parents. Among Millennials who head their own households, only 37 percent are married-couple householders. About the same percentage are nonfamily householders, including 21 percent who live alone.

Married couples account for the 57 to 58 percent majority of households headed by Generation Xers and Boomers. The figure is a smaller 51 percent among the Swing generation and falls to just 32 percent for the World War II generation as widowhood becomes common.

Overall, people who live alone head 27 percent of the nation's households. The percentage is as low as 17 percent among Gen Xers and reaches the 56 percent majority among the World War II generation. Women who live alone account for 43 percent of households headed by the World War II generation, while men who live alone account for a smaller 13 percent.

■ Because the population is aging, the share of households headed by people who live alone should climb steadily in the years ahead.

The married-couple share of households peaks among Generation Xers

(percent of households headed by married couples, by generation, 2009)

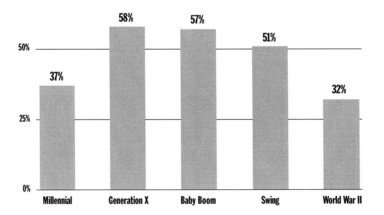

Table 8.3 Households by Age of Householder and Type of Household, 2009

(number and percent distribution of households by age of householder and type of household, 2009; numbers in thousands)

| | total | family households | | | | nonfamily households | | | | |
| | | | | | | | female householder | | male householder | |
		total	married couples	female hh, no spouse present	male hh, no spouse present	total	total	living alone	total	living alone
Total households	**117,181**	**78,850**	**59,118**	**14,480**	**5,252**	**38,331**	**20,637**	**17,899**	**17,694**	**13,758**
Aged 15 to 24	6,357	3,394	1,203	1,356	835	2,963	1,366	667	1,597	871
Aged 25 to 29	9,463	5,951	3,720	1,585	646	3,512	1,359	829	2,153	1,272
Aged 30 to 34	9,839	7,396	5,301	1,553	542	2,443	902	657	1,540	1,038
Aged 35 to 39	10,711	8,540	6,259	1,740	541	2,172	838	699	1,333	1,021
Aged 40 to 44	11,460	9,007	6,656	1,744	608	2,452	918	740	1,535	1,238
Aged 45 to 49	12,437	9,421	7,051	1,749	621	3,016	1,326	1,095	1,690	1,407
Aged 50 to 54	12,196	8,698	6,930	1,314	455	3,497	1,660	1,475	1,838	1,521
Aged 55 to 59	10,596	7,353	6,096	886	371	3,243	1,780	1,620	1,463	1,247
Aged 60 to 64	9,287	6,109	5,321	607	182	3,178	1,921	1,786	1,257	1,097
Aged 65 to 69	7,446	4,741	4,072	541	127	2,705	1,751	1,668	955	866
Aged 70 to 74	5,396	3,163	2,644	443	76	2,234	1,580	1,535	653	588
Aged 75 or older	11,992	5,075	3,864	963	248	6,917	5,236	5,128	1,681	1,593

PERCENT DISTRIBUTION BY AGE OF HOUSEHOLDER

	total	total	married couples	female hh, no spouse present	male hh, no spouse present	total	total	living alone	total	living alone
Total households	**100.0%**	**100.0%**	**100.0%**	**100.0%**	**100.0%**	**100.0%**	**100.0%**	**100.0%**	**100.0%**	**100.0%**
Aged 15 to 24	5.4	4.3	2.0	9.4	15.9	7.7	6.6	3.7	9.0	6.3
Aged 25 to 29	8.1	7.5	6.3	10.9	12.3	9.2	6.6	4.6	12.2	9.2
Aged 30 to 34	8.4	9.4	9.0	10.7	10.3	6.4	4.4	3.7	8.7	7.5
Aged 35 to 39	9.1	10.8	10.6	12.0	10.3	5.7	4.1	3.9	7.5	7.4
Aged 40 to 44	9.8	11.4	11.3	12.0	11.6	6.4	4.4	4.1	8.7	9.0
Aged 45 to 49	10.6	11.9	11.9	12.1	11.8	7.9	6.4	6.1	9.6	10.2
Aged 50 to 54	10.4	11.0	11.7	9.1	8.7	9.1	8.0	8.2	10.4	11.1
Aged 55 to 59	9.0	9.3	10.3	6.1	7.1	8.5	8.6	9.1	8.3	9.1
Aged 60 to 64	7.9	7.7	9.0	4.2	3.5	8.3	9.3	10.0	7.1	8.0
Aged 65 to 69	6.4	6.0	6.9	3.7	2.4	7.1	8.5	9.3	5.4	6.3
Aged 70 to 74	4.6	4.0	4.5	3.1	1.4	5.8	7.7	8.6	3.7	4.3
Aged 75 or older	10.2	6.4	6.5	6.7	4.7	18.0	25.4	28.6	9.5	11.6

PERCENT DISTRIBUTION BY HOUSEHOLD TYPE

	total	total	married couples	female hh, no spouse present	male hh, no spouse present	total	total	living alone	total	living alone
Total households	**100.0%**	**67.3%**	**50.5%**	**12.4%**	**4.5%**	**32.7%**	**17.6%**	**15.3%**	**15.1%**	**11.7%**
Aged 15 to 24	100.0	53.4	18.9	21.3	13.1	46.6	21.5	10.5	25.1	13.7
Aged 25 to 29	100.0	62.9	39.3	16.7	6.8	37.1	14.4	8.8	22.8	13.4
Aged 30 to 34	100.0	75.2	53.9	15.8	5.5	24.8	9.2	6.7	15.7	10.5
Aged 35 to 39	100.0	79.7	58.4	16.2	5.1	20.3	7.8	6.5	12.4	9.5
Aged 40 to 44	100.0	78.6	58.1	15.2	5.3	21.4	8.0	6.5	13.4	10.8
Aged 45 to 49	100.0	75.7	56.7	14.1	5.0	24.3	10.7	8.8	13.6	11.3
Aged 50 to 54	100.0	71.3	56.8	10.8	3.7	28.7	13.6	12.1	15.1	12.5
Aged 55 to 59	100.0	69.4	57.5	8.4	3.5	30.6	16.8	15.3	13.8	11.8
Aged 60 to 64	100.0	65.8	57.3	6.5	2.0	34.2	20.7	19.2	13.5	11.8
Aged 65 to 69	100.0	63.7	54.7	7.3	1.7	36.3	23.5	22.4	12.8	11.6
Aged 70 to 74	100.0	58.6	49.0	8.2	1.4	41.4	29.3	28.4	12.1	10.9
Aged 75 or older	100.0	42.3	32.2	8.0	2.1	57.7	43.7	42.8	14.0	13.3

Note: "hh" means householder.
Source: Bureau of the Census, 2009 Current Population Survey Annual Social and Economic Supplement, Internet site http://www.census.gov/hhes/www/cpstables/032009/hhinc/toc.htm; calculations by New Strategist

Table 8.4 Households by Type and Generation of Householder, 2009

(number and percent distribution of households by type and generation of householder, 2009; numbers in thousands)

	total	family households				nonfamily households				
		total	married couples	female hh, no spouse present	male hh, no spouse present	total	female householder total	female householder living alone	male householder total	male householder living alone
Total households	117,181	78,850	59,118	14,480	5,252	38,331	20,637	17,899	17,694	13,758
Millennial (15–32)	21,723	13,783	8,104	3,873	1,806	7,941	3,266	1,890	4,674	2,766
Generation X (33–44)	26,107	20,505	15,035	4,105	1,366	5,601	2,117	1,702	3,484	2,674
Baby Boom (45–63)	42,659	30,359	24,334	4,435	1,593	12,298	6,303	5,619	5,997	5,053
Swing (64–76)	16,618	9,938	8,398	1,259	279	6,681	4,553	4,381	2,128	1,928
World War II (77+)	10,074	4,265	3,247	808	208	5,809	4,398	4,308	1,411	1,337

PERCENT DISTRIBUTION BY GENERATION OF HOUSEHOLDER

	total	total	married couples	female hh, no spouse present	male hh, no spouse present	total	female total	female living alone	male total	male living alone
Total households	100.0%	100.0%	100.0%	100.0%	100.0%	100.0%	100.0%	100.0%	100.0%	100.0%
Millennial (15–32)	18.5	17.5	13.7	26.7	34.4	20.7	15.8	10.6	26.4	20.1
Generation X (33–44)	22.3	26.0	25.4	28.4	26.0	14.6	10.3	9.5	19.7	19.4
Baby Boom (45–63)	36.4	38.5	41.2	30.6	30.3	32.1	30.5	31.4	33.9	36.7
Swing (64–76)	14.2	12.6	14.2	8.7	5.3	17.4	22.1	24.5	12.0	14.0
World War II (77+)	8.6	5.4	5.5	5.6	4.0	15.2	21.3	24.1	8.0	9.7

PERCENT DISTRIBUTION BY HOUSEHOLD TYPE

	total	total	married couples	female hh, no spouse present	male hh, no spouse present	total	female total	female living alone	male total	male living alone
Total households	100.0%	67.3%	50.5%	12.4%	4.5%	32.7%	17.6%	15.3%	15.1%	11.7%
Millennial (15–32)	100.0	63.4	37.3	17.8	8.3	36.6	15.0	8.7	21.5	12.7
Generation X (33–44)	100.0	78.5	57.6	15.7	5.2	21.5	8.1	6.5	13.3	10.2
Baby Boom (45–63)	100.0	71.2	57.0	10.4	3.7	28.8	14.8	13.2	14.1	11.8
Swing (64–76)	100.0	59.8	50.5	7.6	1.7	40.2	27.4	26.4	12.8	11.6
World War II (77+)	100.0	42.3	32.2	8.0	2.1	57.7	43.7	42.8	14.0	13.3

Note: Households by generation are estimates by New Strategist. "hh" means householder.
Source: Bureau of the Census, 2009 Current Population Survey Annual Social and Economic Supplement, Internet site http://www.census.gov/hhes/www/cpstables/032009/hhinc/toc.htm; calculations by New Strategist

Millennials Are Most Diverse

The World War II generation is the least diverse.

Non-Hispanic whites head 83 million of the nation's 117 million households. The proportion of households headed by non-Hispanic whites increases with each successively older generation. Among Millennials, non-Hispanic whites head only 62 percent of households. In the World War II generation, non-Hispanic whites head 85 percent of households.

The proportion of households headed by Asians is more than twice as great among Millennials as among the World War II generation (5 versus 2 percent). Nearly the same is true for households headed by blacks (15 versus 8 percent). Hispanics head more than three times as many households in the Millennial generation as they do in the World War II generation (17 versus 5 percent).

The Baby-Boom generation accounts for the largest share of households among Asians, blacks, and non-Hispanic whites. Boomers especially dominate non-Hispanic white households. Among Hispanics, the proportion of households headed by Gen Xers is greater than the proportion headed by Boomers.

■ Among Millennials and Generation Xers, households headed by Hispanics outnumber households headed by blacks.

Older householders are more likely to be non-Hispanic white

(percent of households headed by non-Hispanic whites, by generation, 2009)

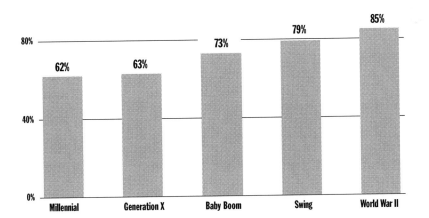

Table 8.5 Households by Age, Race, and Hispanic Origin of Householder, 2009

(number and percent distribution of households by age, race, and Hispanic origin of householder, 2009; numbers in thousands)

	total	Asian	black	Hispanic	non-Hispanic white
Total households	**117,181**	**4,805**	**15,056**	**13,425**	**82,884**
Aged 15 to 24	6,357	281	1,019	1,166	3,869
Aged 25 to 29	9,463	428	1,412	1,557	5,987
Aged 30 to 34	9,839	615	1,453	1,726	5,983
Aged 35 to 39	10,711	636	1,595	1,784	6,638
Aged 40 to 44	11,460	552	1,645	1,608	7,535
Aged 45 to 49	12,437	497	1,644	1,393	8,778
Aged 50 to 54	12,196	497	1,568	1,155	8,857
Aged 55 to 59	10,596	409	1,327	937	7,819
Aged 60 to 64	9,287	291	1,037	624	7,220
Aged 65 to 69	7,446	225	764	542	5,833
Aged 70 to 74	5,396	149	590	370	4,224
Aged 75 or older	11,992	227	1,002	563	10,140

PERCENT DISTRIBUTION BY AGE OF HOUSEHOLDER

Total households	**100.0%**	**100.0%**	**100.0%**	**100.0%**	**100.0%**
Aged 15 to 24	5.4	5.8	6.8	8.7	4.7
Aged 25 to 29	8.1	8.9	9.4	11.6	7.2
Aged 30 to 34	8.4	12.8	9.7	12.9	7.2
Aged 35 to 39	9.1	13.2	10.6	13.3	8.0
Aged 40 to 44	9.8	11.5	10.9	12.0	9.1
Aged 45 to 49	10.6	10.3	10.9	10.4	10.6
Aged 50 to 54	10.4	10.3	10.4	8.6	10.7
Aged 55 to 59	9.0	8.5	8.8	7.0	9.4
Aged 60 to 64	7.9	6.1	6.9	4.6	8.7
Aged 65 to 69	6.4	4.7	5.1	4.0	7.0
Aged 70 to 74	4.6	3.1	3.9	2.8	5.1
Aged 75 or older	10.2	4.7	6.7	4.2	12.2

PERCENT DISTRIBUTION BY RACE AND HISPANIC ORIGIN

Total households	**100.0%**	**4.1%**	**12.8%**	**11.5%**	**70.7%**
Aged 15 to 24	100.0	4.4	16.0	18.3	60.9
Aged 25 to 29	100.0	4.5	14.9	16.5	63.3
Aged 30 to 34	100.0	6.3	14.8	17.5	60.8
Aged 35 to 39	100.0	5.9	14.9	16.7	62.0
Aged 40 to 44	100.0	4.8	14.4	14.0	65.8
Aged 45 to 49	100.0	4.0	13.2	11.2	70.6
Aged 50 to 54	100.0	4.1	12.9	9.5	72.6
Aged 55 to 59	100.0	3.9	12.5	8.8	73.8
Aged 60 to 64	100.0	3.1	11.2	6.7	77.7
Aged 65 to 69	100.0	3.0	10.3	7.3	78.3
Aged 70 to 74	100.0	2.8	10.9	6.9	78.3
Aged 75 or older	100.0	1.9	8.4	4.7	84.6

Note: Numbers by race and Hispanic origin do not sum to total because Asians and blacks include those who identify themselves as being of the race alone and those who identify themselves as being of the race in combination with other races, Hispanics may be of any race, and not all races are shown. Non-Hispanic whites are those who identify themselves as being white alone and not Hispanic.
Source: Bureau of the Census, 2009 Current Population Survey Annual Social and Economic Supplement, Internet site http:// www.census.gov/hhes/www/cpstables/032009/hhinc/toc.htm; calculations by New Strategist

Table 8.6 Households by Generation, Race, and Hispanic Origin of Householder, 2009

(number and percent distribution of households by generation, race, and Hispanic origin of householder, 2009; numbers in thousands)

	total	Asian	black	Hispanic	non-Hispanic white
Total households	**117,181**	**4,805**	**15,056**	**13,425**	**82,884**
Millennial (15–32)	21,723	1,078	3,303	3,759	13,446
Generation X (33–44)	26,107	1,434	3,821	4,082	16,566
Baby Boom (45–63)	42,659	1,636	5,369	3,984	31,230
Swing (64–76)	16,618	469	1,722	1,127	13,123
World War II (77+)	10,074	189	842	473	8,519

PERCENT DISTRIBUTION BY GENERATION OF HOUSEHOLDER

	total	Asian	black	Hispanic	non-Hispanic white
Total households	**100.0%**	**100.0%**	**100.0%**	**100.0%**	**100.0%**
Millennial (15–32)	18.5	22.4	21.9	28.0	16.2
Generation X (33–44)	22.3	29.8	25.4	30.4	20.0
Baby Boom (45–63)	36.4	34.0	35.7	29.7	37.7
Swing (64–76)	14.2	9.8	11.4	8.4	15.8
World War II (77+)	8.6	3.9	5.6	3.5	10.3

PERCENT DISTRIBUTION BY RACE AND HISPANIC ORIGIN

	total	Asian	black	Hispanic	non-Hispanic white
Total households	**100.0%**	**4.1%**	**12.8%**	**11.5%**	**70.7%**
Millennial (15–32)	100.0	5.0	15.2	17.3	61.9
Generation X (33–44)	100.0	5.5	14.6	15.6	63.5
Baby Boom (45–63)	100.0	3.8	12.6	9.3	73.2
Swing (64–76)	100.0	2.8	10.4	6.8	79.0
World War II (77+)	100.0	1.9	8.4	4.7	84.6

Note: Households by generation are estimates by New Strategist. Numbers by race and Hispanic origin do not sum to total because Asians and blacks include those who identify themselves as being of the race alone and those who identify themselves as being of the race in combination with other races, Hispanics may be of any race, and not all races are shown. Non-Hispanic whites are those who identify themselves as being white alone and not Hispanic.
Source: Bureau of the Census, 2009 Current Population Survey Annual Social and Economic Supplement, Internet site http:// www.census.gov/hhes/www/cpstables/032009/hhinc/toc.htm; calculations by New Strategist

Oldest Americans Have the Smallest Households

Many people aged 75 or older live alone.

The average American household is home to 2.57 people. Household size peaks among 35-to-39-year-olds, with an average of 3.35 people in their households. Most people in the 35-to-39 age group have children at home. Households headed by the elderly are much smaller than average. Those headed by people aged 75 or older average only 1.58 people. Small households are the norm among older Americans because so many live alone.

Overall, more than 31 million Americans live by themselves—or 13 percent of the population aged 15 or older. Among men, 12 percent live alone, a figure that does not vary much by age except in the oldest age group, where 23 percent live by themselves. Among women, 14.5 percent live alone, a figure that rises to a high of 49 percent in the 75-or-older age group.

■ Older women are more likely than older men to live alone because of men's higher mortality rate, leaving many women widowed in old age.

Women's chances of living alone rise steeply with age

(percent of women who live alone, by age, 2009)

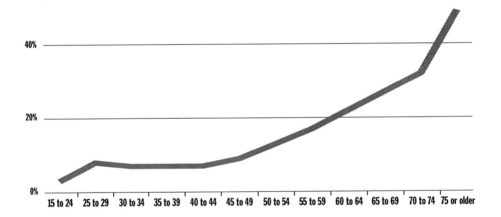

Table 8.7 Average Household Size by Age of Householder, 2009

(number of households and average number of persons per household, by age of householder, 2009; numbers in thousands)

	number of households	average number of persons per household
Total households	**117,181**	**2.57**
Under age 20	843	2.96
Aged 20 to 24	5,514	2.45
Aged 25 to 29	9,463	2.65
Aged 30 to 34	9,839	3.10
Aged 35 to 39	10,711	3.35
Aged 40 to 44	11,460	3.30
Aged 45 to 49	12,437	2.96
Aged 50 to 54	12,196	2.64
Aged 55 to 59	10,596	2.31
Aged 60 to 64	9,287	2.06
Aged 65 to 74	12,842	1.92
Aged 75 or older	11,992	1.58

Source: Bureau of the Census, America's Families and Living Arrangements: 2009, Internet site http://www.census.gov/ population/www/socdemo/hh-fam/cps2009.html; calculations by New Strategist

Table 8.8 People Living Alone by Sex and Age, 2009

(total number of people aged 15 or older, number and percent living alone, and percent distribution of people who live alone, by sex and age, 2009; numbers in thousands)

	total	living alone		
		number	percent	percent distribution
Total people	**240,144**	**31,657**	**13.2%**	**100.0%**
Aged 15 to 24	41,859	1,538	3.7	4.9
Aged 25 to 29	21,256	2,101	9.9	6.6
Aged 30 to 34	19,265	1,695	8.8	5.4
Aged 35 to 39	20,444	1,720	8.4	5.4
Aged 40 to 44	20,878	1,978	9.5	6.2
Aged 45 to 49	22,712	2,502	11.0	7.9
Aged 50 to 54	21,654	2,996	13.8	9.5
Aged 55 to 59	18,754	2,867	15.3	9.1
Aged 60 to 64	15,535	2,883	18.6	9.1
Aged 65 to 69	11,825	2,534	21.4	8.0
Aged 70 to 74	8,579	2,123	24.7	6.7
Aged 75 or older	17,384	6,721	38.7	21.2
Total men	**116,720**	**13,758**	**11.8**	**100.0**
Aged 15 to 24	21,202	871	4.1	6.3
Aged 25 to 29	10,867	1,272	11.7	9.2
Aged 30 to 34	9,574	1,038	10.8	7.5
Aged 35 to 39	10,169	1,021	10.0	7.4
Aged 40 to 44	10,322	1,238	12.0	9.0
Aged 45 to 49	11,162	1,407	12.6	10.2
Aged 50 to 54	10,611	1,521	14.3	11.1
Aged 55 to 59	9,083	1,247	13.7	9.1
Aged 60 to 64	7,423	1,097	14.8	8.0
Aged 65 to 69	5,632	866	15.4	6.3
Aged 70 to 74	3,769	588	15.6	4.3
Aged 75 or older	6,907	1,593	23.1	11.6
Total women	**123,424**	**17,899**	**14.5**	**100.0**
Aged 15 to 24	20,657	667	3.2	3.7
Aged 25 to 29	10,389	829	8.0	4.6
Aged 30 to 34	9,691	657	6.8	3.7
Aged 35 to 39	10,275	699	6.8	3.9
Aged 40 to 44	10,556	740	7.0	4.1
Aged 45 to 49	11,550	1,095	9.5	6.1
Aged 50 to 54	11,043	1,475	13.4	8.2
Aged 55 to 59	9,671	1,620	16.8	9.1
Aged 60 to 64	8,112	1,786	22.0	10.0
Aged 65 to 69	6,193	1,668	26.9	9.3
Aged 70 to 74	4,810	1,535	31.9	8.6
Aged 75 or older	10,477	5,128	48.9	28.6

Source: Bureau of the Census, 2009 Current Population Survey Annual Social and Economic Supplement, Internet site http://www.census.gov/hhes/www/cpstables/032009/hhinc/toc.htm; calculations by New Strategist

Fewer than One-Third of Households include Children under Age 18

Children under age 18 can be found in most Gen X households, however.

Generation Xers, aged 33 to 44 in 2009, are busy raising children. Sixty-three percent of Gen X households include children under age 18. The percentage of households with children under age 18 peaks in the 35-to-39 age group at 68 percent. Generation X is the only generation in which the majority of households include school-aged or younger children. Among households headed by Boomers, only 22 percent have children under age 18 at home. Among Millennials, the proportion is 43 percent.

When children of any age are considered, they can be found in a larger 40 percent of the nation's households. Among married couples, an even larger 54 percent include children of any age. The figure is 50 percent even among Boomer households as adult children delay leaving home or return to their parents' home because they cannot find a job.

■ The Baby-Boom generation has entered the empty-nest lifestage, but many find their children returning home because of the Great Recession.

Most Generation X households include children under age 18

(percent of households with children under age 18, by generation of householder, 2009)

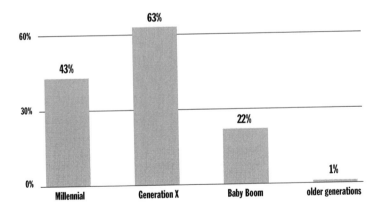

Table 8.9 Households by Age of Householder, Type of Household, and Presence of Children under Age 18, 2009

(number and percent distribution of households by age of householder, type of household, and presence of own children under age 18, and mean age of householder, 2009; numbers in thousands)

	all households		married couples		female-headed families		male-headed families	
	total	with children	total	with children	total	with children	total	with children
Total households	117,181	35,635	59,118	25,129	14,480	8,394	5,252	2,111
Under age 20	843	114	54	22	258	82	212	9
Aged 20 to 24	5,514	1,603	1,149	627	1,098	834	624	142
Aged 25 to 29	9,463	4,041	3,720	2,326	1,585	1,406	646	309
Aged 30 to 34	9,839	5,924	5,301	4,172	1,553	1,443	542	309
Aged 35 to 39	10,711	7,253	6,259	5,308	1,740	1,578	541	368
Aged 40 to 44	11,460	6,909	6,656	5,193	1,744	1,319	608	397
Aged 45 to 49	12,437	5,442	7,051	4,113	1,749	1,032	621	297
Aged 50 to 54	12,196	2,812	6,930	2,192	1,314	449	455	171
Aged 55 to 64	19,883	1,282	11,417	997	1,493	193	552	92
Aged 65 to 74	12,842	203	6,716	150	984	37	204	17
Aged 75 or older	11,992	51	3,864	28	963	22	248	1
Mean age (years)	49.8	39.5	48.3	40.2	43.9	37.0	41.3	39.2

PERCENT DISTRIBUTION BY AGE OF HOUSEHOLDER

	all households		married couples		female-headed families		male-headed families	
Total households	100.0%	100.0%	100.0%	100.0%	100.0%	100.0%	100.0%	100.0%
Under age 20	0.7	0.3	0.1	0.1	1.8	1.0	4.0	0.4
Aged 20 to 24	4.7	4.5	1.9	2.5	7.6	9.9	11.9	6.7
Aged 25 to 29	8.1	11.3	6.3	9.3	10.9	16.8	12.3	14.6
Aged 30 to 34	8.4	16.6	9.0	16.6	10.7	17.2	10.3	14.6
Aged 35 to 39	9.1	20.4	10.6	21.1	12.0	18.8	10.3	17.4
Aged 40 to 44	9.8	19.4	11.3	20.7	12.0	15.7	11.6	18.8
Aged 45 to 49	10.6	15.3	11.9	16.4	12.1	12.3	11.8	14.1
Aged 50 to 54	10.4	7.9	11.7	8.7	9.1	5.3	8.7	8.1
Aged 55 to 64	17.0	3.6	19.3	4.0	10.3	2.3	10.5	4.4
Aged 65 to 74	11.0	0.6	11.4	0.6	6.8	0.4	3.9	0.8
Aged 75 or older	10.2	0.1	6.5	0.1	6.7	0.3	4.7	0.0

PERCENT OF HOUSEHOLDS WITH CHILDREN BY TYPE

	all households		married couples		female-headed families		male-headed families	
Total households	100.0%	30.4%	100.0%	42.5%	100.0%	58.0%	100.0%	40.2%
Under age 20	100.0	13.5	100.0	40.7	100.0	31.8	100.0	4.2
Aged 20 to 24	100.0	29.1	100.0	54.6	100.0	76.0	100.0	22.8
Aged 25 to 29	100.0	42.7	100.0	62.5	100.0	88.7	100.0	47.8
Aged 30 to 34	100.0	60.2	100.0	78.7	100.0	92.9	100.0	57.0
Aged 35 to 39	100.0	67.7	100.0	84.8	100.0	90.7	100.0	68.0
Aged 40 to 44	100.0	60.3	100.0	78.0	100.0	75.6	100.0	65.3
Aged 45 to 49	100.0	43.8	100.0	58.3	100.0	59.0	100.0	47.8
Aged 50 to 54	100.0	23.1	100.0	31.6	100.0	34.2	100.0	37.6
Aged 55 to 64	100.0	6.4	100.0	8.7	100.0	12.9	100.0	16.7
Aged 65 to 74	100.0	1.6	100.0	2.2	100.0	3.8	100.0	8.3
Aged 75 or older	100.0	0.4	100.0	0.7	100.0	2.3	100.0	0.4

Source: Bureau of the Census, America's Families and Living Arrangements: 2009, Internet site http://www.census.gov/population/www/socdemo/hh-fam/cps2009.html; calculations by New Strategist

Table 8.10 Households by Age of Householder, Type of Household, and Presence of Children of Any Age, 2009

(number and percent distribution of households by age of householder, type of household, and presence of own children of any age, and mean age of householder, 2009; numbers in thousands)

	all households		married couples		female-headed families		male-headed families	
	total	with children	total	with children	total	with children	total	with children
Total households	**117,181**	**47,112**	**59,118**	**31,742**	**14,480**	**12,277**	**5,252**	**3,093**
Under age 20	843	114	54	22	258	82	212	9
Aged 20 to 24	5,514	1,603	1,149	627	1,098	834	624	142
Aged 25 to 29	9,463	4,041	3,720	2,326	1,585	1,406	646	309
Aged 30 to 34	9,839	5,958	5,301	4,188	1,553	1,457	542	313
Aged 35 to 39	10,711	7,432	6,259	5,393	1,740	1,660	541	379
Aged 40 to 44	11,460	7,602	6,656	5,540	1,744	1,618	608	443
Aged 45 to 49	12,437	7,279	7,051	5,268	1,749	1,547	621	465
Aged 50 to 54	12,196	5,410	6,930	3,958	1,314	1,119	455	333
Aged 55 to 64	19,883	4,673	11,417	3,219	1,493	1,094	552	360
Aged 65 to 74	12,842	1,730	6,716	884	984	698	204	148
Aged 75 or older	11,992	1,271	3,864	316	963	763	248	192
Mean age (years)	49.8	43.1	48.3	42.8	43.9	43.4	41.3	44.7

PERCENT DISTRIBUTION BY AGE OF HOUSEHOLDER

	all households		married couples		female-headed families		male-headed families	
Total households	**100.0%**	**100.0%**	**100.0%**	**100.0%**	**100.0%**	**100.0%**	**100.0%**	**100.0%**
Under age 20	0.7	0.2	0.1	0.1	1.8	0.7	4.0	0.3
Aged 20 to 24	4.7	3.4	1.9	2.0	7.6	6.8	11.9	4.6
Aged 25 to 29	8.1	8.6	6.3	7.3	10.9	11.5	12.3	10.0
Aged 30 to 34	8.4	12.6	9.0	13.2	10.7	11.9	10.3	10.1
Aged 35 to 39	9.1	15.8	10.6	17.0	12.0	13.5	10.3	12.3
Aged 40 to 44	9.8	16.1	11.3	17.5	12.0	13.2	11.6	14.3
Aged 45 to 49	10.6	15.5	11.9	16.6	12.1	12.6	11.8	15.0
Aged 50 to 54	10.4	11.5	11.7	12.5	9.1	9.1	8.7	10.8
Aged 55 to 64	17.0	9.9	19.3	10.1	10.3	8.9	10.5	11.6
Aged 65 to 74	11.0	3.7	11.4	2.8	6.8	5.7	3.9	4.8
Aged 75 or older	10.2	2.7	6.5	1.0	6.7	6.2	4.7	6.2

PERCENT OF HOUSEHOLDS WITH CHILDREN BY TYPE

	all households		married couples		female-headed families		male-headed families	
Total households	**100.0%**	**40.2%**	**100.0%**	**53.7%**	**100.0%**	**84.8%**	**100.0%**	**58.9%**
Under age 20	100.0	13.5	100.0	40.7	100.0	31.8	100.0	4.2
Aged 20 to 24	100.0	29.1	100.0	54.6	100.0	76.0	100.0	22.8
Aged 25 to 29	100.0	42.7	100.0	62.5	100.0	88.7	100.0	47.8
Aged 30 to 34	100.0	60.6	100.0	79.0	100.0	93.8	100.0	57.7
Aged 35 to 39	100.0	69.4	100.0	86.2	100.0	95.4	100.0	70.1
Aged 40 to 44	100.0	66.3	100.0	83.2	100.0	92.8	100.0	72.9
Aged 45 to 49	100.0	58.5	100.0	74.7	100.0	88.5	100.0	74.9
Aged 50 to 54	100.0	44.4	100.0	57.1	100.0	85.2	100.0	73.2
Aged 55 to 64	100.0	23.5	100.0	28.2	100.0	73.3	100.0	65.2
Aged 65 to 74	100.0	13.5	100.0	13.2	100.0	70.9	100.0	72.5
Aged 75 or older	100.0	10.6	100.0	8.2	100.0	79.2	100.0	77.4

Source: Bureau of the Census, America's Families and Living Arrangements: 2009, Internet site http://www.census.gov/population/www/socdemo/hh-fam/cps2009.html; calculations by New Strategist

Table 8.11   Households by Generation of Householder, Type of Household, and Presence of Children under Age 18, 2009

(number and percent distribution of households by generation of householder, type of household, and presence of own children under age 18, 2009; numbers in thousands)

	all households		married couples		female-headed families		male-headed families	
	total	with children	total	with children	total	with children	total	with children
Total households	**117,181**	**35,635**	**59,118**	**25,129**	**14,480**	**8,394**	**5,252**	**2,111**
Millennial (15–32)	21,723	9,312	8,104	5,478	3,873	3,188	1,807	645
Generation X (33–44)	26,107	16,532	15,035	12,170	4,105	3,474	1,366	889
Baby Boom (45–63)	42,528	9,408	24,256	7,202	4,407	1,655	1,573	551
Swing (64–76)	16,749	339	8,476	254	1,287	60	299	26
World War II (77+)	10,074	44	3,247	25	808	17	207	0

PERCENT DISTRIBUTION BY GENERATION OF HOUSEHOLDER

Total households	**100.0%**	**100.0%**	**100.0%**	**100.0%**	**100.0%**	**100.0%**	**100.0%**	**100.0%**
Millennial (15–32)	18.5	26.1	13.7	21.8	26.7	38.0	34.4	30.6
Generation X (33–44)	22.3	46.4	25.4	48.4	28.4	41.4	26.0	42.1
Baby Boom (45–63)	36.3	26.4	41.0	28.7	30.4	19.7	29.9	26.1
Swing (64–76)	14.3	1.0	14.3	1.0	8.9	0.7	5.7	1.2
World War II (77+)	8.6	0.1	5.5	0.1	5.6	0.2	3.9	0.0

PERCENT OF HOUSEHOLDS WITH CHILDREN BY TYPE

Total households	**100.0%**	**30.4%**	**100.0%**	**42.5%**	**100.0%**	**58.0%**	**100.0%**	**40.2%**
Millennial (15–32)	100.0	42.9	100.0	67.6	100.0	82.3	100.0	35.7
Generation X (33–44)	100.0	63.3	100.0	80.9	100.0	84.6	100.0	65.1
Baby Boom (45–63)	100.0	22.1	100.0	29.7	100.0	37.5	100.0	35.0
Swing (64–76)	100.0	2.0	100.0	3.0	100.0	4.6	100.0	8.8
World War II (77+)	100.0	0.4	100.0	0.8	100.0	2.2	100.0	0.0

Note: Households by generation are estimates by New Strategist.
Source: Bureau of the Census, America's Families and Living Arrangements: 2009, Internet site http://www.census.gov/ population/www/socdemo/hh-fam/cps2009.html; calculations by New Strategist

Table 8.12 Households by Generation of Householder, Type of Household, and Presence of Children of Any Age, 2009

(number and percent distribution of households by generation of householder, type of household, and presence of own children of any age, 2009; numbers in thousands)

	all households		married couples		female-headed families		male-headed families	
	total	with children	total	with children	total	with children	total	with children
Total households	**117,181**	**47,112**	**59,118**	**31,742**	**14,480**	**12,277**	**5,252**	**3,093**
Millennial (15–32)	21,723	9,333	8,104	5,488	3,873	3,196	1,807	648
Generation X (33–44)	26,107	17,417	15,035	12,608	4,105	3,861	1,366	947
Baby Boom (45–63)	42,528	16,895	24,256	12,123	4,407	3,651	1,573	1,122
Swing (64–76)	16,749	2,401	8,476	1,256	1,287	929	299	215
World War II (77+)	10,074	1,067	3,247	266	808	640	207	161

PERCENT DISTRIBUTION BY GENERATION OF HOUSEHOLDER

	all households		married couples		female-headed families		male-headed families	
Total households	**100.0%**	**100.0%**	**100.0%**	**100.0%**	**100.0%**	**100.0%**	**100.0%**	**100.0%**
Millennial (15–32)	18.5	19.8	13.7	17.3	26.7	26.0	34.4	20.9
Generation X (33–44)	22.3	37.0	25.4	39.7	28.4	31.4	26.0	30.6
Baby Boom (45–63)	36.3	35.9	41.0	38.2	30.4	29.7	29.9	36.3
Swing (64–76)	14.3	5.1	14.3	4.0	8.9	7.6	5.7	6.9
World War II (77+)	8.6	2.3	5.5	0.8	5.6	5.2	3.9	5.2

PERCENT OF HOUSEHOLDS WITH CHILDREN BY TYPE

	all households		married couples		female-headed families		male-headed families	
Total households	**100.0%**	**40.2%**	**100.0%**	**53.7%**	**100.0%**	**84.8%**	**100.0%**	**58.9%**
Millennial (15–32)	100.0	43.0	100.0	67.7	100.0	82.5	100.0	35.8
Generation X (33–44)	100.0	66.7	100.0	83.9	100.0	94.0	100.0	69.4
Baby Boom (45–63)	100.0	39.7	100.0	50.0	100.0	82.8	100.0	71.3
Swing (64–76)	100.0	14.3	100.0	14.8	100.0	72.2	100.0	71.8
World War II (77+)	100.0	10.6	100.0	8.2	100.0	79.2	100.0	77.8

Note: Households by generation are estimates by New Strategist.
Source: Bureau of the Census, America's Families and Living Arrangements: 2009, Internet site http://www.census.gov/population/www/socdemo/hh-fam/cps2009.html; calculations by New Strategist

Nearly Half of Hispanic Households include Children under Age 18

Most Asians, blacks, and non-Hispanic whites do not have school-aged or younger children in their home.

Forty-eight percent of Hispanic households include children under age 18. This compares with just 27 percent of non-Hispanic white households, 34 percent of black households, and 37 percent of Asian households.

When children of any age are considered, the proportion of households with children grows substantially. The 59 percent majority of Hispanic households include children of any age. The figure is 49 percent for Asian households, 45 percent for blacks, and 36 percent for non-Hispanic whites.

Interestingly, among Hispanics, Asians, and blacks, the proportion of households with children of any age at home is above 20 percent even among householders aged 65 or older. In contrast, among non-Hispanic whites only 9 to 11 percent of householders aged 65 or older have children living with them.

Whether or not a household includes children differentiates lifestyles. Among householders aged 25 to 29, for example, fully 60 percent of Hispanics have children under age 18 in the home compared with only 23 percent of Asian householders in the age group.

■ Asians are the best educated Americans, which is why many postpone childbearing until they are in their thirties.

Non-Hispanic white households are least likely to include children under age 18

(percent of households that include children under age 18, by race and Hispanic origin of householder, 2009)

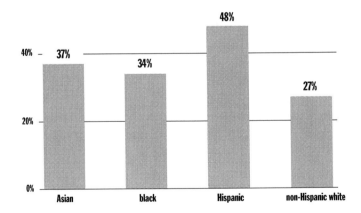

Table 8.13 Households by Age of Householder and Presence of Children, 2009: Asian Households

(number and percent distribution of Asian households by age of householder and presence of own children under age 18 and of any age at home, 2009; numbers in thousands)

	total	with children under 18	with children of any age
Total Asian households	**4,805**	**1,792**	**2,343**
Under age 25	281	30	30
Aged 25 to 29	428	99	99
Aged 30 to 34	615	299	302
Aged 35 to 39	636	435	435
Aged 40 to 44	552	372	395
Aged 45 to 49	497	296	364
Aged 50 to 54	497	167	293
Aged 55 to 64	700	80	287
Aged 65 to 74	374	13	90
Aged 75 or older	227	1	47

PERCENT DISTRIBUTION BY AGE OF HOUSEHOLDER

Total Asian households	**100.0%**	**100.0%**	**100.0%**
Under age 25	5.8	1.7	1.3
Aged 25 to 29	8.9	5.5	4.2
Aged 30 to 34	12.8	16.7	12.9
Aged 35 to 39	13.2	24.3	18.6
Aged 40 to 44	11.5	20.8	16.9
Aged 45 to 49	10.3	16.5	15.5
Aged 50 to 54	10.3	9.3	12.5
Aged 55 to 64	14.6	4.5	12.2
Aged 65 to 74	7.8	0.7	3.8
Aged 75 or older	4.7	0.1	2.0

PERCENT OF HOUSEHOLDS WITH CHILDREN BY TYPE

Total Asian households	**100.0%**	**37.3%**	**48.8%**
Under age 25	100.0	10.7	10.7
Aged 25 to 29	100.0	23.1	23.1
Aged 30 to 34	100.0	48.6	49.1
Aged 35 to 39	100.0	68.4	68.4
Aged 40 to 44	100.0	67.4	71.6
Aged 45 to 49	100.0	59.6	73.2
Aged 50 to 54	100.0	33.6	59.0
Aged 55 to 64	100.0	11.4	41.0
Aged 65 to 74	100.0	3.5	24.1
Aged 75 or older	100.0	0.4	20.7

Note: Asians are those who identify themselves as being of the race alone and those who identy themselves as being of the race in combination with other races.
Source: Bureau of the Census, America's Families and Living Arrangements: 2009, Internet site http://www.census.gov/ population/www/socdemo/hh-fam/cps2009.html; calculations by New Strategist

Table 8.14 Households by Age of Householder and Presence of Children, 2009: Black Households

(number and percent distribution of black households by age of householder and presence of own children under age 18 and of any age at home, 2009; numbers in thousands)

	total	with children under 18	with children of any age
Total black households	**15,056**	**5,141**	**6,847**
Under age 25	1,019	406	406
Aged 25 to 29	1,412	786	786
Aged 30 to 34	1,453	934	947
Aged 35 to 39	1,595	1,007	1,063
Aged 40 to 44	1,645	823	965
Aged 45 to 49	1,644	627	902
Aged 50 to 54	1,568	327	681
Aged 55 to 64	2,364	189	638
Aged 65 to 74	1,354	29	253
Aged 75 or older	1,002	13	205

PERCENT DISTRIBUTION BY AGE OF HOUSEHOLDER

	total	with children under 18	with children of any age
Total black households	**100.0%**	**100.0%**	**100.0%**
Under age 25	6.8	7.9	5.9
Aged 25 to 29	9.4	15.3	11.5
Aged 30 to 34	9.7	18.2	13.8
Aged 35 to 39	10.6	19.6	15.5
Aged 40 to 44	10.9	16.0	14.1
Aged 45 to 49	10.9	12.2	13.2
Aged 50 to 54	10.4	6.4	9.9
Aged 55 to 64	15.7	3.7	9.3
Aged 65 to 74	9.0	0.6	3.7
Aged 75 or older	6.7	0.3	3.0

PERCENT OF HOUSEHOLDS WITH CHILDREN BY TYPE

	total	with children under 18	with children of any age
Total black households	**100.0%**	**34.1%**	**45.5%**
Under age 25	100.0	39.8	39.8
Aged 25 to 29	100.0	55.7	55.7
Aged 30 to 34	100.0	64.3	65.2
Aged 35 to 39	100.0	63.1	66.6
Aged 40 to 44	100.0	50.0	58.7
Aged 45 to 49	100.0	38.1	54.9
Aged 50 to 54	100.0	20.9	43.4
Aged 55 to 64	100.0	8.0	27.0
Aged 65 to 74	100.0	2.1	18.7
Aged 75 or older	100.0	1.3	20.5

Note: Blacks are those who identify themselves as being of the race alone and those who identy themselves as being of the race in combination with other races.
Source: Bureau of the Census, America's Families and Living Arrangements: 2009, Internet site http://www.census.gov/ population/www/socdemo/hh-fam/cps2009.html; calculations by New Strategist

Table 8.15 Households by Age of Householder and Presence of Children, 2009: Hispanic Households

(number and percent distribution of Hispanic households by age of householder and presence of own children under age 18 and of any age at home, 2009; numbers in thousands)

	total	with children under 18	with children of any age
Total Hispanic households	**13,425**	**6,380**	**7,867**
Under age 25	1,166	471	471
Aged 25 to 29	1,557	930	930
Aged 30 to 34	1,726	1,239	1,245
Aged 35 to 39	1,784	1,345	1,380
Aged 40 to 44	1,608	1,101	1,207
Aged 45 to 49	1,393	722	979
Aged 50 to 54	1,155	344	675
Aged 55 to 64	1,561	188	655
Aged 65 to 74	912	31	210
Aged 75 or older	563	11	116

PERCENT DISTRIBUTION BY AGE OF HOUSEHOLDER

Total Hispanic households	**100.0%**	**100.0%**	**100.0%**
Under age 25	8.7	7.4	6.0
Aged 25 to 29	11.6	14.6	11.8
Aged 30 to 34	12.9	19.4	15.8
Aged 35 to 39	13.3	21.1	17.5
Aged 40 to 44	12.0	17.3	15.3
Aged 45 to 49	10.4	11.3	12.4
Aged 50 to 54	8.6	5.4	8.6
Aged 55 to 64	11.6	2.9	8.3
Aged 65 to 74	6.8	0.5	2.7
Aged 75 or older	4.2	0.2	1.5

PERCENT OF HOUSEHOLDS WITH CHILDREN BY TYPE

Total Hispanic households	**100.0%**	**47.5%**	**58.6%**
Under age 25	100.0	40.4	40.4
Aged 25 to 29	100.0	59.7	59.7
Aged 30 to 34	100.0	71.8	72.1
Aged 35 to 39	100.0	75.4	77.4
Aged 40 to 44	100.0	68.5	75.1
Aged 45 to 49	100.0	51.8	70.3
Aged 50 to 54	100.0	29.8	58.4
Aged 55 to 64	100.0	12.0	42.0
Aged 65 to 74	100.0	3.4	23.0
Aged 75 or older	100.0	2.0	20.6

Source: Bureau of the Census, America's Families and Living Arrangements: 2009, Internet site http://www.census.gov/ population/www/socdemo/hh-fam/cps2009.html; calculations by New Strategist

Table 8.16 Households by Age of Householder and Presence of Children, 2009: Non-Hispanic White Households

(number and percent distribution of non-Hispanic white households by age of householder and presence of own children under age 18 and of any age at home, 2009; numbers in thousands)

	total	with children under 18	with children of any age
Total non-Hispanic white households	**82,884**	**22,074**	**29,695**
Under age 25	3,869	800	800
Aged 25 to 29	5,987	2,202	2,202
Aged 30 to 34	5,983	3,415	3,426
Aged 35 to 39	6,638	4,434	4,522
Aged 40 to 44	7,535	4,546	4,960
Aged 45 to 49	8,778	3,764	4,985
Aged 50 to 54	8,857	1,941	3,716
Aged 55 to 64	15,039	816	3,042
Aged 65 to 74	10,057	127	1,146
Aged 75 or older	10,140	28	895

PERCENT DISTRIBUTION BY AGE OF HOUSEHOLDER

Total non-Hispanic white households	**100.0%**	**100.0%**	**100.0%**
Under age 25	4.7	3.6	2.7
Aged 25 to 29	7.2	10.0	7.4
Aged 30 to 34	7.2	15.5	11.5
Aged 35 to 39	8.0	20.1	15.2
Aged 40 to 44	9.1	20.6	16.7
Aged 45 to 49	10.6	17.1	16.8
Aged 50 to 54	10.7	8.8	12.5
Aged 55 to 64	18.1	3.7	10.2
Aged 65 to 74	12.1	0.6	3.9
Aged 75 or older	12.2	0.1	3.0

PERCENT OF HOUSEHOLDS WITH CHILDREN BY TYPE

Total non-Hispanic white households	**100.0%**	**26.6%**	**35.8%**
Under age 25	100.0	20.7	20.7
Aged 25 to 29	100.0	36.8	36.8
Aged 30 to 34	100.0	57.1	57.3
Aged 35 to 39	100.0	66.8	68.1
Aged 40 to 44	100.0	60.3	65.8
Aged 45 to 49	100.0	42.9	56.8
Aged 50 to 54	100.0	21.9	42.0
Aged 55 to 64	100.0	5.4	20.2
Aged 65 to 74	100.0	1.3	11.4
Aged 75 or older	100.0	0.3	8.8

Note: Non-Hispanic whites are those who identify themselves as being white alone and not Hispanic.
Source: Bureau of the Census, America's Families and Living Arrangements: 2009, Internet site http://www.census.gov/ population/www/socdemo/hh-fam/cps2009.html; calculations by New Strategist

Parents in Their Forties Have Teens

Younger parents have younger children.

Preschoolers are most likely to be found in households headed by people aged 30 to 34. Forty-one percent of households in the age group have preschoolers in their home, and 26 percent of the nation's households with preschoolers are headed by people in the 30-to-34 age group. Householders aged 35 to 39 are most likely to have children aged 6 to 11 at home, and householders aged 40 to 44 are most likely to have teenagers. Twenty-six percent of the nation's households with teenagers are headed by 40-to-44-year olds, and half are headed by 40-to-49-year-olds.

Many households include children aged 18 or older. Among households headed by people aged 45 to 49, for example, a 44 percent minority include children under age 18, but the 59 percent majority include children of any age. The figure is 44 percent among householders aged 50 to 54 and a still substantial 24 percent among those aged 55 to 64. Even among the oldest householders, aged 75 or older, 11 percent have children in their home.

■ Although most Boomers are becoming empty nesters, many still have children aged 18 or older at home.

Householders aged 30 to 34 are most likely to have preschoolers

(percent of households with children under age 6 at home, by age of householder, 2009)

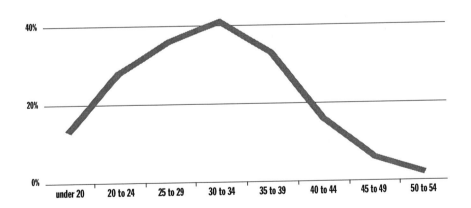

Table 8.17 Households by Age of Householder and Age of Children, 2009

(number and percent distribution of households by age of householder and age of own children living at home, and mean age of householder, 2009; numbers in thousands)

	total households	with children				
		any age	under 18	12 to 17	6 to 11	under 6
Total households	**117,181**	**47,112**	**35,635**	**16,678**	**16,454**	**15,629**
Under age 20	843	114	114	0	9	108
Aged 20 to 24	5,514	1,603	1,603	3	218	1,551
Aged 25 to 29	9,463	4,041	4,041	230	1,701	3,436
Aged 30 to 34	9,839	5,958	5,924	1,443	3,184	4,031
Aged 35 to 39	10,711	7,432	7,253	3,229	4,172	3,573
Aged 40 to 44	11,460	7,602	6,909	4,329	3,785	1,825
Aged 45 to 49	12,437	7,279	5,442	4,022	2,205	706
Aged 50 to 54	12,196	5,410	2,812	2,278	769	212
Aged 55 to 64	19,883	4,673	1,282	983	334	137
Aged 65 to 74	12,842	1,730	203	131	61	35
Aged 75 or older	11,992	1,271	51	30	17	17
Mean age (years)	49.8	43.1	39.5	44.0	38.8	33.8

PERCENT DISTRIBUTION BY AGE OF HOUSEHOLDER

Total households	**100.0%**	**100.0%**	**100.0%**	**100.0%**	**100.0%**	**100.0%**
Under age 20	0.7	0.2	0.3	0.0	0.1	0.7
Aged 20 to 24	4.7	3.4	4.5	0.0	1.3	9.9
Aged 25 to 29	8.1	8.6	11.3	1.4	10.3	22.0
Aged 30 to 34	8.4	12.6	16.6	8.7	19.4	25.8
Aged 35 to 39	9.1	15.8	20.4	19.4	25.4	22.9
Aged 40 to 44	9.8	16.1	19.4	26.0	23.0	11.7
Aged 45 to 49	10.6	15.5	15.3	24.1	13.4	4.5
Aged 50 to 54	10.4	11.5	7.9	13.7	4.7	1.4
Aged 55 to 64	17.0	9.9	3.6	5.9	2.0	0.9
Aged 65 to 74	11.0	3.7	0.6	0.8	0.4	0.2
Aged 75 or older	10.2	2.7	0.1	0.2	0.1	0.1

PERCENT DISTRIBUTION BY AGE OF CHILD

Total households	**100.0%**	**40.2%**	**30.4%**	**14.2%**	**14.0%**	**13.3%**
Under age 20	100.0	13.5	13.5	0.0	1.1	12.8
Aged 20 to 24	100.0	29.1	29.1	0.1	4.0	28.1
Aged 25 to 29	100.0	42.7	42.7	2.4	18.0	36.3
Aged 30 to 34	100.0	60.6	60.2	14.7	32.4	41.0
Aged 35 to 39	100.0	69.4	67.7	30.1	39.0	33.4
Aged 40 to 44	100.0	66.3	60.3	37.8	33.0	15.9
Aged 45 to 49	100.0	58.5	43.8	32.3	17.7	5.7
Aged 50 to 54	100.0	44.4	23.1	18.7	6.3	1.7
Aged 55 to 64	100.0	23.5	6.4	4.9	1.7	0.7
Aged 65 to 74	100.0	13.5	1.6	1.0	0.5	0.3
Aged 75 or older	100.0	10.6	0.4	0.3	0.1	0.1

Note: Numbers do not add to total because many households have children in more than one age group.
Source: Bureau of the Census, America's Families and Living Arrangements: 2009, Internet site http://www.census.gov/population/www/socdemo/hh-fam/cps2009.html; calculations by New Strategist

Householders in Their Thirties Have the Most Kids

Nearly 19 percent of householders aged 35 to 39 have three or more children.

Overall, only 30 percent of the nation's households include children under age 18. Thirteen percent of households have one child under age 18, 11 percent have two, 4 percent have three, and just 2 percent have four or more.

Householders aged 35 to 39 are most likely to have children under age 18 at home, and they also have the largest number of children in their households. Twenty percent of these householders have one child under age 18, 29 percent have two, and 19 percent have three or more.

The proportion of households with only one child under age 18 peaks in the older age groups as the nest begins to empty. Twenty-three percent of householders aged 45 to 49 have one child under age 18 at home—a larger proportion than in any other age group.

■ Although families have gotten smaller, housing and cars have gotten larger. Fewer children means parents have more resources to devote to each child.

Many one-child families are the result of an emptying nest

(percent of households with one child under age 18 at home, by age of householder, 2009)

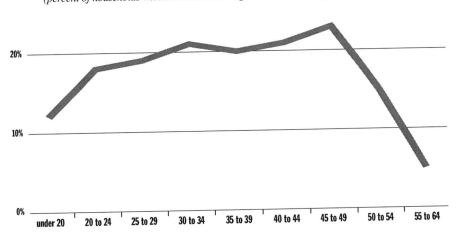

Table 8.18 Households by Age of Householder and Number of Children, 2009

(number and percent distribution of households by age of householder and number of children under age 18 living at home, 2009; numbers in thousands)

	total	with one or more children under age 18				
		total	one	two	three	four or more
Total households	**117,181**	**35,635**	**15,217**	**13,139**	**5,245**	**2,034**
Under age 20	843	114	97	15	1	0
Aged 20 to 24	5,514	1,603	970	476	141	16
Aged 25 to 29	9,463	4,041	1,788	1,425	601	227
Aged 30 to 34	9,839	5,924	2,101	2,274	1,070	480
Aged 35 to 39	10,711	7,253	2,176	3,094	1,403	580
Aged 40 to 44	11,460	6,909	2,421	2,881	1,143	464
Aged 45 to 49	12,437	5,442	2,801	1,864	608	170
Aged 50 to 54	12,196	2,812	1,799	767	180	65
Aged 55 to 64	19,883	1,282	896	280	80	26
Aged 65 to 74	12,842	203	141	47	11	4
Aged 75 or older	11,992	51	28	15	7	1

PERCENT DISTRIBUTION BY AGE OF HOUSEHOLDER

Total households	**100.0%**	**100.0%**	**100.0%**	**100.0%**	**100.0%**	**100.0%**
Under age 20	0.7	0.3	0.6	0.1	0.0	0.0
Aged 20 to 24	4.7	4.5	6.4	3.6	2.7	0.8
Aged 25 to 29	8.1	11.3	11.8	10.8	11.5	11.2
Aged 30 to 34	8.4	16.6	13.8	17.3	20.4	23.6
Aged 35 to 39	9.1	20.4	14.3	23.5	26.7	28.5
Aged 40 to 44	9.8	19.4	15.9	21.9	21.8	22.8
Aged 45 to 49	10.6	15.3	18.4	14.2	11.6	8.4
Aged 50 to 54	10.4	7.9	11.8	5.8	3.4	3.2
Aged 55 to 64	17.0	3.6	5.9	2.1	1.5	1.3
Aged 65 to 74	11.0	0.6	0.9	0.4	0.2	0.2
Aged 75 or older	10.2	0.1	0.2	0.1	0.1	0.0

PERCENT DISTRIBUTION BY NUMBER OF CHILDREN

Total households	**100.0%**	**30.4%**	**13.0%**	**11.2%**	**4.5%**	**1.7%**
Under age 20	100.0	13.5	11.5	1.8	0.1	0.0
Aged 20 to 24	100.0	29.1	17.6	8.6	2.6	0.3
Aged 25 to 29	100.0	42.7	18.9	15.1	6.4	2.4
Aged 30 to 34	100.0	60.2	21.4	23.1	10.9	4.9
Aged 35 to 39	100.0	67.7	20.3	28.9	13.1	5.4
Aged 40 to 44	100.0	60.3	21.1	25.1	10.0	4.0
Aged 45 to 49	100.0	43.8	22.5	15.0	4.9	1.4
Aged 50 to 54	100.0	23.1	14.8	6.3	1.5	0.5
Aged 55 to 64	100.0	6.4	4.5	1.4	0.4	0.1
Aged 65 to 74	100.0	1.6	1.1	0.4	0.1	0.0
Aged 75 or older	100.0	0.4	0.2	0.1	0.1	0.0

Source: Bureau of the Census, America's Families and Living Arrangements: 2009, Internet site http://www.census.gov/population/www/socdemo/hh-fam/cps2009.html; calculations by New Strategist

Householders in the Northeast Are Older

The West has the youngest householders.

Because the South is the nation's most populous region, it is home to the largest share of households in each age group. But there are variations in the age composition of households by region, although the differences are not large.

The Northeast has the smallest share of young householders. Only 19 percent of householders in the Northeast are under age 35 compared with 24 percent in the West. Twenty-three percent of households in the Northeast are headed by people aged 65 or older, versus only 19 percent in the West.

By generation, Millennials are most prevalent in the West, where they account for 20 percent of households. Millennials' smallest share is in the Northeast, where they head just 16 percent of households. The Baby-Boom generation accounts for 35 to 37 percent of householders in every region.

■ Regional differences in households by age are small. Much larger differences by age can be found at the city level, especially in areas hosting universities, military bases, or retirement communities.

The Northeast has the largest share of older householders

(percent of households headed by people under age 30 and aged 65 or older, by region, 2009)

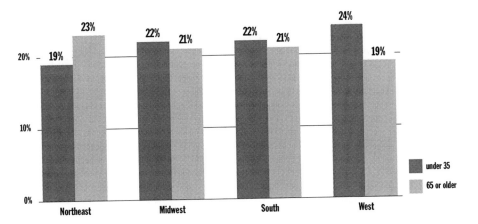

Table 8.19 Households by Age of Householder and Region of Residence, 2009

(number and percent distribution of households by age of householder and region of residence, and mean age, 2009; numbers in thousands)

	total	Northeast	Midwest	South	West
Total households	**117,181**	**21,309**	**26,282**	**43,423**	**26,166**
Under age 20	843	104	161	361	217
Aged 20 to 24	5,514	796	1,256	2,068	1,394
Aged 25 to 29	9,463	1,440	2,163	3,736	2,125
Aged 30 to 34	9,839	1,695	2,137	3,581	2,427
Aged 35 to 39	10,711	1,840	2,332	4,091	2,449
Aged 40 to 44	11,460	2,224	2,473	4,202	2,560
Aged 45 to 49	12,437	2,276	2,896	4,457	2,809
Aged 50 to 54	12,196	2,289	2,821	4,379	2,706
Aged 55 to 64	19,883	3,779	4,477	7,225	4,402
Aged 65 to 74	12,842	2,366	2,740	5,017	2,719
Aged 75 or older	11,992	2,500	2,826	4,307	2,358
Mean age (years)	49.8	51.1	49.9	49.6	48.9

PERCENT DISTRIBUTION BY AGE

	total	Northeast	Midwest	South	West
Total households	**100.0%**	**100.0%**	**100.0%**	**100.0%**	**100.0%**
Under age 20	0.7	0.5	0.6	0.8	0.8
Aged 20 to 24	4.7	3.7	4.8	4.8	5.3
Aged 25 to 29	8.1	6.8	8.2	8.6	8.1
Aged 30 to 34	8.4	8.0	8.1	8.2	9.3
Aged 35 to 39	9.1	8.6	8.9	9.4	9.4
Aged 40 to 44	9.8	10.4	9.4	9.7	9.8
Aged 45 to 49	10.6	10.7	11.0	10.3	10.7
Aged 50 to 54	10.4	10.7	10.7	10.1	10.3
Aged 55 to 64	17.0	17.7	17.0	16.6	16.8
Aged 65 to 74	11.0	11.1	10.4	11.6	10.4
Aged 75 or older	10.2	11.7	10.8	9.9	9.0

PERCENT DISTRIBUTION BY REGION

	total	Northeast	Midwest	South	West
Total households	**100.0%**	**18.2%**	**22.4%**	**37.1%**	**22.3%**
Under age 20	100.0	12.3	19.1	42.8	25.7
Aged 20 to 24	100.0	14.4	22.8	37.5	25.3
Aged 25 to 29	100.0	15.2	22.9	39.5	22.5
Aged 30 to 34	100.0	17.2	21.7	36.4	24.7
Aged 35 to 39	100.0	17.2	21.8	38.2	22.9
Aged 40 to 44	100.0	19.4	21.6	36.7	22.3
Aged 45 to 49	100.0	18.3	23.3	35.8	22.6
Aged 50 to 54	100.0	18.8	23.1	35.9	22.2
Aged 55 to 64	100.0	19.0	22.5	36.3	22.1
Aged 65 to 74	100.0	18.4	21.3	39.1	21.2
Aged 75 or older	100.0	20.8	23.6	35.9	19.7

Source: Bureau of the Census, America's Families and Living Arrangements: 2009, Internet site http://www.census.gov/population/www/socdemo/hh-fam/cps2009.html; calculations by New Strategist

Table 8.20 Households by Generation of Householder and Region of Residence, 2009

(number and percent distribution of households by generation of householder and region of residence, 2009; numbers in thousands)

	total	Northeast	Midwest	South	West
Total households	**117,181**	**21,309**	**26,282**	**43,423**	**26,166**
Millennial (15–32)	21,723	3,357	4,862	8,314	5,192
Generation X (33–44)	26,107	4,742	5,660	9,725	5,980
Baby Boom (45–63)	42,528	7,966	9,746	15,339	9,477
Swing (64–76)	16,749	3,144	3,640	6,429	3,536
World War II (77+)	10,074	2,100	2,374	3,617	1,981

PERCENT DISTRIBUTION BY GENERATION OF HOUSEHOLDER

Total households	**100.0%**	**100.0%**	**100.0%**	**100.0%**	**100.0%**
Millennial (15–32)	18.5	15.8	18.5	19.1	19.8
Generation X (33–44)	22.3	22.3	21.5	22.4	22.9
Baby Boom (45–63)	36.3	37.4	37.1	35.3	36.2
Swing (64–76)	14.3	14.8	13.8	14.8	13.5
World War II (77+)	8.6	9.9	9.0	8.3	7.6

PERCENT DISTRIBUTION BY REGION

Total households	**100.0%**	**18.2%**	**22.4%**	**37.1%**	**22.3%**
Millennial (15–32)	100.0	15.5	22.4	38.3	23.9
Generation X (33–44)	100.0	18.2	21.7	37.3	22.9
Baby Boom (45–63)	100.0	18.7	22.9	36.1	22.3
Swing (64–76)	100.0	18.8	21.7	38.4	21.1
World War II (77+)	100.0	20.8	23.6	35.9	19.7

Note: Households by generation are estimates by New Strategist.
Source: Bureau of the Census, America's Families and Living Arrangements: 2009, Internet site http://www.census.gov/population/www/socdemo/hh-fam/cps2009.html; calculations by New Strategist

Many Children Live with Their Mother Only

Only two out of three live with both parents who are married to each other.

In 2009, 70 percent of children under age 18 lived with both parents and a slightly smaller 67 percent lived with both parents who were married to each other. The percentage of children who live with both parents ranges from a high of 85 percent among Asians to a low of 38 percent among blacks.

Nearly one in four children lives with their mother only. Among Asians, just 10 percent of children live with their mother only. The figure is 50 percent among blacks.

Few children live with their father only, the proportion being 3 to 4 percent regardless of race or Hispanic origin. A slightly larger share of children lives with neither parent, the figure being as high as 8 percent among blacks.

■ Only 6 percent of children live with a stepparent and just 2 percent live with an adoptive parent.

Most children still live with two parents

(percent distribution of children by living arrangement, 2009)

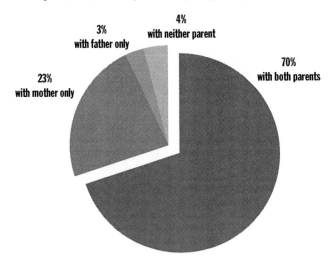

4%
with neither parent

3%
with father only

23%
with mother only

70%
with both parents

Table 8.21 Living Arrangements of Children by Race and Hispanic Origin, 2009

(number and percent distribution of children under age 18 by race, Hispanic origin, and living arrangement, 2009; numbers in thousands)

	total	living with both parents			mother only	father only	neither parent
		total	married to each other	not married to each other			
Total children	**74,230**	**51,836**	**49,550**	**2,286**	**16,911**	**2,504**	**2,979**
Asian	3,035	2,586	2,543	43	311	77	61
Black	11,235	4,281	3,904	377	5,645	378	932
Hispanic	16,360	11,241	10,419	822	4,070	413	637
Non-Hispanic white	41,418	32,330	31,385	945	6,355	1,559	1,173

PERCENT DISTRIBUTION BY LIVING ARRANGEMENT

	total		married to each other	not married to each other	mother only	father only	neither parent
Total children	**100.0%**	**69.8%**	**66.8%**	**3.1%**	**22.8%**	**3.4%**	**4.0%**
Asian	100.0	85.2	83.8	1.4	10.2	2.5	2.0
Black	100.0	38.1	34.7	3.4	50.2	3.4	8.3
Hispanic	100.0	68.7	63.7	5.0	24.9	2.5	3.9
Non-Hispanic white	100.0	78.1	75.8	2.3	15.3	3.8	2.8

PERCENT DISTRIBUTION BY RACE AND HISPANIC ORIGIN

	total		married to each other	not married to each other	mother only	father only	neither parent
Total children	**100.0%**	**100.0%**	**100.0%**	**100.0%**	**100.0%**	**100.0%**	**100.0%**
Asian	4.1	5.0	5.1	1.9	1.8	3.1	2.0
Black	15.1	8.3	7.9	16.5	33.4	15.1	31.3
Hispanic	22.0	21.7	21.0	36.0	24.1	16.5	21.4
Non-Hispanic white	55.8	62.4	63.3	41.3	37.6	62.3	39.4

Source: Bureau of the Census, America's Families and Living Arrangements: 2009, Internet site http://www.census.gov/population/www/socdemo/hh-fam/cps2009.html; calculations by New Strategist

Table 8.22 Children Who Live with Biological, Step, or Adoptive Parents, 2009

(number and percent distribution of children under age 18 who live with biological, step, or adoptive parents, 2009; numbers in thousands)

	number	percent distribution
TOTAL CHILDREN	**74,230**	**100.0%**
Living with two parents	**51,835**	**69.8**
Married parents	49,550	66.8
Unmarried parents	2,286	3.1
Biological mother and father	46,364	62.5
Married parents	44,328	59.7
Biological mother and stepfather	3,316	4.5
Biological father and stepmother	894	1.2
Biological mother and adoptive father	163	0.2
Biological father and adoptive mother	37	0.0
Adoptive mother and father	834	1.1
Other	227	0.3
Living with one parent	**19,415**	**26.2**
Mother only	16,911	22.8
Biological	16,645	22.4
Father only	2,504	3.4
Biological	2,417	3.3
Living with no parents	**2,979**	**4.0**
Grandparents	1,538	2.1
Other	1,441	1.9
At least one biological parent	**69,837**	**94.1**
At least one stepparent	**4,550**	**6.1**
At least one adoptive parent	**1,302**	**1.8**

Source: Bureau of the Census, America's Families and Living Arrangements: 2009, Internet site http://www.census.gov/ population/www/socdemo/hh-fam/cps2009.html; calculations by New Strategist

Nearly 7 Million Children Live with a Grandparent

Most also live with one or both parents.

Nine percent of the nation's children have a grandparent living in the same household. Most with a grandparent in the home (64 percent) live in the grandparent's household. A smaller 36 percent have a grandparent who lives with them in their parents' household.

Children who live in single-parent families are most likely to have a grandparent in the same household. Among children who live with their mother only, 17 percent also have a grandparent in the home. Seventy percent of them live with their mother in their grandparents' household.

■ Of the 7 million children who live with a grandparent, 1.5 million (or 22 percent) do not live with a parent as well.

Few children who live with both parents also live with a grandparent

(percent of children who live with a grandparent, by living arrangement of child, 2009)

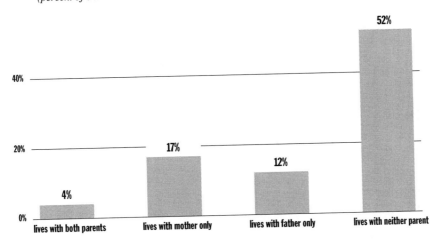

Table 8.23 Children Living with Grandparents by Presence of Parents, 2009

(number and percent distribution of children under age 18 by presence of grandparents and parents in the home, 2009; numbers in thousands)

	total	living with both parents	living with mother only	living with father only	living with neither parent
Total children	**74,230**	**51,835**	**16,911**	**2,504**	**2,979**
No grandparent in home	67,266	49,528	14,090	2,206	1,441
At least one grandparent in home	6,964	2,306	2,821	298	1,538
Grandmother and grandfather in home	2,723	715	1,151	122	735
Grandmother only in home	3,527	1,213	1,438	131	744
Grandfather only in home	714	378	232	45	59
Total children with grandparent in home	**6,964**	**2,306**	**2,821**	**298**	**1,538**
Grandparent is not a householder	2,491	1,547	856	88	0
Grandmother and grandfather in home	454	296	138	20	0
Grandmother only in home	1,652	980	620	52	0
Grandfather only in home	385	271	98	16	0
Grandparent is a householder	4,474	760	1,965	210	1,538
Grandmother and grandfather in home	2,270	419	1,013	102	735
Grandmother only in home	1,875	233	818	80	744
Grandfather only in home	329	108	134	28	59

PERCENT DISTRIBUTION OF CHILDREN BY GRANDPARENT AND PARENT PRESENCE IN HOME

	total	living with both parents	living with mother only	living with father only	living with neither parent
Total children	**100.0%**	**100.0%**	**100.0%**	**100.0%**	**100.0%**
No grandparent in home	90.6	95.5	83.3	88.1	48.4
At least one grandparent in home	9.4	4.4	16.7	11.9	51.6
Grandmother and grandfather in home	3.7	1.4	6.8	4.9	24.7
Grandmother only in home	4.8	2.3	8.5	5.2	25.0
Grandfather only in home	1.0	0.7	1.4	1.8	2.0
Total children with grandparent in home	**100.0**	**100.0**	**100.0**	**100.0**	**100.0**
Grandparent is not a householder	35.8	67.1	30.3	29.5	0.0
Grandmother and grandfather in home	6.5	12.8	4.9	6.7	0.0
Grandmother only in home	23.7	42.5	22.0	17.4	0.0
Grandfather only in home	5.5	11.8	3.5	5.4	0.0
Grandparent is a householder	64.2	33.0	69.7	70.5	100.0
Grandmother and grandfather in home	32.6	18.2	35.9	34.2	47.8
Grandmother only in home	26.9	10.1	29.0	26.8	48.4
Grandfather only in home	4.7	4.7	4.8	9.4	3.8

Source: Bureau of the Census, America's Families and Living Arrangements: 2009, Internet site http://www.census.gov/ population/www/socdemo/hh-fam/cps2009.html; calculations by New Strategist

Living Arrangements Differ by Generation

Many Millennials still live with mom and dad.

The generations are distinguished by their living arrangements. The largest share of Millennials still lives with their parents. Among Generation Xers, Boomers, and members of the Swing generation, most men and women are married-couple householders or spouses. In the World War II generation, the largest share of women lives alone.

Women marry at a younger age than men, and they are more likely than men to be widowed and live alone in old age. In every age group under age 45, women are more likely than men to be a married-couple householder or spouse. From age 50 on, however, men are more likely than women to be married and living with a spouse. The percentage of women who are a married-couple householder or spouse falls below 50 percent in the 75-to-84 age group as a growing share become widows. Sixty percent of women aged 85 or older live alone compared with only 32 percent of men.

■ The wants and needs of men and women diverge as lifestyle differences grow with age.

Women are much more likely than men to live alone in old age

(percent of people aged 85 or older who are living with a spouse or living alone, by sex, 2009)

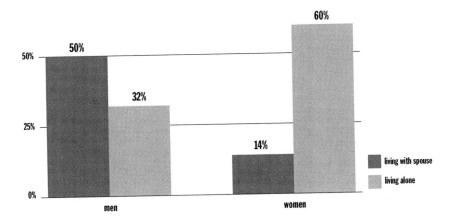

Table 8.24 Men by Living Arrangement and Age, 2009

(number and percent distribution of men aged 15 or older by living arrangement and age, 2009; numbers in thousands)

	total	15–17	18–19	20–24	25–29	30–34	35–39	40–44	45–49	50–54	55–64	65–74	75–84	85+
TOTAL MEN	**116,666**	**6,692**	**4,084**	**10,414**	**10,849**	**9,570**	**10,164**	**10,314**	**11,162**	**10,610**	**16,501**	**9,400**	**5,415**	**1,491**
Living in family household	91,309	6,547	3,743	7,445	7,085	7,136	8,078	8,154	8,882	8,301	13,198	7,630	4,140	972
Living in nonfamily household	25,357	146	342	2,969	3,764	2,433	2,086	2,161	2,279	2,309	3,304	1,769	1,275	520
Householder	**59,099**	**87**	**276**	**2,644**	**4,766**	**5,124**	**5,458**	**6,021**	**6,423**	**6,492**	**10,639**	**6,459**	**3,730**	**981**
Family householder	41,405	83	150	1,178	2,613	3,584	4,125	4,486	4,733	4,654	7,919	4,851	2,543	487
Married-couple householder	36,152	1	20	554	1,967	3,042	3,584	3,878	4,112	4,200	7,366	4,647	2,368	413
Other family householder	5,253	82	130	624	646	542	541	608	621	454	553	204	175	74
Nonfamily householder	17,694	4	126	1,466	2,153	1,540	1,333	1,535	1,690	1,838	2,720	1,608	1,187	494
Living alone	13,758	3	66	801	1,272	1,038	1,021	1,238	1,407	1,521	2,344	1,454	1,114	480
Living with nonrelatives	3,936	1	60	665	882	502	313	297	283	316	376	154	74	14
Not a householder	**57,567**	**6,606**	**3,809**	**7,770**	**6,083**	**4,445**	**4,706**	**4,294**	**4,738**	**4,118**	**5,863**	**2,940**	**1,685**	**511**
In family household	49,904	6,464	3,593	6,267	4,472	3,552	3,953	3,668	4,149	3,647	5,279	2,779	1,597	485
Spouse of householder	22,965	1	4	345	1,328	2,030	2,675	2,602	2,879	2,762	4,322	2,415	1,275	326
Child of householder	20,051	5,921	3,203	5,016	2,248	930	810	587	683	384	250	18	0	0
Other relative of householder	6,888	542	386	906	896	592	468	479	587	501	707	346	322	159
In nonfamily household	7,663	142	216	1,503	1,611	893	753	626	589	471	584	161	88	26

Percent distribution by living arrangement

	total	15–17	18–19	20–24	25–29	30–34	35–39	40–44	45–49	50–54	55–64	65–74	75–84	85+
TOTAL MEN	100.0%	100.0%	100.0%	100.0%	100.0%	100.0%	100.0%	100.0%	100.0%	100.0%	100.0%	100.0%	100.0%	100.0%
Living in family household	78.3	97.8	91.7	71.5	65.3	74.6	79.5	79.1	79.6	78.2	80.0	81.2	76.5	65.2
Living in nonfamily household	21.7	2.2	8.4	28.5	34.7	25.4	20.5	21.0	20.4	21.8	20.0	18.8	23.5	34.9
Householder	**50.7**	**1.3**	**6.8**	**25.4**	**43.9**	**53.5**	**53.7**	**58.4**	**57.5**	**61.2**	**64.5**	**68.7**	**68.9**	**65.8**
Family householder	35.5	1.2	3.7	11.3	24.1	37.5	40.6	43.5	42.4	43.9	48.0	51.6	47.0	32.7
Married-couple householder	31.0	0.0	0.5	5.3	18.1	31.8	35.3	37.6	36.8	39.6	44.6	49.4	43.7	27.7
Other family householder	4.5	1.2	3.2	6.0	6.0	5.7	5.3	5.9	5.6	4.3	3.4	2.2	3.2	5.0
Nonfamily householder	15.2	0.1	3.1	14.1	19.8	16.1	13.1	14.9	15.1	17.3	16.5	17.1	21.9	33.1
Living alone	11.8	0.0	1.6	7.7	11.7	10.8	10.0	12.0	12.6	14.3	14.2	15.5	20.6	32.2
Living with nonrelatives	3.4	0.0	1.5	6.4	8.1	5.2	3.1	2.9	2.5	3.0	2.3	1.6	1.4	0.9
Not a householder	**49.3**	**98.7**	**93.3**	**74.6**	**56.1**	**46.4**	**46.3**	**41.6**	**42.4**	**38.8**	**35.5**	**31.3**	**31.1**	**34.3**
In family household	42.8	96.6	88.0	60.2	41.2	37.1	38.9	35.6	37.2	34.4	32.0	29.6	29.5	32.5
Spouse of householder	19.7	0.0	0.1	3.3	12.2	21.2	26.3	25.2	25.8	26.0	26.2	25.7	23.5	21.9
Child of householder	17.2	88.5	78.4	48.2	20.7	9.7	8.0	5.7	6.1	3.6	1.5	0.2	0.0	0.0
Other relative of householder	5.9	8.1	9.5	8.7	8.3	6.2	4.6	4.6	5.3	4.7	4.3	3.7	5.9	10.7
In nonfamily household	6.6	2.1	5.3	14.4	14.8	9.3	7.4	6.1	5.3	4.4	3.5	1.7	1.6	1.7

Source: Bureau of the Census, America's Families and Living Arrangements: 2009, Internet site http://www.census.gov/population/www/socdemo/hh-fam/cps2009.html; calculations by New Strategist

Table 8.25 Men by Living Arrangement and Generation, 2009

(number and percent distribution of men aged 15 or older by living arrangement and generation, 2009; numbers in thousands)

	total	Millennials (15 to 32)	Generation X (33 to 44)	Baby Boom (45 to 63)	Swing (64 to 76)	World War II (77 or older)
TOTAL MEN	**116,666**	**39,695**	**22,392**	**36,623**	**12,133**	**5,823**
Living in family household	91,309	30,529	17,659	29,061	9,778	4,284
Living in nonfamily household	25,357	9,167	4,734	7,562	2,354	1,540
Householder	**59,099**	**11,872**	**12,504**	**22,490**	**8,269**	**3,965**
Family householder	41,405	6,891	9,328	16,514	6,152	2,521
Married-couple householder	36,152	4,976	8,070	14,941	5,857	2,307
Other family householder	5,253	1,916	1,257	1,573	294	214
Nonfamily householder	17,694	4,981	3,176	5,976	2,117	1,444
Living alone	13,758	2,972	2,467	5,038	1,911	1,371
Living with nonrelatives	3,936	2,010	710	937	206	73
Not a householder	**57,567**	**27,824**	**9,889**	**14,133**	**3,863**	**1,859**
In family household	49,904	23,638	8,331	12,547	3,626	1,763
Spouse of householder	22,965	3,302	5,683	9,531	3,102	1,346
Child of householder	20,051	17,132	1,583	1,292	43	0
Other relative of householder	6,888	3,204	1,065	1,724	481	417
In nonfamily household	7,663	4,186	1,558	1,586	237	96

Percent distribution by living arrangement

	total	Millennials (15 to 32)	Generation X (33 to 44)	Baby Boom (45 to 63)	Swing (64 to 76)	World War II (77 or older)
TOTAL MEN	**100.0%**	**100.0%**	**100.0%**	**100.0%**	**100.0%**	**100.0%**
Living in family household	78.3	76.9	78.9	79.4	80.6	73.6
Living in nonfamily household	21.7	23.1	21.1	20.6	19.4	26.4
Householder	**50.7**	**29.9**	**55.8**	**61.4**	**68.2**	**68.1**
Family householder	35.5	17.4	41.7	45.1	50.7	43.3
Married-couple householder	31.0	12.5	36.0	40.8	48.3	39.6
Other family householder	4.5	4.8	5.6	4.3	2.4	3.7
Nonfamily householder	15.2	12.5	14.2	16.3	17.5	24.8
Living alone	11.8	7.5	11.0	13.8	15.8	23.5
Living with nonrelatives	3.4	5.1	3.2	2.6	1.7	1.3
Not a householder	**49.3**	**70.1**	**44.2**	**38.6**	**31.8**	**31.9**
In family household	42.8	59.5	37.2	34.3	29.9	30.3
Spouse of householder	19.7	8.3	25.4	26.0	25.6	23.1
Child of householder	17.2	43.2	7.1	3.5	0.4	0.0
Other relative of householder	5.9	8.1	4.8	4.7	4.0	7.2
In nonfamily household	6.6	10.5	7.0	4.3	2.0	1.7

Note: Men by generation are estimates by New Strategist.
Source: Bureau of the Census, America's Families and Living Arrangements: 2009, Internet site http://www.census.gov/ population/www/socdemo/hh-fam/cps2009.html; calculations by New Strategist

Table 8.26 Women by Living Arrangement and Age, 2009

(number and percent distribution of women aged 15 or older by living arrangement and age, 2009; numbers in thousands)

	total	15–17	18–19	20–24	25–29	30–34	35–39	40–44	45–49	50–54	55–64	65–74	75–84	85+
TOTAL WOMEN	**123,366**	**6,477**	**3,965**	**10,196**	**10,383**	**9,686**	**10,270**	**10,553**	**11,547**	**11,043**	**17,777**	**11,003**	**7,590**	**2,876**
Living in family household	96,634	6,297	3,499	7,531	7,817	8,141	8,979	9,204	9,789	9,011	13,704	7,529	4,057	1,075
Living in nonfamily household	26,732	180	465	2,664	2,566	1,545	1,291	1,349	1,758	2,033	4,073	3,475	3,532	1,800
Householder	**58,082**	**100**	**380**	**2,870**	**4,697**	**4,714**	**5,253**	**5,439**	**6,014**	**5,704**	**9,245**	**6,384**	**5,144**	**2,136**
Family householder	37,445	87	204	1,693	3,338	3,812	4,415	4,521	4,688	4,044	5,544	3,053	1,667	378
Married-couple householder	22,965	3	31	595	1,754	2,259	2,675	2,777	2,939	2,730	4,051	2,068	941	142
Other family householder	14,480	84	173	1,098	1,584	1,553	1,740	1,744	1,749	1,314	1,493	985	726	236
Nonfamily householder	20,637	13	176	1,177	1,359	902	838	918	1,326	1,660	3,701	3,331	3,477	1,758
Living alone	17,899	8	66	593	829	657	699	740	1,095	1,475	3,406	3,203	3,396	1,732
Living with nonrelatives	2,738	5	110	584	530	245	139	178	231	185	295	128	81	26
Not a householder	**65,284**	**6,377**	**3,584**	**7,325**	**5,686**	**4,972**	**5,017**	**5,114**	**5,533**	**5,340**	**8,532**	**4,620**	**2,445**	**739**
In family household	59,189	6,210	3,295	5,838	4,479	4,329	4,564	4,683	5,101	4,967	8,160	4,476	2,390	697
Spouse of householder	36,152	3	24	1,014	2,633	3,433	3,903	4,039	4,290	4,166	7,064	3,716	1,609	258
Child of householder	15,977	5,696	2,933	3,990	1,376	612	399	272	304	190	181	0	0	0
Other relative of householder	7,060	511	338	834	470	284	262	372	507	611	915	760	781	439
In nonfamily household	6,095	167	289	1,487	1,207	643	453	431	432	373	372	144	55	42

Percent distribution by living arrangement

	total	15-17	18-19	20-24	25-29	30-34	35-39	40-44	45-49	50-54	55-64	65-74	75-84	85+
TOTAL WOMEN	100.0%	100.0%	100.0%	100.0%	100.0%	100.0%	100.0%	100.0%	100.0%	100.0%	100.0%	100.0%	100.0%	100.0%
Living in family household	78.3	97.2	88.2	73.9	75.3	84.0	87.4	87.2	84.8	81.6	77.1	68.4	53.5	37.4
Living in nonfamily household	21.7	2.8	11.7	26.1	24.7	16.0	12.6	12.8	15.2	18.4	22.9	31.6	46.5	62.6
Householder	**47.1**	**1.5**	**9.6**	**28.1**	**45.2**	**48.7**	**51.1**	**51.5**	**52.1**	**51.7**	**52.0**	**58.0**	**67.8**	**74.3**
Family householder	30.4	1.3	5.1	16.6	32.1	39.4	43.0	42.8	40.6	36.6	31.2	27.7	22.0	13.1
Married-couple householder	18.6	0.0	0.8	5.8	16.9	23.3	26.0	26.3	25.5	24.7	22.8	18.8	12.4	4.9
Other family householder	11.7	1.3	4.4	10.8	15.3	16.0	16.9	16.5	15.1	11.9	8.4	9.0	9.6	8.2
Nonfamily householder	16.7	0.2	4.4	11.5	13.1	9.3	8.2	8.7	11.5	15.0	20.8	30.3	45.8	61.1
Living alone	14.5	0.1	1.7	5.8	8.0	6.8	6.8	7.0	9.5	13.4	19.2	29.1	44.7	60.2
Living with nonrelatives	2.2	0.1	2.8	5.7	5.1	2.5	1.4	1.7	2.0	1.7	1.7	1.2	1.1	0.9
Not a householder	**52.9**	**98.5**	**90.4**	**71.8**	**54.8**	**51.3**	**48.9**	**48.5**	**47.9**	**48.4**	**48.0**	**42.0**	**32.2**	**25.7**
In family household	48.0	95.9	83.1	57.3	43.1	44.7	44.4	44.4	44.2	45.0	45.9	40.7	31.5	24.2
Spouse of householder	29.3	0.0	0.6	9.9	25.4	35.4	38.0	38.3	37.2	37.7	39.7	33.8	21.2	9.0
Child of householder	13.0	87.9	74.0	39.1	13.3	6.3	3.9	2.6	2.6	1.7	1.0	0.0	0.0	0.0
Other relative of householder	5.7	7.9	8.5	8.2	4.5	2.9	2.6	3.5	4.4	5.5	5.1	6.9	10.3	15.3
In nonfamily household	4.9	2.6	7.3	14.6	11.6	6.6	4.4	4.1	3.7	3.4	2.1	1.3	0.7	1.5

Source: Bureau of the Census, America's Families and Living Arrangements: 2009, Internet site http://www.census.gov/population/www/socdemo/hh-fam/cps2009.html; calculations by New Strategist

Table 8.27 Women by Living Arrangement and Generation, 2009

(number and percent distribution of women aged 15 or older by living arrangement and age, 2009; numbers in thousands)

	total	Millennials (15 to 32)	Generation X (33 to 44)	Baby Boom (45 to 63)	Swing (64 to 76)	World War II (77 or older)
TOTAL WOMEN	**123,366**	**38,770**	**22,760**	**38,589**	**14,299**	**8,948**
Living in family household	96,634	31,657	19,811	31,134	9,711	4,321
Living in nonfamily household	26,732	7,111	2,949	7,457	4,589	4,626
Householder	**58,082**	**11,818**	**11,635**	**20,039**	**8,337**	**6,251**
Family householder	37,445	8,372	9,698	13,722	3,941	1,712
Married-couple householder	22,965	4,190	5,904	9,315	2,661	895
Other family householder	14,480	4,181	3,795	4,407	1,280	817
Nonfamily householder	20,637	3,447	1,936	6,317	4,397	4,540
Living alone	17,899	2,022	1,570	5,635	4,223	4,449
Living with nonrelatives	2,738	1,425	366	682	174	91
Not a householder	**65,284**	**26,950**	**11,125**	**18,552**	**5,962**	**2,695**
In family household	59,189	23,285	10,113	17,412	5,770	2,609
Spouse of householder	36,152	6,420	8,629	14,814	4,744	1,545
Child of householder	15,977	14,485	793	657	18	0
Other relative of householder	7,060	2,380	691	1,942	1,008	1,064
In nonfamily household	6,095	3,664	1,013	1,140	192	86

Percent distribution by living arrangement

	total	Millennials (15 to 32)	Generation X (33 to 44)	Baby Boom (45 to 63)	Swing (64 to 76)	World War II (77 or older)
TOTAL WOMEN	**100.0%**	**100.0%**	**100.0%**	**100.0%**	**100.0%**	**100.0%**
Living in family household	78.3	81.7	87.0	80.7	67.9	48.3
Living in nonfamily household	21.7	18.3	13.0	19.3	32.1	51.7
Householder	**47.1**	**30.5**	**51.1**	**51.9**	**58.3**	**69.9**
Family householder	30.4	21.6	42.6	35.6	27.6	19.1
Married-couple householder	18.6	10.8	25.9	24.1	18.6	10.0
Other family householder	11.7	10.8	16.7	11.4	8.9	9.1
Nonfamily householder	16.7	8.9	8.5	16.4	30.7	50.7
Living alone	14.5	5.2	6.9	14.6	29.5	49.7
Living with nonrelatives	2.2	3.7	1.6	1.8	1.2	1.0
Not a householder	**52.9**	**69.5**	**48.9**	**48.1**	**41.7**	**30.1**
In family household	48.0	60.1	44.4	45.1	40.4	29.2
Spouse of householder	29.3	16.6	37.9	38.4	33.2	17.3
Child of householder	13.0	37.4	3.5	1.7	0.1	0.0
Other relative of householder	5.7	6.1	3.0	5.0	7.0	11.9
In nonfamily household	4.9	9.5	4.4	3.0	1.3	1.0

Note: Women by generation are estimates by New Strategist.
Source: Bureau of the Census, America's Families and Living Arrangements: 2009, Internet site http://www.census.gov/ population/www/socdemo/hh-fam/cps2009.html; calculations by New Strategist"

Most Americans Are Married

The divorced population peaks in middle age.

The proportion of people who are currently divorced peaks in midlife. Seventeen percent of women and 14 percent of men aged 50 to 54 are currently divorced—the highest proportions among all age groups. (The proportion of people who have ever been divorced is higher because many of the divorced have remarried.)

Because women tend to marry older men, and because men tend to die at a younger age than women, widowhood is far more common for women than for men. Among women age 65 to 74, a substantial 24 percent are currently widowed. The share rises to an enormous 75 percent among women aged 85 or older. Only 6 percent of men aged 65 to 74 are widowers, a figure that climbs to 39 percent among men aged 85 or older.

Most men aged 30 or older are married. Most women are married from age 30 to age 74. From age 75 on, most women are widows.

■ As the women of the Baby-Boom generation age, the number of widows in the population will surpass the number of divorcees.

The marital status of men and women differs greatly in old age

(percent of people aged 85 or older who are currently married or widowed, by sex, 2009)

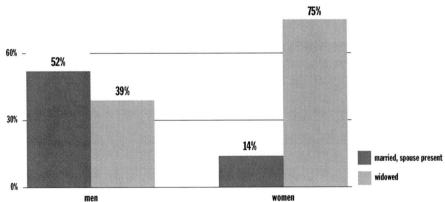

Table 8.28 Marital Status of Men by Age, 2009

(number and percent distribution of men aged 18 or older by age and marital status, 2009; numbers in thousands)

	total	never married	married, spouse present	married, spouse absent	separated	divorced	widowed
Total men	**109,973**	**32,444**	**60,836**	**1,737**	**2,199**	**9,949**	**2,808**
Aged 18 to 19	4,084	4,006	35	14	23	5	1
Aged 20 to 24	10,414	9,055	1,044	105	120	84	5
Aged 25 to 29	10,849	6,626	3,506	197	182	335	3
Aged 30 to 34	9,570	3,345	5,253	167	220	582	3
Aged 35 to 39	10,164	2,288	6,392	230	294	935	24
Aged 40 to 44	10,314	1,894	6,602	212	278	1,280	48
Aged 45 to 49	11,162	1,896	7,140	178	271	1,572	105
Aged 50 to 54	10,610	1,328	7,147	201	269	1,535	131
Aged 55 to 64	16,501	1,297	11,975	230	350	2,265	384
Aged 65 to 74	9,400	448	7,235	81	129	958	549
Aged 75 to 84	5,415	202	3,733	88	54	360	977
Aged 85 or older	1,491	60	773	33	9	40	578
Total men	**100.0%**	**29.5%**	**55.3%**	**1.6%**	**2.0%**	**9.0%**	**2.6%**
Aged 18 to 19	100.0	98.1	0.9	0.3	0.6	0.1	0.0
Aged 20 to 24	100.0	87.0	10.0	1.0	1.2	0.8	0.0
Aged 25 to 29	100.0	61.1	32.3	1.8	1.7	3.1	0.0
Aged 30 to 34	100.0	35.0	54.9	1.7	2.3	6.1	0.0
Aged 35 to 39	100.0	22.5	62.9	2.3	2.9	9.2	0.2
Aged 40 to 44	100.0	18.4	64.0	2.1	2.7	12.4	0.5
Aged 45 to 49	100.0	17.0	64.0	1.6	2.4	14.1	0.9
Aged 50 to 54	100.0	12.5	67.4	1.9	2.5	14.5	1.2
Aged 55 to 64	100.0	7.9	72.6	1.4	2.1	13.7	2.3
Aged 65 to 74	100.0	4.8	77.0	0.9	1.4	10.2	5.8
Aged 75 to 84	100.0	3.7	68.9	1.6	1.0	6.6	18.0
Aged 85 or older	100.0	4.0	51.8	2.2	0.6	2.7	38.8

Source: Bureau of the Census, America's Families and Living Arrangements: 2009, Internet site http://www.census.gov/population/www/socdemo/hh-fam/cps2009.html; calculations by New Strategist

Table 8.29 Marital Status of Women by Age, 2009

(number and percent distribution of women aged 18 or older by age and marital status, 2009; numbers in thousands)

	total	never married	married, spouse present	married, spouse absent	separated	divorced	widowed
Total women	**116,889**	**26,655**	**60,829**	**1,547**	**3,123**	**13,298**	**11,437**
Aged 18 to 19	3,965	3,793	94	34	29	14	2
Aged 20 to 24	10,196	7,893	1,807	111	208	151	26
Aged 25 to 29	10,383	4,803	4,592	131	298	530	30
Aged 30 to 34	9,686	2,543	5,837	156	318	772	60
Aged 35 to 39	10,270	1,681	6,713	165	433	1,166	113
Aged 40 to 44	10,553	1,384	6,965	163	443	1,447	150
Aged 45 to 49	11,547	1,329	7,397	175	408	1,919	319
Aged 50 to 54	11,043	1,107	7,083	143	377	1,918	416
Aged 55 to 64	17,777	1,260	11,374	210	378	3,096	1,459
Aged 65 to 74	11,003	458	5,927	127	173	1,628	2,689
Aged 75 to 84	7,590	285	2,630	89	48	517	4,021
Aged 85 or older	2,876	118	410	44	10	142	2,152
Total women	**100.0%**	**22.8%**	**52.0%**	**1.3%**	**2.7%**	**11.4%**	**9.8%**
Aged 18 to 19	100.0	95.7	2.4	0.9	0.7	0.4	0.1
Aged 20 to 24	100.0	77.4	17.7	1.1	2.0	1.5	0.3
Aged 25 to 29	100.0	46.3	44.2	1.3	2.9	5.1	0.3
Aged 30 to 34	100.0	26.3	60.3	1.6	3.3	8.0	0.6
Aged 35 to 39	100.0	16.4	65.4	1.6	4.2	11.4	1.1
Aged 40 to 44	100.0	13.1	66.0	1.5	4.2	13.7	1.4
Aged 45 to 49	100.0	11.5	64.1	1.5	3.5	16.6	2.8
Aged 50 to 54	100.0	10.0	64.1	1.3	3.4	17.4	3.8
Aged 55 to 64	100.0	7.1	64.0	1.2	2.1	17.4	8.2
Aged 65 to 74	100.0	4.2	53.9	1.2	1.6	14.8	24.4
Aged 75 to 84	100.0	3.8	34.7	1.2	0.6	6.8	53.0
Aged 85 or older	100.0	4.1	14.3	1.5	0.3	4.9	74.8

Source: Bureau of the Census, America's Families and Living Arrangements: 2009, Internet site http://www.census.gov/ population/www/socdemo/hh-fam/cps2009.html; calculations by New Strategist

Younger Generations Stay Single Longer

The World War II generation married early.

Perhaps no trend has so dramatically changed the lifestyle of young adults as the rise of singlehood over the past few decades. In 1970, only 36 percent of women aged 20 to 24 had never married. By 2009, the proportion had more than doubled, reaching 77 percent. Among men, the never-married proportion rose from 55 to 87 percent during those years. The rise in singlehood has not been confined to young adults. Since 1970, the never-married share has grown in every age group under age 65.

The World War II generation created the marriage boom of the 1950s and 1960s by marrying at a younger age and in greater proportions than their parents had. The share of Americans aged 65 or older who have never married is lower today than it was in 1970.

■ The growing importance of a college education has caused many young men and women to postpone marriage.

Young people today are more likely to be single

(percent of people aged 20 to 24 who have never been married, by sex, 1970 and 2009)

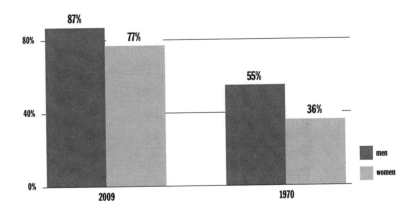

Table 8.30 Never-Married People by Sex and Age, 1970 to 2009

(percent of people who have never been married, by sex and age, 1970 to 2009; percentage point change 1970–2009)

	2009	2000	1990	1980	1970	percentage point change 1970–2009
Men						
Aged 20 to 24	87.0%	83.7%	79.3%	68.8%	54.7%	32.3
Aged 25 to 29	61.1	51.7	45.2	33.1	19.1	42.0
Aged 30 to 34	35.0	30.1	27.0	15.9	9.4	25.6
Aged 35 to 39	22.5	20.3	14.7	7.8	7.2	15.3
Aged 40 to 44	18.4	15.7	10.5	7.1	6.3	12.1
Aged 45 to 54	14.8	9.5	6.3	6.1	7.5	7.3
Aged 55 to 64	7.9	5.5	5.8	5.3	7.8	0.1
Aged 65 or older	4.4	4.2	4.2	4.9	7.5	−3.1
Women						
Aged 20 to 24	77.4	72.8	62.8	50.2	35.8	41.6
Aged 25 to 29	46.3	38.9	31.1	20.9	10.5	35.8
Aged 30 to 34	26.3	21.9	16.4	9.5	6.2	20.1
Aged 35 to 39	16.4	14.3	10.4	6.2	5.4	11.0
Aged 40 to 44	13.1	11.8	8.0	4.8	4.9	8.2
Aged 45 to 54	10.8	8.6	5.0	4.7	4.9	5.9
Aged 55 to 64	7.1	4.9	3.9	4.5	6.8	0.3
Aged 65 or older	4.0	3.6	4.9	5.9	7.7	−3.7

Source: Bureau of the Census, Families and Living Arrangements, Current Population Surveys, Internet site http://www.census .gov/population/www/socdemo/hh-fam.html; calculations by New Strategist

Divorce Is Highest among Men and Women in Their Fifties

At least half of men aged 30 or older are married and still living with their first wife.

Men and women aged 50 to 59 are most likely to have experienced a divorce, according to a Census Bureau study of marriage and divorce. Among women in the age group, 40.7 have been through a divorce. For their male counterparts, the figure is 37.5 percent.

Divorce is much less common for older men and women. Among those aged 70 or older, only 18 percent of women and 21 percent of men have ever divorced. Divorce is also less common among people under age 50, in part because they have not had as much time to get divorced.

Despite the frequency of divorce, more than half of men aged 30 or older have married only once and are still married to their first wife. Among women, most of those in their thirties have married only once and are still living with their first husband. After that, however, the proportion falls with age as women become widows.

■ Divorce is more common among Baby Boomers than older or younger generations for reasons not entirely understood by family experts.

More than one in five adults have experienced divorce

(percent of people aged 15 or older by selected marital history, by sex, 2004)

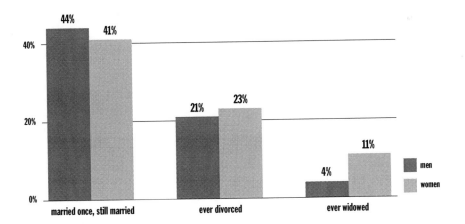

Table 8.31 Marital History of Men by Age, 2004

(number of men aged 15 or older and percent distribution by marital history and age, 2004; numbers in thousands)

	total	15–19	20–24	25–29	30–34	35–39	40–49	50–59	60–69	70+
TOTAL MEN, NUMBER	109,830	10,473	10,022	9,511	9,848	10,121	21,857	17,352	10,571	10,075
TOTAL MEN, PERCENT	100.0%	100.0%	100.0%	100.0%	100.0%	100.0%	100.0%	100.0%	100.0%	100.0%
Never married	31.2	98.1	84.0	53.6	30.3	20.2	14.1	8.7	4.8	3.2
Ever married	68.8	1.9	16.0	46.4	69.7	79.8	85.9	91.3	95.2	96.8
Married once	54.0	1.9	15.9	44.3	62.4	68.1	66.8	63.4	66.8	74.9
Still married	43.8	1.5	14.4	39.7	54.4	56.6	52.8	50.3	54.7	55.1
Married twice	11.8	0.0	0.1	2.0	6.7	10.3	15.7	21.3	20.6	17.0
Still married	9.2	0.0	0.1	1.9	6.0	8.5	12.5	16.1	16.1	12.6
Married three or more times	3.1	0.0	0.0	0.1	0.6	1.4	3.3	6.6	7.7	4.9
Still married	2.3	0.0	0.0	0.0	0.4	1.2	2.7	5.1	5.6	3.1
Ever divorced	20.7	0.1	0.8	5.1	13.1	20.7	30.3	37.5	34.1	20.6
Currently divorced	9.3	0.1	0.7	3.2	6.6	10.9	14.7	16.2	13.0	6.2
Ever widowed	3.6	0.2	0.0	0.1	0.1	0.6	1.1	2.8	7.1	23.8
Currently widowed	2.5	0.2	0.0	0.0	0.1	0.4	0.6	1.4	4.2	18.9

Source: Bureau of the Census, Number, Timing, and Duration of Marriages and Divorces: 2004, Detailed Tables, Internet site http://www.census.gov/population/www/socdemo/marr-div/2004detailed_tables.html

Table 8.32 Marital History of Women by Age, 2004

(number of women aged 15 or older and percent distribution by marital history and age, 2004; numbers in thousands)

	total	15–19	20–24	25–29	30–34	35–39	40–49	50–59	60–69	70+
TOTAL WOMEN, NUMBER	117,677	10,082	10,027	9,484	10,097	10,319	22,818	18,412	11,852	14,586
TOTAL WOMEN, PERCENT	100.0%	100.0%	100.0%	100.0%	100.0%	100.0%	100.0%	100.0%	100.0%	100.0%
Never married	25.8	97.3	73.3	41.3	22.3	16.2	11.9	7.6	4.3	4.9
Ever married	74.2	2.7	26.7	58.7	77.7	83.8	88.1	92.4	95.7	95.1
Married once	57.9	2.7	25.8	55.5	68.4	67.5	65.3	62.8	71.1	77.4
Still married	40.6	2.4	23.0	48.6	57.6	54.6	49.7	44.4	46.2	29.0
Married twice	13.2	0.1	0.8	3.1	8.2	14.1	18.9	22.6	18.7	14.9
Still married	8.8	0.0	0.7	2.8	6.6	11.3	14.0	15.5	11.3	5.3
Married three or more times	3.1	0.0	0.0	0.1	1.2	2.2	3.9	7.0	5.9	2.8
Still married	1.9	0.0	0.0	0.1	0.8	1.6	2.8	4.4	3.6	1.0
Ever divorced	22.9	0.2	2.5	7.0	17.1	25.6	33.9	40.7	32.3	17.8
Currently divorced	10.9	0.1	1.7	4.1	9.1	11.7	16.4	19.4	15.0	7.2
Ever widowed	10.8	0.1	0.1	0.3	0.7	1.1	2.5	7.8	21.2	54.5
Currently widowed	9.6	0.1	0.1	0.2	0.5	0.9	1.6	5.7	18.0	51.6

Source: Bureau of the Census, Number, Timing, and Duration of Marriages and Divorces: 2004, Detailed Tables, Internet site http://www.census.gov/population/www/socdemo/marr-div/2004detailed_tables.html

Population

For more than half a century, economic and cultural trends in the United States have been shaped by baby booms and baby busts. Today, the large Baby-Boom and Millennial generations are moving through the age structure, their size affecting not only the individual members of each generation, but also the nation as a whole. For decades, American society has had to cope with Boomer demands for education, housing, and jobs. Now Boomers are beginning to retire and their claim on Social Security benefits will grow each year. Today, the Millennial generation is crowding the nation's college campuses and entry-level workforce. Soon it might help rescue the housing market.

The small generations on either side of the Baby Boom—the Swing generation and Generation X—are frequently overlooked. The iGeneration, which follows the Millennials, is still forming and has yet to make its mark. These generations are also influencing the economy and culture. For example, Generation X now dominates the nation's parents.

Each generation is unique, with well-defined wants and needs. Some of those wants and needs depend upon lifestage, while others are created by the events that shape each generation as it ages.

What to expect in the future

■ Millennials are the nation's young adults. Their numbers give them confidence and a strong sense of their own importance.

■ Boomers will continue to exert more influence than other generations, especially now that they are in positions of corporate and political power.

■ The differing wants and needs of large and small generations will continue to create conflict. The biggest fight—how to distribute resources equitably among the generations—won't be easily resolved.

Social Trends Mirror Changing Age Structure

The age structure of the population drives the economy.

The changing age structure of the population has greatly influenced American social and economic trends during the past century. It will continue to influence trends as long as there are significant differences in the sizes of various age groups.

The youth movement of the late 1960s was a consequence of the age structure of the population. It is no coincidence that the youth movement arose just when the proportion of young people in the population expanded with the Baby-Boom generation. As Generation X moved into its teens and twenties, the youth population began to shrink to the consternation of businesses long accustomed to serving the young. Now the young-adult market has expanded again as another large generation occupies the under-30 age group. But the youthful share of the population will not reach the levels seen when Boomers inhabited the age groups, limiting the youth market's influence.

The Baby Boom continues to exert a numerical influence on our culture and economy. Boomers have now swelled the ranks of people in fifties and early sixties. This is why the concerns of the middle aged—financial security, health care, and retirement—are getting so much attention.

In 1920, fewer than 5 percent of Americans were aged 65 or older. At that time, there were twice as many people under the age of 5 as aged 65 or older. In 2008, the oldest Americans outnumbered the youngest by nearly 18 million—a figure that will expand sharply as Boomers fill the age group.

■ The aging of the large Baby-Boom generation challenges Americans to come up with innovative ways to provide health care and retirement security.

Children and young adults represent a shrinking share of the population

(percent of the population in selected age groups, 1920 and 2008)

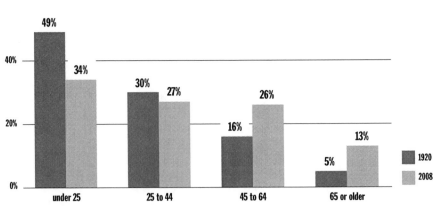

Table 9.1 Population by Age, 1920 to 2008

(number and percent distribution of people by age, and median age, 1920 to 2008; numbers in thousands)

	2008	2000	1990	1980	1970	1960	1950	1940	1930	1920
Total people	**304,060**	**281,422**	**248,791**	**226,546**	**203,212**	**179,323**	**150,697**	**131,669**	**122,775**	**105,711**
Under age 5	21,006	19,176	18,765	16,348	17,154	20,321	16,164	10,542	11,444	11,573
Aged 5 to 14	40,120	41,078	35,109	34,942	40,746	35,465	24,319	22,431	24,612	22,039
Aged 15 to 24	42,573	39,184	37,036	42,487	35,441	24,020	22,098	23,921	22,422	18,708
Aged 25 to 34	40,932	39,892	43,174	37,082	24,907	22,818	23,759	21,339	18,954	17,158
Aged 35 to 44	42,501	45,149	37,444	25,634	23,088	24,081	21,450	18,333	17,199	14,121
Aged 45 to 54	44,372	37,678	25,062	22,800	23,220	20,485	17,343	15,512	13,018	10,498
Aged 55 to 64	33,686	24,275	21,116	21,703	18,590	15,572	13,295	10,572	8,397	6,532
Aged 65 or older	38,870	34,992	31,084	25,550	20,066	16,560	12,270	9,019	6,634	4,933
Median age (years)	36.8	35.3	32.9	30.0	28.1	29.5	30.2	29.0	26.5	25.3
Total people	**100.0%**	**100.0%**	**100.0%**	**100.0%**	**100.0%**	**100.0%**	**100.0%**	**100.0%**	**100.0%**	**100.0%**
Under age 5	6.9	6.8	7.5	7.2	8.4	11.3	10.7	8.0	9.3	10.9
Aged 5 to 14	13.2	14.6	14.1	15.4	20.1	19.8	16.1	17.0	20.0	20.8
Aged 15 to 24	14.0	13.9	14.9	18.8	17.4	13.4	14.7	18.2	18.3	17.7
Aged 25 to 34	13.5	14.2	17.4	16.4	12.3	12.7	15.8	16.2	15.4	16.2
Aged 35 to 44	14.0	16.0	15.1	11.3	11.4	13.4	14.2	13.9	14.0	13.4
Aged 45 to 54	14.6	13.4	10.1	10.1	11.4	11.4	11.5	11.8	10.6	9.9
Aged 55 to 64	11.1	8.6	8.5	9.6	9.1	8.7	8.8	8.0	6.8	6.2
Aged 65 or older	12.8	12.4	12.5	11.3	9.9	9.2	8.1	6.8	5.4	4.7

Note: Numbers by age in 1920 and 1930 do not add to total because "age not stated" is not shown.
Sources: Bureau of the Census, Historical Statistics of the United States, Colonial Times to 1970, Part 1, 1975; and Statistical Abstract of the United States: 2001; and Age: 2000, 2000 Census Brief, C2KBR/01-12, 2001; and Population Estimates, Internet site http://www.census.gov/popest/national/asrh/NC-EST2008-sa.html; calculations by New Strategist

Table 9.2 Population by Age and Generation, 2008

(number and percent distribution of people by age and generation, 2008; numbers in thousands)

	number	percent distribution
Total people	**304,060**	**100.0%**
Under age 5	21,006	6.9
Aged 5 to 9	20,065	6.6
Aged 10 to 14	20,055	6.6
Aged 15 to 19	21,514	7.1
Aged 20 to 24	21,059	6.9
Aged 25 to 29	21,334	7.0
Aged 30 to 34	19,598	6.4
Aged 35 to 39	20,994	6.9
Aged 40 to 44	21,507	7.1
Aged 45 to 49	22,880	7.5
Aged 50 to 54	21,492	7.1
Aged 55 to 59	18,583	6.1
Aged 60 to 64	15,103	5.0
Aged 65 to 69	11,349	3.7
Aged 70 to 74	8,774	2.9
Aged 75 to 79	7,275	2.4
Aged 80 to 84	5,750	1.9
Aged 85 or older	5,722	1.9
Total people	**304,060**	**100.0**
iGeneration (under age 14)	57,115	18.8
Millennial (14 to 31)	75,757	24.9
Generation X (32 to 43)	49,958	16.4
Baby Boom (44 to 62)	76,319	25.1
Swing (63 to 75)	27,619	9.1
World War II (76 or older)	17,292	5.7

Note: Numbers by generation are estimates by New Strategist.
Source: Bureau of the Census, Population Estimates, Internet site http://www.census.gov/popest/national/asrh/ NC-EST2008-sa.html; calculations by New Strategist

Sex Ratio Reverses with Age

Women dominate older Americans, while boys outnumber girls among the young.

In the beginning, boys have the upper hand, at least numerically. More boys than girls are born each year, although no one is quite sure why. By the later years of life, however, the ratio is reversed and women outnumber men. The reversal occurs because males have higher death rates than females at every age.

Among Millennials, there are 1.9 million more males than females. Things equal out in Generation X, where men outnumber women by just 323,000. The Baby Boom is beginning to experience rising mortality rates, with a disproportionate impact on men. Boomer women outnumber Boomer men by 1.6 million.

In the Swing generation, the sex ratio changes more rapidly. There are 2.1 million more women than men. In the World War II generation, men account for only 38 percent of the population.

■ Because women greatly outnumber men among older Americans, women's needs dominate the industries that cater to the old such as health care.

Males are scarce in the World War II generation

(number of males per 100 females, by generation, 2008)

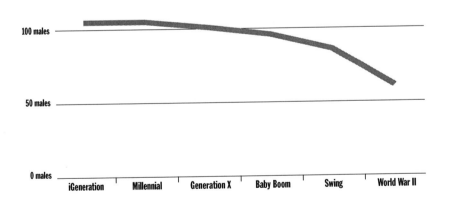

Table 9.3 Population by Age, Generation, and Sex, 2008

(number of people by age, generation, and sex, and sex ratio by age, 2008; numbers in thousands)

	total	female	male	sex ratio
Total people	**304,060**	**154,135**	**149,925**	**97**
Under age 5	21,006	10,258	10,748	105
Aged 5 to 9	20,065	9,806	10,259	105
Aged 10 to 14	20,055	9,792	10,262	105
Aged 15 to 19	21,514	10,487	11,027	105
Aged 20 to 24	21,059	10,214	10,845	106
Aged 25 to 29	21,334	10,393	10,941	105
Aged 30 to 34	19,598	9,639	9,959	103
Aged 35 to 39	20,994	10,425	10,569	101
Aged 40 to 44	21,507	10,762	10,746	100
Aged 45 to 49	22,880	11,566	11,314	98
Aged 50 to 54	21,492	10,954	10,539	96
Aged 55 to 59	18,583	9,569	9,015	94
Aged 60 to 64	15,103	7,867	7,236	92
Aged 65 to 69	11,349	6,042	5,306	88
Aged 70 to 74	8,774	4,816	3,959	82
Aged 75 to 79	7,275	4,178	3,097	74
Aged 80 to 84	5,750	3,510	2,239	64
Aged 85 or older	5,722	3,858	1,864	48
Total people	**304,060**	**154,135**	**149,925**	**97**
iGeneration (under 14)	57,115	27,898	29,217	105
Millennial (14–31)	75,757	36,907	38,850	105
Generation X (32–43)	49,958	24,818	25,141	101
Baby Boom (44–62)	76,319	38,961	37,358	96
Swing (63–75)	27,619	14,840	12,779	86
World War II (76+)	17,292	10,711	6,581	61

Note: The sex ratio is the number of men per 100 women. Numbers by generation are estimates by New Strategist.
Source: Bureau of the Census, Population Estimates, Internet site http://www.census.gov/popest/national/asrh/
NC-EST2008-sa.html; calculations by New Strategist

Greater Diversity among the Young

Just 55 percent of the iGeneration is non-Hispanic white.

The United States is far more diverse today than it was half a century ago. Behind the growing diversity is generational replacement. Due to immigration and higher fertility rates among some racial and ethnic groups, each age group is more diverse than the one preceding it. Among the World War II generation, 83 percent are non-Hispanic white. Among Boomers, the proportion is 72 percent. It drops to 62 percent among Generation Xers and to 60 percent among Millennials. Only 55 percent of the iGeneration is non-Hispanic white.

The nation's racial and ethnic composition is also becoming more complex with many more Hispanics in the mix. Among Gen Xers and younger generations, Hispanics outnumber blacks. Among Boomers and older generations, blacks outnumber Hispanics.

Within racial and ethnic groups, the size of generations varies. Among Hispanics, for example, Boomers are outnumbered by Generation Xers, Millennials, and the iGeneration. In contrast, Boomers account for 28 percent of non-Hispanic whites, while Millennials are a smaller 23 percent and the iGeneration just 16 percent.

■ Understanding the cultural diversity of younger generations is key to reaching them.

Among the young, Hispanics are the largest minority

(Hispanics as a percentage of each generation, 2008)

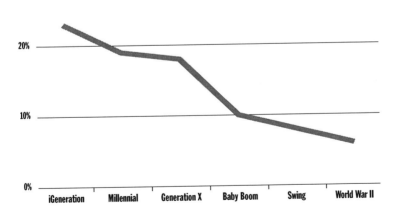

Table 9.4 Population by Age, Race, and Hispanic Origin, 2008

(number and percent distribution of people by age, race, and Hispanic origin, 2008; numbers in thousands)

	total	Asian	black	Hispanic	non-Hispanic white
Total people	**304,060**	**15,480**	**41,127**	**46,944**	**199,491**
Under age 5	21,006	1,242	3,573	5,288	11,065
Aged 5 to 9	20,065	1,107	3,298	4,464	11,222
Aged 10 to 14	20,055	1,033	3,363	3,989	11,660
Aged 15 to 19	21,514	1,018	3,667	3,850	12,903
Aged 20 to 24	21,059	1,027	3,307	3,663	12,949
Aged 25 to 29	21,334	1,206	3,166	4,141	12,740
Aged 30 to 34	19,598	1,334	2,724	4,041	11,456
Aged 35 to 39	20,994	1,404	2,823	3,730	12,981
Aged 40 to 44	21,507	1,210	2,847	3,279	14,085
Aged 45 to 49	22,880	1,107	2,882	2,795	15,964
Aged 50 to 54	21,492	986	2,563	2,187	15,615
Aged 55 to 59	18,583	829	2,068	1,650	13,907
Aged 60 to 64	15,103	612	1,471	1,204	11,706
Aged 65 to 69	11,349	443	1,075	853	8,899
Aged 70 to 74	8,774	339	829	653	6,899
Aged 75 to 79	7,275	255	614	496	5,871
Aged 80 to 84	5,750	176	438	346	4,763
Aged 85 or older	5,722	154	419	313	4,807

PERCENT DISTRIBUTION BY RACE AND HISPANIC ORIGIN

Total people	**100.0%**	**5.1%**	**13.5%**	**15.4%**	**65.6%**
Under age 5	100.0	5.9	17.0	25.2	52.7
Aged 5 to 9	100.0	5.5	16.4	22.2	55.9
Aged 10 to 14	100.0	5.1	16.8	19.9	58.1
Aged 15 to 19	100.0	4.7	17.0	17.9	60.0
Aged 20 to 24	100.0	4.9	15.7	17.4	61.5
Aged 25 to 29	100.0	5.7	14.8	19.4	59.7
Aged 30 to 34	100.0	6.8	13.9	20.6	58.5
Aged 35 to 39	100.0	6.7	13.4	17.8	61.8
Aged 40 to 44	100.0	5.6	13.2	15.2	65.5
Aged 45 to 49	100.0	4.8	12.6	12.2	69.8
Aged 50 to 54	100.0	4.6	11.9	10.2	72.7
Aged 55 to 59	100.0	4.5	11.1	8.9	74.8
Aged 60 to 64	100.0	4.1	9.7	8.0	77.5
Aged 65 to 69	100.0	3.9	9.5	7.5	78.4
Aged 70 to 74	100.0	3.9	9.5	7.4	78.6
Aged 75 to 79	100.0	3.5	8.4	6.8	80.7
Aged 80 to 84	100.0	3.1	7.6	6.0	82.8
Aged 85 or older	100.0	2.7	7.3	5.5	84.0

Note: Numbers by race and Hispanic origin do not sum to total because Asians and blacks include those who identified them-selves as being of the race alone or in combination with other races, Hispanics may be of any race, and not all races are shown. Non-Hispanic whites are those who identified themselves as being white alone and not Hispanic.
Source: Bureau of the Census, Population Estimates, Internet site http://www.census.gov/popest/national/asrh/ NC-EST2008-asrh.html; calculations by New Strategist

Table 9.5 Population by Generation, Race, and Hispanic Origin, 2008

(number and percent distribution of people by generation, race, and Hispanic origin, 2008; numbers in thousands)

	total	Asian	black	Hispanic	non-Hispanic white
Total people	**304,060**	**15,480**	**41,127**	**46,944**	**199,491**
iGeneration (under age 14)	57,115	3,174	9,562	12,944	31,615
Millennial (14 to 31)	75,757	3,991	11,902	14,068	45,506
Generation X (32 to 43)	49,958	3,172	6,735	8,778	31,123
Baby Boom (44 to 62)	76,319	3,531	8,965	8,011	55,326
Swing (63 to 75)	27,619	1,078	2,616	2,086	21,654
World War II (76 or older)	17,292	534	1,348	1,056	14,267

PERCENT DISTRIBUTION BY RACE AND HISPANIC ORIGIN

	total	Asian	black	Hispanic	non-Hispanic white
Total people	**100.0%**	**5.1%**	**13.5%**	**15.4%**	**65.6%**
iGeneration (under age 14)	100.0	5.6	16.7	22.7	55.4
Millennial (14 to 31)	100.0	5.3	15.7	18.6	60.1
Generation X (32 to 43)	100.0	6.3	13.5	17.6	62.3
Baby Boom (44 to 62)	100.0	4.6	11.7	10.5	72.5
Swing (63 to 75)	100.0	3.9	9.5	7.6	78.4
World War II (76 or older)	100.0	3.1	7.8	6.1	82.5

PERCENT DISTRIBUTION BY GENERATION

	total	Asian	black	Hispanic	non-Hispanic white
Total people	**100.0%**	**100.0%**	**100.0%**	**100.0%**	**100.0%**
iGeneration (under age 14)	18.8	20.5	23.2	27.6	15.8
Millennial (14 to 31)	24.9	25.8	28.9	30.0	22.8
Generation X (32 to 43)	16.4	20.5	16.4	18.7	15.6
Baby Boom (44 to 62)	25.1	22.8	21.8	17.1	27.7
Swing (63 to 75)	9.1	7.0	6.4	4.4	10.9
World War II (76 or older)	5.7	3.4	3.3	2.3	7.2

Note: Numbers by race and Hispanic origin do not sum to total because Asians and blacks include those who identified themselves as being of the race alone or in combination with other races, Hispanics may be of any race, and not all races are shown. Non-Hispanic whites are those who identified themselves as being white alone and not Hispanic.
Source: Bureau of the Census, Population Estimates, Internet site http://www.census.gov/popest/national/asrh/NC-EST2008-asrh.html; calculations by New Strategist

Number of People in Their Sixties to Grow Rapidly

Between 2010 and 2020, expect rapid growth in the number of people aged 65 to 74.

As large and small generations grow older, age groups expand and contract. Between 2010 and 2020, the largest expansion will be among 70-to-74-year-olds as the oldest Boomers begin to enter their seventies. The age group is projected to grow by 57 percent during those years.

Several age groups will shrink as they fill with the small Generation X. The number of 45-to-49-year-olds is projected to fall by 9 percent.

■ The generations that follow Generation X (Millennials and the iGeneration) do not vary as much in size, which will dampen future fluctuations in age groups.

Declines are projected for the 45-to-54 age group

(percent change in size of selected age groups, 2010 to 2020)

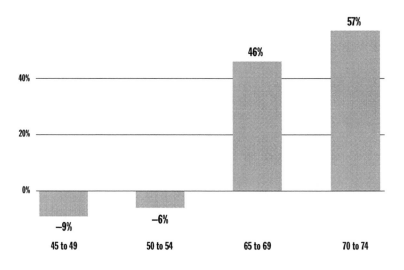

Table 9.6 Population by Age, 2010 and 2020

(number of people by age, 2010 to 2020; percent change, 2010–20; numbers in thousands)

	2010	2020	percent change 2010–20
Total people	**310,233**	**341,387**	**10.0%**
Under age 5	21,100	22,846	8.3
Aged 5 to 9	20,886	22,732	8.8
Aged 10 to 14	20,395	22,571	10.7
Aged 15 to 19	21,770	22,554	3.6
Aged 20 to 24	21,779	21,799	0.1
Aged 25 to 29	21,418	22,949	7.1
Aged 30 to 34	20,400	23,112	13.3
Aged 35 to 39	20,267	22,586	11.4
Aged 40 to 44	21,010	21,078	0.3
Aged 45 to 49	22,596	20,502	–9.3
Aged 50 to 54	22,109	20,852	–5.7
Aged 55 to 59	19,517	21,994	12.7
Aged 60 to 64	16,758	21,009	25.4
Aged 65 to 69	12,261	17,861	45.7
Aged 70 to 74	9,202	14,452	57.1
Aged 75 to 79	7,282	9,656	32.6
Aged 80 to 84	5,733	6,239	8.8
Aged 85 or older	5,751	6,597	14.7

Source: Bureau of the Census, Internet site http://www.census.gov/population/www/projections/2009projections.html; calculations by New Strategist

Minorities Are Close to Becoming the Majority

Among children under age 5, half will be minorities in 2020.

Children are far more diverse than older Americans, and this diversity will intensify over the next decade. In 2020, only 50 percent of children under age 5 will be non-Hispanic white. More than one in four (27 percent) will be Hispanic. In contrast, 81 percent of people aged 85 or older will be non-Hispanic white and only 8 percent will be Hispanic. The number of Hispanics will climb by 33 percent between 2010 and 2020. Asians are projected to increase by 31 percent, blacks by 13 percent, and non-Hispanic whites by only 2 percent. Asians and Hispanics will experience gains in every age group during those years, while blacks and non-Hispanic whites will see rapid growth in some age groups and declines in others as large and small generations pass through the age structure.

■ The Hispanic share of the 45-to-49 age group is projected to climb sharply between 2010 and 2020, from 13 to 20 percent.

The generation gap will be a racial and ethnic divide

(minority share of selected age groups, 2020)

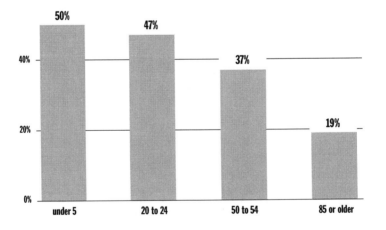

Table 9.7 Population by Age, Race, and Hispanic Origin, 2010

(number and percent distribution of people by age, race, and Hispanic origin, 2010; numbers in thousands)

	total	Asian	black	Hispanic	non-Hispanic white
Total people	**310,233**	**16,472**	**42,163**	**49,726**	**200,853**
Under age 5	21,100	1,251	3,475	5,053	11,375
Aged 5 to 9	20,886	1,204	3,397	4,888	11,448
Aged 10 to 14	20,395	1,125	3,343	4,513	11,440
Aged 15 to 19	21,770	1,133	3,662	4,473	12,472
Aged 20 to 24	21,779	1,115	3,513	4,010	13,049
Aged 25 to 29	21,418	1,223	3,246	3,887	12,959
Aged 30 to 34	20,400	1,382	2,955	4,039	11,974
Aged 35 to 39	20,267	1,494	2,778	3,868	12,078
Aged 40 to 44	21,010	1,299	2,785	3,431	13,423
Aged 45 to 49	22,596	1,154	2,901	3,002	15,415
Aged 50 to 54	22,109	1,035	2,706	2,425	15,800
Aged 55 to 59	19,517	898	2,214	1,862	14,409
Aged 60 to 64	16,758	746	1,705	1,417	12,769
Aged 65 to 69	12,261	511	1,153	974	9,534
Aged 70 to 74	9,202	370	861	710	7,201
Aged 75 to 79	7,282	250	630	514	5,848
Aged 80 to 84	5,733	160	434	354	4,759
Aged 85 or older	5,751	121	404	305	4,902

PERCENT DISTRIBUTION BY RACE AND HISPANIC ORIGIN

	total	Asian	black	Hispanic	non-Hispanic white
Total people	**100.0%**	**5.3%**	**13.6%**	**16.0%**	**64.7%**
Under age 5	100.0	5.9	16.5	23.9	53.9
Aged 5 to 9	100.0	5.8	16.3	23.4	54.8
Aged 10 to 14	100.0	5.5	16.4	22.1	56.1
Aged 15 to 19	100.0	5.2	16.8	20.5	57.3
Aged 20 to 24	100.0	5.1	16.1	18.4	59.9
Aged 25 to 29	100.0	5.7	15.2	18.1	60.5
Aged 30 to 34	100.0	6.8	14.5	19.8	58.7
Aged 35 to 39	100.0	7.4	13.7	19.1	59.6
Aged 40 to 44	100.0	6.2	13.3	16.3	63.9
Aged 45 to 49	100.0	5.1	12.8	13.3	68.2
Aged 50 to 54	100.0	4.7	12.2	11.0	71.5
Aged 55 to 59	100.0	4.6	11.3	9.5	73.8
Aged 60 to 64	100.0	4.5	10.2	8.5	76.2
Aged 65 to 69	100.0	4.2	9.4	7.9	77.8
Aged 70 to 74	100.0	4.0	9.4	7.7	78.3
Aged 75 to 79	100.0	3.4	8.7	7.1	80.3
Aged 80 to 84	100.0	2.8	7.6	6.2	83.0
Aged 85 or older	100.0	2.1	7.0	5.3	85.2

Note: Numbers by race and Hispanic origin do not sum to total because Asians and blacks include those who identified themselves as being of the race alone or in combination with other races, Hispanics may be of any race, and not all races are shown. Non-Hispanic whites are those who identified themselves as being white alone and not Hispanic.
Source: Bureau of the Census, Internet site http://www.census.gov/population/www/projections/summarytables.html; calculations by New Strategist

Table 9.8 Population by Age, Race, and Hispanic Origin, 2020

(number and percent distribution of people by age, race, and Hispanic origin, 2020; numbers in thousands)

	total	Asian	black	Hispanic	non-Hispanic white
Total people	**341,387**	**21,586**	**47,748**	**66,365**	**205,255**
Under age 5	22,846	1,460	3,835	6,266	11,426
Aged 5 to 9	22,732	1,428	3,762	6,059	11,582
Aged 10 to 14	22,571	1,447	3,610	6,036	11,564
Aged 15 to 19	22,554	1,467	3,559	5,983	11,632
Aged 20 to 24	21,799	1,387	3,469	5,441	11,561
Aged 25 to 29	22,949	1,423	3,750	5,152	12,619
Aged 30 to 34	23,112	1,555	3,617	4,591	13,277
Aged 35 to 39	22,586	1,668	3,333	4,376	13,122
Aged 40 to 44	21,078	1,675	2,989	4,356	12,019
Aged 45 to 49	20,502	1,683	2,753	4,043	11,981
Aged 50 to 54	20,852	1,434	2,694	3,529	13,130
Aged 55 to 59	21,994	1,257	2,730	3,063	14,830
Aged 60 to 64	21,009	1,119	2,462	2,452	14,847
Aged 65 to 69	17,861	946	1,922	1,826	13,049
Aged 70 to 74	14,452	729	1,382	1,307	10,932
Aged 75 to 79	9,656	441	839	827	7,482
Aged 80 to 84	6,239	261	532	528	4,879
Aged 85 or older	6,597	205	510	531	5,324

PERCENT DISTRIBUTION BY RACE AND HISPANIC ORIGIN

Total people	**100.0%**	**6.3%**	**14.0%**	**19.4%**	**60.1%**
Under age 5	100.0	6.4	16.8	27.4	50.0
Aged 5 to 9	100.0	6.3	16.5	26.7	51.0
Aged 10 to 14	100.0	6.4	16.0	26.7	51.2
Aged 15 to 19	100.0	6.5	15.8	26.5	51.6
Aged 20 to 24	100.0	6.4	15.9	25.0	53.0
Aged 25 to 29	100.0	6.2	16.3	22.4	55.0
Aged 30 to 34	100.0	6.7	15.6	19.9	57.4
Aged 35 to 39	100.0	7.4	14.8	19.4	58.1
Aged 40 to 44	100.0	7.9	14.2	20.7	57.0
Aged 45 to 49	100.0	8.2	13.4	19.7	58.4
Aged 50 to 54	100.0	6.9	12.9	16.9	63.0
Aged 55 to 59	100.0	5.7	12.4	13.9	67.4
Aged 60 to 64	100.0	5.3	11.7	11.7	70.7
Aged 65 to 69	100.0	5.3	10.8	10.2	73.1
Aged 70 to 74	100.0	5.0	9.6	9.0	75.6
Aged 75 to 79	100.0	4.6	8.7	8.6	77.5
Aged 80 to 84	100.0	4.2	8.5	8.5	78.2
Aged 85 or older	100.0	3.1	7.7	8.0	80.7

Note: Numbers by race and Hispanic origin do not sum to total because Asians and blacks include those who identified themselves as being of the race alone or in combination with other races, Hispanics may be of any race, and not all races are shown. Non-Hispanic whites are those who identified themselves as being white alone and not Hispanic.
Source: Bureau of the Census, Internet site http://www.census.gov/population/www/projections/summarytables.html; calculations by New Strategist

Table 9.9 Population Change by Age, Race, and Hispanic Origin, 2010 to 2020

(number of people by age, race, and Hispanic origin, 2010 and 2020, and numerical and percent change, 2010–20; numbers in thousands)

	Asian				black			
			change				change	
	2010	2020	numerical	percent	2010	2020	numerical	percent
Total people	16,472	21,586	5,114	31.0%	42,163	47,748	5,585	13.2%
Under age 5	1,251	1,460	209	16.7	3,475	3,835	360	10.4
Aged 5 to 9	1,204	1,428	224	18.6	3,397	3,762	365	10.7
Aged 10 to 14	1,125	1,447	322	28.6	3,343	3,610	267	8.0
Aged 15 to 19	1,133	1,467	334	29.5	3,662	3,559	–103	–2.8
Aged 20 to 24	1,115	1,387	272	24.4	3,513	3,469	–44	–1.3
Aged 25 to 29	1,223	1,423	200	16.4	3,246	3,750	504	15.5
Aged 30 to 34	1,382	1,555	173	12.5	2,955	3,617	662	22.4
Aged 35 to 39	1,494	1,668	174	11.6	2,778	3,333	555	20.0
Aged 40 to 44	1,299	1,675	376	28.9	2,785	2,989	204	7.3
Aged 45 to 49	1,154	1,683	529	45.8	2,901	2,753	–148	–5.1
Aged 50 to 54	1,035	1,434	399	38.6	2,706	2,694	–12	–0.4
Aged 55 to 59	898	1,257	359	40.0	2,214	2,730	516	23.3
Aged 60 to 64	746	1,119	373	50.0	1,705	2,462	757	44.4
Aged 65 to 69	511	946	435	85.1	1,153	1,922	769	66.7
Aged 70 to 74	370	729	359	97.0	861	1,382	521	60.5
Aged 75 to 79	250	441	191	76.4	630	839	209	33.2
Aged 80 to 84	160	261	101	63.1	434	532	98	22.6
Aged 85 or older	121	205	84	69.4	404	510	106	26.2

	Hispanic				non-Hispanic white			
			change				change	
	2010	2020	numerical	percent	2010	2020	numerical	percent
Total people	49,726	66,365	16,639	33.5%	200,853	205,255	4,402	2.2%
Under age 5	5,053	6,266	1,213	24.0	11,375	11,426	51	0.4
Aged 5 to 9	4,888	6,059	1,171	24.0	11,448	11,582	134	1.2
Aged 10 to 14	4,513	6,036	1,523	33.7	11,440	11,564	124	1.1
Aged 15 to 19	4,473	5,983	1,510	33.8	12,472	11,632	–840	–6.7
Aged 20 to 24	4,010	5,441	1,431	35.7	13,049	11,561	–1,488	–11.4
Aged 25 to 29	3,887	5,152	1,265	32.5	12,959	12,619	–340	–2.6
Aged 30 to 34	4,039	4,591	552	13.7	11,974	13,277	1,303	10.9
Aged 35 to 39	3,868	4,376	508	13.1	12,078	13,122	1,044	8.6
Aged 40 to 44	3,431	4,356	925	27.0	13,423	12,019	–1,404	–10.5
Aged 45 to 49	3,002	4,043	1,041	34.7	15,415	11,981	–3,434	–22.3
Aged 50 to 54	2,425	3,529	1,104	45.5	15,800	13,130	–2,670	–16.9
Aged 55 to 59	1,862	3,063	1,201	64.5	14,409	14,830	421	2.9
Aged 60 to 64	1,417	2,452	1,035	73.0	12,769	14,847	2,078	16.3
Aged 65 to 69	974	1,826	852	87.5	9,534	13,049	3,515	36.9
Aged 70 to 74	710	1,307	597	84.1	7,201	10,932	3,731	51.8
Aged 75 to 79	514	827	313	60.9	5,848	7,482	1,634	27.9
Aged 80 to 84	354	528	174	49.2	4,759	4,879	120	2.5
Aged 85 or older	305	531	226	74.1	4,902	5,324	422	8.6

Note: Numbers by race and Hispanic origin do not sum to total because Asians and blacks include those who identified themselves as being of the race alone or in combination with other races, Hispanics may be of any race, and not all races are shown. Non-Hispanic whites are those who identified themselves as being white alone and not Hispanic.
Source: Bureau of the Census, Internet site http://www.census.gov/population/www/projections/summarytables.html; calculations by New Strategist

Immigration Contributes to Diversity

Twenty percent of 35-to-44-year-olds are immigrants.

Overall, 12 percent of Americans were born outside the United States, according to the 2008 American Community Survey. By age, the largest proportion of foreign-born is found among people aged 35 to 44. Twenty percent of the age group was born in another country.

More than 1 million people legally immigrated to the United States in 2008. The number of immigrants coming to the United States may set a record during this decade, although immigration probably has slowed considerably since 2008 because of the Great Recession. People come to the United States for a variety of reasons, but substantial numbers are looking for jobs. That explains why more than 70 percent of immigrants are of prime working age—between the ages of 25 and 54.

■ High levels of immigration, combined with the greater fertility of recent immigrants, means the U.S. population will become increasingly diverse.

Most Americans live in their state of birth

(percent distribution of population by place of birth, 2008)

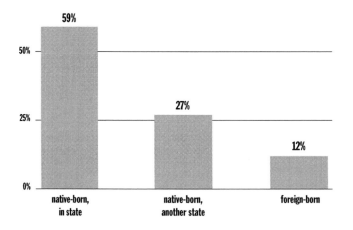

Table 9.10 Population by Age and Place of Birth, 2008

(number and percent distribution of people by age and place of birth, 2008; numbers in thousands)

	born in the United States			citizen born outside U.S.	foreign-born
	total	in state	outside state		
Total people	**304,060**	**179,133**	**82,935**	**4,031**	**37,961**
Under age 5	20,910	18,585	1,924	122	280
Aged 5 to 17	53,012	41,245	8,698	554	2,514
Aged 18 to 24	30,108	19,262	7,108	438	3,299
Aged 25 to 34	40,319	21,347	10,681	631	7,659
Aged 35 to 44	42,745	20,735	12,750	709	8,550
Aged 45 to 54	44,436	22,430	14,636	701	6,670
Aged 55 to 59	18,443	9,282	6,526	247	2,388
Aged 60 to 61	7,175	3,545	2,665	92	874
Aged 62 to 64	8,100	3,834	3,092	113	1,061
Aged 65 to 74	20,166	9,650	7,669	229	2,618
Aged 75 or older	18,647	9,218	7,185	195	2,049

PERCENT DISTRIBUTION BY PLACE OF BIRTH

Total people	**100.0%**	**58.9%**	**27.3%**	**1.3%**	**12.5%**
Under age 5	100.0	88.9	9.2	0.6	1.3
Aged 5 to 17	100.0	77.8	16.4	1.0	4.7
Aged 18 to 24	100.0	64.0	23.6	1.5	11.0
Aged 25 to 34	100.0	52.9	26.5	1.6	19.0
Aged 35 to 44	100.0	48.5	29.8	1.7	20.0
Aged 45 to 54	100.0	50.5	32.9	1.6	15.0
Aged 55 to 59	100.0	50.3	35.4	1.3	12.9
Aged 60 to 61	100.0	49.4	37.1	1.3	12.2
Aged 62 to 64	100.0	47.3	38.2	1.4	13.1
Aged 65 to 74	100.0	47.9	38.0	1.1	13.0
Aged 75 or older	100.0	49.4	38.5	1.0	11.0

PERCENT DISTRIBUTION BY AGE

Total people	**100.0%**	**100.0%**	**100.0%**	**100.0%**	**100.0%**
Under age 5	6.9	10.4	2.3	3.0	0.7
Aged 5 to 17	17.4	23.0	10.5	13.7	6.6
Aged 18 to 24	9.9	10.8	8.6	10.9	8.7
Aged 25 to 34	13.3	11.9	12.9	15.7	20.2
Aged 35 to 44	14.1	11.6	15.4	17.6	22.5
Aged 45 to 54	14.6	12.5	17.6	17.4	17.6
Aged 55 to 59	6.1	5.2	7.9	6.1	6.3
Aged 60 to 61	2.4	2.0	3.2	2.3	2.3
Aged 62 to 64	2.7	2.1	3.7	2.8	2.8
Aged 65 to 74	6.6	5.4	9.2	5.7	6.9
Aged 75 or older	6.1	5.1	8.7	4.8	5.4

Source: Bureau of the Census, 2008 American Community Survey, Internet site http://factfinder.census.gov/home/saff/main .html?_lang=en; calculations by New Strategist

Table 9.11 **Legal Immigrants by Age, 2008**

(number and percent distribution of immigrants admitted for legal permanent residence, by age, fiscal year 2008)

	number	percent distribution
Total legal immigrants	**1,107,126**	**100.0%**
Under age 1	8,280	0.7
Aged 1 to 4	29,998	2.7
Aged 5 to 9	52,993	4.8
Aged 10 to 14	74,608	6.7
Aged 15 to 19	94,697	8.6
Aged 20 to 24	104,332	9.4
Aged 25 to 29	121,416	11.0
Aged 30 to 34	140,132	12.7
Aged 35 to 39	124,341	11.2
Aged 40 to 44	92,627	8.4
Aged 45 to 64	203,091	18.3
Aged 45 to 49	69,868	6.3
Aged 50 to 54	53,848	4.9
Aged 55 to 59	43,789	4.0
Aged 60 to 64	35,586	3.2
Aged 65 to 74	45,399	4.1
Aged 75 or older	15,205	1.4

Note: Immigrants are those granted legal permanent residence in the United States. They either arrive in the United States with immigrant visas issued abroad or adjust their status in the United States from temporary to permanent residence. Numbers may not sum to total because "age not stated" is not shown.
Source: Department of Homeland Security, 2008 Yearbook of Immigration Statistics, Internet site http://www.uscis.gov/graphics/shared/statistics/yearbook/index.htm

The West Is the Youngest Region

Millennials outnumber Boomers in the West.

Time marches on, and as it does younger generations replace older ones. In 2008, the two youngest generations (Millennial and iGeneration) outnumber the three oldest generations (Baby Boom, Swing, and World War II) in every region except the Northeast. In the West, the gap is considerable, with the two younger generations accounting for 46 percent of the population and the three oldest generations accounting for only 38 percent.

There is little variation in the distribution of generations by region. The South, which is the most populous region, is home to more than one-third of each generation. The West is home to about one in four members of the younger generations and a slightly smaller share of the older generations. The Northeast has the smallest share of each generation, including only 17 percent of Millennials and 16 percent of the iGeneration.

■ Most Americans live in the South or West.

The Northeast is the oldest region

(percent of population in selected generations, by region, 2008)

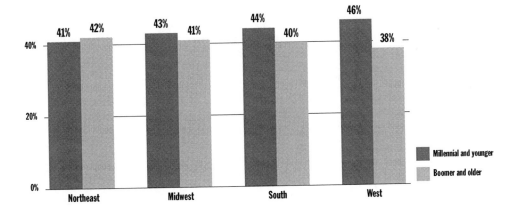

Legend: Millennial and younger / Boomer and older

- Northeast: 41%, 42%
- Midwest: 43%, 41%
- South: 44%, 40%
- West: 46%, 38%

Table 9.12 Regional Populations by Age, 2008

(number and percent distribution of people by age and region, 2008; numbers in thousands)

	total	Northeast	Midwest	South	West
Total people	**304,060**	**54,925**	**66,561**	**111,719**	**70,855**
Under age 5	21,006	3,339	4,463	7,971	5,232
Aged 5 to 9	20,065	3,309	4,343	7,573	4,840
Aged 10 to 14	20,055	3,468	4,429	7,355	4,802
Aged 15 to 19	21,514	3,899	4,769	7,749	5,097
Aged 20 to 24	21,059	3,739	4,619	7,627	5,074
Aged 25 to 29	21,334	3,477	4,573	7,957	5,327
Aged 30 to 34	19,598	3,354	4,126	7,261	4,857
Aged 35 to 39	20,994	3,767	4,416	7,776	5,035
Aged 40 to 44	21,507	4,105	4,614	7,844	4,944
Aged 45 to 49	22,880	4,374	5,112	8,238	5,156
Aged 50 to 54	21,492	4,094	4,877	7,702	4,819
Aged 55 to 59	18,583	3,514	4,186	6,729	4,155
Aged 60 to 64	15,103	2,865	3,302	5,624	3,312
Aged 65 to 69	11,349	2,140	2,511	4,269	2,428
Aged 70 to 74	8,774	1,673	1,946	3,289	1,866
Aged 75 to 79	7,275	1,436	1,626	2,686	1,527
Aged 80 to 84	5,750	1,175	1,310	2,067	1,197
Aged 85 or older	5,722	1,197	1,339	2,000	1,186
PERCENT DISTRIBUTION BY REGION					
Total people	**100.0%**	**18.1%**	**21.9%**	**36.7%**	**23.3%**
Under age 5	100.0	15.9	21.2	37.9	24.9
Aged 5 to 9	100.0	16.5	21.6	37.7	24.1
Aged 10 to 14	100.0	17.3	22.1	36.7	23.9
Aged 15 to 19	100.0	18.1	22.2	36.0	23.7
Aged 20 to 24	100.0	17.8	21.9	36.2	24.1
Aged 25 to 29	100.0	16.3	21.4	37.3	25.0
Aged 30 to 34	100.0	17.1	21.1	37.0	24.8
Aged 35 to 39	100.0	17.9	21.0	37.0	24.0
Aged 40 to 44	100.0	19.1	21.5	36.5	23.0
Aged 45 to 49	100.0	19.1	22.3	36.0	22.5
Aged 50 to 54	100.0	19.0	22.7	35.8	22.4
Aged 55 to 59	100.0	18.9	22.5	36.2	22.4
Aged 60 to 64	100.0	19.0	21.9	37.2	21.9
Aged 65 to 69	100.0	18.9	22.1	37.6	21.4
Aged 70 to 74	100.0	19.1	22.2	37.5	21.3
Aged 75 to 79	100.0	19.7	22.4	36.9	21.0
Aged 80 to 84	100.0	20.4	22.8	36.0	20.8
Aged 85 or older	100.0	20.9	23.4	34.9	20.7

	total	Northeast	Midwest	South	West
PERCENT DISTRIBUTION BY AGE					
Total people	100.0%	100.0%	100.0%	100.0%	100.0%
Under age 5	6.9	6.1	6.7	7.1	7.4
Aged 5 to 9	6.6	6.0	6.5	6.8	6.8
Aged 10 to 14	6.6	6.3	6.7	6.6	6.8
Aged 15 to 19	7.1	7.1	7.2	6.9	7.2
Aged 20 to 24	6.9	6.8	6.9	6.8	7.2
Aged 25 to 29	7.0	6.3	6.9	7.1	7.5
Aged 30 to 34	6.4	6.1	6.2	6.5	6.9
Aged 35 to 39	6.9	6.9	6.6	7.0	7.1
Aged 40 to 44	7.1	7.5	6.9	7.0	7.0
Aged 45 to 49	7.5	8.0	7.7	7.4	7.3
Aged 50 to 54	7.1	7.5	7.3	6.9	6.8
Aged 55 to 59	6.1	6.4	6.3	6.0	5.9
Aged 60 to 64	5.0	5.2	5.0	5.0	4.7
Aged 65 to 69	3.7	3.9	3.8	3.8	3.4
Aged 70 to 74	2.9	3.0	2.9	2.9	2.6
Aged 75 to 79	2.4	2.6	2.4	2.4	2.2
Aged 80 to 84	1.9	2.1	2.0	1.9	1.7
Aged 85 or older	1.9	2.2	2.0	1.8	1.7

Source: Bureau of the Census, State Population Estimates, Internet site http://www.census.gov/popest/states/asrh/; calculations by New Strategist

Table 9.13 Regional Populations by Generation, 2008

(number and percent distribution of people by generation and region, 2008; numbers in thousands)

	total	Northeast	Midwest	South	West
Total people	**304,060**	**54,925**	**66,561**	**111,719**	**70,855**
iGeneration (under age 14)	57,115	9,422	12,350	21,429	13,914
Millennial (14 to 31)	75,757	13,150	16,497	27,709	18,401
Generation X (32 to 43)	49,958	9,063	10,583	18,408	11,905
Baby Boom (44 to 62)	76,319	14,522	17,078	27,612	17,106
Swing (63 to 75)	27,619	5,246	6,104	10,345	5,924
World War II (76 or older)	17,292	3,522	3,950	6,216	3,605
PERCENT DISTRIBUTION BY GENERATION					
Total people	**100.0%**	**100.0%**	**100.0%**	**100.0%**	**100.0%**
iGeneration (under age 14)	18.8	17.2	18.6	19.2	19.6
Millennial (14 to 31)	24.9	23.9	24.8	24.8	26.0
Generation X (32 to 43)	16.4	16.5	15.9	16.5	16.8
Baby Boom (44 to 62)	25.1	26.4	25.7	24.7	24.1
Swing (63 to 75)	9.1	9.6	9.2	9.3	8.4
World War II (76 or older)	5.7	6.4	5.9	5.6	5.1
PERCENT DISTRIBUTION BY REGION					
Total people	**100.0%**	**18.1%**	**21.9%**	**36.7%**	**23.3%**
iGeneration (under age 14)	100.0	16.5	21.6	37.5	24.4
Millennial (14 to 31)	100.0	17.4	21.8	36.6	24.3
Generation X (32 to 43)	100.0	18.1	21.2	36.8	23.8
Baby Boom (44 to 62)	100.0	19.0	22.4	36.2	22.4
Swing (63 to 75)	100.0	19.0	22.1	37.5	21.4
World War II (76 or older)	100.0	20.4	22.8	35.9	20.8

Note: Numbers of people by generation are estimates by New Strategist.
Source: Bureau of the Census, Population Estimates, Internet site http://www.census.gov/popest/national/asrh/
NC-EST2006-sa.html; calculations by New Strategist

Diversity Is Growing in Every Region

North, South, East, West—younger generations are more diverse.

Non-Hispanic whites dominate older generations of Americans, while they are in the minority among younger generations in some regions. In the Midwest, 91 percent of the World War II generation is non-Hispanic white, according to the 2008 American Community Survey. In other regions, the non-Hispanic white share of the older population ranges from 75 to 86 percent.

Non-Hispanic whites are a far smaller share of children and young adults—Millennials and the iGeneration. In the West, non-Hispanic whites account for only 49 percent of Millennials and an even smaller 42 percent of the iGeneration (under age 14 in 2008). Hispanics account for 40 percent of the iGeneration in the West.

The Midwest is the least diverse region, with non-Hispanic whites dominating even the youngest residents of the region. Seventy-one percent of the iGeneration in the Midwest are non-Hispanic white. This compares with 62 percent of the youngest generation in the Northeast and 52 percent in the South.

■ The differences in racial and ethnic composition by region will persist, even as regions become more diverse, because immigrants tend to settle in areas with large immigrant populations.

More diversity among the young in every region

(non-Hispanic white share of selected generations, by region, 2008)

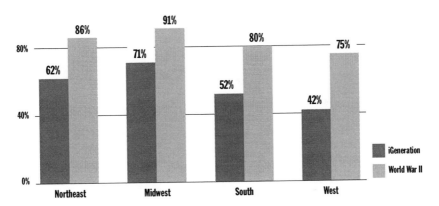

Table 9.14 Population of the Northeast by Age, Race, and Hispanic Origin, 2008

(number and percent distribution of people in the Northeast by age, race, and Hispanic origin, 2008; numbers in thousands)

	total	Asian	black	Hispanic	non-Hispanic white
Total, Northeast	**54,925**	**2,841**	**6,398**	**6,416**	**38,659**
Under age 5	3,333	191	465	641	1,948
Aged 5 to 9	3,292	183	446	513	2,073
Aged 10 to 14	3,488	168	492	516	2,239
Aged 15 to 17	2,272	103	331	308	1,492
Aged 18 to 19	1,670	81	239	221	1,105
Aged 20 to 24	3,725	190	514	510	2,464
Aged 25 to 29	3,431	220	461	539	2,176
Aged 30 to 34	3,327	260	415	533	2,085
Aged 35 to 44	7,898	528	940	1,008	5,355
Aged 45 to 54	8,488	419	898	757	6,355
Aged 55 to 64	6,385	271	592	459	5,027
Aged 65 to 74	3,819	145	347	248	3,062
Aged 75 to 84	2,642	65	186	127	2,256
Aged 85 or older	1,155	17	73	37	1,022
Total, Northeast	**100.0%**	**5.2%**	**11.6%**	**11.7%**	**70.4%**
Under age 5	100.0	5.7	14.0	19.2	58.4
Aged 5 to 9	100.0	5.6	13.5	15.6	63.0
Aged 10 to 14	100.0	4.8	14.1	14.8	64.2
Aged 15 to 17	100.0	4.5	14.6	13.6	65.7
Aged 18 to 19	100.0	4.8	14.3	13.2	66.1
Aged 20 to 24	100.0	5.1	13.8	13.7	66.1
Aged 25 to 29	100.0	6.4	13.4	15.7	63.4
Aged 30 to 34	100.0	7.8	12.5	16.0	62.7
Aged 35 to 44	100.0	6.7	11.9	12.8	67.8
Aged 45 to 54	100.0	4.9	10.6	8.9	74.9
Aged 55 to 64	100.0	4.2	9.3	7.2	78.7
Aged 65 to 74	100.0	3.8	9.1	6.5	80.2
Aged 75 to 84	100.0	2.5	7.0	4.8	85.4
Aged 85 or older	100.0	1.5	6.3	3.2	88.5

Note: Numbers do not add to total because Asians and blacks include only those who identified themselves as being of the race alone, not all races are shown, and Hispanics may be of any race. Non-Hispanic whites are those who identified themselves as being white alone and not Hispanic.
Source: Bureau of the Census, 2008 American Community Survey, Internet site http://factfinder.census.gov/home/saff/main .html?_lang=en; calculations by New Strategist

Table 9.15 Population of the Northeast by Generation, Race, and Hispanic Origin, 2008

(number and percent distribution of people in the Northeast by generation, race, and Hispanic origin, 2008; numbers in thousands)

	total	Asian	black	Hispanic	non-Hispanic white
Total Northeast	**54,925**	**2,841**	**6,398**	**6,416**	**38,659**
iGeneration (under age 14)	9,416	508	1,304	1,566	5,812
Millennial (14 to 31)	13,127	731	1,809	1,895	8,519
Generation X (32 to 43)	9,104	632	1,095	1,227	6,071
Baby Boom (44 to 62)	14,386	689	1,465	1,225	10,912
Swing (63 to 75)	5,360	206	484	352	4,293
World War II (76 or older)	3,533	76	240	151	3,053
Total Northeast	**100.0%**	**5.2%**	**11.6%**	**11.7%**	**70.4%**
iGeneration (under age 14)	100.0	5.4	13.9	16.6	61.7
Millennial (14 to 31)	100.0	5.6	13.8	14.4	64.9
Generation X (32 to 43)	100.0	6.9	12.0	13.5	66.7
Baby Boom (44 to 62)	100.0	4.8	10.2	8.5	75.9
Swing (63 to 75)	100.0	3.8	9.0	6.6	80.1
World War II (76 or older)	100.0	2.1	6.8	4.3	86.4

Note: Numbers do not add to total because Asians and blacks include only those who identified themselves as being of the race alone, not all races are shown, and Hispanics may be of any race. Non-Hispanic whites are those who identified themselves as being white alone and not Hispanic. Number of people by generation are estimates by New Strategist.
Source: Bureau of the Census, 2008 American Community Survey, Internet site http://factfinder.census.gov/home/saff/main .html?_lang=en; calculations by New Strategist

Table 9.16 Population of the Midwest by Age, Race, and Hispanic Origin, 2008

(number and percent distribution of people in the Midwest by age, race, and Hispanic origin, 2008; numbers in thousands)

	total	Asian	black	Hispanic	non-Hispanic white
Total, Midwest	**66,561**	**1,572**	**6,696**	**4,248**	**52,628**
Under age 5	4,455	118	517	529	3,072
Aged 5 to 9	4,333	116	511	452	3,070
Aged 10 to 14	4,441	96	554	385	3,247
Aged 15 to 17	2,838	59	374	210	2,105
Aged 18 to 19	2,010	51	259	143	1,497
Aged 20 to 24	4,611	126	509	347	3,521
Aged 25 to 29	4,499	133	502	381	3,392
Aged 30 to 34	4,090	159	434	388	3,035
Aged 35 to 44	9,053	282	932	622	7,074
Aged 45 to 54	10,019	193	916	409	8,362
Aged 55 to 64	7,492	133	604	215	6,458
Aged 65 to 74	4,460	69	330	99	3,920
Aged 75 to 84	2,989	29	190	54	2,698
Aged 85 or older	1,270	8	65	14	1,178
Total, Midwest	**100.0%**	**2.4%**	**10.1%**	**6.4%**	**79.1%**
Under age 5	100.0	2.6	11.6	11.9	69.0
Aged 5 to 9	100.0	2.7	11.8	10.4	70.8
Aged 10 to 14	100.0	2.2	12.5	8.7	73.1
Aged 15 to 17	100.0	2.1	13.2	7.4	74.2
Aged 18 to 19	100.0	2.5	12.9	7.1	74.5
Aged 20 to 24	100.0	2.7	11.0	7.5	76.4
Aged 25 to 29	100.0	3.0	11.2	8.5	75.4
Aged 30 to 34	100.0	3.9	10.6	9.5	74.2
Aged 35 to 44	100.0	3.1	10.3	6.9	78.1
Aged 45 to 54	100.0	1.9	9.1	4.1	83.5
Aged 55 to 64	100.0	1.8	8.1	2.9	86.2
Aged 65 to 74	100.0	1.6	7.4	2.2	87.9
Aged 75 to 84	100.0	1.0	6.3	1.8	90.2
Aged 85 or older	100.0	0.6	5.1	1.1	92.7

Note: Numbers do not add to total because Asians and blacks include only those who identified themselves as being of the race alone, not all races are shown, and Hispanics may be of any race. Non-Hispanic whites are those who identified themselves as being white alone and not Hispanic.
Source: Bureau of the Census, 2008 American Community Survey, Internet site http://factfinder.census.gov/home/saff/main .html?_lang=en; calculations by New Strategist

Table 9.17 Population of the Midwest by Generation, Race, and Hispanic Origin, 2008

(number and percent distribution of people in the Midwest by generation, race, and Hispanic origin, 2008; numbers in thousands)

	total	Asian	black	Hispanic	non-Hispanic white
Total Midwest	**66,561**	**1,572**	**6,696**	**4,248**	**52,628**
iGeneration (under age 14)	12,341	310	1,471	1,289	8,739
Millennial (14 to 31)	16,483	452	1,929	1,313	12,378
Generation X (32 to 43)	10,602	350	1,100	792	8,188
Baby Boom (44 to 62)	16,918	327	1,492	643	14,236
Swing (63 to 75)	6,257	99	469	148	5,481
World War II (76 or older)	3,960	34	235	63	3,605
Total Midwest	**100.0%**	**2.4%**	**10.1%**	**6.4%**	**79.1%**
iGeneration (under age 14)	100.0	2.5	11.9	10.4	70.8
Millennial (14 to 31)	100.0	2.7	11.7	8.0	75.1
Generation X (32 to 43)	100.0	3.3	10.4	7.5	77.2
Baby Boom (44 to 62)	100.0	1.9	8.8	3.8	84.1
Swing (63 to 75)	100.0	1.6	7.5	2.4	87.6
World War II (76 or older)	100.0	0.9	5.9	1.6	91.0

Note: Numbers do not add to total because Asians and blacks include only those who identified themselves as being of the race alone, not all races are shown, and Hispanics may be of any race. Non-Hispanic whites are those who identified themselves as being white alone and not Hispanic. Number of people by generation are estimates by New Strategist.
Source: Bureau of the Census, 2008 American Community Survey, Internet site http://factfinder.census.gov/home/saff/main .html?_lang=en; calculations by New Strategist

Table 9.18 Population of the South by Age, Race, and Hispanic Origin, 2008

(number and percent distribution of people in the South by age, race, and Hispanic origin, 2008; numbers in thousands)

	total	Asian	black	Hispanic	non-Hispanic white
Total, South	**111,719**	**2,824**	**21,182**	**16,486**	**69,049**
Under age 5	7,910	200	1,622	1,889	3,896
Aged 5 to 9	7,448	194	1,595	1,521	3,887
Aged 10 to 14	7,530	180	1,655	1,360	4,104
Aged 15 to 17	4,644	99	1,097	755	2,564
Aged 18 to 19	3,307	74	806	518	1,824
Aged 20 to 24	7,615	183	1,691	1,274	4,309
Aged 25 to 29	7,748	216	1,580	1,436	4,378
Aged 30 to 34	7,157	262	1,372	1,433	3,967
Aged 35 to 44	15,769	536	3,055	2,497	9,449
Aged 45 to 54	15,948	400	2,967	1,745	10,599
Aged 55 to 64	12,368	271	1,956	1,033	8,949
Aged 65 to 74	7,584	139	1,028	572	5,763
Aged 75 to 84	4,858	55	549	344	3,876
Aged 85 or older	1,832	14	210	111	1,485
Total, South	**100.0%**	**2.5%**	**19.0%**	**14.8%**	**61.8%**
Under age 5	100.0	2.5	20.5	23.9	49.2
Aged 5 to 9	100.0	2.6	21.4	20.4	52.2
Aged 10 to 14	100.0	2.4	22.0	18.1	54.5
Aged 15 to 17	100.0	2.1	23.6	16.3	55.2
Aged 18 to 19	100.0	2.2	24.4	15.6	55.1
Aged 20 to 24	100.0	2.4	22.2	16.7	56.6
Aged 25 to 29	100.0	2.8	20.4	18.5	56.5
Aged 30 to 34	100.0	3.7	19.2	20.0	55.4
Aged 35 to 44	100.0	3.4	19.4	15.8	59.9
Aged 45 to 54	100.0	2.5	18.6	10.9	66.5
Aged 55 to 64	100.0	2.2	15.8	8.4	72.4
Aged 65 to 74	100.0	1.8	13.6	7.5	76.0
Aged 75 to 84	100.0	1.1	11.3	7.1	79.8
Aged 85 or older	100.0	0.8	11.5	6.1	81.1

Note: Numbers do not add to total because Asians and blacks include only those who identified themselves as being of the race alone, not all races are shown, and Hispanics may be of any race. Non-Hispanic whites are those who identified themselves as being white alone and not Hispanic.
Source: Bureau of the Census, 2008 American Community Survey, Internet site http://factfinder.census.gov/home/saff/main .html?_lang=en; calculations by New Strategist

Table 9.19 Population of the South by Generation, Race, and Hispanic Origin, 2008

(number and percent distribution of people in the South by generation, race, and Hispanic origin, 2008; numbers in thousands)

	total	Asian	black	Hispanic	non-Hispanic white
Total South	**111,719**	**2,824**	**21,182**	**16,486**	**69,049**
iGeneration (under age 14)	21,382	538	4,541	4,497	11,066
Millennial (14 to 31)	27,683	714	6,053	4,827	15,482
Generation X (32 to 43)	18,486	639	3,573	3,107	10,885
Baby Boom (44 to 62)	27,419	671	4,837	2,822	18,703
Swing (63 to 75)	10,543	198	1,474	813	7,940
World War II (76 or older)	6,204	63	704	420	4,973
Total South	**100.0%**	**2.5%**	**19.0%**	**14.8%**	**61.8%**
iGeneration (under age 14)	100.0	2.5	21.2	21.0	51.8
Millennial (14 to 31)	100.0	2.6	21.9	17.4	55.9
Generation X (32 to 43)	100.0	3.5	19.3	16.8	58.9
Baby Boom (44 to 62)	100.0	2.4	17.6	10.3	68.2
Swing (63 to 75)	100.0	1.9	14.0	7.7	75.3
World War II (76 or older)	100.0	1.0	11.3	6.8	80.2

Note: Numbers do not add to total because Asians and blacks include only those who identified themselves as being of the race alone, not all races are shown, and Hispanics may be of any race. Non-Hispanic whites are those who identified themselves as being white alone and not Hispanic. Number of people by generation are estimates by New Strategist.
Source: Bureau of the Census, 2008 American Community Survey, Internet site http://factfinder.census.gov/home/saff/main .html?_lang=en; calculations by New Strategist

Table 9.20 Population of the West by Age, Race, and Hispanic Origin, 2008

(number and percent distribution of people in the West by age, race, and Hispanic origin, 2008; numbers in thousands)

	total	Asian	black	Hispanic	non-Hispanic white
Total, West	**70,855**	**6,177**	**3,311**	**19,741**	**38,607**
Under age 5	5,212	346	233	2,194	2,087
Aged 5 to 9	4,786	332	237	1,868	2,043
Aged 10 to 14	4,878	344	258	1,841	2,134
Aged 15 to 17	3,062	223	171	1,071	1,420
Aged 18 to 19	2,109	167	128	684	1,008
Aged 20 to 24	5,059	402	274	1,585	2,546
Aged 25 to 29	5,248	431	246	1,721	2,635
Aged 30 to 34	4,819	496	219	1,656	2,263
Aged 35 to 44	10,025	1,064	491	2,909	5,196
Aged 45 to 54	9,981	936	476	2,050	6,186
Aged 55 to 64	7,473	683	292	1,138	5,135
Aged 65 to 74	4,303	399	166	585	3,038
Aged 75 to 84	2,772	265	87	338	2,031
Aged 85 or older	1,129	89	32	103	885
Total, West	**100.0%**	**8.7%**	**4.7%**	**27.9%**	**54.5%**
Under age 5	100.0	6.6	4.5	42.1	40.0
Aged 5 to 9	100.0	6.9	4.9	39.0	42.7
Aged 10 to 14	100.0	7.1	5.3	37.7	43.7
Aged 15 to 17	100.0	7.3	5.6	35.0	46.4
Aged 18 to 19	100.0	7.9	6.1	32.4	47.8
Aged 20 to 24	100.0	7.9	5.4	31.3	50.3
Aged 25 to 29	100.0	8.2	4.7	32.8	50.2
Aged 30 to 34	100.0	10.3	4.6	34.4	47.0
Aged 35 to 44	100.0	10.6	4.9	29.0	51.8
Aged 45 to 54	100.0	9.4	4.8	20.5	62.0
Aged 55 to 64	100.0	9.1	3.9	15.2	68.7
Aged 65 to 74	100.0	9.3	3.9	13.6	70.6
Aged 75 to 84	100.0	9.6	3.1	12.2	73.3
Aged 85 or older	100.0	7.9	2.8	9.1	78.4

Note: Numbers do not add to total because Asians and blacks include only those who identified themselves as being of the race alone, not all races are shown, and Hispanics may be of any race. Non-Hispanic whites are those who identified themselves as being white alone and not Hispanic.
Source: Bureau of the Census, 2008 American Community Survey, Internet site http://factfinder.census.gov/home/saff/main .html?_lang=en; calculations by New Strategist

Table 9.21 Population of the West by Generation, Race, and Hispanic Origin, 2008

(number and percent distribution of people in the West by generation, race, and Hispanic origin, 2008; numbers in thousands)

	total	Asian	black	Hispanic	non-Hispanic white
Total West	**70,855**	**6,177**	**3,311**	**19,741**	**38,607**
iGeneration (under age 14)	13,900	953	675	5,534	5,837
Millennial (14 to 31)	18,381	1,490	959	6,092	8,941
Generation X (32 to 43)	11,914	1,255	574	3,611	6,034
Baby Boom (44 to 62)	16,962	1,589	759	3,251	10,813
Swing (63 to 75)	6,075	562	234	846	4,268
World War II (76 or older)	3,624	328	110	407	2,713
Total West	**100.0%**	**8.7%**	**4.7%**	**27.9%**	**54.5%**
iGeneration (under age 14)	100.0	6.9	4.9	39.8	42.0
Millennial (14 to 31)	100.0	8.1	5.2	33.1	48.6
Generation X (32 to 43)	100.0	10.5	4.8	30.3	50.6
Baby Boom (44 to 62)	100.0	9.4	4.5	19.2	63.8
Swing (63 to 75)	100.0	9.3	3.8	13.9	70.3
World War II (76 or older)	100.0	9.0	3.0	11.2	74.9

Note: Numbers do not add to total because Asians and blacks include only those who identified themselves as being of the race alone, not all races are shown, and Hispanics may be of any race. Non-Hispanic whites are those who identified themselves as being white alone and not Hispanic. Number of people by generation are estimates by New Strategist.
Source: Bureau of the Census, 2008 American Community Survey, Internet site http://factfinder.census.gov/home/saff/main .html?_lang=en; calculations by New Strategist

Young and Old Are Drawn to Different States

Millennials are the largest generation in many states.

Utah is one of the most youthful states in the nation, demographically speaking, while Florida is the oldest. Only 10 percent of people living in Utah are members of the older generations—Swing and World War II (aged 63 or older in 2008), while Florida's share is twice as great at 20 percent.

Utah is the only state in which more than half the population belongs to the iGeneration or the Millennial generation (under age 32). Twenty-five percent are members of the iGeneration and 30 percent are Millennials—both far surpassing the 19 percent in the Baby Boom generation. The reason for Utah's youthful population is the preponderance of the Mormon religion, which encourages large families.

Florida's population is the oldest in the nation because the state has attracted retirees to its warm winter climate. Other states with above-average older populations are those in which older people have been left behind by young adults seeking opportunity elsewhere, such as West Virginia.

■ The elderly population will increase in every state as the large Baby-Boom generation ages.

Old and young are concentrated in different states

(percent of people in the two youngest and two oldest generations in Florida and Utah, 2008)

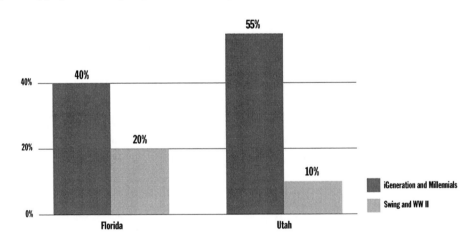

Table 9.22 State Populations by Age, 2008

(number of people by state and age, 2008; numbers in thousands)

	total	under 5	5 to 14	15 to 19	20 to 24	25 to 29	30 to 34	35 to 44	45 to 54	55 to 64	65 to 74	75 or older
United States	**304,060**	**21,006**	**40,120**	**21,514**	**21,059**	**21,334**	**19,598**	**42,501**	**44,372**	**33,686**	**20,123**	**18,747**
Alabama	4,662	311	615	328	319	321	287	623	674	542	345	297
Alaska	686	52	96	51	55	57	47	95	108	75	31	19
Arizona	6,500	516	918	444	431	488	445	871	846	678	445	418
Arkansas	2,855	202	381	197	186	202	179	373	396	331	215	193
California	36,757	2,705	5,027	2,769	2,718	2,714	2,541	5,350	5,152	3,667	2,127	1,988
Colorado	4,939	358	651	324	341	388	356	720	743	547	279	232
Connecticut	3,501	212	452	250	224	205	200	512	561	408	237	241
Delaware	873	59	111	62	59	56	53	121	128	102	64	57
District of Columbia	592	36	56	41	54	61	48	85	77	63	37	34
Florida	18,328	1,141	2,163	1,159	1,149	1,202	1,094	2,487	2,609	2,138	1,536	1,652
Georgia	9,686	741	1,387	688	653	716	669	1,462	1,379	1,010	553	428
Hawaii	1,288	87	150	81	92	97	85	174	180	152	90	100
Idaho	1,524	122	223	111	104	115	98	193	208	167	98	84
Illinois	12,902	894	1,738	940	919	920	868	1,809	1,873	1,366	812	763
Indiana	6,377	443	869	452	427	445	409	871	938	709	423	390
Iowa	3,003	201	385	217	215	195	175	381	444	344	214	231
Kansas	2,802	203	380	200	211	197	171	360	408	306	180	187
Kentucky	4,269	285	549	283	273	310	277	593	632	502	308	258
Louisiana	4,411	311	604	329	336	329	265	568	639	489	289	251
Maine	1,316	71	150	88	78	76	73	182	220	178	103	96
Maryland	5,634	372	728	407	377	380	351	825	875	639	366	314
Massachusetts	6,498	384	784	460	465	428	404	951	1,003	748	429	442
Michigan	10,003	626	1,320	740	679	650	595	1,383	1,537	1,169	680	624
Minnesota	5,220	358	677	367	360	368	328	720	812	580	330	320

	total	under 5	5 to 14	15 to 19	20 to 24	25 to 29	30 to 34	35 to 44	45 to 54	55 to 64	65 to 74	75 or older
Mississippi	2,939	221	414	224	214	205	180	379	410	320	198	174
Missouri	5,912	399	771	413	399	421	362	787	882	673	416	389
Montana	967	61	119	67	69	66	54	116	152	126	72	65
Nebraska	1,783	132	239	129	133	124	108	225	257	195	117	124
Nevada	2,600	199	361	165	155	200	188	382	362	292	171	126
New Hampshire	1,316	75	162	93	83	78	73	194	223	165	89	81
New Jersey	8,683	557	1,129	590	540	522	545	1,312	1,359	976	585	566
New Mexico	1,984	148	269	144	144	144	123	250	278	224	137	123
New York	19,490	1,208	2,396	1,403	1,400	1,309	1,251	2,795	2,911	2,209	1,332	1,276
North Carolina	9,222	653	1,218	629	627	620	615	1,341	1,325	1,055	618	521
North Dakota	641	42	76	48	60	46	35	74	94	72	44	51
Ohio	11,486	744	1,497	809	763	775	689	1,556	1,751	1,333	807	764
Oklahoma	3,642	267	487	252	270	274	224	459	512	407	259	232
Oregon	3,790	243	472	248	243	278	256	510	560	476	262	242
Pennsylvania	12,448	737	1,509	890	829	754	711	1,693	1,926	1,488	922	989
Rhode Island	1,051	61	125	80	77	67	63	148	161	121	70	78
South Carolina	4,480	303	576	321	304	302	279	611	641	545	327	270
South Dakota	804	59	105	57	60	55	46	96	117	93	56	60
Tennessee	6,215	416	808	413	392	442	403	875	912	735	449	371
Texas	24,327	2,027	3,630	1,765	1,759	1,868	1,710	3,439	3,299	2,357	1,332	1,140
Utah	2,736	269	454	213	243	251	195	326	313	225	132	115
Vermont	621	33	71	45	42	37	34	85	104	85	46	41
Virginia	7,769	523	988	536	545	551	513	1,139	1,157	876	514	427
Washington	6,549	433	836	442	441	488	438	925	990	772	416	368
West Virginia	1,814	105	212	117	110	119	113	240	274	241	150	135
Wisconsin	5,628	362	715	398	393	380	339	768	875	647	379	371
Wyoming	533	38	68	37	39	40	32	65	83	65	35	30

Source: Bureau of the Census, State Population Estimates, Internet site http://www.census.gov/popest/states/asrh/SC-EST2008-02.html; calculations by New Strategist

Table 9.23 Distribution of State Populations by Age, 2008

(distribution of state populations by age, 2008)

	total	under 5	5 to 14	15 to 19	20 to 24	25 to 29	30 to 34	35 to 44	45 to 54	55 to 64	65 to 74	75 or older
United States	100.0%	6.9%	13.2%	7.1%	6.9%	7.0%	6.4%	14.0%	14.6%	11.1%	6.6%	6.2%
Alabama	100.0	6.7	13.2	7.0	6.8	6.9	6.2	13.4	14.5	11.6	7.4	6.4
Alaska	100.0	7.6	13.9	7.5	8.0	8.4	6.8	13.8	15.8	10.9	4.5	2.8
Arizona	100.0	7.9	14.1	6.8	6.6	7.5	6.8	13.4	13.0	10.4	6.8	6.4
Arkansas	100.0	7.1	13.3	6.9	6.5	7.1	6.3	13.1	13.9	11.6	7.5	6.7
California	100.0	7.4	13.7	7.5	7.4	7.4	6.9	14.6	14.0	10.0	5.8	5.4
Colorado	100.0	7.3	13.2	6.6	6.9	7.9	7.2	14.6	15.0	11.1	5.6	4.7
Connecticut	100.0	6.0	12.9	7.1	6.4	5.9	5.7	14.6	16.0	11.7	6.8	6.9
Delaware	100.0	6.8	12.7	7.1	6.7	6.4	6.0	13.9	14.7	11.7	7.4	6.6
District of Columbia	100.0	6.1	9.5	6.9	9.1	10.2	8.2	14.3	13.0	10.7	6.2	5.7
Florida	100.0	6.2	11.8	6.3	6.3	6.6	6.0	13.6	14.2	11.7	8.4	9.0
Georgia	100.0	7.6	14.3	7.1	6.7	7.4	6.9	15.1	14.2	10.4	5.7	4.4
Hawaii	100.0	6.8	11.6	6.3	7.1	7.5	6.6	13.5	14.0	11.8	7.0	7.8
Idaho	100.0	8.0	14.6	7.3	6.8	7.5	6.4	12.7	13.7	11.0	6.4	5.5
Illinois	100.0	6.9	13.5	7.3	7.1	7.1	6.7	14.0	14.5	10.6	6.3	5.9
Indiana	100.0	6.9	13.6	7.1	6.7	7.0	6.4	13.7	14.7	11.1	6.6	6.1
Iowa	100.0	6.7	12.8	7.2	7.2	6.5	5.8	12.7	14.8	11.5	7.1	7.7
Kansas	100.0	7.2	13.6	7.1	7.5	7.0	6.1	12.9	14.6	10.9	6.4	6.7
Kentucky	100.0	6.7	12.9	6.6	6.4	7.3	6.5	13.9	14.8	11.8	7.2	6.1
Louisiana	100.0	7.0	13.7	7.5	7.6	7.5	6.0	12.9	14.5	11.1	6.6	5.7
Maine	100.0	5.4	11.4	6.7	6.0	5.8	5.5	13.9	16.7	13.5	7.8	7.3
Maryland	100.0	6.6	12.9	7.2	6.7	6.7	6.2	14.6	15.5	11.3	6.5	5.6
Massachusetts	100.0	5.9	12.1	7.1	7.2	6.6	6.2	14.6	15.4	11.5	6.6	6.8
Michigan	100.0	6.3	13.2	7.4	6.8	6.5	6.0	13.8	15.4	11.7	6.8	6.2
Minnesota	100.0	6.9	13.0	7.0	6.9	7.0	6.3	13.8	15.6	11.1	6.3	6.1

	total	under 5	5 to 14	15 to 19	20 to 24	25 to 29	30 to 34	35 to 44	45 to 54	55 to 64	65 to 74	75 or older
Mississippi	100.0%	7.5%	14.1%	7.6%	7.3%	7.0%	6.1%	12.9%	13.9%	10.9%	6.7%	5.9%
Missouri	100.0	6.8	13.0	7.0	6.8	7.1	6.1	13.3	14.9	11.4	7.0	6.6
Montana	100.0	6.3	12.3	6.9	7.1	6.8	5.5	12.0	15.7	13.0	7.4	6.8
Nebraska	100.0	7.4	13.4	7.2	7.5	7.0	6.1	12.6	14.4	10.9	6.6	6.9
Nevada	100.0	7.7	13.9	6.3	5.9	7.7	7.2	14.7	13.9	11.2	6.6	4.8
New Hampshire	100.0	5.7	12.3	7.0	6.3	5.9	5.5	14.8	16.9	12.6	6.8	6.1
New Jersey	100.0	6.4	13.0	6.8	6.2	6.0	6.3	15.1	15.6	11.2	6.7	6.5
New Mexico	100.0	7.5	13.5	7.3	7.3	7.3	6.2	12.6	14.0	11.3	6.9	6.2
New York	100.0	6.2	12.3	7.2	7.2	6.7	6.4	14.3	14.9	11.3	6.8	6.5
North Carolina	100.0	7.1	13.2	6.8	6.8	6.7	6.7	14.5	14.4	11.4	6.7	5.6
North Dakota	100.0	6.5	11.8	7.5	9.4	7.1	5.4	11.6	14.7	11.3	6.8	7.9
Ohio	100.0	6.5	13.0	7.0	6.6	6.7	6.0	13.5	15.2	11.6	7.0	6.6
Oklahoma	100.0	7.3	13.4	6.9	7.4	7.5	6.2	12.6	14.0	11.2	7.1	6.4
Oregon	100.0	6.4	12.5	6.5	6.4	7.3	6.8	13.5	14.8	12.6	6.9	6.4
Pennsylvania	100.0	5.9	12.1	7.2	6.7	6.1	5.7	13.6	15.5	12.0	7.4	7.9
Rhode Island	100.0	5.8	11.9	7.6	7.4	6.4	6.0	14.1	15.4	11.5	6.7	7.4
South Carolina	100.0	6.8	12.9	7.2	6.8	6.8	6.2	13.6	14.3	12.2	7.3	6.0
South Dakota	100.0	7.3	13.1	7.1	7.4	6.8	5.7	11.9	14.6	11.5	6.9	7.5
Tennessee	100.0	6.7	13.0	6.6	6.3	7.1	6.5	14.1	14.7	11.8	7.2	6.0
Texas	100.0	8.3	14.9	7.3	7.2	7.7	7.0	14.1	13.6	9.7	5.5	4.7
Utah	100.0	9.8	16.6	7.8	8.9	9.2	7.1	11.9	11.5	8.2	4.8	4.2
Vermont	100.0	5.3	11.4	7.3	6.8	5.9	5.5	13.6	16.7	13.6	7.4	6.6
Virginia	100.0	6.7	12.7	6.9	7.0	7.1	6.6	14.7	14.9	11.3	6.6	5.5
Washington	100.0	6.6	12.8	6.7	6.7	7.5	6.7	14.1	15.1	11.8	6.4	5.6
West Virginia	100.0	5.8	11.7	6.4	6.1	6.5	6.2	13.2	15.1	13.3	8.3	7.5
Wisconsin	100.0	6.4	12.7	7.1	7.0	6.8	6.0	13.6	15.5	11.5	6.7	6.6
Wyoming	100.0	7.2	12.8	7.0	7.3	7.5	6.0	12.3	15.5	12.2	6.6	5.7

Source: Bureau of the Census, State Population Estimates, Internet site http://www.census.gov/popest/states/asrh/SC-EST2008-02.html; calculations by New Strategist

Table 9.24 State Populations by Generation, 2008

(number of people by state and generation, 2008; numbers in thousands)

	total	iGeneration (under 14)	Millennials (14 to 31)	Generation X (32 to 43)	Baby Boom (44 to 62)	Swing (63 to 75)	World War II (76 or older)
United States	**304,060**	**57,115**	**75,757**	**49,958**	**76,319**	**27,619**	**17,292**
Alabama	4,662	864	1,145	732	1,180	468	273
Alaska	686	138	192	113	181	45	17
Arizona	6,500	1,344	1,631	1,053	1,484	603	385
Arkansas	2,855	545	695	443	703	292	177
California	36,757	7,224	9,724	6,342	8,706	2,925	1,834
Colorado	4,939	946	1,258	863	1,266	393	213
Connecticut	3,501	617	806	577	949	329	224
Delaware	873	159	209	140	224	88	53
District of Columbia	592	87	180	106	137	51	31
Florida	18,328	3,087	4,164	2,887	4,597	2,065	1,528
Georgia	9,686	1,993	2,459	1,719	2,353	770	392
Hawaii	1,288	222	319	208	321	125	93
Idaho	1,524	323	391	233	364	134	78
Illinois	12,902	2,458	3,300	2,148	3,180	1,111	705
Indiana	6,377	1,225	1,574	1,028	1,610	579	360
Iowa	3,003	548	735	447	767	291	214
Kansas	2,802	545	714	426	696	247	173
Kentucky	4,269	779	1,031	699	1,104	419	237
Louisiana	4,411	855	1,160	669	1,100	396	231
Maine	1,316	206	287	207	385	143	88
Maryland	5,634	1,026	1,378	950	1,486	505	289
Massachusetts	6,498	1,088	1,595	1,093	1,717	596	410
Michigan	10,003	1,810	2,442	1,598	2,641	936	576
Minnesota	5,220	967	1,294	842	1,366	454	297
Mississippi	2,939	593	756	449	710	269	160
Missouri	5,912	1,092	1,455	924	1,513	568	359
Montana	967	168	235	137	268	99	60
Nebraska	1,783	348	453	267	441	160	115
Nevada	2,600	525	631	457	637	236	115
New Hampshire	1,316	220	299	218	379	125	74
New Jersey	8,683	1,572	1,985	1,502	2,296	805	522
New Mexico	1,984	391	509	298	487	187	113
New York	19,490	3,360	4,857	3,257	5,013	1,826	1,178
North Carolina	9,222	1,752	2,241	1,577	2,320	854	478
North Dakota	641	110	176	88	162	60	47
Ohio	11,486	2,088	2,774	1,810	3,008	1,102	704
Oklahoma	3,642	706	934	547	890	352	214
Oregon	3,790	668	918	614	1,002	365	224
Pennsylvania	12,448	2,091	2,913	1,943	3,324	1,261	916
Rhode Island	1,051	173	262	170	276	97	72
South Carolina	4,480	822	1,096	717	1,147	450	248

	total	iGeneration (under 14)	Millennials (14 to 31)	Generation X (32 to 43)	Baby Boom (44 to 62)	Swing (63 to 75)	World War II (76 or older)
South Dakota	804	153	201	114	204	76	56
Tennessee	6,215	1,143	1,489	1,028	1,600	614	340
Texas	24,327	5,307	6,426	4,130	5,575	1,842	1,047
Utah	2,736	680	828	413	530	180	105
Vermont	621	96	145	96	183	64	38
Virginia	7,769	1,413	1,935	1,332	1,990	707	392
Washington	6,549	1,185	1,630	1,096	1,718	582	339
West Virginia	1,814	296	412	283	496	204	124
Wisconsin	5,628	1,005	1,379	891	1,490	520	343
Wyoming	533	99	136	78	143	49	28

Note: Number of people by generation are estimates by New Strategist.
Source: Bureau of the Census, State Population Estimates, Internet site http://www.census.gov/popest/states/asrh/
SC-EST2008-02.html; calculations by New Strategist

Table 9.25 Distribution of State Populations by Generation, 2008

(percent distribution of people by state and generation, 2008)

	total	iGeneration (under 14)	Millennials (14 to 31)	Generation X (32 to 43)	Baby Boom (44 to 62)	Swing (63 to 75)	World War II (76 or older)
United States	**100.0%**	**18.8%**	**24.9%**	**16.4%**	**25.1%**	**9.1%**	**5.7%**
Alabama	100.0	18.5	24.6	15.7	25.3	10.0	5.8
Alaska	100.0	20.1	28.0	16.5	26.3	6.5	2.5
Arizona	100.0	20.7	25.1	16.2	22.8	9.3	5.9
Arkansas	100.0	19.1	24.4	15.5	24.6	10.2	6.2
California	100.0	19.7	26.5	17.3	23.7	8.0	5.0
Colorado	100.0	19.2	25.5	17.5	25.6	8.0	4.3
Connecticut	100.0	17.6	23.0	16.5	27.1	9.4	6.4
Delaware	100.0	18.2	23.9	16.1	25.6	10.1	6.0
District of Columbia	100.0	14.7	30.4	17.8	23.1	8.5	5.3
Florida	100.0	16.8	22.7	15.8	25.1	11.3	8.3
Georgia	100.0	20.6	25.4	17.7	24.3	7.9	4.1
Hawaii	100.0	17.2	24.8	16.1	25.0	9.7	7.2
Idaho	100.0	21.2	25.7	15.3	23.9	8.8	5.1
Illinois	100.0	19.0	25.6	16.6	24.7	8.6	5.5
Indiana	100.0	19.2	24.7	16.1	25.3	9.1	5.6
Iowa	100.0	18.3	24.5	14.9	25.5	9.7	7.1
Kansas	100.0	19.5	25.5	15.2	24.8	8.8	6.2
Kentucky	100.0	18.2	24.1	16.4	25.9	9.8	5.6
Louisiana	100.0	19.4	26.3	15.2	24.9	9.0	5.2
Maine	100.0	15.6	21.8	15.7	29.3	10.9	6.7
Maryland	100.0	18.2	24.5	16.9	26.4	9.0	5.1
Massachusetts	100.0	16.7	24.5	16.8	26.4	9.2	6.3
Michigan	100.0	18.1	24.4	16.0	26.4	9.4	5.8
Minnesota	100.0	18.5	24.8	16.1	26.2	8.7	5.7
Mississippi	100.0	20.2	25.7	15.3	24.2	9.2	5.4
Missouri	100.0	18.5	24.6	15.6	25.6	9.6	6.1
Montana	100.0	17.3	24.3	14.1	27.7	10.2	6.2
Nebraska	100.0	19.5	25.4	15.0	24.7	9.0	6.4
Nevada	100.0	20.2	24.2	17.6	24.5	9.1	4.4
New Hampshire	100.0	16.7	22.7	16.5	28.8	9.5	5.7
New Jersey	100.0	18.1	22.9	17.3	26.4	9.3	6.0
New Mexico	100.0	19.7	25.6	15.0	24.5	9.4	5.7
New York	100.0	17.2	24.9	16.7	25.7	9.4	6.0
North Carolina	100.0	19.0	24.3	17.1	25.2	9.3	5.2
North Dakota	100.0	17.1	27.4	13.7	25.2	9.3	7.3
Ohio	100.0	18.2	24.1	15.8	26.2	9.6	6.1
Oklahoma	100.0	19.4	25.6	15.0	24.4	9.7	5.9
Oregon	100.0	17.6	24.2	16.2	26.4	9.6	5.9
Pennsylvania	100.0	16.8	23.4	15.6	26.7	10.1	7.4
Rhode Island	100.0	16.5	25.0	16.2	26.3	9.3	6.9
South Carolina	100.0	18.4	24.5	16.0	25.6	10.0	5.5

	total	iGeneration (under 14)	Millennials (14 to 31)	Generation X (32 to 43)	Baby Boom (44 to 62)	Swing (63 to 75)	World War II (76 or older)
South Dakota	100.0%	19.1%	25.0%	14.1%	25.3%	9.5%	7.0%
Tennessee	100.0	18.4	24.0	16.5	25.7	9.9	5.5
Texas	100.0	21.8	26.4	17.0	22.9	7.6	4.3
Utah	100.0	24.9	30.2	15.1	19.4	6.6	3.8
Vermont	100.0	15.4	23.4	15.5	29.4	10.3	6.1
Virginia	100.0	18.2	24.9	17.1	25.6	9.1	5.0
Washington	100.0	18.1	24.9	16.7	26.2	8.9	5.2
West Virginia	100.0	16.3	22.7	15.6	27.3	11.2	6.9
Wisconsin	100.0	17.9	24.5	15.8	26.5	9.2	6.1
Wyoming	100.0	18.7	25.5	14.7	26.8	9.2	5.2

Note: Number of people by generation are estimates by New Strategist.
Source: Bureau of the Census, State Population Estimates, Internet site http://www.census.gov/popest/states/asrh/
SC-EST2008-02.html; calculations by New Strategist

10

Spending

Spending is directly linked to lifestage. Young adults are just starting out, and because their incomes are low, they have little to spend. The middle aged, on the other hand, have higher incomes and larger households, which means they spend more.

The spending of middle-aged householders has always been above average thanks to their higher incomes. Today, the Baby-Boom generation is leaving the peak-spending age group (45 to 54), but Boomers still dominate spending on many products and services. In some categories, however, Boomers are less important than other generations. Older generations dominate health care spending. Generation Xers are now the most important customers of products and services for children, but Millennials are close behind.

What to expect in the future

■ As Boomers age into their sixties and postpone retirement, the average spending of households headed by 55-to-64-year-olds will grow along with labor force participation rates.

■ The Millennial generation, now in the 25-to-34 age group, will have a harder time gaining a foothold in the middle class because of student loan debt, tighter mortgage standards, and soaring health care costs.

■ The spending of older Americans is rising to meet the average. As Boomers fill the older age groups, expect the spending patterns and lifestyles of elderly Americans to become more like those of younger adults.

At All Ages, Housing Is the Largest Expense

Transportation ranks second in the household budget.

The average household spent $50,486 in 2008, but spending varies greatly by age. The biggest spenders are householders ranging in age from 45 to 54, averaging just over $61,000 in annual expenditures. Householders in this age group spend the most because their nest is still crowded and they are in their peak-earning years. Householders under age 25 spend the least, just $29,325 in 2008.

Regardless of age, housing is the largest expenditure for the average household. Housing expenses absorb from 32 to 38 percent of total spending regardless of age. Spending on transportation is more variable, with the youngest householders devoting a larger share of spending to transportation than older householders. Transportation accounts for 19 percent of spending by householders under age 25. The figure bottoms out at 14 percent among householders aged 75 or older. The oldest householders spend as much on health care as they do on transportation.

The youngest householders devote a larger share of their budget to food away from home than older households do. Seven percent of the budget of householders under age 25 is spent on food away from home compared with only 4 percent for householders aged 75 or older.

■ Householders under age 25 devote as much of the household budget to education (5.8 percent) as they do to entertainment (5.5 percent) as they pursue the credentials they need to get ahead.

Health care spending rises sharply with age

(health care spending as a percent of total spending, by age of householder, 2008)

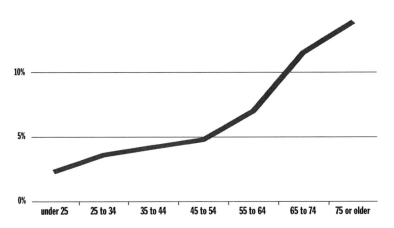

Table 10.1 Average Spending by Age of Householder, 2008

(average annual spending of consumer units (CUs) by product and service category and age of consumer unit reference person, 2008)

	total consumer units	under 25	25 to 34	35 to 44	45 to 54	55 to 64	aged 65 or older total	65 to 74	75 or older
Number of consumer units (in 000s)	120,770	8,227	20,208	22,834	25,614	19,826	24,062	12,580	11,481
Average number of persons per CU	2.5	2.0	2.8	3.3	2.7	2.1	1.7	1.8	1.5
Average annual spending of CUs	$50,486	$29,325	$48,159	$58,808	$61,179	$54,783	$36,844	$41,433	$31,692
FOOD	**6,443**	**4,447**	**6,229**	**7,849**	**7,696**	**6,357**	**4,692**	**5,338**	**3,935**
Food at home	3,744	2,330	3,393	4,509	4,452	3,710	3,075	3,421	2,667
Cereals and bakery products	507	281	454	620	600	492	435	473	390
Cereals and cereal products	170	103	169	213	203	152	131	142	118
Bakery products	337	178	286	407	397	340	304	332	271
Meats, poultry, fish, and eggs	846	573	742	1,014	1,018	845	687	781	576
Beef	239	165	213	288	290	243	182	206	154
Pork	163	108	137	196	187	166	145	173	113
Other meats	106	66	91	129	132	102	89	102	74
Poultry	159	112	152	197	195	153	112	131	89
Fish and seafood	128	89	104	145	157	129	114	123	103
Eggs	51	33	46	60	57	53	45	48	42
Dairy products	430	256	395	518	506	419	362	406	309
Fresh milk and cream	168	109	164	214	192	153	136	148	123
Other dairy products	261	147	231	304	315	267	225	259	186
Fruits and vegetables	657	370	583	754	779	682	577	616	531
Fresh fruits	222	114	196	259	262	230	197	212	179
Fresh vegetables	212	114	186	238	249	235	184	196	170
Processed fruits	116	78	103	132	140	111	106	110	101
Processed vegetables	107	63	98	125	128	107	90	97	80
Other food at home	1,305	851	1,219	1,603	1,549	1,272	1,015	1,145	863
Sugar and other sweets	129	79	103	154	149	135	121	132	107
Fats and oils	104	60	93	118	123	107	96	106	83
Miscellaneous foods	680	450	680	850	796	636	508	564	441
Nonalcoholic beverages	342	246	310	431	424	321	250	285	207
Food prepared by consumer unit on trips	49	15	34	51	57	74	41	57	24
Food away from home	2,698	2,117	2,836	3,340	3,244	2,646	1,617	1,917	1,268
ALCOHOLIC BEVERAGES	**444**	**448**	**491**	**462**	**505**	**525**	**251**	**343**	**144**
HOUSING	**17,109**	**9,975**	**17,318**	**20,649**	**19,562**	**17,611**	**12,993**	**13,845**	**12,035**
Shelter	10,183	6,530	10,935	12,689	11,629	10,122	6,933	7,281	6,553
Owned dwellings	6,760	1,383	5,873	9,056	8,606	7,387	4,685	5,334	3,974
Mortgage interest and charges	3,826	918	4,151	6,194	4,943	3,613	1,288	1,836	688
Property taxes	1,758	282	1,059	1,965	2,185	2,284	1,766	1,865	1,657
Maintenance, repair, insurance, other expenses	1,176	184	663	896	1,477	1,489	1,631	1,634	1,629
Rented dwellings	2,724	4,940	4,734	3,013	2,037	1,607	1,658	1,294	2,057
Other lodging	698	206	328	621	986	1,128	590	652	522
Utilities, fuels, and public services	3,649	1,875	3,152	4,130	4,247	3,974	3,314	3,538	3,067
Natural gas	531	211	400	588	623	603	539	552	526
Electricity	1,353	739	1,179	1,549	1,544	1,462	1,232	1,325	1,131

	total consumer units	under 25	25 to 34	35 to 44	45 to 54	55 to 64	aged 65 or older total	65 to 74	75 or older
Fuel oil and other fuels	$192	$25	$97	$167	$213	$254	$279	$251	$309
Telephone services	1,127	732	1,120	1,315	1,360	1,148	823	947	688
Water and other public services	446	167	356	511	506	507	440	464	413
Household services	**998**	**326**	**1,137**	**1,376**	**964**	**879**	**884**	**750**	**1,032**
Personal services	383	140	721	766	251	70	218	86	362
Other household services	614	185	417	609	713	809	667	664	670
Housekeeping supplies	**654**	**303**	**594**	**664**	**765**	**743**	**627**	**747**	**485**
Laundry and cleaning supplies	148	83	150	178	166	153	115	135	91
Other household products	350	155	294	361	438	400	322	380	253
Postage and stationery	156	66	150	126	161	190	190	232	141
Household furnishings and equipment	**1,624**	**942**	**1,499**	**1,789**	**1,956**	**1,894**	**1,235**	**1,529**	**898**
Household textiles	126	36	105	105	191	158	101	142	54
Furniture	388	284	459	479	416	411	228	267	184
Floor coverings	45	8	26	46	50	61	51	49	53
Major appliances	204	104	171	238	228	264	160	185	131
Small appliances and misc. housewares	113	49	85	97	130	161	116	133	96
Miscellaneous household equipment	749	460	654	824	941	839	579	753	379
APPAREL AND RELATED SERVICES	**1,801**	**1,351**	**1,965**	**2,235**	**2,228**	**1,622**	**1,092**	**1,381**	**755**
Men and boys	**427**	**296**	**436**	**623**	**488**	**391**	**239**	**340**	**121**
Men, aged 16 or older	344	261	321	451	401	354	220	309	115
Boys, aged 2 to 15	83	35	115	172	87	37	19	30	7
Women and girls	**718**	**439**	**708**	**824**	**977**	**671**	**487**	**567**	**393**
Women, aged 16 or older	597	410	562	589	821	615	448	500	387
Girls, aged 2 to 15	121	29	146	236	156	57	39	68	6
Children under age 2	**93**	**170**	**192**	**125**	**56**	**45**	**28**	**38**	**17**
Footwear	**314**	**253**	**346**	**404**	**411**	**243**	**179**	**219**	**132**
Other apparel products and services	**248**	**192**	**284**	**259**	**296**	**272**	**159**	**218**	**93**
TRANSPORTATION	**8,604**	**5,464**	**8,699**	**9,797**	**10,691**	**9,377**	**5,620**	**6,740**	**4,392**
Vehicle purchases	**2,755**	**1,988**	**3,149**	**3,122**	**3,351**	**2,999**	**1,502**	**1,920**	**1,044**
Cars and trucks, new	1,305	615	1,336	1,420	1,588	1,572	885	1,115	634
Cars and trucks, used	1,315	1,114	1,679	1,555	1,634	1,253	565	759	352
Other vehicles	134	259	134	148	129	174	52	46	58
Gasoline and motor oil	**2,715**	**1,974**	**2,754**	**3,347**	**3,298**	**2,818**	**1,629**	**2,045**	**1,173**
Other vehicle expenses	**2,621**	**1,273**	**2,380**	**2,798**	**3,414**	**2,921**	**2,039**	**2,261**	**1,793**
Vehicle finance charges	312	233	418	397	366	308	116	175	52
Maintenance and repairs	731	412	600	747	990	856	555	609	496
Vehicle insurance	1,113	427	856	1,100	1,514	1,223	1,073	1,106	1,035
Vehicle rentals, leases, licenses, other charges	465	202	506	554	544	534	294	371	209
Public transportation	**513**	**229**	**416**	**530**	**628**	**638**	**450**	**513**	**382**
HEALTH CARE	**2,976**	**682**	**1,737**	**2,499**	**2,930**	**3,825**	**4,605**	**4,779**	**4,413**
Health insurance	1,653	389	983	1,341	1,523	1,945	2,844	2,901	2,783
Medical services	727	143	472	711	838	1,022	793	853	728
Drugs	482	117	215	349	432	714	821	880	756
Medical supplies	114	33	67	98	138	144	145	145	146
ENTERTAINMENT	**2,835**	**1,608**	**2,766**	**3,603**	**3,297**	**3,036**	**1,914**	**2,418**	**1,349**
Fees and admissions	616	271	524	823	805	643	389	498	268
Audio and visual equipment and services	1,036	681	1,105	1,168	1,174	1,113	763	885	628
Pets, toys, and playground equipment	704	380	696	992	787	728	431	574	266
Other entertainment products and services	479	276	441	621	531	552	331	461	187

	total consumer units	under 25	25 to 34	35 to 44	45 to 54	55 to 64	aged 65 or older		
							total	65 to 74	75 or older
PERSONAL CARE PRODUCTS AND SERVICES	$616	$370	$547	$728	$736	$630	$512	$559	$456
READING	116	48	79	102	124	157	142	152	132
EDUCATION	1,046	1,691	759	953	2,012	867	272	345	192
TOBACCO PRODUCTS AND SMOKING SUPPLIES	317	251	298	354	437	354	161	227	88
MISCELLANEOUS	840	280	726	862	957	1,316	588	659	507
CASH CONTRIBUTIONS	1,737	427	1,036	1,550	2,152	2,163	2,156	2,033	2,291
PERSONAL INSURANCE AND PENSIONS	5,605	2,283	5,510	7,165	7,853	6,943	1,846	2,616	1,003
Life and other personal insurance	317	37	155	284	394	519	330	461	187
Pensions and Social Security	5,288	2,246	5,354	6,881	7,458	6,424	1,516	2,155	815
PERSONAL TAXES	1,789	219	1,069	1,905	3,307	2,644	500	830	139
Federal income taxes	1,817	467	1,346	2,033	2,982	2,465	695	975	388
2008 tax stimulus	−784	−451	−882	−1,017	−818	−761	−576	−637	−509
State and local income taxes	542	182	510	712	847	650	119	178	54
Other taxes	213	21	96	177	296	289	263	314	206
GIFTS FOR PEOPLE IN OTHER HOUSEHOLDS	1,209	429	579	856	2,037	1,752	1,016	1,291	700

Note: Spending by category does not add to total spending because gift spending is also included in the preceding product and service categories and personal taxes are not included in the total.
Source: Bureau of Labor Statistics, 2008 Consumer Expenditure Survey, Internet site http://www.bls.gov/cex/; calculations by New Strategist.

Table 10.2 Percent Distribution of Spending by Product Category and Age, 2008

(percent distribution of average annual spending of consumer units by product category and age of reference person, 2008)

	total consumer units	under 25	25 to 34	35 to 44	45 to 54	55 to 64	aged 65 or older total	65 to 74	75 or older
Average annual spending	100.0%	100.0%	100.0%	100.0%	100.0%	100.0%	100.0%	100.0%	100.0%
FOOD	**12.8**	**15.2**	**12.9**	**13.3**	**12.6**	**11.6**	**12.7**	**12.9**	**12.4**
Food at home	**7.4**	**7.9**	**7.0**	**7.7**	**7.3**	**6.8**	**8.3**	**8.3**	**8.4**
Cereals and bakery products	1.0	1.0	0.9	1.1	1.0	0.9	1.2	1.1	1.2
Cereals and cereal products	0.3	0.4	0.4	0.4	0.3	0.3	0.4	0.3	0.4
Bakery products	0.7	0.6	0.6	0.7	0.6	0.6	0.8	0.8	0.9
Meats, poultry, fish, and eggs	1.7	2.0	1.5	1.7	1.7	1.5	1.9	1.9	1.8
Beef	0.5	0.6	0.4	0.5	0.5	0.4	0.5	0.5	0.5
Pork	0.3	0.4	0.3	0.3	0.3	0.3	0.4	0.4	0.4
Other meats	0.2	0.2	0.2	0.2	0.2	0.2	0.2	0.2	0.2
Poultry	0.3	0.4	0.3	0.3	0.3	0.3	0.3	0.3	0.3
Fish and seafood	0.3	0.3	0.2	0.2	0.3	0.2	0.3	0.3	0.3
Eggs	0.1	0.1	0.1	0.1	0.1	0.1	0.1	0.1	0.1
Dairy products	0.9	0.9	0.8	0.9	0.8	0.8	1.0	1.0	1.0
Fresh milk and cream	0.3	0.4	0.3	0.4	0.3	0.3	0.4	0.4	0.4
Other dairy products	0.5	0.5	0.5	0.5	0.5	0.5	0.6	0.6	0.6
Fruits and vegetables	1.3	1.3	1.2	1.3	1.3	1.2	1.6	1.5	1.7
Fresh fruits	0.4	0.4	0.4	0.4	0.4	0.4	0.5	0.5	0.6
Fresh vegetables	0.4	0.4	0.4	0.4	0.4	0.4	0.5	0.5	0.5
Processed fruits	0.2	0.3	0.2	0.2	0.2	0.2	0.3	0.3	0.3
Processed vegetables	0.2	0.2	0.2	0.2	0.2	0.2	0.2	0.2	0.3
Other food at home	2.6	2.9	2.5	2.7	2.5	2.3	2.8	2.8	2.7
Sugar and other sweets	0.3	0.3	0.2	0.3	0.2	0.2	0.3	0.3	0.3
Fats and oils	0.2	0.2	0.2	0.2	0.2	0.2	0.3	0.3	0.3
Miscellaneous foods	1.3	1.5	1.4	1.4	1.3	1.2	1.4	1.4	1.4
Nonalcoholic beverages	0.7	0.8	0.6	0.7	0.7	0.6	0.7	0.7	0.7
Food prepared by consumer unit on trips	0.1	0.1	0.1	0.1	0.1	0.1	0.1	0.1	0.1
Food away from home	**5.3**	**7.2**	**5.9**	**5.7**	**5.3**	**4.8**	**4.4**	**4.6**	**4.0**
ALCOHOLIC BEVERAGES	**0.9**	**1.5**	**1.0**	**0.8**	**0.8**	**1.0**	**0.7**	**0.8**	**0.5**
HOUSING	**33.9**	**34.0**	**36.0**	**35.1**	**32.0**	**32.1**	**35.3**	**33.4**	**38.0**
Shelter	**20.2**	**22.3**	**22.7**	**21.6**	**19.0**	**18.5**	**18.8**	**17.6**	**20.7**
Owned dwellings	13.4	4.7	12.2	15.4	14.1	13.5	12.7	12.9	12.5
Mortgage interest and charges	7.6	3.1	8.6	10.5	8.1	6.6	3.5	4.4	2.2
Property taxes	3.5	1.0	2.2	3.3	3.6	4.2	4.8	4.5	5.2
Maintenance, repair, insurance, other expenses	2.3	0.6	1.4	1.5	2.4	2.7	4.4	3.9	5.1
Rented dwellings	5.4	16.8	9.8	5.1	3.3	2.9	4.5	3.1	6.5
Other lodging	1.4	0.7	0.7	1.1	1.6	2.1	1.6	1.6	1.6
Utilities, fuels, and public services	**7.2**	**6.4**	**6.5**	**7.0**	**6.9**	**7.3**	**9.0**	**8.5**	**9.7**
Natural gas	1.1	0.7	0.8	1.0	1.0	1.1	1.5	1.3	1.7
Electricity	2.7	2.5	2.4	2.6	2.5	2.7	3.3	3.2	3.6

	total consumer units	under 25	25 to 34	35 to 44	45 to 54	55 to 64	aged 65 or older		
							total	65 to 74	75 or older
Fuel oil and other fuels	0.4%	0.1%	0.2%	0.3%	0.3%	0.5%	0.8%	0.6%	1.0%
Telephone services	2.2	2.5	2.3	2.2	2.2	2.1	2.2	2.3	2.2
Water and other public services	0.9	0.6	0.7	0.9	0.8	0.9	1.2	1.1	1.3
Household services	**2.0**	**1.1**	**2.4**	**2.3**	**1.6**	**1.6**	**2.4**	**1.8**	**3.3**
Personal services	0.8	0.5	1.5	1.3	0.4	0.1	0.6	0.2	1.1
Other household services	1.2	0.6	0.9	1.0	1.2	1.5	1.8	1.6	2.1
Housekeeping supplies	**1.3**	**1.0**	**1.2**	**1.1**	**1.3**	**1.4**	**1.7**	**1.8**	**1.5**
Laundry and cleaning supplies	0.3	0.3	0.3	0.3	0.3	0.3	0.3	0.3	0.3
Other household products	0.7	0.5	0.6	0.6	0.7	0.7	0.9	0.9	0.8
Postage and stationery	0.3	0.2	0.3	0.2	0.3	0.3	0.5	0.6	0.4
Household furnishings and equipment	**3.2**	**3.2**	**3.1**	**3.0**	**3.2**	**3.5**	**3.4**	**3.7**	**2.8**
Household textiles	0.2	0.1	0.2	0.2	0.3	0.3	0.3	0.3	0.2
Furniture	0.8	1.0	1.0	0.8	0.7	0.8	0.6	0.6	0.6
Floor coverings	0.1	0.0	0.1	0.1	0.1	0.1	0.1	0.1	0.2
Major appliances	0.4	0.4	0.4	0.4	0.4	0.5	0.4	0.4	0.4
Small appliances and misc. housewares	0.2	0.2	0.2	0.2	0.2	0.3	0.3	0.3	0.3
Miscellaneous household equipment	1.5	1.6	1.4	1.4	1.5	1.5	1.6	1.8	1.2
APPAREL AND RELATED SERVICES	**3.6**	**4.6**	**4.1**	**3.8**	**3.6**	**3.0**	**3.0**	**3.3**	**2.4**
Men and boys	**0.8**	**1.0**	**0.9**	**1.1**	**0.8**	**0.7**	**0.6**	**0.8**	**0.4**
Men, aged 16 or older	0.7	0.9	0.7	0.8	0.7	0.6	0.6	0.7	0.4
Boys, aged 2 to 15	0.2	0.1	0.2	0.3	0.1	0.1	0.1	0.1	0.0
Women and girls	**1.4**	**1.5**	**1.5**	**1.4**	**1.6**	**1.2**	**1.3**	**1.4**	**1.2**
Women, aged 16 or older	1.2	1.4	1.2	1.0	1.3	1.1	1.2	1.2	1.2
Girls, aged 2 to 15	0.2	0.1	0.3	0.4	0.3	0.1	0.1	0.2	0.0
Children under age 2	**0.2**	**0.6**	**0.4**	**0.2**	**0.1**	**0.1**	**0.1**	**0.1**	**0.1**
Footwear	**0.6**	**0.9**	**0.7**	**0.7**	**0.7**	**0.4**	**0.5**	**0.5**	**0.4**
Other apparel products and services	**0.5**	**0.7**	**0.6**	**0.4**	**0.5**	**0.5**	**0.4**	**0.5**	**0.3**
TRANSPORTATION	**17.0**	**18.6**	**18.1**	**16.7**	**17.5**	**17.1**	**15.3**	**16.3**	**13.9**
Vehicle purchases	**5.5**	**6.8**	**6.5**	**5.3**	**5.5**	**5.5**	**4.1**	**4.6**	**3.3**
Cars and trucks, new	2.6	2.1	2.8	2.4	2.6	2.9	2.4	2.7	2.0
Cars and trucks, used	2.6	3.8	3.5	2.6	2.7	2.3	1.5	1.8	1.1
Other vehicles	0.3	0.9	0.3	0.3	0.2	0.3	0.1	0.1	0.2
Gasoline and motor oil	**5.4**	**6.7**	**5.7**	**5.7**	**5.4**	**5.1**	**4.4**	**4.9**	**3.7**
Other vehicle expenses	**5.2**	**4.3**	**4.9**	**4.8**	**5.6**	**5.3**	**5.5**	**5.5**	**5.7**
Vehicle finance charges	0.6	0.8	0.9	0.7	0.6	0.6	0.3	0.4	0.2
Maintenance and repairs	1.4	1.4	1.2	1.3	1.6	1.6	1.5	1.5	1.6
Vehicle insurance	2.2	1.5	1.8	1.9	2.5	2.2	2.9	2.7	3.3
Vehicle rentals, leases, licenses, other charges	0.9	0.7	1.1	0.9	0.9	1.0	0.8	0.9	0.7
Public transportation	**1.0**	**0.8**	**0.9**	**0.9**	**1.0**	**1.2**	**1.2**	**1.2**	**1.2**
HEALTH CARE	**5.9**	**2.3**	**3.6**	**4.2**	**4.8**	**7.0**	**12.5**	**11.5**	**13.9**
Health insurance	3.3	1.3	2.0	2.3	2.5	3.6	7.7	7.0	8.8
Medical services	1.4	0.5	1.0	1.2	1.4	1.9	2.2	2.1	2.3
Drugs	1.0	0.4	0.4	0.6	0.7	1.3	2.2	2.1	2.4
Medical supplies	0.2	0.1	0.1	0.2	0.2	0.3	0.4	0.3	0.5
ENTERTAINMENT	**5.6**	**5.5**	**5.7**	**6.1**	**5.4**	**5.5**	**5.2**	**5.8**	**4.3**
Fees and admissions	1.2	0.9	1.1	1.4	1.3	1.2	1.1	1.2	0.8
Audio and visual equipment and services	2.1	2.3	2.3	2.0	1.9	2.0	2.1	2.1	2.0
Pets, toys, and playground equipment	1.4	1.3	1.4	1.7	1.3	1.3	1.2	1.4	0.8
Other entertainment products and services	0.9	0.9	0.9	1.1	0.9	1.0	0.9	1.1	0.6

	total consumer units	under 25	25 to 34	35 to 44	45 to 54	55 to 64	aged 65 or older total	65 to 74	75 or older
PERSONAL CARE PRODUCTS AND SERVICES	1.2%	1.3%	1.1%	1.2%	1.2%	1.1%	1.4%	1.3%	1.4%
READING	0.2	0.2	0.2	0.2	0.2	0.3	0.4	0.4	0.4
EDUCATION	2.1	5.8	1.6	1.6	3.3	1.6	0.7	0.8	0.6
TOBACCO PRODUCTS AND SMOKING SUPPLIES	0.6	0.9	0.6	0.6	0.7	0.6	0.4	0.5	0.3
MISCELLANEOUS	1.7	1.0	1.5	1.5	1.6	2.4	1.6	1.6	1.6
CASH CONTRIBUTIONS	3.4	1.5	2.2	2.6	3.5	3.9	5.9	4.9	7.2
PERSONAL INSURANCE AND PENSIONS	11.1	7.8	11.4	12.2	12.8	12.7	5.0	6.3	3.2
Life and other personal insurance	0.6	0.1	0.3	0.5	0.6	0.9	0.9	1.1	0.6
Pensions and Social Security	10.5	7.7	11.1	11.7	12.2	11.7	4.1	5.2	2.6
PERSONAL TAXES	3.5	0.7	2.2	3.2	5.4	4.8	1.4	2.0	0.4
Federal income taxes	3.6	1.6	2.8	3.5	4.9	4.5	1.9	2.4	1.2
2008 tax stimulus	–	–	–	–	–	–	–	–	–
State and local income taxes	1.1	0.6	1.1	1.2	1.4	1.2	0.3	0.4	0.2
Other taxes	0.4	0.1	0.2	0.3	0.5	0.5	0.7	0.8	0.7
GIFTS FOR PEOPLE IN OTHER HOUSEHOLDS	2.4	1.5	1.2	1.5	3.3	3.2	2.8	3.1	2.2

Note: Spending by category does not add to total spending because gift spending is also included in the preceding product and service categories and personal taxes are not included in the total.
Source: Bureau of Labor Statistics, 2008 Consumer Expenditure Survey, Internet site http://www.bls.gov/cex/

Under Age 25: Transition to Adulthood

Many young adults are in school, limiting their spending.

The nation's householders under age 25 (the youngest members of the Millennial generation) accounted for 7 percent of total household spending in 2008. Consumer units headed by people under age 25 spend only 58 percent as much as the average household—$29,325 versus the $50,486 spent by the average household in 2008.

Householders under age 25 spend less than average in almost every category. There are exceptions, however. They spend an average amount on alcoholic beverages. They spend 81 percent more than average on rental housing and account for 12 percent of the rental market. They spend 62 percent more than the average household on education. They spend 83 percent more than average on clothes for children under age 2. The spending of this age group on "other vehicles" (mostly motorcycles) is 93 percent above average.

■ Because of the high cost of education and housing, young adults are finding it increasingly difficult to gain a foothold in the middle class.

Young adults are not big spenders on restaurant meals, entertainment, or clothes

(indexed spending of householders under age 25 on selected categories, 2008)

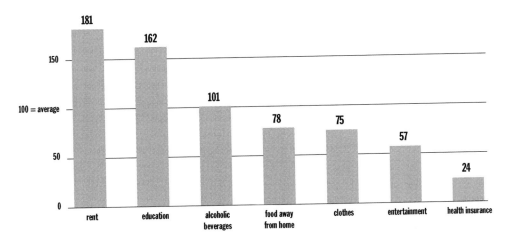

Table 10.3 Spending by Householders under Age 25, 2008

(average annual spending of total consumer units and those headed by people under age 25, indexed spending and share of total spending accounted for by consumer units under age 25; by product category, 2008)

	avg. spending of total consumer units	consumer units headed by people under age 25		
		average spending	indexed spending	market share
Number of consumer units (in 000s)	120,770	8,227	–	6.8%
Average annual spending	$50,486	$29,325	58	4.0
FOOD	6,443	4,447	69	4.7
Food at home	3,744	2,330	62	4.2
Cereals and bakery products	507	281	55	3.8
Cereals and cereal products	170	103	61	4.1
Bakery products	337	178	53	3.6
Meats, poultry, fish, and eggs	846	573	68	4.6
Beef	239	165	69	4.7
Pork	163	108	66	4.5
Other meats	106	66	62	4.2
Poultry	159	112	70	4.8
Fish and seafood	128	89	70	4.7
Eggs	51	33	65	4.4
Dairy products	430	256	60	4.1
Fresh milk and cream	168	109	65	4.4
Other dairy products	261	147	56	3.8
Fruits and vegetables	657	370	56	3.8
Fresh fruits	222	114	51	3.5
Fresh vegetables	212	114	54	3.7
Processed fruits	116	78	67	4.6
Processed vegetables	107	63	59	4.0
Other food at home	1,305	851	65	4.4
Sugar and other sweets	129	79	61	4.2
Fats and oils	104	60	58	3.9
Miscellaneous foods	680	450	66	4.5
Nonalcoholic beverages	342	246	72	4.9
Food prepared by consumer unit on trips	49	15	31	2.1
Food away from home	2,698	2,117	78	5.3
ALCOHOLIC BEVERAGES	444	448	101	6.9
HOUSING	17,109	9,975	58	4.0
Shelter	10,183	6,530	64	4.4
Owned dwellings	6,760	1,383	20	1.4
Mortgage interest and charges	3,826	918	24	1.6
Property taxes	1,758	282	16	1.1
Maintenance, repair, insurance, other expenses	1,176	184	16	1.1
Rented dwellings	2,724	4,940	181	12.4
Other lodging	698	206	30	2.0
Utilities, fuels, and public services	3,649	1,875	51	3.5
Natural gas	531	211	40	2.7
Electricity	1,353	739	55	3.7

	avg. spending of total consumer units	consumer units headed by people under age 25		
		average spending	indexed spending	market share
Fuel oil and other fuels	$192	$25	13	0.9%
Telephone services	1,127	732	65	4.4
Water and other public services	446	167	37	2.6
Household services	**998**	**326**	**33**	**2.2**
Personal services	383	140	37	2.5
Other household services	614	185	30	2.1
Housekeeping supplies	**654**	**303**	**46**	**3.2**
Laundry and cleaning supplies	148	83	56	3.8
Other household products	350	155	44	3.0
Postage and stationery	156	66	42	2.9
Household furnishings and equipment	**1,624**	**942**	**58**	**4.0**
Household textiles	126	36	29	1.9
Furniture	388	284	73	5.0
Floor coverings	45	8	18	1.2
Major appliances	204	104	51	3.5
Small appliances and miscellaneous housewares	113	49	43	3.0
Miscellaneous household equipment	749	460	61	4.2
APPAREL AND RELATED SERVICES	**1,801**	**1,351**	**75**	**5.1**
Men and boys	**427**	**296**	**69**	**4.7**
Men, aged 16 or older	344	261	76	5.2
Boys, aged 2 to 15	83	35	42	2.9
Women and girls	**718**	**439**	**61**	**4.2**
Women, aged 16 or older	597	410	69	4.7
Girls, aged 2 to 15	121	29	24	1.6
Children under age 2	**93**	**170**	**183**	**12.5**
Footwear	**314**	**253**	**81**	**5.5**
Other apparel products and services	**248**	**192**	**77**	**5.3**
TRANSPORTATION	**8,604**	**5,464**	**64**	**4.3**
Vehicle purchases	**2,755**	**1,988**	**72**	**4.9**
Cars and trucks, new	1,305	615	47	3.2
Cars and trucks, used	1,315	1,114	85	5.8
Other vehicles	134	259	193	13.2
Gasoline and motor oil	**2,715**	**1,974**	**73**	**5.0**
Other vehicle expenses	**2,621**	**1,273**	**49**	**3.3**
Vehicle finance charges	312	233	75	5.1
Maintenance and repairs	731	412	56	3.8
Vehicle insurance	1,113	427	38	2.6
Vehicle rentals, leases, licenses, other charges	465	202	43	3.0
Public transportation	**513**	**229**	**45**	**3.0**
HEALTH CARE	**2,976**	**682**	**23**	**1.6**
Health insurance	1,653	389	24	1.6
Medical services	727	143	20	1.3
Drugs	482	117	24	1.7
Medical supplies	114	33	29	2.0
ENTERTAINMENT	**2,835**	**1,608**	**57**	**3.9**
Fees and admissions	616	271	44	3.0
Audio and visual equipment and services	1,036	681	66	4.5
Pets, toys, and playground equipment	704	380	54	3.7
Other entertainment products and services	479	276	58	3.9

	avg. spending of total consumer units	consumer units headed by people under age 25		
		average spending	indexed spending	market share
PERSONAL CARE PRODUCTS AND SERVICES	$616	$370	60	4.1%
READING	116	48	41	2.8
EDUCATION	1,046	1,691	162	11.0
TOBACCO PRODUCTS AND SMOKING SUPPLIES	317	251	79	5.4
MISCELLANEOUS	840	280	33	2.3
CASH CONTRIBUTIONS	1,737	427	25	1.7
PERSONAL INSURANCE AND PENSIONS	5,605	2,283	41	2.8
Life and other personal insurance	317	37	12	0.8
Pensions and Social Security	5,288	2,246	42	2.9
PERSONAL TAXES	**1,789**	**219**	**12**	**0.8**
Federal income taxes	1,817	467	26	1.8
2008 tax stimulus	−784	−451	58	–
State and local income taxes	542	182	34	2.3
Other taxes	213	21	10	0.7
GIFTS FOR PEOPLE IN OTHER HOUSEHOLDS	**1,209**	**429**	**35**	**2.4**

Note: Spending by category does not add to total spending because gift spending is also included in the preceding product and service categories and personal taxes are not included in the total.
Source: Bureau of Labor Statistics, 2008 Consumer Expenditure Survey, Internet site http://www.bls.gov/cex/; calculcations by New Strategist

25-to-34-Year-Olds: Spending on Children

Children determine the spending priorities of householders aged 25 to 34.

Households headed by people aged 25 to 34 controlled 16 percent of total household spending in 2008, slightly less than their 17 percent share of households. Spending by households in the age group is close to the average in most categories. If their spending exceeds the average, it usually involves children.

Most households headed by people aged 25 to 34 include children. This is why they spend 88 percent more than the average household on personal services, primarily day care expenses. They spend nearly twice the average on clothing for children under age 2 and account for 35 percent of the market for this category.

In this age group, most people are not yet homeowners, which is why households headed by 25-to-34-year-olds spend 74 percent more than average on rent. They also spend more than average on alcoholic beverages and used cars and trucks. Surprisingly, they spend slightly less than the average household on entertainment.

■ Householders aged 25 to 34 are the primary market for goods and services for infants and young children.

Householders aged 25 to 34 spend more than average on clothes for infants

(indexed spending of householders aged 25 to 34 on selected categories, 2008)

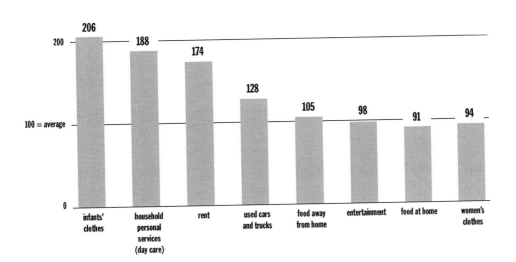

Table 10.4 Spending by Householders Aged 25 to 34, 2008

(average annual spending of total consumer units and those headed by people aged 25 to 34, indexed spending and share of total spending accounted for by consumer units aged 25 to 34; by category, 2008)

	avg. spending of total consumer units	consumer units headed by people aged 25 to 34		
		average spending	indexed spending	market share
Number of consumer units (in 000s)	120,770	20,208	–	16.7%
Average annual spending	$50,486	$48,159	95	16.0
FOOD	**6,443**	**6,229**	**97**	**16.2**
Food at home	**3,744**	**3,393**	**91**	**15.2**
Cereals and bakery products	507	454	90	15.0
Cereals and cereal products	170	169	99	16.6
Bakery products	337	286	85	14.2
Meats, poultry, fish, and eggs	846	742	88	14.7
Beef	239	213	89	14.9
Pork	163	137	84	14.1
Other meats	106	91	86	14.4
Poultry	159	152	96	16.0
Fish and seafood	128	104	81	13.6
Eggs	51	46	90	15.1
Dairy products	430	395	92	15.4
Fresh milk and cream	168	164	98	16.3
Other dairy products	261	231	89	14.8
Fruits and vegetables	657	583	89	14.8
Fresh fruits	222	196	88	14.8
Fresh vegetables	212	186	88	14.7
Processed fruits	116	103	89	14.9
Processed vegetables	107	98	92	15.3
Other food at home	1,305	1,219	93	15.6
Sugar and other sweets	129	103	80	13.4
Fats and oils	104	93	89	15.0
Miscellaneous foods	680	680	100	16.7
Nonalcoholic beverages	342	310	91	15.2
Food prepared by consumer unit on trips	49	34	69	11.6
Food away from home	**2,698**	**2,836**	**105**	**17.6**
ALCOHOLIC BEVERAGES	**444**	**491**	**111**	**18.5**
HOUSING	**17,109**	**17,318**	**101**	**16.9**
Shelter	**10,183**	**10,935**	**107**	**18.0**
Owned dwellings	6,760	5,873	87	14.5
Mortgage interest and charges	3,826	4,151	108	18.2
Property taxes	1,758	1,059	60	10.1
Maintenance, repair, insurance, other expenses	1,176	663	56	9.4
Rented dwellings	2,724	4,734	174	29.1
Other lodging	698	328	47	7.9
Utilities, fuels, and public services	**3,649**	**3,152**	**86**	**14.5**
Natural gas	531	400	75	12.6
Electricity	1,353	1,179	87	14.6

	avg. spending of total consumer units	consumer units headed by people aged 25 to 34		
		average spending	indexed spending	market share
Fuel oil and other fuels	$192	$97	51	8.5%
Telephone services	1,127	1,120	99	16.6
Water and other public services	446	356	80	13.4
Household services	**998**	**1,137**	**114**	**19.1**
Personal services	383	721	188	31.5
Other household services	614	417	68	11.4
Housekeeping supplies	**654**	**594**	**91**	**15.2**
Laundry and cleaning supplies	148	150	101	17.0
Other household products	350	294	84	14.1
Postage and stationery	156	150	96	16.1
Household furnishings and equipment	**1,624**	**1,499**	**92**	**15.4**
Household textiles	126	105	83	13.9
Furniture	388	459	118	19.8
Floor coverings	45	26	58	9.7
Major appliances	204	171	84	14.0
Small appliances and miscellaneous housewares	113	85	75	12.6
Miscellaneous household equipment	749	654	87	14.6
APPAREL AND RELATED SERVICES	**1,801**	**1,965**	**109**	**18.3**
Men and boys	**427**	**436**	**102**	**17.1**
Men, aged 16 or older	344	321	93	15.6
Boys, aged 2 to 15	83	115	139	23.2
Women and girls	**718**	**708**	**99**	**16.5**
Women, aged 16 or older	597	562	94	15.8
Girls, aged 2 to 15	121	146	121	20.2
Children under age 2	**93**	**192**	**206**	**34.5**
Footwear	**314**	**346**	**110**	**18.4**
Other apparel products and services	**248**	**284**	**115**	**19.2**
TRANSPORTATION	**8,604**	**8,699**	**101**	**16.9**
Vehicle purchases	**2,755**	**3,149**	**114**	**19.1**
Cars and trucks, new	1,305	1,336	102	17.1
Cars and trucks, used	1,315	1,679	128	21.4
Other vehicles	134	134	100	16.7
Gasoline and motor oil	**2,715**	**2,754**	**101**	**17.0**
Other vehicle expenses	**2,621**	**2,380**	**91**	**15.2**
Vehicle finance charges	312	418	134	22.4
Maintenance and repairs	731	600	82	13.7
Vehicle insurance	1,113	856	77	12.9
Vehicle rentals, leases, licenses, other charges	465	506	109	18.2
Public transportation	**513**	**416**	**81**	**13.6**
HEALTH CARE	**2,976**	**1,737**	**58**	**9.8**
Health insurance	1,653	983	59	10.0
Medical services	727	472	65	10.9
Drugs	482	215	45	7.5
Medical supplies	114	67	59	9.8
ENTERTAINMENT	**2,835**	**2,766**	**98**	**16.3**
Fees and admissions	616	524	85	14.2
Audio and visual equipment and services	1,036	1,105	107	17.8
Pets, toys, and playground equipment	704	696	99	16.5
Other entertainment products and services	479	441	92	15.4

	avg. spending of total consumer units	consumer units headed by people aged 25 to 34		
		average spending	indexed spending	market share
PERSONAL CARE PRODUCTS AND SERVICES	**$616**	**$547**	**89**	**14.9%**
READING	**116**	**79**	**68**	**11.4**
EDUCATION	**1,046**	**759**	**73**	**12.1**
TOBACCO PRODUCTS AND SMOKING SUPPLIES	**317**	**298**	**94**	**15.7**
MISCELLANEOUS	**840**	**726**	**86**	**14.5**
CASH CONTRIBUTIONS	**1,737**	**1,036**	**60**	**10.0**
PERSONAL INSURANCE AND PENSIONS	**5,605**	**5,510**	**98**	**16.4**
Life and other personal insurance	317	155	49	8.2
Pensions and Social Security	5,288	5,354	101	16.9
PERSONAL TAXES	**1,789**	**1,069**	**60**	**10.0**
Federal income taxes	1,817	1,346	74	12.4
2008 tax stimulus	−784	−882	113	–
State and local income taxes	542	510	94	15.7
Other taxes	213	96	45	7.5
GIFTS FOR PEOPLE IN OTHER HOUSEHOLDS	**1,209**	**579**	**48**	**8.0**

Note: Spending by category does not add to total spending because gift spending is also included in the preceding product and service categories and personal taxes are not included in the total.
Source: Bureau of Labor Statistics, 2008 Consumer Expenditure Survey, Internet site http://www.bls.gov/cex/; calculcations by New Strategist

35-to-44-Year-Olds: More Mouths to Feed

Households in the age group control a large share of spending.

Householders aged 35 to 44 spend almost as much as those aged 45 to 54—nearly $59,000 on average in 2008. They account for a substantial 22 percent of total household spending, but lag behind the 26 percent of spending controlled by householders aged 45 to 54. Behind the high level of spending by householders aged 35 to 44 is the size of their households. The average household headed by a 35-to-44-year-old includes 3.3 people, well above the 2.5 people in the average household.

Because householders aged 35 to 44 are in their childrearing years, their spending is above average on most categories of products and services. The age group spends much more than average on food—both at home (with an index of 120) and at restaurants (124). Because many in this age group became homeowners when housing prices were peaking, they spend 62 percent more than the average household on mortgage interest—far more than any other age group. Their spending on entertainment is 27 percent above average. They spend about twice the average on clothes for girls and boys.

■ Much of the spending of householders aged 35 to 44 is nondiscretionary, devoted to mortgages, car payments, food, and clothes.

Householders aged 35 to 44 spend more than average on most things

(indexed spending of householders aged 35 to 44 on selected categories, 2008)

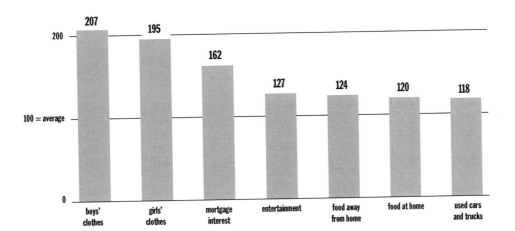

Table 10.5 Spending by Householders Aged 35 to 44, 2008

(average annual spending of total consumer units and those headed by people aged 35 to 44, indexed spending and share of total spending accounted for by consumer units aged 35 to 44; by category, 2008)

| | avg. spending of total consumer units | consumer units headed by people aged 35 to 44 | | |
		average spending	indexed spending	market share
Number of consumer units (in 000s)	120,770	22,834	–	18.9%
Average annual spending	$50,486	$58,808	116	22.0
FOOD	6,443	7,849	122	23.0
Food at home	3,744	4,509	120	22.8
Cereals and bakery products	507	620	122	23.1
Cereals and cereal products	170	213	125	23.7
Bakery products	337	407	121	22.8
Meats, poultry, fish, and eggs	846	1,014	120	22.7
Beef	239	288	121	22.8
Pork	163	196	120	22.7
Other meats	106	129	122	23.0
Poultry	159	197	124	23.4
Fish and seafood	128	145	113	21.4
Eggs	51	60	118	22.2
Dairy products	430	518	120	22.8
Fresh milk and cream	168	214	127	24.1
Other dairy products	261	304	116	22.0
Fruits and vegetables	657	754	115	21.7
Fresh fruits	222	259	117	22.1
Fresh vegetables	212	238	112	21.2
Processed fruits	116	132	114	21.5
Processed vegetables	107	125	117	22.1
Other food at home	1,305	1,603	123	23.2
Sugar and other sweets	129	154	119	22.6
Fats and oils	104	118	113	21.5
Miscellaneous foods	680	850	125	23.6
Nonalcoholic beverages	342	431	126	23.8
Food prepared by consumer unit on trips	49	51	104	19.7
Food away from home	2,698	3,340	124	23.4
ALCOHOLIC BEVERAGES	444	462	104	19.7
HOUSING	17,109	20,649	121	22.8
Shelter	10,183	12,689	125	23.6
Owned dwellings	6,760	9,056	134	25.3
Mortgage interest and charges	3,826	6,194	162	30.6
Property taxes	1,758	1,965	112	21.1
Maintenance, repair, insurance, other expenses	1,176	896	76	14.4
Rented dwellings	2,724	3,013	111	20.9
Other lodging	698	621	89	16.8
Utilities, fuels, and public services	3,649	4,130	113	21.4
Natural gas	531	588	111	20.9
Electricity	1,353	1,549	114	21.6

	avg. spending of total consumer units	consumer units headed by people aged 35 to 44		
		average spending	indexed spending	market share
Fuel oil and other fuels	$192	$167	87	16.4%
Telephone services	1,127	1,315	117	22.1
Water and other public services	446	511	115	21.7
Household services	**998**	**1,376**	**138**	**26.1**
Personal services	383	766	200	37.8
Other household services	614	609	99	18.8
Housekeeping supplies	**654**	**664**	**102**	**19.2**
Laundry and cleaning supplies	148	178	120	22.7
Other household products	350	361	103	19.5
Postage and stationery	156	126	81	15.3
Household furnishings and equipment	**1,624**	**1,789**	**110**	**20.8**
Household textiles	126	105	83	15.8
Furniture	388	479	123	23.3
Floor coverings	45	46	102	19.3
Major appliances	204	238	117	22.1
Small appliances and miscellaneous housewares	113	97	86	16.2
Miscellaneous household equipment	749	824	110	20.8
APPAREL AND RELATED SERVICES	**1,801**	**2,235**	**124**	**23.5**
Men and boys	**427**	**623**	**146**	**27.6**
Men, aged 16 or older	344	451	131	24.8
Boys, aged 2 to 15	83	172	207	39.2
Women and girls	**718**	**824**	**115**	**21.7**
Women, aged 16 or older	597	589	99	18.7
Girls, aged 2 to 15	121	236	195	36.9
Children under age 2	**93**	**125**	**134**	**25.4**
Footwear	**314**	**404**	**129**	**24.3**
Other apparel products and services	**248**	**259**	**104**	**19.7**
TRANSPORTATION	**8,604**	**9,797**	**114**	**21.5**
Vehicle purchases	**2,755**	**3,122**	**113**	**21.4**
Cars and trucks, new	1,305	1,420	109	20.6
Cars and trucks, used	1,315	1,555	118	22.4
Other vehicles	134	148	110	20.9
Gasoline and motor oil	**2,715**	**3,347**	**123**	**23.3**
Other vehicle expenses	**2,621**	**2,798**	**107**	**20.2**
Vehicle finance charges	312	397	127	24.1
Maintenance and repairs	731	747	102	19.3
Vehicle insurance	1,113	1,100	99	18.7
Vehicle rentals, leases, licenses, other charges	465	554	119	22.5
Public transportation	**513**	**530**	**103**	**19.5**
HEALTH CARE	**2,976**	**2,499**	**84**	**15.9**
Health insurance	1,653	1,341	81	15.3
Medical services	727	711	98	18.5
Drugs	482	349	72	13.7
Medical supplies	114	98	86	16.3
ENTERTAINMENT	**2,835**	**3,603**	**127**	**24.0**
Fees and admissions	616	823	134	25.3
Audio and visual equipment and services	1,036	1,168	113	21.3
Pets, toys, and playground equipment	704	992	141	26.6
Other entertainment products and services	479	621	130	24.5

	avg. spending of total consumer units	consumer units headed by people aged 35 to 44		
		average spending	indexed spending	market share
PERSONAL CARE PRODUCTS AND SERVICES	**$616**	**$728**	**118**	**22.3%**
READING	**116**	**102**	**88**	**16.6**
EDUCATION	**1,046**	**953**	**91**	**17.2**
TOBACCO PRODUCTS AND SMOKING SUPPLIES	**317**	**354**	**112**	**21.1**
MISCELLANEOUS	**840**	**862**	**103**	**19.4**
CASH CONTRIBUTIONS	**1,737**	**1,550**	**89**	**16.9**
PERSONAL INSURANCE AND PENSIONS	**5,605**	**7,165**	**128**	**24.2**
Life and other personal insurance	317	284	90	16.9
Pensions and Social Security	5,288	6,881	130	24.6
PERSONAL TAXES	**1,789**	**1,905**	**106**	**20.1**
Federal income taxes	1,817	2,033	112	21.2
2008 tax stimulus	−784	−1,017	130	–
State and local income taxes	542	712	131	24.8
Other taxes	213	177	83	15.7
GIFTS FOR PEOPLE IN OTHER HOUSEHOLDS	**1,209**	**856**	**71**	**13.4**

Note: Spending by category does not add to total spending because gift spending is also included in the preceding product and service categories and personal taxes are not included in the total.
Source: Bureau of Labor Statistics, 2008 Consumer Expenditure Survey, Internet site http://www.bls.gov/cex/; calculcations by New Strategist

45-to-54-Year-Olds: Big Spenders

They are in their peak earning—and spending—years.

Households headed by people aged 45 to 54 have the highest incomes and are also the biggest spenders. This age group accounts for 21 percent of households and 26 percent of household spending. Households headed by 45-to-54-year-olds spend 21 percent more than the average household.

Householders aged 45 to 54 spend more than average in almost every category. On some categories, spending by householders aged 45 to 54 is far above average. They spent 20 percent more than average on food away from home, 29 percent more than average on mortgage interest, and 16 percent more than average on entertainment.

Many 45-to-54-year-olds have teenagers and young adults in their household. Consequently, they spend 92 percent more than average on education. They spend 24 percent more than average on used cars and trucks, often buying vehicles for their children. They spend 31 percent more than average on fees and admission to entertainment events, such as movie tickets. They spend 21 percent more than average on telephone service.

■ As Boomers exit the 45-to-54 age group in the coming decade, the share of spending controlled by the age group will decline.

Householders aged 45 to 54 spend more than average on most items

(indexed spending of householders aged 45 to 54 on selected categories, 2008)

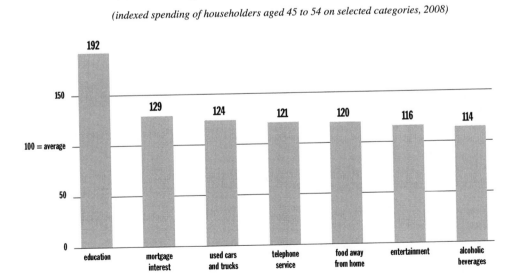

Table 10.6 Spending by Householders Aged 45 to 54, 2008

(average annual spending of total consumer units and those headed by people aged 45 to 54, indexed spending and share of total spending accounted for by consumer units aged 45 to 54; by category, 2008)

| | avg. spending of total consumer units | consumer units headed by people aged 45 to 54 | | |
		average spending	indexed spending	market share
Number of consumer units (in 000s)	120,770	25,614	–	21.2%
Average annual spending	$50,486	$61,179	121	25.7
FOOD	**6,443**	**7,696**	**119**	**25.3**
Food at home	**3,744**	**4,452**	**119**	**25.2**
Cereals and bakery products	507	600	118	25.1
Cereals and cereal products	170	203	119	25.3
Bakery products	337	397	118	25.0
Meats, poultry, fish, and eggs	846	1,018	120	25.5
Beef	239	290	121	25.7
Pork	163	187	115	24.3
Other meats	106	132	125	26.4
Poultry	159	195	123	26.0
Fish and seafood	128	157	123	26.0
Eggs	51	57	112	23.7
Dairy products	430	506	118	25.0
Fresh milk and cream	168	192	114	24.2
Other dairy products	261	315	121	25.6
Fruits and vegetables	657	779	119	25.1
Fresh fruits	222	262	118	25.0
Fresh vegetables	212	249	117	24.9
Processed fruits	116	140	121	25.6
Processed vegetables	107	128	120	25.4
Other food at home	1,305	1,549	119	25.2
Sugar and other sweets	129	149	116	24.5
Fats and oils	104	123	118	25.1
Miscellaneous foods	680	796	117	24.8
Nonalcoholic beverages	342	424	124	26.3
Food prepared by consumer unit on trips	49	57	116	24.7
Food away from home	**2,698**	**3,244**	**120**	**25.5**
ALCOHOLIC BEVERAGES	**444**	**505**	**114**	**24.1**
HOUSING	**17,109**	**19,562**	**114**	**24.2**
Shelter	**10,183**	**11,629**	**114**	**24.2**
Owned dwellings	6,760	8,606	127	27.0
Mortgage interest and charges	3,826	4,943	129	27.4
Property taxes	1,758	2,185	124	26.4
Maintenance, repair, insurance, other expenses	1,176	1,477	126	26.6
Rented dwellings	2,724	2,037	75	15.9
Other lodging	698	986	141	30.0
Utilities, fuels, and public services	**3,649**	**4,247**	**116**	**24.7**
Natural gas	531	623	117	24.9
Electricity	1,353	1,544	114	24.2

	avg. spending of total consumer units	consumer units headed by people aged 45 to 54		
		average spending	indexed spending	market share
Fuel oil and other fuels	$192	$213	111	23.5%
Telephone services	1,127	1,360	121	25.6
Water and other public services	446	506	113	24.1
Household services	**998**	**964**	**97**	**20.5**
Personal services	383	251	66	13.9
Other household services	614	713	116	24.6
Housekeeping supplies	**654**	**765**	**117**	**24.8**
Laundry and cleaning supplies	148	166	112	23.8
Other household products	350	438	125	26.5
Postage and stationery	156	161	103	21.9
Household furnishings and equipment	**1,624**	**1,956**	**120**	**25.5**
Household textiles	126	191	152	32.2
Furniture	388	416	107	22.7
Floor coverings	45	50	111	23.6
Major appliances	204	228	112	23.7
Small appliances and miscellaneous housewares	113	130	115	24.4
Miscellaneous household equipment	749	941	126	26.6
APPAREL AND RELATED SERVICES	**1,801**	**2,228**	**124**	**26.2**
Men and boys	**427**	**488**	**114**	**24.2**
Men, aged 16 or older	344	401	117	24.7
Boys, aged 2 to 15	83	87	105	22.2
Women and girls	**718**	**977**	**136**	**28.9**
Women, aged 16 or older	597	821	138	29.2
Girls, aged 2 to 15	121	156	129	27.3
Children under age 2	**93**	**56**	**60**	**12.8**
Footwear	**314**	**411**	**131**	**27.8**
Other apparel products and services	**248**	**296**	**119**	**25.3**
TRANSPORTATION	**8,604**	**10,691**	**124**	**26.4**
Vehicle purchases	**2,755**	**3,351**	**122**	**25.8**
Cars and trucks, new	1,305	1,588	122	25.8
Cars and trucks, used	1,315	1,634	124	26.4
Other vehicles	134	129	96	20.4
Gasoline and motor oil	**2,715**	**3,298**	**121**	**25.8**
Other vehicle expenses	**2,621**	**3,414**	**130**	**27.6**
Vehicle finance charges	312	366	117	24.9
Maintenance and repairs	731	990	135	28.7
Vehicle insurance	1,113	1,514	136	28.9
Vehicle rentals, leases, licenses, other charges	465	544	117	24.8
Public transportation	**513**	**628**	**122**	**26.0**
HEALTH CARE	**2,976**	**2,930**	**98**	**20.9**
Health insurance	1,653	1,523	92	19.5
Medical services	727	838	115	24.4
Drugs	482	432	90	19.0
Medical supplies	114	138	121	25.7
ENTERTAINMENT	**2,835**	**3,297**	**116**	**24.7**
Fees and admissions	616	805	131	27.7
Audio and visual equipment and services	1,036	1,174	113	24.0
Pets, toys, and playground equipment	704	787	112	23.7
Other entertainment products and services	479	531	111	23.5

	avg. spending of total consumer units	consumer units headed by people aged 45 to 54		
		average spending	indexed spending	market share
PERSONAL CARE PRODUCTS AND SERVICES	**$616**	**$736**	**119**	**25.3%**
READING	**116**	**124**	**107**	**22.7**
EDUCATION	**1,046**	**2,012**	**192**	**40.8**
TOBACCO PRODUCTS AND SMOKING SUPPLIES	**317**	**437**	**138**	**29.2**
MISCELLANEOUS	**840**	**957**	**114**	**24.2**
CASH CONTRIBUTIONS	**1,737**	**2,152**	**124**	**26.3**
PERSONAL INSURANCE AND PENSIONS	**5,605**	**7,853**	**140**	**29.7**
Life and other personal insurance	317	394	124	26.4
Pensions and Social Security	5,288	7,458	141	29.9
PERSONAL TAXES	**1,789**	**3,307**	**185**	**39.2**
Federal income taxes	1,817	2,982	164	34.8
2008 tax stimulus	−784	−818	104	−
State and local income taxes	542	847	156	33.1
Other taxes	213	296	139	29.5
GIFTS FOR PEOPLE IN OTHER HOUSEHOLDS	**1,209**	**2,037**	**168**	**35.7**

Note: Spending by category does not add to total spending because gift spending is also included in the preceding product and service categories and personal taxes are not included in the total.
Source: Bureau of Labor Statistics, 2008 Consumer Expenditure Survey, Internet site http://www.bls.gov/cex/; calculcations by New Strategist

55-to-64-Year-Olds: Spending More than Average

This age group spends more than average on many discretionary items, including entertainment.

Householders aged 55 to 64 spend less than those aged 45 to 54 for two reasons: One, their households are smaller because their children are grown; and two, many in the age group are retired. Consequently, the spending of households headed by people aged 55 to 64 is only slightly above average. In 2008, householders aged 55 to 64 spent 9 percent more than the average household.

Although their overall spending is only slightly above average, households headed by 55-to-64-year-olds are big spenders on many discretionary items. They spend 62 percent more than average on "other lodging" (mostly hotel and motel expenses), 24 percent more on public transportation (mostly airline fares), and 7 percent more on entertainment.

Health care expenses increase in the 55-to-64 age group. Householders aged 55 to 64 spend 48 percent more than average on drugs and 41 percent more on medical services. Their homes are still a major expense, with spending 27 percent above average on maintenance and insurance for owned homes.

■ The spending of households headed by 55-to-64-year-olds will rise in the years ahead as early retirement becomes less common.

Householders aged 55 to 64 spend more than average on alcohol

(indexed spending of householders aged 55 to 64 on selected categories, 2008)

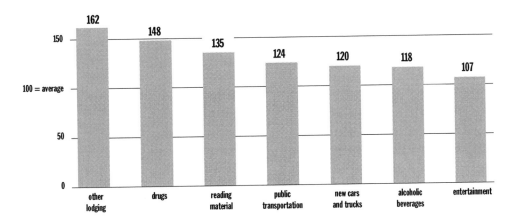

Table 10.7 Spending by Householders Aged 55 to 64, 2008

(average annual spending of total consumer units and those headed by people aged 55 to 64, indexed spending and share of total spending accounted for by consumer units aged 55 to 64; by category, 2008)

	avg. spending of total consumer units	consumer units headed by people aged 55 to 64		
		average spending	indexed spending	market share
Number of consumer units (in 000s)	120,770	19,826	–	16.4%
Average annual spending	$50,486	$54,783	109	17.8
FOOD	6,443	6,357	99	16.2
Food at home	3,744	3,710	99	16.3
Cereals and bakery products	507	492	97	15.9
Cereals and cereal products	170	152	89	14.7
Bakery products	337	340	101	16.6
Meats, poultry, fish, and eggs	846	845	100	16.4
Beef	239	243	102	16.7
Pork	163	166	102	16.7
Other meats	106	102	96	15.8
Poultry	159	153	96	15.8
Fish and seafood	128	129	101	16.5
Eggs	51	53	104	17.1
Dairy products	430	419	97	16.0
Fresh milk and cream	168	153	91	15.0
Other dairy products	261	267	102	16.8
Fruits and vegetables	657	682	104	17.0
Fresh fruits	222	230	104	17.0
Fresh vegetables	212	235	111	18.2
Processed fruits	116	111	96	15.7
Processed vegetables	107	107	100	16.4
Other food at home	1,305	1,272	97	16.0
Sugar and other sweets	129	135	105	17.2
Fats and oils	104	107	103	16.9
Miscellaneous foods	680	636	94	15.4
Nonalcoholic beverages	342	321	94	15.4
Food prepared by consumer unit on trips	49	74	151	24.8
Food away from home	2,698	2,646	98	16.1
ALCOHOLIC BEVERAGES	444	525	118	19.4
HOUSING	17,109	17,611	103	16.9
Shelter	10,183	10,122	99	16.3
Owned dwellings	6,760	7,387	109	17.9
Mortgage interest and charges	3,826	3,613	94	15.5
Property taxes	1,758	2,284	130	21.3
Maintenance, repair, insurance, other expenses	1,176	1,489	127	20.8
Rented dwellings	2,724	1,607	59	9.7
Other lodging	698	1,128	162	26.5
Utilities, fuels, and public services	3,649	3,974	109	17.9
Natural gas	531	603	114	18.6
Electricity	1,353	1,462	108	17.7

	avg. spending of total consumer units	consumer units headed by people aged 55 to 64		
		average spending	indexed spending	market share
Fuel oil and other fuels	$192	$254	132	21.7%
Telephone services	1,127	1,148	102	16.7
Water and other public services	446	507	114	18.7
Household services	**998**	**879**	**88**	**14.5**
Personal services	383	70	18	3.0
Other household services	614	809	132	21.6
Housekeeping supplies	**654**	**743**	**114**	**18.7**
Laundry and cleaning supplies	148	153	103	17.0
Other household products	350	400	114	18.8
Postage and stationery	156	190	122	20.0
Household furnishings and equipment	**1,624**	**1,894**	**117**	**19.1**
Household textiles	126	158	125	20.6
Furniture	388	411	106	17.4
Floor coverings	45	61	136	22.3
Major appliances	204	264	129	21.2
Small appliances and miscellaneous housewares	113	161	142	23.4
Miscellaneous household equipment	749	839	112	18.4
APPAREL AND RELATED SERVICES	**1,801**	**1,622**	**90**	**14.8**
Men and boys	**427**	**391**	**92**	**15.0**
Men, aged 16 or older	344	354	103	16.9
Boys, aged 2 to 15	83	37	45	7.3
Women and girls	**718**	**671**	**93**	**15.3**
Women, aged 16 or older	597	615	103	16.9
Girls, aged 2 to 15	121	57	47	7.7
Children under age 2	**93**	**45**	**48**	**7.9**
Footwear	**314**	**243**	**77**	**12.7**
Other apparel products and services	**248**	**272**	**110**	**18.0**
TRANSPORTATION	**8,604**	**9,377**	**109**	**17.9**
Vehicle purchases	**2,755**	**2,999**	**109**	**17.9**
Cars and trucks, new	1,305	1,572	120	19.8
Cars and trucks, used	1,315	1,253	95	15.6
Other vehicles	134	174	130	21.3
Gasoline and motor oil	**2,715**	**2,818**	**104**	**17.0**
Other vehicle expenses	**2,621**	**2,921**	**111**	**18.3**
Vehicle finance charges	312	308	99	16.2
Maintenance and repairs	731	856	117	19.2
Vehicle insurance	1,113	1,223	110	18.0
Vehicle rentals, leases, licenses, other charges	465	534	115	18.9
Public transportation	**513**	**638**	**124**	**20.4**
HEALTH CARE	**2,976**	**3,825**	**129**	**21.1**
Health insurance	1,653	1,945	118	19.3
Medical services	727	1,022	141	23.1
Drugs	482	714	148	24.3
Medical supplies	114	144	126	20.7
ENTERTAINMENT	**2,835**	**3,036**	**107**	**17.6**
Fees and admissions	616	643	104	17.1
Audio and visual equipment and services	1,036	1,113	107	17.6
Pets, toys, and playground equipment	704	728	103	17.0
Other entertainment products and services	479	552	115	18.9

	avg. spending of total consumer units	consumer units headed by people aged 55 to 64		
		average spending	indexed spending	market share
PERSONAL CARE PRODUCTS AND SERVICES	**$616**	**$630**	**102**	**16.8%**
READING	**116**	**157**	**135**	**22.2**
EDUCATION	**1,046**	**867**	**83**	**13.6**
TOBACCO PRODUCTS AND SMOKING SUPPLIES	**317**	**354**	**112**	**18.3**
MISCELLANEOUS	**840**	**1,316**	**157**	**25.7**
CASH CONTRIBUTIONS	**1,737**	**2,163**	**125**	**20.4**
PERSONAL INSURANCE AND PENSIONS	**5,605**	**6,943**	**124**	**20.3**
Life and other personal insurance	317	519	164	26.9
Pensions and Social Security	5,288	6,424	121	19.9
PERSONAL TAXES	**1,789**	**2,644**	**148**	**24.3**
Federal income taxes	1,817	2,465	136	22.3
2008 tax stimulus	−784	−761	97	−
State and local income taxes	542	650	120	19.7
Other taxes	213	289	136	22.3
GIFTS FOR PEOPLE IN OTHER HOUSEHOLDS	**1,209**	**1,752**	**145**	**23.8**

Note: Spending by category does not add to total spending because gift spending is also included in the preceding product and service categories and personal taxes are not included in the total.
Source: Bureau of Labor Statistics, 2008 Consumer Expenditure Survey, Internet site http://www.bls.gov/cex/; calculcations by New Strategist

65-to-74-Year-Olds: Average Spenders

Householders aged 65 to 74 spend less than average on many items, partly because their households are smaller.

Householders aged 65 to 74 spend 18 percent less than the average household. Averaging only 1.8 people in their households compared with 2.5 people in the average household, householders aged 65 to 74 do not need to spend as much to live as well.

Many expenses are reduced for older householders. They spend far less than the average household on mortgage interest since most own their homes free and clear. But because their homes are older, they spend 39 percent more than average on maintenance and repair of owned homes.

Householders aged 65 to 74 spend more than the average household on many discretionary items such as household textiles (with an index of 113), floor coverings (109), and reading material such as books and newspapers (131).

Householders aged 65 to 74 spend considerably more than average on health care. They spend 61 percent more than average on health care overall and 83 percent more on drugs. They spend 17 percent more than average on cash contributions—a large portion of which is donated to religious institutions.

■ The spending of householders aged 65 to 74 is likely to rise as Boomers enter the age group and labor force participation rates rise.

Householders aged 65 to 74 are big spenders on maintenance and repairs for owned homes

(indexed spending of householders aged 65 to 74 on selected categories, 2008)

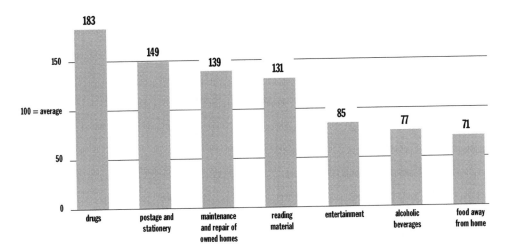

Table 10.8 Spending by Householders 65 to 74, 2008

(average annual spending of total consumer units and those headed by people aged 65 to 74, indexed spending and share of total spending accounted for by consumer units aged 65 to 74; by category, 2008)

	avg. spending of total consumer units	consumer units headed by people aged 65 to 74		
		average spending	indexed spending	market share
Number of consumer units (in 000s)	120,770	12,580	–	10.4%
Average annual spending	$50,486	$41,433	82	8.5
FOOD	6,443	5,338	83	8.6
Food at home	3,744	3,421	91	9.5
Cereals and bakery products	507	473	93	9.7
Cereals and cereal products	170	142	84	8.7
Bakery products	337	332	99	10.3
Meats, poultry, fish, and eggs	846	781	92	9.6
Beef	239	206	86	9.0
Pork	163	173	106	11.1
Other meats	106	102	96	10.0
Poultry	159	131	82	8.6
Fish and seafood	128	123	96	10.0
Eggs	51	48	94	9.8
Dairy products	430	406	94	9.8
Fresh milk and cream	168	148	88	9.2
Other dairy products	261	259	99	10.3
Fruits and vegetables	657	616	94	9.8
Fresh fruits	222	212	95	9.9
Fresh vegetables	212	196	92	9.6
Processed fruits	116	110	95	9.9
Processed vegetables	107	97	91	9.4
Other food at home	1,305	1,145	88	9.1
Sugar and other sweets	129	132	102	10.7
Fats and oils	104	106	102	10.6
Miscellaneous foods	680	564	83	8.6
Nonalcoholic beverages	342	285	83	8.7
Food prepared by consumer unit on trips	49	57	116	12.1
Food away from home	2,698	1,917	71	7.4
ALCOHOLIC BEVERAGES	444	343	77	8.0
HOUSING	17,109	13,845	81	8.4
Shelter	10,183	7,281	72	7.4
Owned dwellings	6,760	5,334	79	8.2
Mortgage interest and charges	3,826	1,836	48	5.0
Property taxes	1,758	1,865	106	11.1
Maintenance, repair, insurance, other expenses	1,176	1,634	139	14.5
Rented dwellings	2,724	1,294	48	4.9
Other lodging	698	652	93	9.7
Utilities, fuels, and public services	3,649	3,538	97	10.1
Natural gas	531	552	104	10.8
Electricity	1,353	1,325	98	10.2

	avg. spending of total consumer units	consumer units headed by people aged 65 to 74		
		average spending	indexed spending	market share
Fuel oil and other fuels	$192	$251	131	13.6%
Telephone services	1,127	947	84	8.8
Water and other public services	446	464	104	10.8
Household services	**998**	**750**	**75**	**7.8**
Personal services	383	86	–	2.3
Other household services	614	664	108	11.3
Housekeeping supplies	**654**	**747**	**114**	**11.9**
Laundry and cleaning supplies	148	135	91	9.5
Other household products	350	380	109	11.3
Postage and stationery	156	232	149	15.5
Household furnishings and equipment	**1,624**	**1,529**	**94**	**9.8**
Household textiles	126	142	113	11.7
Furniture	388	267	69	7.2
Floor coverings	45	49	109	11.3
Major appliances	204	185	91	9.4
Small appliances and miscellaneous housewares	113	133	118	12.3
Miscellaneous household equipment	749	753	101	10.5
APPAREL AND RELATED SERVICES	**1,801**	**1,381**	**77**	**8.0**
Men and boys	**427**	**340**	**80**	**8.3**
Men, aged 16 or older	344	309	90	9.4
Boys, aged 2 to 15	83	30	36	3.8
Women and girls	**718**	**567**	**79**	**8.2**
Women, aged 16 or older	597	500	84	8.7
Girls, aged 2 to 15	121	68	56	5.9
Children under age 2	**93**	**38**	**41**	**4.3**
Footwear	**314**	**219**	**70**	**7.3**
Other apparel products and services	**248**	**218**	**88**	**9.2**
TRANSPORTATION	**8,604**	**6,740**	**78**	**8.2**
Vehicle purchases	**2,755**	**1,920**	**70**	**7.3**
Cars and trucks, new	1,305	1,115	85	8.9
Cars and trucks, used	1,315	759	58	6.0
Other vehicles	134	46	34	3.6
Gasoline and motor oil	**2,715**	**2,045**	**75**	**7.8**
Other vehicle expenses	**2,621**	**2,261**	**86**	**9.0**
Vehicle finance charges	312	175	56	5.8
Maintenance and repairs	731	609	83	8.7
Vehicle insurance	1,113	1,106	99	10.4
Vehicle rentals, leases, licenses, other charges	465	371	80	8.3
Public transportation	**513**	**513**	**100**	**10.4**
HEALTH CARE	**2,976**	**4,779**	**161**	**16.7**
Health insurance	1,653	2,901	175	18.3
Medical services	727	853	117	12.2
Drugs	482	880	183	19.0
Medical supplies	114	145	127	13.2
ENTERTAINMENT	**2,835**	**2,418**	**85**	**8.9**
Fees and admissions	616	498	81	8.4
Audio and visual equipment and services	1,036	885	85	8.9
Pets, toys, and playground equipment	704	574	82	8.5
Other entertainment products and services	479	461	96	10.0

	avg. spending of total consumer units	consumer units headed by people aged 65 to 74		
		average spending	indexed spending	market share
PERSONAL CARE PRODUCTS AND SERVICES	**$616**	**$559**	**91**	**9.5%**
READING	**116**	**152**	**131**	**13.6**
EDUCATION	**1,046**	**345**	**33**	**3.4**
TOBACCO PRODUCTS AND SMOKING SUPPLIES	**317**	**227**	**72**	**7.5**
MISCELLANEOUS	**840**	**659**	**78**	**8.2**
CASH CONTRIBUTIONS	**1,737**	**2,033**	**117**	**12.2**
PERSONAL INSURANCE AND PENSIONS	**5,605**	**2,616**	**47**	**4.9**
Life and other personal insurance	317	461	145	15.1
Pensions and Social Security	5,288	2,155	41	4.2
PERSONAL TAXES	**1,789**	**830**	**46**	**4.8**
Federal income taxes	1,817	975	54	5.6
2008 tax stimulus	−784	−637	81	–
State and local income taxes	542	178	33	3.4
Other taxes	213	314	147	15.4
GIFTS FOR PEOPLE IN OTHER HOUSEHOLDS	**1,209**	**1,291**	**107**	**11.1**

Note: Spending by category does not add to total spending because gift spending is also included in the preceding product and service categories and personal taxes are not included in the total.
Source: Bureau of Labor Statistics, 2008 Consumer Expenditure Survey, Internet site http://www.bls.gov/cex/; calculcations by New Strategist

75 or Older: Spending on Health Care

As people age, health care spending rises sharply.

Households headed by people aged 75 or older spent an average of $4,413 on health care in 2008, much more than the $2,976 spent by the average household on this item. For the oldest households, health care accounts for a larger share of the budget than groceries.

The oldest householders spend far less than average on most items. They spend only 32 percent as much as the average household on alcoholic beverages, 65 percent as much as the average on women's clothing, and 48 percent as much as the average on entertainment. One factor behind the lower spending is the smaller size of the households headed by the oldest Americans.

Householders aged 75 or older spend 39 percent more than average on maintenance and repair of owned homes. They spend 14 percent more on reading material and 32 percent more on cash contributions.

■ Although their spending on entertainment is below average, households headed by people aged 75 or older spend almost as much on entertainment as householders under age 25.

The oldest householders are big spenders on health insurance (Medicare)

(indexed spending of householders aged 75 or older on selected categories, 2008)

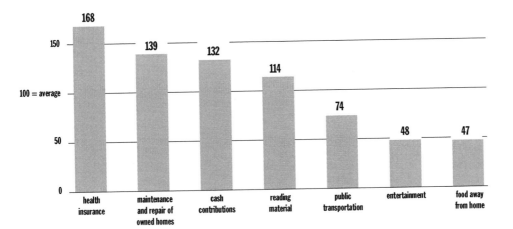

Table 10.9 Spending by Householders Aged 75 or Older, 2008

(average annual spending of total consumer units and those headed by people aged 75 or older, indexed spending and share of total spending accounted for by consumer units aged 75 or older, by category, 2008)

	avg. spending of total consumer units	consumer units headed by people aged 75 or older		
		average spending	indexed spending	market share
Number of consumer units (in 000s)	120,770	11,481	–	9.5%
Average annual spending	$50,486	$31,692	63	6.0
FOOD	6,443	3,935	61	5.8
Food at home	3,744	2,667	71	6.8
Cereals and bakery products	507	390	77	7.3
Cereals and cereal products	170	118	69	6.6
Bakery products	337	271	80	7.6
Meats, poultry, fish, and eggs	846	576	68	6.5
Beef	239	154	64	6.1
Pork	163	113	69	6.6
Other meats	106	74	70	6.6
Poultry	159	89	56	5.3
Fish and seafood	128	103	80	7.6
Eggs	51	42	82	7.8
Dairy products	430	309	72	6.8
Fresh milk and cream	168	123	73	7.0
Other dairy products	261	186	71	6.8
Fruits and vegetables	657	531	81	7.7
Fresh fruits	222	179	81	7.7
Fresh vegetables	212	170	80	7.6
Processed fruits	116	101	87	8.3
Processed vegetables	107	80	75	7.1
Other food at home	1,305	863	66	6.3
Sugar and other sweets	129	107	83	7.9
Fats and oils	104	83	80	7.6
Miscellaneous foods	680	441	65	6.2
Nonalcoholic beverages	342	207	61	5.8
Food prepared by consumer unit on trips	49	24	49	4.7
Food away from home	2,698	1,268	47	4.5
ALCOHOLIC BEVERAGES	444	144	32	3.1
HOUSING	17,109	12,035	70	6.7
Shelter	10,183	6,553	64	6.1
Owned dwellings	6,760	3,974	59	5.6
Mortgage interest and charges	3,826	688	18	1.7
Property taxes	1,758	1,657	94	9.0
Maintenance, repair, insurance, other expenses	1,176	1,629	139	13.2
Rented dwellings	2,724	2,057	76	7.2
Other lodging	698	522	75	7.1
Utilities, fuels, and public services	3,649	3,067	84	8.0
Natural gas	531	526	99	9.4
Electricity	1,353	1,131	84	7.9

	avg. spending of total consumer units	consumer units headed by people aged 75 or older		
		average spending	indexed spending	market share
Fuel oil and other fuels	$192	$309	161	15.3%
Telephone services	1,127	688	61	5.8
Water and other public services	446	413	93	8.8
Household services	**998**	**1,032**	**103**	**9.8**
Personal services	383	362	95	9.0
Other household services	614	670	109	10.4
Housekeeping supplies	**654**	**485**	**74**	**7.0**
Laundry and cleaning supplies	148	91	61	5.8
Other household products	350	253	72	6.9
Postage and stationery	156	141	90	8.6
Household furnishings and equipment	**1,624**	**898**	**55**	**5.3**
Household textiles	126	54	43	4.1
Furniture	388	184	47	4.5
Floor coverings	45	53	118	11.2
Major appliances	204	131	64	6.1
Small appliances and miscellaneous housewares	113	96	85	8.1
Miscellaneous household equipment	749	379	51	4.8
APPAREL AND RELATED SERVICES	**1,801**	**755**	**42**	**4.0**
Men and boys	**427**	**121**	**28**	**2.7**
Men, aged 16 or older	344	115	33	3.2
Boys, aged 2 to 15	83	7	8	0.8
Women and girls	**718**	**393**	**55**	**5.2**
Women, aged 16 or older	597	387	65	6.2
Girls, aged 2 to 15	121	6	5	0.5
Children under age 2	**93**	**17**	**18**	**1.7**
Footwear	**314**	**132**	**42**	**4.0**
Other apparel products and services	**248**	**93**	**38**	**3.6**
TRANSPORTATION	**8,604**	**4,392**	**51**	**4.9**
Vehicle purchases	**2,755**	**1,044**	**38**	**3.6**
Cars and trucks, new	1,305	634	49	4.6
Cars and trucks, used	1,315	352	27	2.5
Other vehicles	134	58	43	4.1
Gasoline and motor oil	**2,715**	**1,173**	**43**	**4.1**
Other vehicle expenses	**2,621**	**1,793**	**68**	**6.5**
Vehicle finance charges	312	52	17	1.6
Maintenance and repairs	731	496	68	6.5
Vehicle insurance	1,113	1,035	93	8.8
Vehicle rentals, leases, licenses, other charges	465	209	45	4.3
Public transportation	**513**	**382**	**74**	**7.1**
HEALTH CARE	**2,976**	**4,413**	**148**	**14.1**
Health insurance	1,653	2,783	168	16.0
Medical services	727	728	100	9.5
Drugs	482	756	157	14.9
Medical supplies	114	146	128	12.2
ENTERTAINMENT	**2,835**	**1,349**	**48**	**4.5**
Fees and admissions	616	268	44	4.1
Audio and visual equipment and services	1,036	628	61	5.8
Pets, toys, and playground equipment	704	266	38	3.6
Other entertainment products and services	479	187	39	3.7

	avg. spending of total consumer units	consumer units headed by people aged 75 or older		
		average spending	indexed spending	market share
PERSONAL CARE PRODUCTS AND SERVICES	**$616**	**$456**	**74**	**7.0%**
READING	**116**	**132**	**114**	**10.8**
EDUCATION	**1,046**	**192**	**18**	**1.7**
TOBACCO PRODUCTS AND SMOKING SUPPLIES	**317**	**88**	**28**	**2.6**
MISCELLANEOUS	**840**	**507**	**60**	**5.7**
CASH CONTRIBUTIONS	**1,737**	**2,291**	**132**	**12.5**
PERSONAL INSURANCE AND PENSIONS	**5,605**	**1,003**	**18**	**1.7**
Life and other personal insurance	317	187	59	5.6
Pensions and Social Security	5,288	815	15	1.5
PERSONAL TAXES	**1,789**	**139**	**8**	**0.7**
Federal income taxes	1,817	388	21	2.0
2008 tax stimulus	−784	−509	65	–
State and local income taxes	542	54	10	0.9
Other taxes	213	206	97	9.2
GIFTS FOR PEOPLE IN OTHER HOUSEHOLDS	**1,209**	**700**	**58**	**5.5**

Note: Spending by category does not add to total spending because gift spending is also included in the preceding product and service categories and personal taxes are not included in the total.
Source: Bureau of Labor Statistics, 2008 Consumer Expenditure Survey, Internet site http://www.bls.gov/cex/; calculcations by New Strategist

11

Time Use

How people spend their time is determined by their life stage, attitudes, and values. Each generation of Americans is at a different life stage, and each has distinct attitudes and values. Consequently, the generations spend their time differently, as is documented by the Bureau of Labor Statistics American Time Use Survey. The survey reveals that young adults spend more time with computers, middle-aged adults are busy raising children, and older Americans spend the most time watching television.

The life stage demands confronting each age group, as well as generational preferences, determine how involved the generations are with technology, religion, politics, and community organizations. By knowing who is doing what, businesses and policymakers can hone their products and programs to best meet the wants and needs of the American public.

What to expect in the future

■ Gen X and Millennials devote more leisure time to computers than to reading. As they get older, electronic media will increasingly dominate print media as a source of entertainment and information.

■ Americans are busier than ever, and no one is busier juggling work and family than the middle aged. The consequence is little leisure time and less sleep than younger or older generations.

■ Boomers are leaving the crowded-nest lifestage, but they cannot look forward to having as much leisure time as their parents had during the empty-nest lifestage because many will have to postpone retirement.

Leisure Activities Rank Second in Time Use among Americans

Work ranks third in time use.

The American Time Use Survey asks a representative sample of Americans to detail their activities during the past 24 hours. These diary data are combined and analyzed by type of activity and demographic characteristic, revealing how much time people devote to eating, shopping, working, and playing.

The time use survey results show, not surprisingly, that people spend the most time in personal care activities, which include sleeping, bathing, and dressing—an average of 9.38 hours per day in 2008. Ranking second are socializing, relaxing, and leisure, absorbing 4.62 hours per day on average. Work comes in third, at 3.45 hours per day (the figure is relatively low because it includes both workers and those not in the labor force). Household activities, traveling (i.e., commuting), and eating and drinking are next in line.

The amount of time people spend doing activities varies by demographic characteristic. The youngest and the oldest adults spend more time than the middle aged in personal care activities, in large part because they have more free time. Teenagers and young adults spend much more time than the average person engaged in educational activities. People aged 25 to 54 spend 32 to 33 percent more time than average working. Older Americans spend more time than the average person engaged in socializing and leisure.

■ Researchers use the results of time use surveys to determine how people balance work and family issues.

Teens spend the most time sleeping

(average number of hours per day spent sleeping, by age, 2008)

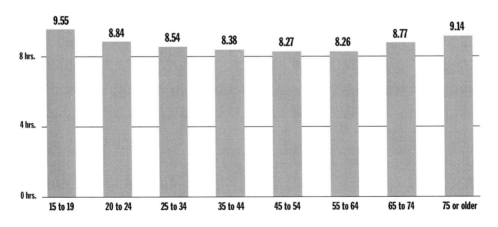

Table 11.1 Time Use by Primary Activity and Age, 2008

(average number of hours per day spent in primary activities, and index of time use by age to average, 2008)

	total	15–19	20–24	25–34	35–44	45–54	55–64	65–74	75+
Total, all activities (hours)	**24.00**	**24.00**	**24.00**	**24.00**	**24.00**	**24.00**	**24.00**	**24.00**	**24.00**
Personal care	9.38	10.35	9.61	9.28	9.11	9.09	9.03	9.51	10.02
Household activities	1.77	0.74	1.05	1.50	1.89	1.94	2.14	2.34	2.42
Caring for and helping household members	0.45	0.09	0.48	0.93	0.87	0.32	0.16	0.07	0.06
Caring for and helping people in other households	0.16	0.15	0.17	0.09	0.10	0.16	0.32	0.24	0.11
Work and work-related activities	3.45	1.28	4.01	4.57	4.56	4.60	3.28	1.14	0.34
Education	0.44	2.92	1.11	0.29	0.08	0.08	0.02	0.01	0.03
Consumer purchases (store, telephone, Internet)	0.38	0.30	0.40	0.37	0.43	0.36	0.42	0.42	0.33
Professional and personal care services	0.08	0.05	0.04	0.06	0.06	0.08	0.12	0.13	0.16
Eating and drinking	1.11	0.90	0.99	1.04	1.08	1.08	1.20	1.32	1.44
Socializing, relaxing, and leisure	4.62	4.53	4.03	3.82	3.68	4.20	5.22	6.56	7.27
Sports, exercise, and recreation	0.33	0.80	0.40	0.28	0.30	0.28	0.25	0.33	0.18
Religious and spiritual activities	0.14	0.10	0.06	0.10	0.12	0.15	0.17	0.25	0.26
Volunteer activities	0.15	0.14	0.04	0.08	0.14	0.17	0.19	0.23	0.22
Telephone calls	0.13	0.27	0.17	0.09	0.07	0.10	0.12	0.13	0.20
Traveling	1.20	1.16	1.32	1.31	1.32	1.21	1.17	1.05	0.70
INDEX OF TIME USE BY AGE TO AVERAGE									
Total, all activities	**100**	**100**	**100**	**100**	**100**	**100**	**100**	**100**	**100**
Personal care	100	110	102	99	97	97	96	101	107
Household activities	100	42	59	85	107	110	121	132	137
Caring for and helping household members	100	20	107	207	193	71	36	16	13
Caring for and helping people in other households	100	94	106	56	63	100	200	150	69
Work and work-related activities	100	37	116	132	132	133	95	33	10
Education	100	664	252	66	18	18	5	2	7
Consumer purchases (store, telephone, Internet)	100	79	105	97	113	95	111	111	87
Professional and personal care services	100	63	50	75	75	100	150	163	200
Eating and drinking	100	81	89	94	97	97	108	119	130
Socializing, relaxing, and leisure	100	98	87	83	80	91	113	142	157
Sports, exercise, and recreation	100	242	121	85	91	85	76	100	55
Religious and spiritual activities	100	71	43	71	86	107	121	179	186
Volunteer activities	100	93	27	53	93	113	127	153	147
Telephone calls	100	208	131	69	54	77	92	100	154
Traveling	100	97	110	109	110	101	98	88	58

Note: Primary activities are those respondents identified as their main activity. Other activities done simultaneously, such as eating while watching TV, are not included.
Source: Bureau of Labor Statistics, unpublished tables from the 2008 American Time Use Survey, Internet site http://www.bls.gov/tus/home.htm; calculations by New Strategist

Table 11.2 Time Spent Sleeping by Age and Sex, 2008

(hours per day spent sleeping as a primary activity and index of time to average, by age and sex, 2008)

	total	men	women
Aged 15 or older	**8.60**	**8.56**	**8.64**
Aged 15 to 19	9.55	9.64	9.46
Aged 20 to 24	8.84	8.89	8.78
Aged 25 to 34	8.54	8.48	8.57
Aged 35 to 44	8.38	8.31	8.44
Aged 45 to 54	8.27	8.16	8.39
Aged 55 to 64	8.26	8.24	8.29
Aged 65 to 74	8.77	8.88	8.67
Aged 75 or older	9.14	9.03	9.22
INDEX OF TIME TO AVERAGE			
Aged 15 or older	**100**	**100**	**100**
Aged 15 to 19	111	112	110
Aged 20 to 24	103	103	102
Aged 25 to 34	99	99	100
Aged 35 to 44	97	97	98
Aged 45 to 54	96	95	98
Aged 55 to 64	96	96	96
Aged 65 to 74	102	103	101
Aged 75 or older	106	105	107

Note: Primary activities are those respondents identified as their main activity. Other activities done simultaneously, such as eating while watching TV, are not included.
Source: Bureau of Labor Statistics, unpublished tables from the 2008 American Time Use Survey, Internet site http://www.bls .gov/tus/home.htm; calculations by New Strategist

Older Adults Spend the Most Time in Leisure Pursuits

People aged 35 to 44 have the least amount of leisure time.

The average American spends 4.62 hours a day in leisure activities, more than half of that time being spent in front of a television set. After personal care activities (sleeping, bathing, dressing, etc.), leisure activities take up the largest share of the average person's day including 2.77 hours a day of watching television. Older men and women spend the most time watching TV, with men aged 65 or older spending more than four hours a day watching television as a primary activity.

Socializing and communicating is the second-most-time-consuming leisure activity after watching television, but on average people spend only 0.64 hours socializing each day (or 38 minutes). Teenagers spend the most time socializing, with 15-to-19-year-olds spending 34 percent more time socializing than the average person. Reading is the third-ranking leisure pursuit, but only among women. Men spend more time participating in sports than reading. Teenage girls spend more time than anyone else using a computer for leisure (except gaming), and teenage boys spend more time than anyone else playing games (a category that includes computer gaming as well as board and card games).

Older adults spend the most time reading

(indexed average hours per day that people spend reading for personal interest as a primary activity, by age, 2008; time spent by the average person equals 100)

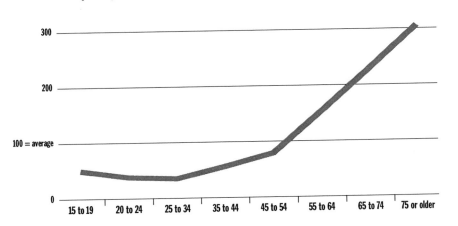

Table 11.3 Time Spent Watching Television by Age and Sex, 2008

(hours per day spent watching television as the primary activity and index of time to average, by age and sex, 2008)

	total	men	women
Aged 15 or older	**2.77**	**3.01**	**2.54**
Aged 15 to 19	2.16	2.23	2.08
Aged 20 to 24	2.20	2.41	1.99
Aged 25 to 34	2.25	2.34	2.16
Aged 35 to 44	2.29	2.42	2.17
Aged 45 to 54	2.76	3.09	2.44
Aged 55 to 64	3.27	3.81	2.76
Aged 65 to 74	4.00	4.60	3.49
Aged 75 or older	4.19	4.66	3.89
INDEX OF TIME TO AVERAGE			
Aged 15 or older	**100**	**109**	**92**
Aged 15 to 19	78	81	75
Aged 20 to 24	79	87	72
Aged 25 to 34	81	84	78
Aged 35 to 44	83	87	78
Aged 45 to 54	100	112	88
Aged 55 to 64	118	138	100
Aged 65 to 74	144	166	126
Aged 75 or older	151	168	140

Note: Primary activities are those respondents identified as their main activity. Other activities done simultaneously, such as eating while watching TV, are not included.
Source: Bureau of Labor Statistics, unpublished tables from the 2008 American Time Use Survey, Internet site http://www.bls .gov/tus/home.htm; calculations by New Strategist

Table 11.4 Time Spent Socializing and Communicating by Age and Sex, 2008

(hours per day spent socializing and communicating as the primary activity and index of time to average, by age and sex, 2008)

	total	men	women
Aged 15 or older	**0.64**	**0.59**	**0.68**
Aged 15 to 19	0.86	0.87	0.85
Aged 20 to 24	0.77	0.82	0.73
Aged 25 to 34	0.66	0.61	0.70
Aged 35 to 44	0.56	0.52	0.59
Aged 45 to 54	0.52	0.46	0.58
Aged 55 to 64	0.65	0.56	0.74
Aged 65 to 74	0.66	0.56	0.75
Aged 75 or older	0.57	0.55	0.58
INDEX OF TIME TO AVERAGE			
Aged 15 or older	**100**	**92**	**106**
Aged 15 to 19	134	136	133
Aged 20 to 24	120	128	114
Aged 25 to 34	103	95	109
Aged 35 to 44	88	81	92
Aged 45 to 54	81	72	91
Aged 55 to 64	102	88	116
Aged 65 to 74	103	88	117
Aged 75 or older	89	86	91

Note: Primary activities are those respondents identified as their main activity. Other activities done simultaneously, such as eating while watching TV, are not included.
Source: Bureau of Labor Statistics, unpublished tables from the 2008 American Time Use Survey, Internet site http://www.bls .gov/tus/home.htm; calculations by New Strategist

Table 11.5 Time Spent Reading by Age and Sex, 2008

(hours per day spent reading as the primary activity and index of time to average, by age and sex, 2008)

	total	men	women
Aged 15 or older	**0.34**	**0.29**	**0.40**
Aged 15 to 19	0.17	0.16	0.18
Aged 20 to 24	0.13	0.10	0.15
Aged 25 to 34	0.12	0.07	0.16
Aged 35 to 44	0.19	0.14	0.24
Aged 45 to 54	0.27	0.24	0.31
Aged 55 to 64	0.52	0.48	0.57
Aged 65 to 74	0.78	0.69	0.87
Aged 75 or older	1.04	1.02	1.05
INDEX OF TIME TO AVERAGE			
Aged 15 or older	**100**	**85**	**118**
Aged 15 to 19	50	47	53
Aged 20 to 24	38	29	44
Aged 25 to 34	35	21	47
Aged 35 to 44	56	41	71
Aged 45 to 54	79	71	91
Aged 55 to 64	153	141	168
Aged 65 to 74	229	203	256
Aged 75 or older	306	300	309

Note: Primary activities are those respondents identified as their main activity. Other activities done simultaneously, such as eating while watching TV, are not included.
Source: Bureau of Labor Statistics, unpublished tables from the 2008 American Time Use Survey, Internet site http://www.bls .gov/tus/home.htm; calculations by New Strategist

Table 11.6 Time Spent Participating in Sports, Exercise, or Recreation by Age and Sex, 2008

(hours per day spent participating in sports, exercise, or recreation as the primary activity and index of time to average, by age and sex, 2008)

	total	men	women
Aged 15 or older	**0.29**	**0.40**	**0.20**
Aged 15 to 19	0.70	1.00	0.39
Aged 20 to 24	0.35	0.44	0.26
Aged 25 to 34	0.25	0.32	0.18
Aged 35 to 44	0.25	0.33	0.18
Aged 45 to 54	0.25	0.32	0.18
Aged 55 to 64	0.23	0.31	0.17
Aged 65 to 74	0.30	0.50	0.13
Aged 75 or older	0.18	0.20	0.16
INDEX OF TIME TO AVERAGE			
Aged 15 or older	**100**	**138**	**69**
Aged 15 to 19	241	345	134
Aged 20 to 24	121	152	90
Aged 25 to 34	86	110	62
Aged 35 to 44	86	114	62
Aged 45 to 54	86	110	62
Aged 55 to 64	79	107	59
Aged 65 to 74	103	172	45
Aged 75 or older	62	69	55

Note: Primary activities are those respondents identified as their main activity. Other activities done simultaneously, such as eating while watching TV, are not included.
Source: Bureau of Labor Statistics, unpublished tables from the 2008 American Time Use Survey, Internet site http://www.bls .gov/tus/home.htm; calculations by New Strategist

Table 11.7 Time Spent Relaxing and Thinking by Age and Sex, 2008

(hours per day spent relaxing and thinking as the primary activity and index of time to average, by age and sex, 2008)

	total	men	women
Aged 15 or older	**0.27**	**0.27**	**0.26**
Aged 15 to 19	0.14	0.12	0.15
Aged 20 to 24	0.18	0.14	0.22
Aged 25 to 34	0.19	0.22	0.16
Aged 35 to 44	0.15	0.15	0.15
Aged 45 to 54	0.27	0.29	0.25
Aged 55 to 64	0.28	0.31	0.25
Aged 65 to 74	0.45	0.43	0.46
Aged 75 or older	0.74	0.87	0.65
INDEX OF TIME TO AVERAGE			
Aged 15 or older	**100**	**100**	**96**
Aged 15 to 19	52	44	56
Aged 20 to 24	67	52	81
Aged 25 to 34	70	81	59
Aged 35 to 44	56	56	56
Aged 45 to 54	100	107	93
Aged 55 to 64	104	115	93
Aged 65 to 74	167	159	170
Aged 75 or older	274	322	241

Note: Primary activities are those respondents identified as their main activity. Other activities done simultaneously, such as eating while watching TV, are not included.
Source: Bureau of Labor Statistics, unpublished tables from the 2008 American Time Use Survey, Internet site http://www.bls.gov/tus/home.htm; calculations by New Strategist

Table 11.8 Time Spent Playing Games and Using the Computer for Leisure by Age and Sex, 2008

(hours per day spent playing games and using the computer for leisure as the primary activities and index of time to average, by age and sex, 2008)

	playing games			leisure computer use		
	total	men	women	total	men	women
Aged 15 or older	**0.20**	**0.25**	**0.15**	**0.14**	**0.15**	**0.14**
Aged 15 to 19	0.48	0.76	0.19	0.31	0.27	0.35
Aged 20 to 24	0.34	0.57	0.12	0.10	0.11	0.08
Aged 25 to 34	0.19	0.28	0.10	0.18	0.18	0.18
Aged 35 to 44	0.12	0.13	0.10	0.15	0.16	0.14
Aged 45 to 54	0.09	0.06	0.11	0.09	0.09	0.09
Aged 55 to 64	0.13	0.08	0.17	0.10	0.13	0.08
Aged 65 to 74	0.23	0.19	0.27	0.13	0.14	0.12
Aged 75 or older	0.29	0.25	0.31	0.10	0.13	0.08
INDEX OF TIME TO AVERAGE						
Aged 15 or older	**100**	**125**	**75**	**100**	**107**	**100**
Aged 15 to 19	240	380	95	221	193	250
Aged 20 to 24	170	285	60	71	79	57
Aged 25 to 34	95	140	50	129	129	129
Aged 35 to 44	60	65	50	107	114	100
Aged 45 to 54	45	30	55	64	64	64
Aged 55 to 64	65	40	85	71	93	57
Aged 65 to 74	115	95	135	93	100	86
Aged 75 or older	145	125	155	71	93	57

Note: The category "leisure computer use" does not include playing computer games. The category "playing games" includes computer and videogames, board games, and card games. Primary activities are those respondents identified as their main activity. Other activities done simultaneously, such as eating while watching TV, are not included.
Source: Bureau of Labor Statistics, unpublished tables from the 2008 American Time Use Survey, Internet site http://www.bls.gov/tus/home.htm; calculations by New Strategist

Older Women Spend the Most Time Cooking

Older men spend the most time caring for their lawns.

Older Americans, both men and women, spend more time than younger adults doing housework. Women aged 65 to 74 spend the most time cooking and cleaning the house. Men aged 55 or older spend more than twice as much time as the average person tending their lawns and gardens.

Older people spend more time than younger ones puttering around the house because younger adults are too busy working and raising children to have much time for domestic chores. The time devoted to caring for household children is above average among women aged 20 to 44 and men aged 25 to 44. As the demands of children ease, pets take up the slack. The time people spend caring for pets rises above average among people aged 55 or older.

■ Women still spend much more time than men doing housework. Men spend more time at work.

Older Americans devote the most time to pet care

(indexed average number of hours per day people spend caring for animals and pets as a primary activity, by age, 2008)

Table 11.9 Time Spent Housecleaning by Age and Sex, 2008

(hours per day spent housecleaning as the primary activity and index of time to average, by age and sex, 2008)

	total	men	women
Aged 15 or older	**0.37**	**0.17**	**0.55**
Aged 15 to 19	0.23	0.14	0.33
Aged 20 to 24	0.25	0.14	0.39
Aged 25 to 34	0.38	0.21	0.56
Aged 35 to 44	0.40	0.17	0.62
Aged 45 to 54	0.36	0.16	0.55
Aged 55 to 64	0.35	0.17	0.52
Aged 65 to 74	0.47	0.16	0.74
Aged 75 or older	0.47	0.16	0.67
INDEX OF TIME TO AVERAGE			
Aged 15 or older	**100**	**46**	**149**
Aged 15 to 19	62	38	89
Aged 20 to 24	68	38	105
Aged 25 to 34	103	57	151
Aged 35 to 44	108	46	168
Aged 45 to 54	97	43	149
Aged 55 to 64	95	46	141
Aged 65 to 74	127	43	200
Aged 75 or older	127	43	181

Note: Primary activities are those respondents identified as their main activity. Other activities done simultaneously, such as eating while watching TV, are not included.
Source: Bureau of Labor Statistics, unpublished tables from the 2008 American Time Use Survey, Internet site http://www.bls .gov/tus/home.htm; calculations by New Strategist

Table 11.10 Time Spent Doing the Laundry by Age and Sex, 2008

(hours per day spent doing the laundry as the primary activity and index of time to average, by age and sex, 2008)

	total	men	women
Aged 15 or older	**0.17**	**0.06**	**0.28**
Aged 15 to 19	0.04	0.03	0.06
Aged 20 to 24	0.11	0.06	0.15
Aged 25 to 34	0.16	0.07	0.25
Aged 35 to 44	0.21	0.07	0.35
Aged 45 to 54	0.21	0.08	0.33
Aged 55 to 64	0.19	0.06	0.31
Aged 65 to 74	0.19	0.05	0.31
Aged 75 or older	0.19	0.04	0.29
INDEX OF TIME TO AVERAGE			
Aged 15 or older	**100**	**35**	**165**
Aged 15 to 19	24	18	35
Aged 20 to 24	65	35	88
Aged 25 to 34	94	41	147
Aged 35 to 44	124	41	206
Aged 45 to 54	124	47	194
Aged 55 to 64	112	35	182
Aged 65 to 74	112	29	182
Aged 75 or older	112	24	171

Note: Primary activities are those respondents identified as their main activity. Other activities done simultaneously, such as eating while watching TV, are not included.
Source: Bureau of Labor Statistics, unpublished tables from the 2008 American Time Use Survey, Internet site http://www.bls .gov/tus/home.htm; calculations by New Strategist

Table 11.11 Time Spent Cooking by Age and Sex, 2008

(hours per day spent in food and drink preparation as the primary activity and index of time to average, by age and sex, 2008)

	total	men	women
Aged 15 or older	**0.40**	**0.25**	**0.55**
Aged 15 to 19	0.10	0.07	0.13
Aged 20 to 24	0.25	0.18	0.33
Aged 25 to 34	0.41	0.26	0.56
Aged 35 to 44	0.47	0.28	0.65
Aged 45 to 54	0.44	0.27	0.59
Aged 55 to 64	0.44	0.28	0.60
Aged 65 to 74	0.49	0.29	0.66
Aged 75 or older	0.50	0.29	0.65
INDEX OF TIME TO AVERAGE			
Aged 15 or older	**100**	**63**	**138**
Aged 15 to 19	25	18	33
Aged 20 to 24	63	45	83
Aged 25 to 34	103	65	140
Aged 35 to 44	118	70	163
Aged 45 to 54	110	68	148
Aged 55 to 64	110	70	150
Aged 65 to 74	123	73	165
Aged 75 or older	125	73	163

Note: Primary activities are those respondents identified as their main activity. Other activities done simultaneously, such as eating while watching TV, are not included.
Source: Bureau of Labor Statistics, unpublished tables from the 2008 American Time Use Survey, Internet site http://www.bls .gov/tus/home.htm; calculations by New Strategist

Table 11.12 Time Spent Cleaning Up in the Kitchen by Age and Sex, 2008

(hours per day spent cleaning up in the kitchen as the primary activity and index of time to average, by age and sex, 2008)

	total	men	women
Aged 15 or older	**0.12**	**0.05**	**0.18**
Aged 15 to 19	0.03	0.02	0.03
Aged 20 to 24	0.03	0.01	0.06
Aged 25 to 34	0.12	0.06	0.17
Aged 35 to 44	0.13	0.05	0.22
Aged 45 to 54	0.12	0.05	0.20
Aged 55 to 64	0.14	0.06	0.21
Aged 65 to 74	0.14	0.05	0.22
Aged 75 or older	0.18	0.10	0.24
INDEX OF TIME TO AVERAGE			
Aged 15 or older	**100**	**42**	**150**
Aged 15 to 19	25	17	25
Aged 20 to 24	25	8	50
Aged 25 to 34	100	50	142
Aged 35 to 44	108	42	183
Aged 45 to 54	100	42	167
Aged 55 to 64	117	50	175
Aged 65 to 74	117	42	183
Aged 75 or older	150	83	200

Note: Primary activities are those respondents identified as their main activity. Other activities done simultaneously, such as eating while watching TV, are not included.
Source: Bureau of Labor Statistics, unpublished tables from the 2008 American Time Use Survey, Internet site http://www.bls .gov/tus/home.htm; calculations by New Strategist

Table 11.13 Time Spent on Lawn, Garden, and Houseplant Care by Age and Sex, 2008

(hours per day spent in lawn, garden, and houseplant care as the primary activity and index of time to average, by age and sex, 2008)

	total	men	women
Aged 15 or older	**0.19**	**0.26**	**0.12**
Aged 15 to 19	0.03	0.05	0.02
Aged 20 to 24	0.07	0.13	0.00
Aged 25 to 34	0.09	0.12	0.05
Aged 35 to 44	0.16	0.23	0.09
Aged 45 to 54	0.23	0.31	0.15
Aged 55 to 64	0.32	0.42	0.23
Aged 65 to 74	0.32	0.47	0.19
Aged 75 or older	0.32	0.45	0.24
INDEX OF TIME TO AVERAGE			
Aged 15 or older	**100**	**137**	**63**
Aged 15 to 19	16	26	11
Aged 20 to 24	37	68	0
Aged 25 to 34	47	63	26
Aged 35 to 44	84	121	47
Aged 45 to 54	121	163	79
Aged 55 to 64	168	221	121
Aged 65 to 74	168	247	100
Aged 75 or older	168	237	126

Note: Primary activities are those respondents identified as their main activity. Other activities done simultaneously, such as eating while watching TV, are not included.
Source: Bureau of Labor Statistics, unpublished tables from the 2008 American Time Use Survey, Internet site http://www.bls .gov/tus/home.htm; calculations by New Strategist

Table 11.14 Time Spent Caring for Household Children by Age and Sex, 2008

(hours per day spent caring for household children as the primary activity and index of time to average, by age and sex, 2008)

	total	men	women
Aged 15 or older	**0.37**	**0.25**	**0.48**
Aged 15 to 19	0.07	0.03	0.11
Aged 20 to 24	0.43	0.14	0.72
Aged 25 to 34	0.84	0.52	1.17
Aged 35 to 44	0.74	0.52	0.96
Aged 45 to 54	0.23	0.22	0.25
Aged 55 to 64	0.06	0.06	0.06
Aged 65 to 74	0.02	0.02	0.03
Aged 75 or older	0.01	0.00	0.01
INDEX OF TIME TO AVERAGE			
Aged 15 or older	**100**	**68**	**130**
Aged 15 to 19	19	8	30
Aged 20 to 24	116	38	195
Aged 25 to 34	227	141	316
Aged 35 to 44	200	141	259
Aged 45 to 54	62	59	68
Aged 55 to 64	16	16	16
Aged 65 to 74	5	5	8
Aged 75 or older	3	0	3

Note: Primary activities are those respondents identified as their main activity. Other activities done simultaneously, such as eating while watching TV, are not included.
Source: Bureau of Labor Statistics, unpublished tables from the 2008 American Time Use Survey, Internet site http://www.bls .gov/tus/home.htm; calculations by New Strategist

Table 11.15 Time Spent on Pet Care by Age and Sex, 2008

(hours per day spent on animal and pet care as the primary activity and index of time to average, by age and sex, 2008)

	total	men	women
Aged 15 or older	**0.09**	**0.08**	**0.10**
Aged 15 to 19	0.05	0.05	0.05
Aged 20 to 24	0.09	0.13	0.05
Aged 25 to 34	0.07	0.05	0.09
Aged 35 to 44	0.08	0.07	0.09
Aged 45 to 54	0.09	0.07	0.11
Aged 55 to 64	0.13	0.10	0.15
Aged 65 to 74	0.10	0.12	0.09
Aged 75 or older	0.13	0.14	0.12
INDEX OF TIME TO AVERAGE			
Aged 15 or older	**100**	**89**	**111**
Aged 15 to 19	56	56	56
Aged 20 to 24	100	144	56
Aged 25 to 34	78	56	100
Aged 35 to 44	89	78	100
Aged 45 to 54	100	78	122
Aged 55 to 64	144	111	167
Aged 65 to 74	111	133	100
Aged 75 or older	144	156	133

Note: Primary activities are those respondents identified as their main activity. Other activities done simultaneously, such as eating while watching TV, are not included.
Source: Bureau of Labor Statistics, unpublished tables from the 2008 American Time Use Survey, Internet site http://www.bls .gov/tus/home.htm; calculations by New Strategist

Young Adults Spend the Most Time on the Phone

The middle aged spend the most time traveling from one activity to another.

The average American travels more than one hour a day, making travel one of the most time-consuming daily activities. Travel time peaks among people aged 20 to 44 primarily because of the commute to work.

It is no surprise that teenagers spend the most time on the telephone as a primary activity. Teenage girls spend nearly three times the average amount of time on the phone. Women aged 75 or older spend more than twice as much time on the phone as the average person. People aged 65 or older spend the most time involved in religious activities.

Grocery shopping peaks among older Americans. The oldest men spend more time in the grocery store on an average day than middle-aged women.

■ Time spent volunteering is lowest among people aged 20 to 34, when childrearing demands are at a peak.

People aged 65 or older spend the most time involved in religious activities

(indexed average hours per day people spend involved in religious activities as a primary activity, by age, 2008)

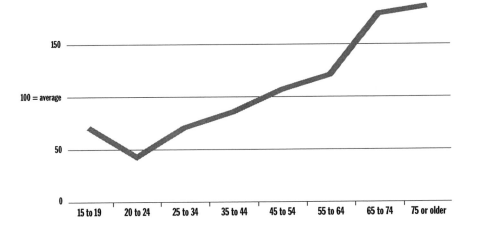

Table 11.16 Time Spent Shopping for Groceries by Age and Sex, 2008

(hours per day spent shopping for groceries as the primary activity and index of time to average, by age and sex, 2008)

	total	men	women
Aged 15 or older	**0.10**	**0.06**	**0.13**
Aged 15 to 19	0.04	0.03	0.05
Aged 20 to 24	0.07	0.06	0.08
Aged 25 to 34	0.09	0.07	0.12
Aged 35 to 44	0.10	0.06	0.14
Aged 45 to 54	0.10	0.06	0.15
Aged 55 to 64	0.11	0.07	0.15
Aged 65 to 74	0.14	0.11	0.18
Aged 75 or older	0.11	0.17	0.13
INDEX OF TIME TO AVERAGE			
Aged 15 or older	**100**	**60**	**130**
Aged 15 to 19	40	30	50
Aged 20 to 24	70	60	80
Aged 25 to 34	90	70	120
Aged 35 to 44	100	60	140
Aged 45 to 54	100	60	150
Aged 55 to 64	110	70	150
Aged 65 to 74	140	110	180
Aged 75 or older	110	170	130

Note: Primary activities are those respondents identified as their main activity. Other activities done simultaneously, such as eating while watching TV, are not included.
Source: Bureau of Labor Statistics, unpublished tables from the 2008 American Time Use Survey, Internet site http://www.bls .gov/tus/home.htm; calculations by New Strategist

Table 11.17 Time Spent Shopping (Except for Food or Gas) by Age and Sex, 2008

(hours per day spent shopping for consumer goods except food or gas as the primary activity and index of time to average, by age and sex, 2008)

	total	men	women
Aged 15 or older	**0.25**	**0.19**	**0.31**
Aged 15 to 19	0.22	0.13	0.31
Aged 20 to 24	0.30	0.13	0.46
Aged 25 to 34	0.24	0.19	0.28
Aged 35 to 44	0.30	0.23	0.36
Aged 45 to 54	0.22	0.17	0.28
Aged 55 to 64	0.28	0.19	0.36
Aged 65 to 74	0.26	0.26	0.26
Aged 75 or older	0.21	0.21	0.21
INDEX OF TIME TO AVERAGE			
Aged 15 or older	**100**	**76**	**124**
Aged 15 to 19	88	52	124
Aged 20 to 24	120	52	184
Aged 25 to 34	96	76	112
Aged 35 to 44	120	92	144
Aged 45 to 54	88	68	112
Aged 55 to 64	112	76	144
Aged 65 to 74	104	104	104
Aged 75 or older	84	84	84

Note: Primary activities are those respondents identified as their main activity. Other activities done simultaneously, such as eating while watching TV, are not included.
Source: Bureau of Labor Statistics, unpublished tables from the 2008 American Time Use Survey, Internet site http://www.bls.gov/tus/home.htm; calculations by New Strategist

Table 11.18 Time Spent Participating in Religious Activities by Age and Sex, 2008

(hours per day spent participating in religious activities as the primary activity and index of time to average, by age and sex, 2008)

	total	men	women
Aged 15 or older	**0.14**	**0.12**	**0.17**
Aged 15 to 19	0.10	0.08	0.11
Aged 20 to 24	0.06	0.05	0.06
Aged 25 to 34	0.10	0.08	0.12
Aged 35 to 44	0.12	0.10	0.14
Aged 45 to 54	0.15	0.13	0.17
Aged 55 to 64	0.17	0.11	0.22
Aged 65 to 74	0.25	0.21	0.28
Aged 75 or older	0.26	0.28	0.25
INDEX OF TIME TO AVERAGE			
Aged 15 or older	**100**	**86**	**121**
Aged 15 to 19	71	57	79
Aged 20 to 24	43	36	43
Aged 25 to 34	71	57	86
Aged 35 to 44	86	71	100
Aged 45 to 54	107	93	121
Aged 55 to 64	121	79	157
Aged 65 to 74	179	150	200
Aged 75 or older	186	200	179

Note: Primary activities are those respondents identified as their main activity. Other activities done simultaneously, such as eating while watching TV, are not included.
Source: Bureau of Labor Statistics, unpublished tables from the 2008 American Time Use Survey, Internet site http://www.bls .gov/tus/home.htm; calculations by New Strategist

Table 11.19 Time Spent Volunteering by Age and Sex, 2008

(hours per day spent volunteering as the primary activity and index of time to average, by age and sex, 2008)

	total	men	women
Aged 15 or older	**0.15**	**0.14**	**0.16**
Aged 15 to 19	0.14	0.15	0.12
Aged 20 to 24	0.04	0.03	0.04
Aged 25 to 34	0.08	0.06	0.11
Aged 35 to 44	0.14	0.10	0.18
Aged 45 to 54	0.17	0.19	0.15
Aged 55 to 64	0.19	0.16	0.21
Aged 65 to 74	0.23	0.26	0.21
Aged 75 or older	0.22	0.24	0.20
INDEX OF TIME TO AVERAGE			
Aged 15 or older	**100**	**93**	**107**
Aged 15 to 19	93	100	80
Aged 20 to 24	27	20	27
Aged 25 to 34	53	40	73
Aged 35 to 44	93	67	120
Aged 45 to 54	113	127	100
Aged 55 to 64	127	107	140
Aged 65 to 74	153	173	140
Aged 75 or older	147	160	133

Note: Primary activities are those respondents identified as their main activity. Other activities done simultaneously, such as eating while watching TV, are not included.
Source: Bureau of Labor Statistics, unpublished tables from the 2008 American Time Use Survey, Internet site http://www.bls .gov/tus/home.htm; calculations by New Strategist

Table 11.20 Time Spent Talking on the Telephone by Age and Sex, 2008

(hours per day spent on the telephone as the primary activity and index of time to average, by age and sex, 2008)

	total	men	women
Aged 15 or older	**0.13**	**0.07**	**0.18**
Aged 15 to 19	0.27	0.18	0.38
Aged 20 to 24	0.17	0.12	0.23
Aged 25 to 34	0.09	0.06	0.12
Aged 35 to 44	0.07	0.05	0.10
Aged 45 to 54	0.10	0.04	0.16
Aged 55 to 64	0.12	0.05	0.18
Aged 65 to 74	0.13	0.08	0.16
Aged 75 or older	0.20	0.08	0.27
INDEX OF TIME TO AVERAGE			
Aged 15 or older	**100**	**54**	**138**
Aged 15 to 19	208	138	292
Aged 20 to 24	131	92	177
Aged 25 to 34	69	46	92
Aged 35 to 44	54	38	77
Aged 45 to 54	77	31	123
Aged 55 to 64	92	38	138
Aged 65 to 74	100	62	123
Aged 75 or older	154	62	208

Note: Primary activities are those respondents identified as their main activity. Other activities done simultaneously, such as eating while watching TV, are not included.
Source: Bureau of Labor Statistics, unpublished tables from the 2008 American Time Use Survey, Internet site http://www.bls .gov/tus/home.htm; calculations by New Strategist

Table 11.21 Time Spent Traveling by Age and Sex, 2008

(hours per day spent traveling and index of time to average, by age and sex, 2008)

	total	men	women
Aged 15 or older	**1.20**	**1.23**	**1.17**
Aged 15 to 19	1.16	1.19	1.14
Aged 20 to 24	1.32	1.27	1.38
Aged 25 to 34	1.31	1.38	1.24
Aged 35 to 44	1.32	1.37	1.28
Aged 45 to 54	1.21	1.25	1.18
Aged 55 to 64	1.17	1.16	1.18
Aged 65 to 74	1.05	0.98	1.12
Aged 75 or older	0.70	0.85	0.60
INDEX OF TIME TO AVERAGE			
Aged 15 or older	**100**	**103**	**98**
Aged 15 to 19	97	99	95
Aged 20 to 24	110	106	115
Aged 25 to 34	109	115	103
Aged 35 to 44	110	114	107
Aged 45 to 54	101	104	98
Aged 55 to 64	98	97	98
Aged 65 to 74	88	82	93
Aged 75 or older	58	71	50

Note: Primary activities are those respondents identified as their main activity. Other activities done simultaneously, such as eating while watching TV, are not included.
Source: Bureau of Labor Statistics, unpublished tables from the 2008 American Time Use Survey, Internet site http://www.bls .gov/tus/home.htm; calculations by New Strategist

Older Americans Are Much Less Likely to Be Online

More than nine out of 10 young adults are connected.

Seventy-nine percent of Americans aged 18 or older were Internet users in 2009, up substantially from the 49 percent of 2000, according to surveys by the Pew Internet & American Life Project. Young adults are most likely to use the Internet, with 92 percent doing so in 2009. Internet use falls with age. Only 42 percent of people aged 65 or older are online.

Among people who use the Internet, the percentage who were online yesterday is highest among young adults (77 percent). It is lowest among those aged 65 or older (62 percent).

■ Look for the percentage of Internet users in the 65or-older age group to surge as Boomers age into their late sixties.

The oldest Americans are least likely to use the Internet

(percent of people who use the Internet, by age, 2009)

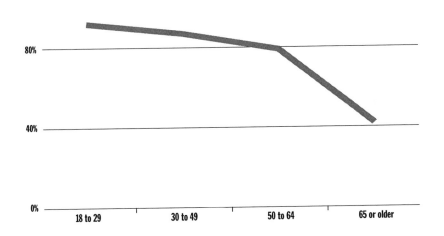

Table 11.22 Internet Use by Age, 2000 and 2009

(percent of people aged 18 or older who use the Internet and who used the Internet yesterday, by age, April 2000 and April 2009; and percentage point change, 2000–09)

	2009	2000	percentage point change
USE THE INTERNET			
Total people	**79%**	**49%**	**30**
Aged 18 to 29	92	69	23
Aged 30 to 49	87	60	27
Aged 50 to 64	79	45	34
Aged 65 or older	42	14	28
WERE ONLINE YESTERDAY (OF THOSE USING THE INTERNET)			
Total people	**73**	**55**	**18**
Aged 18 to 29	77	54	23
Aged 30 to 49	76	54	22
Aged 50 to 64	69	58	11
Aged 65 or older	62	59	3

Source: Pew Internet & American Life Project, Latest Trends—Usage Over Time, Internet site http://www.pewinternet.org/ trends.asp#demographics; calculations by New Strategist

Voting Rate Fell among All but the Youngest Americans

People aged 65 or older are still more likely to vote than any other age group.

The older people are, the more likely they are to vote. This has long been true, but the gap between young and old has widened over the years. In the 1972 presidential election (the first in which 18-to-20-year-olds could vote), 63.5 percent of people aged 65 or older voted compared with 49.6 percent of those aged 18 to 24. In the 2008 election, 68.1 percent of people aged 65 or older voted versus only 44.3 percent of people aged 18 to 24—a 24 percentage point difference.

Despite all the excitement generated by Barack Obama during the presidential campaign, the voting rate fell slightly between 2004 and 2008. Young adults were the only ones who boosted their voting rate, the percentage of 18-to-24-year-olds who voted rising from 41.9 to 44.3 percent between 2004 and 2008.

■ Because older adults are most likely to vote, politicians pay closer attention to the issues affecting the aged than to the concerns of young adults.

Fewer than half of young adults vote

(percent of people who voted in the 2008 presidential election, by age)

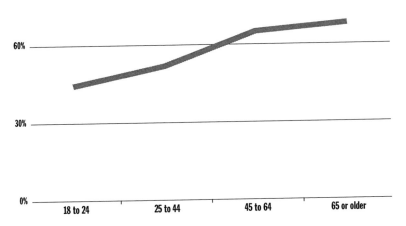

Table 11.23 Voting Rate in Presidential Elections by Age, 1964 to 2008

(percent of people of voting age who reported voting in presidential elections by age, 1964 to 2008; percentage point change for selected years)

	total people of voting age	18 to 24	25 to 44	45 to 64	65 or older
2008	58.2%	44.3%	51.9%	65.0%	68.1%
2004	58.3	41.9	52.2	66.6	68.9
2000	54.7	32.3	49.8	64.1	67.6
1996	54.2	32.4	49.2	64.4	67.0
1992	61.3	42.8	58.3	70.0	70.1
1988	57.4	36.2	54.0	67.9	68.8
1984	59.9	40.8	58.4	69.8	67.7
1980	59.3	39.9	58.7	69.3	65.1
1976	59.2	42.2	58.7	68.7	62.2
1972	63.0	49.6	62.7	70.8	63.5
1968	67.8	50.4	66.6	74.9	65.8
1964	69.3	50.9	69.0	75.9	66.3
Percentage point change					
2004 to 2008	−0.1	2.4	−0.3	−1.6	−0.8
1964 to 2008	−11.1	−6.6	−17.1	−10.9	1.8

Note: Before 1972, data for 18-to-24-year-olds include only 21-to-24-year-olds.
Source: Bureau of the Census, Voting and Registration, Historical Time Series Tables, Internet site http://www.census.gov/ population/www/socdemo/voting.html; calculations by New Strategist

Wealth

Every three years the federal government surveys the wealth of American households with its Survey of Consumer Finances. The most recent survey results, from 2007, provide a snapshot of household wealth just as the housing bubble peaked. That picture is presented in this chapter, along with the Federal Reserve Board's estimates (in the accompanying text) of how much net worth, stock values, and housing values have declined since then.

Despite the ups and downs in the economy, the pattern of wealth accumulation remains the same. Older householders are wealthier than younger householders, largely because they are more likely to own a home. Homes are the single most important asset for the average American household. In 2007, median net worth peaked in the 55-to-64 age group at $253,700. In contrast, the net worth of householders under age 35 was just $11,800. Behind the difference is homeownership. Only 41 percent of householders under age 35 were homeowners in 2007 versus 81 percent of householders aged 55 to 64.

In retirement, older Americans must live off their accumulated wealth—either personal savings or retirement benefits earned through years of work. The disappearance of defined-benefit retirement plans has reduced the wealth of workers, and few are making up the difference through personal savings. Most have saved little. Only 36 percent of workers aged 55 or older have saved $100,000 or more, according to the Employee Benefit Research Institute's Retirement Confidence Survey.

What to expect in the future

■ The collapse of the housing market, combined with more debt, has greatly reduced the net worth of Americans regardless of age.

■ The retirement plans of the Baby-Boom generation have been transformed by the Great Recession, with most older Boomers planning to work to age 66 or beyond.

■ With unemployment high and the cost of necessities rising, it has become harder than ever for Americans to save for retirement. Expect Social Security to be the most important source of income for the largest share of Boomers in retirement.

Net Worth Climbed Sharply during the Housing Bubble

Inflated housing values drove up net worth.

Net worth is what remains when a household's debts are subtracted from its assets. During this decade's housing bubble, housing values rose faster than mortgage debt. Consequently, net worth grew substantially—up 18 percent between 2004 and 2007 (the latest data available), after adjusting for inflation. The gains did not last, however. The Federal Reserve Board estimates that by October 2008, median household net worth had fallen to $99,000—3 percent less than in 2004.

Net worth typically rises with age as people pay off their debts. In 2007, net worth peaked in the 55-to-64 age group at $253,700. Although this age group had the highest net worth, it experienced a 7 percent decline in net worth between 2004 and 2007 as debt climbed more rapidly than assets. The net worth of householders under age 35 also fell because of the growing debt of households in the age group.

■ Net worth will continue to decline until home values stabilize.

Net worth has fallen since reaching a peak in 2007

(median household net worth, 2004 to 2008; in 2007 dollars)

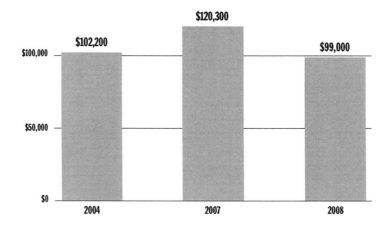

Table 12.1 Net Worth of Households by Age of Householder, 2004 to 2007

(median net worth of households by age of householder, 2004 to 2007; percent change, 2004–07; in 2007 dollars)

	2007	2004	percent change 2004–07
Total households	**$120,300**	**$102,200**	**17.7%**
Under age 35	11,800	15,600	−24.4
Aged 35 to 44	86,600	76,200	13.6
Aged 45 to 54	182,500	158,900	14.9
Aged 55 to 64	253,700	273,100	−7.1
Aged 65 to 74	239,400	208,800	14.7
Aged 75 or older	213,500	179,100	19.2

Source: Federal Reserve Board, Changes in U.S. Family Finances from 2004 to 2007: Evidence from the Survey of Consumer Finances, Federal Reserve Bulletin, February 2009, Internet site http://www.federalreserve.gov/pubs/oss/oss2/2007/scf2007home.html; calculations by New Strategist

Financial Asset Values Rose between 2004 and 2007

For most households, the gains made between 2004 and 2007 were erased by the decline in the stock market in 2008.

Most households own financial assets, which range from transaction accounts (checking and saving) to stocks, mutual funds, retirement accounts, and life insurance. The median value of the financial assets owned by the average household stood at $28,800 in 2007, up 14 percent since 2004 after adjusting for inflation. The stock market plunge of 2008 greatly reduced the value of the financial assets owned by the average household, however.

Transaction accounts, the most commonly owned financial asset, are held by 92 percent of households. Retirement accounts are the second most commonly owned financial asset, and 53 percent of households have one. In 2007, the 51 percent majority of households owned stock either directly or indirectly through retirement accounts and mutual funds. The median value of the stock owned by the average household fell 2 percent between 2004 and 2007, to $35,000 after adjusting for inflation. The loss since then has been much greater. According to estimates by the Federal Reserve Board, the median value of the stock owned by the average household fell to $22,500 by October 2008—a 36 percent decline between 2007 and 2008.

■ The median value of financial assets peaks in the 55-to-64 age group—at $72,400 in 2007.

Retirement accounts are modest, even among those approaching retirement age

(median value of retirement accounts owned by households, by age of householder, 2007)

Table 12.2 Financial Assets of Households by Age of Householder, 2004 and 2007

(percentage of households owning financial assets and median value of assets for owners, by age of householder, 2004 and 2007; percentage point change in ownership and percent change in value of asset, 2004–07; in 2007 dollars)

	2007	2004	percentage point change
PERCENT OWNING ANY FINANCIAL ASSET			
Total households	**93.9%**	**93.8%**	**0.1**
Under age 35	89.2	90.1	−0.9
Aged 35 to 44	93.1	93.6	−0.5
Aged 45 to 54	93.3	93.6	−0.3
Aged 55 to 64	97.8	95.2	2.6
Aged 65 to 74	96.1	96.5	−0.4
Aged 75 or older	97.4	97.6	−0.2

	2007	2004	percent change
MEDIAN VALUE OF FINANCIAL ASSETS			
Total households	**$28,800**	**$25,300**	**13.8%**
Under age 35	6,800	5,700	19.3
Aged 35 to 44	25,800	20,900	23.4
Aged 45 to 54	54,000	42,400	27.4
Aged 55 to 64	72,400	85,700	−15.5
Aged 65 to 74	68,100	39,600	72.0
Aged 75 or older	41,500	42,600	−2.6

Source: Federal Reserve Board, Changes in U.S. Family Finances from 2004 to 2007: Evidence from the Survey of Consumer Finances, Federal Reserve Bulletin, February 2009, Internet site http://www.federalreserve.gov/pubs/oss/oss2/2007/scf2007home.html; calculations by New Strategist

Table 12.3 Financial Assets of Households by Type of Asset and Age of Householder, 2007

(percentage of households owning financial assets, and median value of asset for owners, by type of asset and age of householder, 2007)

	total	under 35	35 to 44	45 to 54	55 to 64	65 to 74	75 or older
PERCENT OWNING ASSET							
Any financial asset	**93.9%**	**89.2%**	**93.1%**	**93.3%**	**97.8%**	**96.1%**	**97.4%**
Transaction accounts	92.1	87.3	91.2	91.7	96.4	94.6	95.3
Certificates of deposit	16.1	6.7	9.0	14.3	20.5	24.2	37.0
Savings bonds	14.9	13.7	16.8	19.0	16.2	10.3	7.9
Bonds	1.6	–	0.7	1.1	2.1	4.2	3.5
Stocks	17.9	13.7	17.0	18.6	21.3	19.1	30.2
Pooled investment funds	11.4	5.3	11.6	12.6	14.3	14.6	13.2
Retirement accounts	52.6	41.6	57.5	64.7	60.9	51.7	30.0
Cash value life insurance	23.0	11.4	17.5	22.3	35.2	34.3	27.6
Other managed assets	5.8	–	2.2	5.1	7.7	13.2	14.0
Other financial assets	9.3	10.0	9.6	10.5	9.2	9.4	5.3
MEDIAN VALUE OF ASSET							
Any financial asset	**$28,800**	**$6,800**	**$25,800**	**$54,000**	**$72,400**	**$68,100**	**$41,500**
Transaction accounts	4,000	2,400	3,400	5,000	5,200	7,700	6,100
Certificates of deposit	20,000	5,000	5,000	15,000	23,000	23,200	30,000
Savings bonds	1,000	700	1,000	1,000	1,900	1,000	20,000
Bonds	80,000	–	9,700	200,000	90,800	50,000	100,000
Stocks	17,000	3,000	15,000	18,500	24,000	38,000	40,000
Pooled investment funds	56,000	18,000	22,500	50,000	112,000	86,000	75,000
Retirement accounts	45,000	10,000	36,000	67,000	98,000	77,000	35,000
Cash value life insurance	8,000	2,800	8,300	10,000	10,000	10,000	5,000
Other managed assets	70,000	–	24,000	45,000	59,000	70,000	100,000
Other financial assets	6,000	1,500	8,000	6,000	20,000	10,000	15,000

Note: "–" means sample is too small to make a reliable estimate.
Source: Federal Reserve Board, Changes in U.S. Family Finances from 2004 to 2007: Evidence from the Survey of Consumer Finances, Federal Reserve Bulletin, February 2009, Internet site http://www.federalreserve.gov/pubs/oss/oss2/2007/scf2007home.html; calculations by New Strategist

Table 12.4 Stock Ownership of Households by Age of Householder, 2004 and 2007

(percentage of households owning stocks directly or indirectly, median value of stock for owners, and share of total household financial assets accounted for by stock holdings, by age of householder, 2004 and 2007; percent and percentage point change, 2004–07; in 2007 dollars)

	2007	2004	percentage point point change
PERCENT OWNING STOCK			
Total households	**51.1%**	**50.2%**	**0.9**
Under age 35	38.6	40.8	−2.2
Aged 35 to 44	53.5	54.5	−1.0
Aged 45 to 54	60.4	56.5	3.9
Aged 55 to 64	58.9	62.8	−3.9
Aged 65 to 74	52.1	46.9	5.2
Aged 75 or older	40.1	34.8	5.3
	2007	**2004**	**percent change**
MEDIAN VALUE OF STOCK			
Total households	**$35,000**	**$35,700**	**−2.0%**
Under age 35	7,000	8,800	−20.5
Aged 35 to 44	26,000	22,000	18.2
Aged 45 to 54	45,000	54,900	−18.0
Aged 55 to 64	78,000	78,000	0.0
Aged 65 to 74	57,000	76,900	−25.9
Aged 75 or older	41,000	94,300	−56.5
	2007	**2004**	**percentage point change**
STOCK AS SHARE OF FINANCIAL ASSETS			
Total households	**53.3%**	**51.3%**	**2.0**
Under age 35	44.3	40.3	4.0
Aged 35 to 44	53.7	53.5	0.2
Aged 45 to 54	53.0	53.8	−0.8
Aged 55 to 64	55.0	55.0	0.0
Aged 65 to 74	55.3	51.5	3.8
Aged 75 or older	48.1	39.3	8.8

Source: Federal Reserve Board, Changes in U.S. Family Finances from 2004 to 2007: Evidence from the Survey of Consumer Finances, Federal Reserve Bulletin, February 2009, Internet site http://www.federalreserve.gov/pubs/oss/oss2/2007/scf2007home.html; calculations by New Strategist

Nonfinancial Assets Are the Foundation of Household Wealth

For the average household, nonfinancial assets are six times as valuable as financial assets.

The median value of the nonfinancial assets owned by the average American household stood at $177,400 in 2007, much greater than the $28,800 median in financial assets. Between 2004 and 2007, the value of the nonfinancial assets owned by the average household grew 9 percent, after adjusting for inflation. Rising housing prices were behind the increase, and the collapse of the housing market in the past few years substantially lowered the value of nonfinancial assets.

Eighty-seven percent of households own a vehicle, the most commonly held nonfinancial asset. The second most commonly owned nonfinancial asset is a home, owned by 69 percent. Homes are by far the most valuable asset owned by Americans, and they account for the largest share of net worth. In 2007, the median value of the average owned home stood at $200,000. The decline in housing prices since 2007 has lowered housing values. The Federal Reserve Board estimates that the median value of the average home fell to $181,600 by October 2008—still 3 percent higher than in 2004, after adjusting for inflation.

■ The drop in housing values is the primary cause of the decline in household net worth since 2007.

Median housing value peaks in the 45-to-54 age group

(median value of the primary residence among homeowners, by age of householder, 2007)

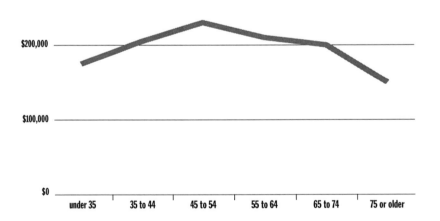

Table 12.5 Nonfinancial Assets of Households by Age of Householder, 2004 and 2007

(percentage of households owning nonfinancial assets and median value of assets for owners, by age of house-holder, 2004 and 2007; percentage point change in ownership and percent change in value of asset, 2004–07; in 2007 dollars)

	2007	2004	percentage point change
PERCENT OWNING ANY NONFINANCIAL ASSET			
Total households	**92.0%**	**92.5%**	**−0.5**
Under age 35	88.2	88.6	−0.4
Aged 35 to 44	91.3	93.0	−1.7
Aged 45 to 54	95.0	94.7	0.3
Aged 55 to 64	95.6	92.6	3.0
Aged 65 to 74	94.5	95.6	−1.1
Aged 75 or older	87.3	92.5	−5.2

	2007	2004	percent change
MEDIAN VALUE OF NONFINANCIAL ASSETS			
Total households	**$177,400**	**$162,300**	**9.3%**
Under age 35	30,900	35,500	−13.0
Aged 35 to 44	182,600	166,200	9.9
Aged 45 to 54	224,900	202,600	11.0
Aged 55 to 64	233,100	248,600	−6.2
Aged 65 to 74	212,200	177,000	19.9
Aged 75 or older	157,100	150,600	4.3

Source: Federal Reserve Board, Changes in U.S. Family Finances from 2004 to 2007: Evidence from the Survey of Consumer Finances, Federal Reserve Bulletin, February 2009, Internet site http://www.federalreserve.gov/pubs/oss/oss2/2007/scf2007home.html; calculations by New Strategist

Table 12.6 Nonfinancial Assets of Households by Type of Asset and Age of Householder, 2007

(percentage of households owning nonfinancial assets, and median value of asset for owners, by type of asset and age of householder, 2007)

	total	under 35	35 to 44	45 to 54	55 to 64	65 to 74	75 or older
PERCENT OWNING ASSET							
Any nonfinancial asset	**92.0%**	**88.2%**	**91.3%**	**95.0%**	**95.6%**	**94.5%**	**87.3%**
Vehicles	87.0	85.4	87.5	90.3	92.2	90.6	71.5
Primary residence	68.6	40.7	66.1	77.3	81.0	85.5	77.0
Other residential property	13.7	5.6	12.0	15.7	20.9	18.9	13.4
Equity in nonresidential property	8.1	3.2	7.5	9.5	11.5	12.3	6.8
Business equity	12.0	6.8	16.0	15.2	16.3	10.1	3.8
Other nonfinancial assets	7.2	5.9	5.5	8.7	8.5	9.1	5.8
MEDIAN VALUE OF ASSET							
Total nonfinancial assets	**$177,400**	**$30,900**	**$182,600**	**$224,900**	**$233,100**	**$212,200**	**$157,100**
Vehicles	15,500	13,300	17,400	18,700	17,400	14,600	9,400
Primary residence	200,000	175,000	205,000	230,000	210,000	200,000	150,000
Other residential property	146,000	85,000	150,000	150,000	157,000	150,000	100,000
Equity in nonresidential property	75,000	50,000	50,000	80,000	90,000	75,000	110,000
Business equity	100,500	59,900	86,000	100,000	116,300	415,000	250,000
Other nonfinancial assets	14,000	8,000	10,000	15,000	20,000	20,000	25,000

Source: Federal Reserve Board, Changes in U.S. Family Finances from 2004 to 2007: Evidence from the Survey of Consumer Finances, Federal Reserve Bulletin, February 2009, Internet site http://www.federalreserve.gov/pubs/oss/oss2/2007/scf2007home.html; calculations by New Strategist

Table 12.7 Household Ownership of Primary Residence by Age of Householder, 2004 and 2007

(percentage of households owning their primary residence, median value of asset for owners, and median value of home-secured debt for owners, by age of householder, 2004 and 2007; percentage point change in ownership and percent change in value of asset, 2004–07; in 2007 dollars)

	2007	2004	percentage point change
PERCENT OWNING PRIMARY RESIDENCE			
Total households	**68.6%**	**69.1%**	**–0.5**
Under age 35	40.7	41.6	–0.9
Aged 35 to 44	66.1	68.3	–2.2
Aged 45 to 54	77.3	77.3	0.0
Aged 55 to 64	81.0	79.1	1.9
Aged 65 to 74	85.5	81.3	4.2
Aged 75 or older	77.0	85.2	–8.2

	2007	2004	percent change
MEDIAN VALUE OF PRIMARY RESIDENCE			
Total households	**$200,000**	**$175,700**	**13.8%**
Under age 35	175,000	148,300	18.0
Aged 35 to 44	205,000	175,700	16.7
Aged 45 to 54	230,000	186,700	23.2
Aged 55 to 64	210,000	218,700	–4.0
Aged 65 to 74	200,000	164,700	21.4
Aged 75 or older	150,000	137,300	9.2

	2007	2004	percent change
MEDIAN VALUE OF HOME–SECURED DEBT			
Total households	**$100,000**	**$95,600**	**4.6%**
Under age 35	78,000	68,600	13.7
Aged 35 to 44	101,600	82,400	23.3
Aged 45 to 54	82,000	95,600	–14.2
Aged 55 to 64	130,000	119,500	8.8
Aged 65 to 74	125,000	109,800	13.8
Aged 75 or older	50,000	42,800	16.8

Source: Federal Reserve Board, Changes in U.S. Family Finances from 2004 to 2007: Evidence from the Survey of Consumer Finances, Federal Reserve Bulletin, February 2009, Internet site http://www.federalreserve.gov/pubs/oss/oss2/2007/scf2007home.html; calculations by New Strategist

Most Households Are in Debt

More than three of four households owe money on mortgages, credits cards, or other types of loans.

Seventy-seven percent of households have debt, owing a median of $67,300 in 2007. The median amount of debt owed by the average debtor household increased by 11 percent between 2004 and 2007, after adjusting for inflation.

Householders aged 35 to 54 are most likely to be in debt, with 86 to 87 percent owing money. Debt declines with age, falling to a low of 31 percent among householders aged 75 or older.

Three types of debt are most common—home-secured debt such as mortgages (49 percent of households have this type of debt), installment loans such as for vehicles (47 percent), and credit card debt (46 percent). Mortgages account for the largest share of debt. The median amount owed by the average homeowner for the primary residence stood at $107,000 in 2007.

Most households either do not have a credit card or pay off their cards in full each month. Among householders aged 35 to 54, however, most had a balance remaining on their credit card after they paid their last bill.

■ As Americans attempt to pay down their debt following the collapse of the housing bubble and the downturn in the stock market, consumer demand has declined.

Debt declines with age

(median amount of debt owed by households by age of householder, 2004)

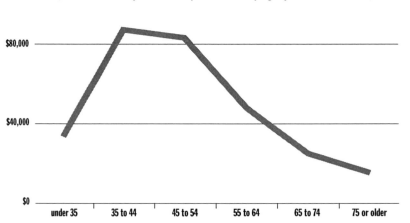

Table 12.8 Debt of Households by Age of Householder, 2004 and 2007

(percentage of households with debt and median amount of debt for debtors, by age of householder, 2004 and 2007; percentage point change in households with debt and percent change in amount of debt, 2004–07; in 2007 dollars)

	2007	2004	percentage point change
PERCENT WITH DEBT			
Total households	**77.0%**	**76.4%**	**0.6**
Under age 35	83.5	79.8	3.7
Aged 35 to 44	86.2	88.6	–2.4
Aged 45 to 54	86.8	88.4	–1.6
Aged 55 to 64	81.8	76.3	5.5
Aged 65 to 74	65.5	58.8	6.7
Aged 75 or older	31.4	40.3	–8.9

	2007	2004	percent change
MEDIAN AMOUNT OF DEBT			
Total households	**$67,300**	**$60,700**	**10.9%**
Under age 35	36,200	36,900	–1.9
Aged 35 to 44	106,200	95,800	10.9
Aged 45 to 54	95,900	91,400	4.9
Aged 55 to 64	60,300	52,700	14.4
Aged 65 to 74	40,100	27,500	45.8
Aged 75 or older	13,000	16,900	–23.1

Source: Federal Reserve Board, Changes in U.S. Family Finances from 2004 to 2007: Evidence from the Survey of Consumer Finances, Federal Reserve Bulletin, February 2009, Internet site http://www.federalreserve.gov/pubs/oss/oss2/2007/scf2007home.html; calculations by New Strategist

Table 12.9 Debt of of Households by Type of Debt and Age of Householder, 2007

(percentage of households with debt, and median value of debt for those with debt, by type of debt and age of householder, 2007)

	total	under 35	35 to 44	45 to 54	55 to 64	65 to 74	75 or older
PERCENT WITH DEBT							
Any debt	**77.0%**	**83.5%**	**86.2%**	**86.8%**	**81.8%**	**65.5%**	**31.4%**
Secured by residential property							
Primary residence	48.7	37.3	59.5	65.5	55.3	42.9	13.9
Other	5.5	3.3	6.5	8.0	7.8	5.0	0.6
Lines of credit not secured by residential property	1.7	2.1	2.2	1.9	1.2	1.5	–
Installment loans	46.9	65.2	56.2	51.9	44.6	26.1	7.0
Credit card balances	46.1	48.5	51.7	53.6	49.9	37.0	18.8
Other debt	6.8	5.9	7.5	9.8	8.7	4.4	1.3
MEDIAN AMOUNT OF DEBT							
Any debt	**$67,300**	**$36,200**	**$106,200**	**$95,900**	**$60,300**	**$40,100**	**$13,000**
Secured by residential property							
Primary residence	107,000	135,300	128,000	110,000	85,000	69,000	40,000
Other	100,000	78,000	101,600	82,000	130,000	125,000	50,000
Lines of credit not secured by residential property	3,800	1,000	4,600	6,000	10,000	30,000	–
Installment loans	13,000	15,000	13,500	12,900	10,900	10,300	8,000
Credit card balances	3,000	1,800	3,500	3,600	3,600	3,000	800
Other debt	5,000	4,500	5,000	4,500	6,000	5,000	4,500

Note: "–" means sample is too small to make a reliable estimate.
Source: Federal Reserve Board, Changes in U.S. Family Finances from 2004 to 2007: Evidence from the Survey of Consumer Finances, Federal Reserve Bulletin, February 2009, Internet site http://www.federalreserve.gov/pubs/oss/oss2/2007/scf2007home.html; calculations by New Strategist

Retirement Plan Participation Peaks in the 45-to-64 Age Group

Many Americans are worried about economic security in retirement.

Only 40 percent of American workers participated in an employment-based retirement plan in 2008, according to an analysis of government statistics by the Employee Benefit Research Institute (EBRI). Retirement coverage peaks among workers aged 45 to 64, at about 50 percent. Among wage and salary workers, those in the private sector are much less likely than public sector workers to participate in a retirement plan, 40.7 versus 74.5 percent.

Another EBRI study shows that only 31 percent of households own an IRA. The median value of the IRAs owned in 2007 had fallen by 15 percent by 2009. Similarly, the 41 percent of households with a worker who participated in an employer-sponsored defined-contribution retirement plan saw the value of their savings fall by 16 percent between 2007 and 2009.

With minimal savings, it is no surprise that many Americans are worried about retirement. Only 16 percent of workers are "very confident" they will have enough money to live comfortably throughout retirement. The figure is an even lower 13 percent among workers aged 55 or older. Among workers aged 55 or older, the percentage who expect to retire at age 66 or later climbed from 28 to 52 percent between 2000 and 2010.

■ The expected age of retirement has soared as the economy has soured.

Most workers aged 55 or older expect to retire at age 66 or later

(percent of workers aged 55 or older who expect to retire at age 66 or older, including "never retire," 2000 and 2010)

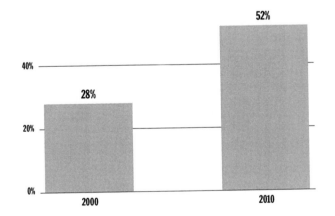

Table 12.10 Retirement Plan Coverage by Age, 2008

(total number of workers, percent whose employer offers a retirement plan, and percent participating in plan, by type of employment and age of worker, 2008; numbers in thousands)

	number of workers	percent with employer that sponsors a retirement plan	percent of all workers participating in a plan
Total workers	**157,843**	**50.6%**	**40.4%**
Under age 21	9,880	24.1	4.8
Aged 21 to 24	12,659	36.4	18.7
Aged 25 to 34	33,717	50.5	38.3
Aged 35 to 44	34,430	54.7	46.1
Aged 45 to 54	36,193	57.2	50.3
Aged 55 to 64	23,339	57.4	50.5
Aged 65 or older	7,625	38.7	28.1
PRIVATE WAGE AND SALARY WORKERS AGED 21 TO 64			
Total workers	**110,687**	**51.0**	**40.7**
Aged 21 to 24	11,261	35.0	17.6
Aged 25 to 34	28,130	48.0	35.1
Aged 35 to 44	27,238	53.1	43.8
Aged 45 to 54	27,400	55.7	47.9
Aged 55 to 64	16,658	55.7	48.5
PUBLIC WAGE AND SALARY WORKERS AGED 21 TO 64			
Total workers	**20,724**	**83.0**	**74.5**
Aged 21 to 24	1,131	57.4	33.7
Aged 25 to 34	4,202	80.4	69.7
Aged 35 to 44	4,969	84.5	77.1
Aged 45 to 54	5,983	85.9	80.4
Aged 55 to 64	4,439	86.4	78.3

Source: Employee Benefit Research Institute, Employment-Based Retirement Plan Participation: Geographic Differences and Trends, 2008, Issue Brief, No. 336, November 2009; Internet site http://www.ebri.org/

Table 12.11 Ownership and Value of Individual Retirement Accounts by Age, 2007 and 2009

(percentage of households that owned an indidivudal retirement account in 2007, and median value of IRA in 2007 and 2009; percent change in value, 2007–09; in 2009 dollars)

	percent owning	median value		percent change in value
		2007	2009	
Total households	**30.6%**	**$34,000**	**$28,955**	**–14.8%**
Under age 35	16.2	8,300	6,644	–20.0
Aged 35 to 44	28.8	24,000	18,717	–22.0
Aged 45 to 54	35.3	36,000	29,853	–17.1
Aged 55 to 64	39.5	65,000	52,220	–19.7
Aged 65 to 74	43.0	66,000	55,901	–15.3
Aged 75 or older	27.3	35,000	32,879	–6.1

Source: Employee Benefit Research Institute, Individual Account Retirement Plans: An Analysis of the 2007 Survey of Consumer Finances, with Market Adjustments to June 2009, by Craig Copeland, Issue Brief, No. 333, August 2009; Internet site http://www.ebri.org/publications/ib/index.cfm?fa=ibDisp&content_id=4326

Table 12.12 Participation in and Value of Employer-Based Defined-Contribution Retirement Plans by Age, 2007 and 2009

(percentage of households that participated in an employer-based defined-contribution retirement plan in 2007, and median value of plan in 2007 and 2009; percent change in value, 2007–09; in 2009 dollars)

	percent participatimg	median value		percent change in value
		2007	2009	
Total households	**40.6%**	**$31,800**	**$26,578**	**–16.4%**
Under age 35	40.0	8,000	6,306	–21.2
Aged 35 to 44	52.2	29,000	22,460	–22.6
Aged 45 to 54	58.5	50,000	43,797	–12.4
Aged 55 to 64	46.7	81,000	69,127	–14.7
Aged 65 to 74	14.3	60,000	56,212	–6.3
Aged 75 or older	1.9	–	–	–

Note: "–" means sample is too small to make a reliable estimate.
Source: Employee Benefit Research Institute, Individual Account Retirement Plans: An Analysis of the 2007 Survey of Consumer Finances, with Market Adjustments to June 2009, by Craig Copeland, Issue Brief, No. 333, August 2009; Internet site http://www.ebri.org/publications/ib/index.cfm?fa=ibDisp&content_id=4326

Table 12.13 Retirement Planning by Age, 2010

(percentage of workers aged 25 or older responding by age, 2010)

	total	25 to 34	35 to 44	45 to 54	55 or older
Very confident in having enough money to live comfortably throughout retirement	16%	22%	15%	13%	13%
Very confident in having enough money to take care of medical expenses in retirement	12	12	16	10	11
Worker and/or spouse have saved for retirement	69	58	61	78	81
Worker and/or spouse are currently saving for retirement	60	50	54	67	72
Contribute to a workplace retirement savings plan	40	33	37	48	43
Have an IRA that includes money saved outside of employer's retirement plan	46	44	45	47	50
Expected retirement age					
Under age 60	9	17	9	6	2
Aged 60 to 64	19	21	16	19	17
Aged 65	24	26	22	29	19
Aged 66 or older	33	29	31	33	42
Never retire	9	4	14	7	10
Don't know/refused	6	3	7	5	9
Total savings and investments (not including value of primary residence or defined-benefit plans)					
Less than $10,000	43	56	46	38	29
$10,000 to $24,999	11	15	14	8	8
$25,000 to $49,999	12	12	11	13	11
$50,000 to $99,999	11	8	11	11	15
$100,000 to $249,999	11	6	11	17	13
$250,000 or more	11	4	8	14	23

Source: Employee Benefit Research Institute and Mathew Greenwald & Associates, Inc., 2010 Retirement Confidence Survey, Internet site http://www.ebri.org/surveys/rcs/2010/

Table 12.14 Expected Age of Retirement by Age, 2000 and 2010

(percentage of workers aged 25 or older by expected age of retirement, by age, 2000 and 2010)

	2010	2000	percentage point change
Total workers			
Under age 60	9%	22%	−13
Aged 60 to 64	19	22	−3
Aged 65	24	28	−4
Aged 66 or older	33	19	14
Never retire	9	4	5
Don't know/refused	6	5	1
Workers aged 25 to 34			
Under age 60	17	30	−13
Aged 60 to 64	21	21	0
Aged 65	26	29	−3
Aged 66 or older	29	12	17
Never retire	4	1	3
Don't know/refused	3	6	−3
Workers aged 35 to 44			
Under age 60	9	18	−9
Aged 60 to 64	16	20	−4
Aged 65	22	32	−10
Aged 66 or older	31	24	7
Never retire	14	2	12
Don't know/refused	7	4	3
Workers aged 45 to 54			
Under age 60	6	24	−18
Aged 60 to 64	19	21	−2
Aged 65	29	28	1
Aged 66 or older	33	18	15
Never retire	7	5	2
Don't know/refused	5	3	2
Workers aged 55 or older			
Under age 60	2	12	−10
Aged 60 to 64	17	28	−11
Aged 65	19	20	−1
Aged 66 or older	42	20	22
Never retire	10	8	2
Don't know/refused	9	13	−4

Source: Employee Benefit Research Institute and Mathew Greenwald & Associates, Inc., Retirement Confidence Surveys, Internet site http://www.ebri.org/surveys/rcs/

Glossary

adjusted for inflation Income or a change in income that has been adjusted for the rise in the cost of living, or the consumer price index (CPI-U-RS).

American Community Survey The ACS is an on-going nationwide survey of 250,000 households per month, providing detailed demographic data at the community level. Designed to replace the census long-form questionnaire, the ACS includes more than 60 questions that formerly appeared on the long form, such as language spoken at home, income, and education. ACS data are available for areas as small as census tracts.

American Housing Survey The AHS collects national and metropolitan-level data on the nation's housing, including apartments, single-family homes, and mobile homes. The nationally representative survey, with a sample of 55,000 homes, is conducted by the Census Bureau for the Department of Housing and Urban Development every other year.

American Indians In this book, American Indians include Alaska Natives.

American Time Use Survey Under contract with the Bureau of Labor Statistics, the Census Bureau collects ATUS information, revealing how people spend their time. The ATUS sample is drawn from U.S. households completing their final month of interviews for the Current Population Survey. One individual from each selected household is chosen to participate in ATUS. Respondents are interviewed by telephone about their time use during the previous 24 hours. About 26,300 households are included in the sample, with 13,300 completed interviews.

Asian Includes Native Hawaiians and other Pacific Islanders unless those groups are shown separately.

Baby Boom Americans born between 1946 and 1964.

Baby Bust Americans born between 1965 and 1976, also known as Generation X.

Behavioral Risk Factor Surveillance System The BRFSS is a collaborative project of the Centers for Disease Control and Prevention and U.S. states and territories. It is an ongoing data collection program designed to measure behavioral risk factors in the adult population aged 18 or older. All 50 states, three territories, and the District of Columbia take part in the survey, making the BRFSS the primary source of information on the health-related behaviors of Americans.

black Includes those who identified themselves as "black" or "African American."

Consumer Expenditure Survey The CEX is an ongoing study of the day-to-day spending of American households administered by the Bureau of Labor Statistics. The CEX includes an interview survey and a diary survey. The average spending figures shown in this book are the integrated data from both the diary and interview components of the survey. Two separate, nationally representative samples are used for the interview and diary surveys. For the interview survey, about 7,500 consumer units are interviewed on a rotating panel basis each quarter for five consecutive quarters. For the diary survey, 7,500 consumer units keep weekly diaries of spending for two consecutive weeks.

consumer unit *(on spending tables only)* For convenience, the term consumer unit and households are used interchangeably in the spending section of this book, although consumer units are somewhat different from the Census Bureau's households. Consumer units are all related members of a household, or financially independent members of a household. A household may include more than one consumer unit.

Current Population Survey The CPS is a nationally representative survey of the civilian noninstitutional population aged 15 or older. It is taken monthly by the Census Bureau for the Bureau of Labor Statistics, collecting information from more than 50,000 households on employment and unemployment. In March of each year, the survey includes the Annual Social and Economic Supplement, which is the source of most national data on the characteristics of Americans, such as educational attainment, living arrangements, and incomes.

disability The National Health Interview Survey estimates the number of people aged 18 or older who have difficulty in physical functioning, probing whether respondents could perform nine activities by themselves without using special equipment. The categories are walking a quarter mile; standing for two hours; sitting for two hours; walking up 10 steps without resting;

stooping, bending, kneeling; reaching over one's head; grasping or handling small objects; carrying a 10-pound object; and pushing/pulling a large object. Adults who reported that any of these activities was very difficult or they could not do it at all were defined as having physical difficulties.

dual-earner couple A married couple in which both the householder and the householder's spouse are in the labor force.

earnings A type of income, earnings is the amount of money a person receives from his or her job. *See also* Income.

employed All civilians who did any work as a paid employee or farmer/self-employed worker, or who worked 15 hours or more as an unpaid farm worker or in a family-owned business, during the reference period. All those who have jobs but who are temporarily absent from their jobs due to illness, bad weather, vacation, labor management dispute, or personal reasons are considered employed.

expenditure The transaction cost including excise and sales taxes of goods and services acquired during the survey period. The full cost of each purchase is recorded even though full payment may not have been made at the date of purchase. Average expenditure figures may be artificially low for infrequently purchased items such as cars because figures are calculated using all consumer units within a demographic segment rather than just purchasers. Expenditure estimates include money spent on gifts for others.

family A group of two or more people (one of whom is the householder) related by birth, marriage, or adoption and living in the same household.

family household A household maintained by a householder who lives with one or more people related to him or her by blood, marriage, or adoption.

female/male householder A woman or man who maintains a household without a spouse present. May head family or nonfamily households.

foreign-born population People who are not U.S. citizens at birth.

full-time employment Full-time is 35 or more hours of work per week during a majority of the weeks worked.

full-time, year-round Indicates 50 or more weeks of full-time employment during the previous calendar year.

General Social Survey The GSS is a biennial survey of the attitudes of Americans taken by the University of Chicago's National Opinion Research Center. NORC conducts the GSS through face-to-face interviews with an independently drawn, representative sample of 3,000 to 4,000 noninstitutionalized people aged 18 or older who live in the United States.

Generation X Americans born between 1965 and 1976, also known as the baby-bust generation.

Hispanic Because Hispanic is an ethnic origin rather than a race, Hispanics may be of any race. While most Hispanics are white, there are black, Asian, American Indian, and even Native Hawaiian Hispanics.

household All the persons who occupy a housing unit. A household includes the related family members and all the unrelated persons, if any, such as lodgers, foster children, wards, or employees who share the housing unit. A person living alone is counted as a household. A group of unrelated people who share a housing unit as roommates or unmarried partners is also counted as a household. Households do not include group quarters such as college dormitories, prisons, or nursing homes.

household, race/ethnicity of Households are categorized according to the race or ethnicity of the householder only.

householder The person (or one of the persons) in whose name the housing unit is owned or rented or, if there is no such person, any adult member. With married couples, the householder may be either the husband or wife. The householder is the reference person for the household.

householder, age of The age of the householder is used to categorize households into age groups such as those used in this book. Married couples, for example, are classified according to the age of either the husband or wife, depending on which one identified him or herself as the householder.

housing unit A house, an apartment, a group of rooms, or a single room occupied or intended for occupancy as separate living quarters. Separate living quarters are those in which the occupants do not live and eat with any other persons in the structure and that have direct access from the outside of the building or through a common hall that is used or intended for use by the occupants of another unit or by the general public. The occupants may be a single family, one person living alone, two or more families living together, or any other group of related or unrelated persons who share living arrangements.

Housing Vacancy Survey The HVS is a supplement to the Current Population Survey, providing quarterly and annual data on rental and homeowner vacancy rates, characteristics of units available for occupancy, and homeownership rates by age, household type, region, state, and metropolitan area. The Current Population Survey sample includes 51,000 occupied housing units and 9,000 vacant units.

housing value The respondent's estimate of how much his or her house and lot would sell for if it were for sale.

iGeneration Americans born in 1995 through the present.

immigration The relatively permanent movement (change of residence) of people into the country of reference.

income Money received in the preceding calendar year by each person aged 15 or older from each of the following sources: (1) earnings from longest job (or self-employment), (2) earnings from jobs other than longest job, (3) unemployment compensation, (4) workers' compensation, (5) Social Security, (6) Supplemental Security income, (7) public assistance, (8) veterans' payments, (9) survivor benefits, (10) disability benefits, (11) retirement pensions, (12) interest, (13) dividends, (14) rents and royalties or estates and trusts, (15) educational assistance, (16) alimony, (17) child support, (18) financial assistance from outside the household, and other periodic income. Income is reported in several ways in this book. Household income is the combined income of all household members. Income of persons is all income accruing to a person from all sources. Earnings are the money a person receives from his or her job.

job tenure The length of time a person has been employed continuously by the same employer.

labor force The labor force tables in this book show the civilian labor force only. The labor force includes both the employed and the unemployed (people who are looking for work). People are counted as in the labor force if they were working or looking for work during the reference week in which the Census Bureau fields the Current Population Survey.

labor force participation rate The percent of the civilian noninstitutional population that is in the civilian labor force, which includes both the employed and the unemployed.

married couples with or without children under age 18 Refers to married couples with or without own children under age 18 living in the same household. Couples without children under age 18 may be parents of grown children who live elsewhere, or they could be childless couples.

median The amount that divides the population or households into two equal portions: one below and one above the median. Medians can be calculated for income, age, and many other characteristics.

median income The amount that divides the income distribution into two equal groups, half having incomes above the median, half having incomes below the median. The medians for households or families are based on all households or families. The median for persons are based on all persons aged 15 or older with income.

Millennial generation Americans born between 1977 and 1994.

mobility status People are classified according to their mobility status on the basis of a comparison between their place of residence at the time of the March Current Population Survey and their place of residence in March of the previous year. Nonmovers are people living in the same house at the end of the period as at the beginning of the period. Movers are people living in a different house at the end of the period than at the beginning of the period. Movers from abroad are either citizens or aliens whose place of residence is outside the United States at the beginning of the period, that is, in an outlying area under the jurisdiction of the United States or in a foreign country. The mobility status for children is fully allocated from the mother if she is in the household; otherwise it is allocated from the householder.

National Ambulatory Medical Care Survey The NAMCS is an annual survey of visits to nonfederally employed office-based physicians who are primarily engaged in direct patient care. Data are collected from physicians rather than patients, with each physician assigned a one-week reporting period. During that week the physician or office staff records a systematic random sample of visit characteristics.

National Health and Nutrition Examination Survey The NHANES is a continuous survey of a representative sample of the U.S. civilian noninstitutionalized population. Respondents are interviewed at home about their health and nutrition, and the interview is followed up by a physical examination that measures such things as height and weight in mobile examination centers.

National Health Interview Survey The NHIS is a continuing nationwide sample survey of the civilian noninstitutional population of the U.S. conducted by the Census Bureau for the National Center for Health Statistics. In interviews each year, data are collected from more than 100,000 people about their illnesses, injuries, impairments, chronic and acute conditions, activity limitations, and use of health services.

National Hospital Ambulatory Medical Care Survey The NHAMCS, sponsored by the National Center for Health Statistics, is an annual national probability sample survey of visits to emergency departments and outpatient departments at non-Federal, short stay and general hospitals. Hospital staff collect data from patient records.

National Survey of Family Growth The 2002 NSFG, sponsored by the National Center for Health Statistics, is a nationally representative survey of the civilian noninstitutionalized population aged 15 to 44. In-person interviews were completed with 12,571 men and women, collecting data on marriage, divorce, contraception, and infertility. The 2002 survey updates previous NSFG surveys taken in 1973, 1976, 1988, and 1995.

National Survey on Drug Use and Health The NSDUH is an annual survey of a nationally representative sample of more than 68,000 people aged 12 or older living in households, noninstitutional group quarters (such as college dorms), and military bases in the United States. It is the primary source of information about illegal drug use in the United States and has been conducted since 1971. Interviews are held in person and incorporate procedures (such as anonymity and computer-assisted interviewing) that will increase respondents' cooperation and willingness to report honestly about their illicit drug use behavior.

nonfamily household A household maintained by a householder who lives alone or who lives with people to whom he or she is not related.

nonfamily householder A householder who lives alone or with nonrelatives.

non-Hispanic People who do not identify themselves as Hispanic are classified as non-Hispanic. Non-Hispanics may be of any race.

non-Hispanic white People who identify their race as white and who do not indicate a Hispanic origin.

occupation Occupational classification is based on the kind of work a person did at his or her job during the previous calendar year. If a person changed jobs during the year, the data refer to the occupation of the job held the longest during that year.

occupied housing units A housing unit is classified as occupied if a person or group of people is living in it or if the occupants are only temporarily absent—on vacation, example. By definition, the count of occupied housing units is the same as the count of households.

own children Sons and daughters, including stepchildren and adopted children, of the householder. The totals include never-married children living away from home in college dormitories.

owner occupied A housing unit in which the owner lives in the unit, even if it is mortgaged or not fully paid for. A cooperative or condominium unit is "owner occupied" only if the owner lives in it. All other occupied units are classified as "renter occupied."

part-time employment Less than 35 hours of work per week in a majority of the weeks worked during the year.

percent change The change (either positive or negative) in a measure that is expressed as a proportion of the starting measure. When median income changes from $20,000 to $25,000, for example, this is a 25 percent increase.

percentage point change The change (either positive or negative) in a value which is already expressed as a percentage. When a labor force participation rate changes from 70 percent of 75 percent, for example, this is a 5 percentage point increase.

poverty level The official income threshold below which families and people are classified as living in poverty. The threshold rises each year with inflation and varies depending on family size and age of householder.

proportion or share The value of a part expressed as a percentage of the whole. If there are 4 million people aged 25 and 3 million of them are white, then the white proportion is 75 percent.

race Race is self-reported and can be defined in three ways. The "race alone" population comprises people who identify themselves as only one race. The "race in combination" population comprises people who identify themselves as more than one race, such as white and black. The "race, alone or in combination" population includes both those who identify themselves as one race and those who identify themselves as more than one race.

regions The four major regions and nine census divisions of the United States are the state groupings as shown below:

Northeast:
—New England: Connecticut, Maine, Massachusetts, New Hampshire, Rhode Island, and Vermont
—Middle Atlantic: New Jersey, New York, and Pennsylvania

Midwest:
—East North Central: Illinois, Indiana, Michigan, Ohio, and Wisconsin
—West North Central: Iowa, Kansas, Minnesota, Missouri, Nebraska, North Dakota, and South Dakota

South:
—South Atlantic: Delaware, District of Columbia, Florida, Georgia, Maryland, North Carolina, South Carolina, Virginia, and West Virginia
—East South Central: Alabama, Kentucky, Mississippi, and Tennessee
—West South Central: Arkansas, Louisiana, Oklahoma, and Texas

West:
—Mountain: Arizona, Colorado, Idaho, Montana, Nevada, New Mexico, Utah, and Wyoming
—Pacific: Alaska, California, Hawaii, Oregon, and Washington

renter occupied *See* Owner Occupied.

Retirement Confidence Survey The RCS, sponsored by the Employee Benefit Research Institute and Mathew Greenwald & Associates, is an annual survey of a nationally representative sample of 1,000 people aged 25 or older. Respondents are asked a core set of questions that have been asked since 1996, measuring attitudes and behavior towards retirement. Additional questions are asked about current retirement issues.

rounding Percentages are rounded to the nearest tenth of a percent; therefore, the percentages in a distribution do not always add exactly to 100.0 percent. The totals, however, are always shown as 100.0. Moreover, individual figures are rounded to the nearest thousand without being adjusted to group totals, which are independently rounded; percentages are based on the unrounded numbers.

self-employment A person is categorized as self-employed if he or she was self-employed in the job held longest during the reference period. Persons who report self-employment from a second job are excluded, but those who report wage-and-salary income from a second job are included. Unpaid workers in family businesses are excluded. Self-employment statistics include only nonagricultural workers and exclude people who work for themselves in incorporated business.

sex ratio The number of men per 100 women.

Survey of Consumer Finances A triennial survey taken by the Federal Reserve Board. It collects data on the assets, debts, and net worth of American households. For the 2007 survey, the Federal Reserve Board interviewed a representative sample of 4,422 households.

unemployed People who, during the survey period, had no employment but were available and looking for work. Those who were laid off from their jobs and were waiting to be recalled are also classified as unemployed.

white Includes many Hispanics (who may be of any race) unless the term "non-Hispanic white" is used.

Youth Risk Behavior Surveillance System The YRBSS was created by the Centers for Disease Control to monitor health risks being taken by young people at the national, state, and local level. The national survey is taken every two years based on a nationally representative sample of 16,000 students in 9th through 12th grade in public and private schools.

Bibliography

Bureau of Labor Statistics

Internet site http://www.bls.gov

—2008 American Time Use Survey, Internet site http://www.bls.gov/tus/home.htm

—2008 Consumer Expenditure Survey, Internet site http://www.bls.gov/cex/home.htm

—2009 Current Population Survey, Labor Force Statistics, Internet site http://www.bls.gov/cps/tables.htm#empstat

—Characteristics of Minimum Wage Workers: 2009, Internet site http://www.bls.gov/cps/minwage2009.htm

—Employee Tenure, Internet site http://www.bls.gov/news.release/tenure.toc.htm

—Employment Characteristics of Families, Internet site http://www.bls.gov/news.release/famee.toc.htm

—"Labor force projections to 2018: older workers staying more active," *Monthly Labor Review*, November 2009, Internet site http://www.bls.gov/opub/mlr/2009/11/contents.htm

—Public Query Data Tool, Internet site http://www.bls.gov/data

Bureau of the Census

Internet site http://www.census.gov/

—2000 Census, American FactFinder, Internet site http://factfinder.census.gov/home/saff/main.html?_lang=en

—2008 American Community Survey, Internet site http://factfinder.census.gov/home/saff/main.html?_lang=en

—2009 Current Population Survey Annual Social and Economic Supplement, Detailed Income Tabulations from the CPS, Internet site http://www.census.gov/hhes/www/income/dinctabs.html

—2009 Current Population Survey Annual Social and Economic Supplement, Detailed Poverty Tabulations from the CPS, Internet site http://www.census.gov/hhes/www/poverty/poverty.html

—Age: 2000, *2000 Census Brief*, C2KBR/01-12, 2001

—American Housing Survey for the United States: 2007, Internet site http://www.census.gov/hhes/www/housing/ahs/ahs07/ahs07.html

—America's Families and Living Arrangements: 2009, Detailed Tables, Internet site http://www.census.gov/population/www/socdemo/hh-fam/cps2009.html

—America's Families and Living Arrangements, Historical Time Series, Internet site http://www.census.gov/population/www/socdemo/hh-fam.html

—Educational Attainment in the United States: 2009, detailed tables, Internet site http://www.census.gov/population/www/socdemo/education/cps2009.html

—Fertility of American Women, Historical Time Series Tables, Internet site http://www.census.gov/population/www/socdemo/fertility.html#hist

— Geographic Mobility: 2008 to 2009, Detailed Tables, Internet site http://www.census.gov/population/www/socdemo/migrate/cps2009.html

—Historical Health Insurance Tables, Internet site http://www.census.gov/hhes/www/cpstables/032009/health/toc.htm

—Historical income data, Current Population Survey Annual Demographic Supplements, Internet site http://www.census.gov/hhes/www/income/histinc/histinctb.html

—Historical poverty data, Current Population Survey Annual Demographic Supplements, Internet site http://www.census.gov/hhes/income/histinc/histpovtb.html

—*Historical Statistics of the United States, Colonial Times to 1970,* Part 1, 1975

—Housing Vacancies and Homeownership Survey, Internet site http://www.census.gov/hhes/www/housing/hvs/hvs.html

—Number, Timing, and Duration of Marriages and Divorces: 2004, Detailed Tables, Internet site http://www.census.gov/population/www/socdemo/marr-div/2004detailed_tables.html

—Population Estimate*s,* Internet site http://www.census.gov/popest/national/asrh/NC-EST2008-sa.html

—Population Projections, Internet site http://www.census.gov/population/www/projections/2009projections.html

—School Enrollment, Historical Tables, Internet site http://www.census.gov/population/www/socdemo/school.html

—School Enrollment—Social and Economic Characteristics of Students: October 2008, detailed tables, Internet site http://www.census.gov/population/www/socdemo/school/cps2008.html

—State Population Estimates, Internet site http://www.census.gov/popest/states/asrh/

—*Statistical Abstract of the United States: 2001,* Internet site http://www.census.gov/compendia/statab/

—Voting and Registration, Historical Time Series Tables, Internet site http://www.census.gov/population/www/socdemo/voting.html

Centers for Disease Control and Prevention

Internet site http://www.cdc.gov

—Behavioral Risk Factor Surveillance System, Prevalence Data, Internet site http://www.apps.nccd.cdc.gov/brfss/

—Health Related Quality of Life, Behavioral Risk Factor Surveillance System, Prevalence Data, Internet site http://apps.nccd.cdc.gov/HRQOL/

—"Youth Risk Behavior Surveillance—United States, 2007," *Morbidity and Mortality Weekly Report*, Surveillance Summaries, Vol. 57/SS-4, June 6, 2008 Internet site http://www.cdc.gov/HealthyYouth/yrbs/index.htm

Department of Homeland Security

Internet site http://www.dhs.gov

— 2008 Yearbook of Immigration Statistics, Internet site http://www.uscis.gov/graphics/shared/statistics/yearbook/index.htm

Employee Benefit Research Institute

Internet site http://www.ebri.org/

— "Employment-Based Retirement Plan Participation: Geographic Differences and Trends, 2008," *Issue Brief*, No. 336, November 2009; Internet site http://www.ebri.org/

— "Individual Account Retirement Plans: An Analysis of the 2007 Survey of Consumer Finances, with Market Adjustments to June 2009," Craig Copeland, *Issue Brief*, Vol. 29, No. 333, August 2009, Internet site http://www.ebri.org/

Employee Benefit Research Institute and Mathew Greenwald & Associates
Internet site http://www.ebri.org/
—Retirement Confidence Surveys, Internet site http://www.ebri.org/surveys/rcs/

Federal Reserve Board
Internet site http://www.federalreserve.gov/pubs/oss/oss2/scfindex.html
—"Recent Changes in U.S. Family Finances: Evidence from 2004 to 2007: Evidence from the Survey of Consumer Finances," *Federal Reserve Bulletin*, February 2009, Internet site http://www.federalreserve.gov/pubs/oss/oss2/2007/scf2007home.html

National Center for Education Statistics
Internet site http://nces.ed.gov
—Projections of Education Statistics to 2018, Internet site http://nces.ed.gov/programs/projections/tables.asp

National Center for Health Statistics
Internet site http://www.cdc.gov/nchs
—*Ambulatory Medical Care Utilization Estimates for 2006*, National Health Statistics Reports, No. 8, 2008, Internet site http://www.cdc.gov/nchs/ahcd/ahcd_reports.htm
—*Anthropometric Reference Data for Children and Adults: United States, 2003–2006*, National Health Statistics Reports, No. 10, 2008, Internet site http://www.cdc.gov/nchs/products/nhsr.htm
—*Births: Final Data for 2006,* National Vital Statistics Reports, Vol. 57, No. 7, 2009, Internet site http://www.cdc.gov/nchs/births.htm
—*Births: Preliminary Data for 2008,* National Vital Statistics Reports, Vol. 58, No. 16, 2010, Internet site http://www.cdc.gov/nchs/products/nvsr.htm
—*Deaths: Preliminary Data for 2007,* National Vital Statistics Reports, Vol. 58, No. 1, 2009, Internet site http://www.cdc.gov/nchs/products/nvsr.htm#vol58
—*Health United States 2009,* Internet site http://www.cdc.gov/nchs/hus.htm
—*Mean Body Weight, Height, and Body Mass Index, United States 1960–2002*, Advance Data, No. 347, 2004, Internet site http://www.cdc.gov/nchs/pressroom/04news/americans.htm
—*National Ambulatory Medical Care Survey: 2006 Summary*, National Health Statistics Reports, No. 3, 2008; Internet site http://www.cdc.gov/nchs/ahcd/ahcd_reports.htm
—*Summary Health Statistics for the U.S. Population: National Health Interview Survey, 2008*, Series 10, No. 243, 2009, Internet site http://www.cdc.gov/nchs/nhis/nhis_series.htm
—*Summary Health Statistics for U.S. Adults: National Health Interview Survey, 2008*, Series 10, No. 242, 2009, Internet site http://www.cdc.gov/nchs/nhis.htm
—*Summary Health Statistics for U.S. Children: National Health Interview Survey, 2008*, Series 10, No. 244, 2009, Internet site http://www.cdc.gov/nchs/nhis/nhis_series.htm
—*Use of Contraception and Use of Family Planning Services in the United States: 1982—2002*, Advance Data, No. 350, 2004, Internet site http://www.cdc.gov/nchs/nsfg.htm

Pew Internet & American Life Project

    Internet site http://www.pewinternet.org

    —Latest Trends—Usage Over Time, Internet site http://www.pewinternet.org/trends
    .asp#demographics

Social Security Administration

    Internet site http://www.ssa.gov/

    — *Income of the Population 55 or Older, 2008*, April 2010, Internet site http://www.ssa
    .gov/policy/docs/statcomps/income_pop55/

Substance Abuse and Mental Health Services Administration

    Internet site http://www.samhsa.gov

    —National Survey on Drug Use and Health, 2008, Internet site http://www.oas.samhsa
    .gov/NSDUH/2K8NSDUH/tabs/toc.htm

Survey Documentation and Analysis, University of California—Berkeley

    Internet site http://sda.berkeley.edu

    —General Social Surveys Cumulative Data File, 1972–2008, Internet site http://sda
    .berkeley.edu/cgi-bin/hsda?harcsda+gss08

Index

Hinduism, 40
Hispanics
    births to, 89–90
    by region, 327–335
    educational attainment, 68–71
    health conditions of children, 133–137
    homeownership, 163–164
    households, 263–265, 274, 277
    income, 203–204, 207
    labor force, 230–232
    living arrangements of children, 286–287
    population, 311–313, 316–319, 327–335
    poverty status, 215–216
    weight, 100–101
home, as nonfinancial asset, 418, 420–421
homeownership status. See also Housing.
    by household type, 161–162
    by race and Hispanic origin, 163–164
    by region, 168–170
    historical, 165–170
    number of owners and renters, 159–160
homicide, as cause of death, 149–150
homosexual. See Sexual orientation.
homosexuality, attitude toward, 43, 45–46
hospital emergency department visits, 142–143
hospital outpatient visits, 142–143
hospital stays, 145–146
housecleaning, time spent, 392–393
household services, spending on, 346–380
households
    assets of, 414–421
    by presence of children, 269–282
    by race and Hispanic origin, 263–265, 274–278
    by region, 283–285
    by size, 266–268
    by type, 260–262, 269–273
    debt of, 422–424
    historical, 258–259
    income of, 186–208
    net worth of, 412–413
    spending by, 346–380
households, family, female-headed
    by presence of children, 270–273
    homeownership of, 161–162
    income of, 193–202
    labor force participation by presence of
        children, 244
    number of, 260–262, 270–273
households, family, male-headed
    by presence of children, 270–273
    homeownership of, 161–162
    income of, 193–202
    labor force participation by presence of
        children, 244
    number of, 260–262, 270–273

households, family, married-couple
    by presence of children, 269–273
    dual-earner, 240–242, 244
    homeownership of, 161–162
    income of, 193–202
    labor force participation by presence of
        children, 242, 244
    number of, 260–262, 269–273
households, nonfamily. See also People
        living alone.
    income of, 193–202
    number of, 260–262
housework, time spent, 392–396
housing. See also Homeownership status.
    as nonfinancial asset, 418, 420–421
    by type, 171–172
    spending on, 346–380
    value, 418, 420–421
hypertension. See High blood pressure.

immigrants, 320, 322. See also Movers from
        abroad.
income. See also Financial situation and Poverty
        status.
    by household type, 193–202
    by quintile, 188–189
    by race and Hispanic origin, 203–208
    by sex, 174–185
    health conditions of children by family,
        134–137
    historical, 174–177, 186–187
    household, 186–208
    minimum wage, 252–253
    of full-time workers, 178–179, 181–182,
        184–185
    relative to other families, 53–54
    sources of, 209–211
independent, 50–51
influenza and pneumonia, as cause of death,
        148–151
installment debt, 422, 424
insurance, health. See Health insurance.
insurance, personal. See Personal insurance and
        pensions, spending on.
interest income, as source of income, 209–211
Internet
    as source of news, 34–37
    use, 407–408
IRAs, 425, 427–428

Jewish religion, 40
job tenure, 245–247

kidney disease, 128–130
kitchen clean-up, time spent, 392, 396

socializing
    time spent, 383, 385, 387
    with friends, 56–57
    with relatives, 56–57
South. *See* Regions.
sports, time spent participating in, 383, 389
standard of living, 53, 55, 425, 428
state
    born in, 320–321
    moved to different, 156–158
    population by, 336–344
stepparents, 286, 288
stocks, as financial asset, 414, 416–417
stroke, 128–130
suicide
    as cause of death, 149–151
    contemplated by high school students, 123–124
survivors' benefits, as source of income, 210

taxes. *See* Personal taxes, spending on.
telephone, time spent, 383, 400, 405
television
    as source of news, 34–37
    time spent watching, 385–386
tobacco products and smoking supplies, spending
        on, 346–380
tobacco use
    chewing tobacco, 113
    cigarette smoking 111–113
    cigars, 113
transaction accounts, as financial asset, 414, 416
transportation, spending on, 346–380
traveling, time spent, 383, 400, 406
trust in others, 47–48

ulcers, 128–130
unemployed. *See* Labor force.
unemployment insurance, as source of income, 210
union representation, 248–249
utilities, fuels, public services, spending on,
        346–380

vehicles
    as nonfinancial asset, 418, 420
    spending on, 346–380
veteran benefits, as source of income, 210
visual impairments, 128–130
volunteering, time spent, 383, 400, 404
voting, 409–410

wages and salaries, as source of income, 209–211
water. *See* Utilities, fuels, and public services,
        spending on.
weight
    by sex, 97–102
    of children, 100–102

West. *See* Regions.
whites, in labor force, 230–232. *See also* Whites,
        non-Hispanic.
whites, non-Hispanic. *See also* Whites.
    births to, 89–90
    by region, 327–335
    educational attainment, 68–71
    health conditions of children, 133–137
    households, 263–265, 274, 278
    income, 203–204, 208
    living arrangements of children, 286–287
    population, 311–313, 316–319, 327–335
    poverty status, 215–216
    weight, 100–101
widowhood, 298–300, 303–304
women
    AIDS, diagnosed with, 131–132
    births, 89–94
    blood pressure, high, 107–108
    childless, 95–96
    cholesterol, high, 105–106
    college enrollment, 76–77, 80–81
    contraceptive use, 120–122
    educational attainment, 63, 66–68, 71
    full-time workers, 181–182, 184–185, 237–238,
        242–244
    income, 176–177, 181–185
    job tenure, 245–247
    labor force, 220–226, 230–231, 242–244,
        250–251, 254–255
    life expectancy, 152–153
    living alone, 260–262, 266, 268, 291, 295–297
    living arrangements, 291, 295–297
    marital history, 303–304
    marital status, 298, 300–304
    part-time workers, 237–239, 242–244
    physician visits, 142, 144
    population, 309–310
    poverty status, 212, 214, 217–218
    risk behavior, 123–124
    school enrollment, 74–75
    self-employed, 250–251
    sexual behavior, 120, 122, 124
    time use, 384–407
    unemployed, 222–224, 230, 232
    union representation, 248–249
    weight status, 97–102
    working mothers, 44, 242–244
work. *See* Labor force.
worker's compensation, as source of income, 210
working, time spent, 383